Reclaiming Men's Spirituality

Reclaiming Men's Spirituality

Spiritual Direction of Men through the Lens of Saint John of the Cross

CHRISTOPHER FELIX BEZZINA

Foreword by George Pattison

☙PICKWICK *Publications* · Eugene, Oregon

RECLAIMING MEN'S SPIRITUALITY
Spiritual Direction of Men through the Lens of Saint John of the Cross

Copyright © 2024 Christopher Felix Bezzina. All rights reserved. Except for brief quotations in critical publications or reviews, no part of this book may be reproduced in any manner without prior written permission from the publisher. Write: Permissions, Wipf and Stock Publishers, 199 W. 8th Ave., Suite 3, Eugene, OR 97401.

Pickwick Publications
An Imprint of Wipf and Stock Publishers
199 W. 8th Ave., Suite 3
Eugene, OR 97401

www.wipfandstock.com

PAPERBACK ISBN: 978-1-6667-6352-2
HARDCOVER ISBN: 978-1-6667-6353-9
EBOOK ISBN: 978-1-6667-6354-6

Cataloguing-in-Publication data:

Names: Bezzina, Christopher Felix, author. | Pattison, George, foreword.

Title: Reclaiming men's spirituality : spiritual direction of men through the lens of Saint John of the Cross / Christopher Felix Bezzina ; foreword by George Pattison.

Description: Eugene, OR: Pickwick Publications, 2024. | Includes bibliographical references and index.

Identifiers: ISBN 978-1-6667-6352-2 (paperback). | ISBN 978-1-6667-6353-9 (hardcover). | ISBN 978-1-6667-6354-6 (ebook).

Subjects: LCSH: Men—Religious aspects—Christianity. | Men (Christian theology. | Spiritual direction. | Spiritual life—Christianity. | John of the Cross, Saint, 1542–1591.

Classification: BT703.5 B49 2024 (print). | BT703.5 (epub).

02/15/24

To a soul
gone hastily
casting shades
in memory.

Contents

List of Tables — ix
Foreword by George Pattison — xi
Acknowledgments — xiii
Abbreviations — xv
Introduction — 1
Chapter 1   The Spiritual Doctrine of John of the Cross — 14
Chapter 2   Ten Spiritual Narratives of Men — 54
Chapter 3   Strangers of the *Dark Night* — 108
Chapter 4   Companions of the *Dark Night* — 155
Chapter 5   Theoretical Considerations of Spirituality and Masculinity — 200
Conclusion — 268
Bibliography — 273
Index — 287

Tables

Table 1 Maltese Educational Institutions Teaching Spiritual Direction   7
Table 2 Spiritual Directors Gatekeepers   8
Table 3 Map of the *Dark Night*   110

Foreword

Since E. Allison Peers's 1930s translations of John of the Cross, the Spanish mystic has entered the mainstream of spiritual life in the Anglophone world. Often, it has to be said, he is not cited beyond that wonderfully evocative phrase 'the dark night of the soul', a phrase that has become a commonplace of the English language. At a more serious level, John's vision of spiritual life has been growing in influence on those venturing the challenge of living out a spiritual life in the conditions of late modernity. The question, of course, is how this sixteenth-century monastic figure, seemingly so remote from our time with regard to his intellectual and cultural presuppositions, can be a resource for people living in a secular world and subject to the manifold pressures that this involves. The question is a serious one and merits a careful response that is as attentive to specifics as it is to larger theological horizons. Christopher Bezzina's study is just such a response. By combining detailed case-studies with a careful reading of John's spiritual doctrine he shows just how relevant the saint's work is to real-life concerns in the contemporary world.

There is, however, an interesting twist. It is not as if the subjects on whom Bezzina focusses are themselves preoccupied with how to apply John's thought to their lives. Rather, Bezzina shows that what John does is supply a theoretical framework for making sense of the process through which they are going and therefore also yielding criteria by which to assess their progress and the challenges they must face next. In this sense, John offers an explication of the process of spiritual formation that provides an important complement to any more secular approach.

Specifically, Bezzina focusses on the spiritual lives of men and the issues that arise in the process of spiritual direction for men. Men's studies have in recent years—understandably and for good reasons—had a much lower profile than women's studies. Of course, these should not be seen as being in competition and it should be obvious that progress in one requires progress in the other. Practically, however, and despite the existence of much excellent research, there is clearly a deficit in men's studies that needs to be filled, not least with regard to religious life. Bezzina's study makes an important contribution to addressing this deficit. Although—or, rather, because—his empirical focus is on just a few real-life cases, he is able to bring into focus some of the deepest issues facing men who are attempting to live out the spiritual life today.

As Bezzina several times reminds us, Malta is a distinctive society in which the Church retains a kind of presence that is very different from that in northern Europe or the United States. Nevertheless, the stories told here will resonate with contemporary men's experience in many societies. His examples include gay, straight, married, and single men, and there will be few readers who do not recognize the situations they are dealing with from their own or their friends' lives. These are not ultra-pious types from the religious ghetto but real men struggling with real issues that also confront those who have not chosen the spiritual option. As often, qualitative research takes us to a point of universality that mass statistics can attain only with difficulty.

I count myself privileged to have been the supervisor of the thesis on which this book is based. However, the word 'supervisor' probably implies too much. From the outset, Bezzina was thoroughly self-motivated, planning and executing his research with an impressive professionalism that shines through the finished text. The result is a work that provides a valuable resource for those working in the sociology and psychology of religion, while also speaking to the needs of those seeking or practicing spiritual direction. As such, it is a superlative example of applied theology and merits a wide international readership.

—George Pattison

Acknowledgments

Grateful acknowledgment is made to Professor George Pattison and Professor Charlotte Methuen for their academic guidance. Their expertise was vital in refining my thinking and bringing my work to a higher level.

I would like to acknowledge Rev. Dr. Charlo Camilleri and Rev. Dr. Glen Attard for their academic aid, especially at the proposal stage, and for providing the Carmelite Institute with a location where interviews could be conducted. Furthermore, I would also like to thank the gatekeepers and participants in this research. Without their participation, this study could not have come to fruition.

I am also profoundly grateful to Professor Albert Borg and Ms. Laura Camilleri Sghendo for translating Maltese quotations to English and Mr. Thomas Pace for his meticulous proofreading of Maltese segments.

Finally, I could not have completed this study without the support of relatives and friends. Their empathic availability encouraged me with spaces outside of my research to rest my mind.

Abbreviations

Ascent	*The Ascent of Mount Carmel*
Canticle	*The Spiritual Canticle*
Dark	*The Dark Night*
Flame	*The Living Flame of Love*
Counsel	*Counsels to a Religious*
Sayings	*Sayings of Light and Love*

Introduction

MOTIVATION

Over the last three decades, discourse about masculinity has continued to grow. A single search on an internet search engine brings up various opinions, often contrasting views about men's characters, problems, and lifestyles. Moreover, in a period when men's studies has established itself as a specialized field in academia, expanding into other disciplines beyond the sociological, culture has given rise to a variety of men's movements, from conservative religious-inspired movements to men's rights groups and the *mythopoetics* also referred to as men's spiritual movements.[1] The position of religion with these movements is mixed. Some authors have appropriated the ideas of *mythopoetics* and related them to Christian themes.[2] Others involved with theories of men's studies investigated religious traditions, while some theologians have begun exploring biblical masculinity.[3] All these movements reveal how men are not united under one single understanding of gender dynamics. While some men have taken on board feminist ideas, others resist and defend the status quo.[4] Although these movements began in the United States, their ideas and spirit of disagreement permeate and influence the world in academia and the public domain.

---

1. For men's studies, see Kimmel, *Handbook of Studies on Men and Masculinities*; Adams and Savran, *Masculinity Studies Reader*. Some men movements' authors include Bly, *Iron John*; Keen, *Fire in the Belly*.

2. Examples: Rohr, *Adams' Return*; Pable, *Quest for the Male Soul*.

3. Examples of studies on biblical masculinities include Moore and Anderson, *New Testament Masculinities*; Conway, *Behold the Man: Jesus and Greco-Roman Masculinity*. See also Delap and Morgan, *Men, Masculinities and Religious Change in Twentieth-Century Britain*; Gelfer, *Numen, Old Men*.

4. See Messner et al., *Some Men*; Jordan, *New Politics of Fatherhood*.

What inspired this research endeavor was none of these trends. Instead, it all began with a question in Timothy Radcliffe's book: *Why be a Christian?*[5] Trying to answer this question, one could opt to refer to doctrine or the theological merits of the faith, but in reality, an honest and intimate answer to the question brings a gendered reality: *why be a Christian man or woman?* We bring our own gendered experience to explore if it is worth being Christian. Moreover, to answer such a question honestly, life cannot remain unexamined, even if it entails distancing oneself from some aspects of Christianity. By exploring life and sometimes the other side of the fence, the self compares lifestyles and questions the call to believe or what to believe. The self demands proof for believing, which often carries a shadow of sin since we are taught that a believer should not doubt. As Mark Muesse puts it, "what I [he] needed was a method, a technique, a discipline for change. I [He] needed a conversion of practice more than a conversion of belief."[6] Often this conversion of practice is taken for granted unless challenging life circumstances force us to doubt whom we think we are, how much others, including our friends, relatives, and institutions, know us, and how uncomfortably we rest in the ready-made all-encompassing definitions of what a Christian man or woman should be. It is a question that cuts deep into the core of our being, but it equally unveils possibilities if the person is ready to risk finding the Truth. The self can test other lifestyles, explore books about masculinity or renounce Christianity altogether. We live in a period where possibilities are endless, and lifestyles have become fluid, or so we think.

These thoughts are essential for this research. Instead of jumping on any sociological, theological, or popular bandwagon, this study temporarily suspends all the present discourses about masculinity. Although it does not discredit their import, this study seeks answers by returning to men who, through their lived experience, relate to us their unfinished spiritual narratives. Furthermore, this study steps into uncharted territory in the realm of men's research by entering into dialogue with questions of masculinity in conversation with the mystics or mystical theology, particularly John of the Cross.[7]

Mystical theology is not just the other side of theology. Instead, it is the fulcrum that evokes the spirit of the believer.[8] It is the motivational force

---

5. Radcliffe, *What Is the Point of Being Christian?*

6. Muesse, "Don't Just Do Something, Sit There," 7.

7. Although feminist thoughts propelled a rediscovery of feminine spirituality in conversation with Christian mystics, very few studies have engaged mystics in the area of masculinity. For an example, see the chapter on Saint Bernard of Clairvaux by Wiethaus, "Christian Piety and the Legacy of Medieval Masculinity."

8. For an introduction to mystical theology, see Howells and McIntosh, *Oxford*

INTRODUCTION

that leads the person to participate, engage, and reflect upon God's presence and hiddenness in their actual lives.[9] In the realm of mystical theology, we are not primarily concerned with how much one sticks to fixed dogmatic teachings but, similar to the early Christians, who did not possess a clear set of beliefs, possessed a new consciousness that Christ has brought into effect. Rowan Williams describes mystical theology as "both the condition and the result of a certain style of Christian living."[10] To quote Thomas Merton:

> Without mysticism there is no real theology, and without theology there is no real mysticism. Hence the emphasis will be on mysticism as theology, to bring out clearly the mystical dimensions of our theology, hence to help us to do what we must really do: live our theology. Some think it is sufficient to come to the monastery to live the rule. More is required—we must live our theology, fully, deeply, in its totality. Without this, there is no sanctity. The separation of theology from 'spirituality' is a disaster.[11]

These observations gave birth to the title for this thesis: reclaiming men's spirituality. As much as it is about men's needs to reclaim a neglected or closeted spirituality, it attempts to reclaim a practice of doing theological research without ignoring the spiritual or mystical ingredient. By mystical, it is not simply inquiring about supernatural incidents one has of God but how mystery supersedes and permeates any rational configuration that this world might dictate or predict.

AIM OF THE STUDY

Having explored what motivates this study, this section addresses the research objectives and the style of inquiry. This study explores the need to examine men's spirituality by taking onboard three research questions: can a form of spirituality about men be identified and described, how can this spirituality be examined, and what is it that needs to be reclaimed? These questions suggest three hypotheses underlying this study:

1. **Hypothesis 1**: Men's spirituality can be observed and documented. It permeates all forms of publicly displayed spiritualties. Such a spirituality carries a variety of features, expressions, and contours that tie

---

Handbook of Mystical Theology; Bernard, *Teologia Mistica*.

9. Williams, "Mystical Theology and Christian Self-Understanding," 14.
10. Williams, "Mystical Theology and Christian Self-Understanding," 16.
11. Merton, *Course in Christian Mysticism*, 1.

closely to men's being. These features expose a form and the background scenarios that allow such a spirituality to arise. The first hypothesis concerns itself with the material object under investigation.

2. **Hypothesis 2**: John of the Cross' spiritual framework is relevant for contemporary discourse on masculinity and spirituality. The second hypothesis considers John of the Cross' spiritual doctrine a valid instrument to provide in-depth insight. His doctrine demonstrates the operations, goals, and problems of men's spirituality and recommends appropriate guidance. Although John originally wrote to religious men and females, his ideas have been applied beyond the monastery's walls to fulfill the call for perfection promulgated by the Vatican Council II.[12]

3. **Hypothesis 3**: Men need to reclaim their spirituality. The third hypothesis attends to the need to reclaim men's spirituality in three ways: firstly, by making space in the theological sphere that respects and takes into consideration men's lived experiences, an activity that would expose an often hidden voice of men who live their commitment towards their relationship with God quietly. As a result, distinct insights proper for theological and other academic fields are discovered. Second, a reclamation that respects dialogue and accessible participation in the debate about masculinity without ending reactive, reductive, defensive or fanatical. No ideology or popular opinion takes precedence, but rather it opts to listen attentively and empathetically to what men have to say about themselves, their relation to the Triune God, and the transformative results of such interaction. Allowing men to recount their stories is a reclamation in itself. Thirdly, a reclamation to the continuous discovery of what it means to be a Christian man. Reclamation calls for discernment that disengages from presumptive, rigid and insensitive characterizations about masculinity and Christianity. Hence this is a reclamation of mystery yet to unfold.

METHODOLOGY

This section lays out the approaches used to answer the three research questions. The study of spirituality, if lived in the context of faith in a personal God, demands critical analysis of divine and human interaction based on two primary conditions: the process of transformation occurring within the relationship and a systematic account of that transformative process which

---

12. *Dogmatic Constitution on the Church: Lumen Gentium*, 40. See also Gula, *Call to Holiness*.

arises from the lived experience. These two prerequisites call for a methodology that incorporates interdisciplinary instruments.[13] Conscious that debates surrounding the study of spirituality are still evolving, this project adheres to a methodological framework proposed by Kees Waaijman.[14] Waaijman seeks the historical foundations of spirituality in light of its praxis (lived experience)[15] and the scientific instruments used to examine it.[16] His deep analysis considers the universalistic phenomena of spirituality beyond the Judeo-Christian tradition. The definition of spirituality that develops, which applies to this research project, is the following:

> On the basis of lived spirituality, listening to the basic words of praxis and instructed by the scientific traditions, we can describe spirituality as the divine-human relational process (material object) viewed from the perspective of transformation (formal object).[17]

While an experience of life provides a sense of being alive, lived experience "collects and embraces the totality of a person's experiences during their life."[18] An identity emerges over time. Transformation is noticeable when one retrospectively observes how lifestyles alterations have been brought forth by relationships. Identities mold themselves out of encounters and over time. Here the emphasis is on the divine-human relationship and the multi-layered progressions resulting from such a relationship.[19]

To remain faithful to how transformation materializes and to respect as much as possible men's personal experiences without a presupposed bias, theories relating to masculinity and men's studies are introduced only at the

---

13. On the study of spirituality, see Bernard, *Teologia Spirituale*, vol. 30; Col, "Spirituality and the Search for a Triple Unity"; Downey, *Understanding Christian Spirituality*; Schneiders, "Spirituality in the Academy," 4; Schneiders, "Religion and Spirituality," 2; Sheldrake, "Study of Spirituality," 39; Waaijman, "Spirituality as Transformation Demands a Dynamic-Structural Approach," 1; Waaijman, "Towards a Phenomenological Definition of Spirituality"; Dreyer and Burrows, *Minding the Spirit*. Also see conference proceeding in "Study of Christian Spirituality E La Teologia Spirituale," 2.

14. Waaijman, *Spirituality*.

15. Waaijman, *Spirituality*, 313.

16. Waaijman, *Spirituality*, 367.

17. Waaijman, *Spirituality*, 305; Waaijman, "Towards a Phenomenological Definition of Spirituality."

18. "The difference between experience and lived experience does not lie in the former's awareness of the latter's unreflectedness, but in the fact that experience refers to a singular fact while lived experience embraces a spectrum of experiences." Col, "Spirituality and the Search for a Triple Unity," 6.

19. Waaijman, *Spirituality*, 424.

final stages of this research. Therefore, this study deviates from the practice of beginning its inquiry with a standard literature review. In order to give voice to the participants, only after their personal stories have been analyzed in the light of the doctrine of John of the Cross does a fuller discussion with theories of masculinity occur.

Although the matter under investigation is men's spirituality, it is impossible to explore all the forms of spiritualties in which men partake in one piece of research. What can be explored is a particular spirituality in a specific social-religious setting. This study opted to study Maltese men.[20] The research sample composition is discussed in the next section.

Sample Composition

Although the Catholic population in Malta is broad, this research is concerned with laymen who have a constant and intimate relationship with the divine and therefore relate to faith as more than just a socio-religious label. The same premise underpinned the choice of spiritual directors. The assumption that all Catholic priests are spiritual directors is misleading. Although all priests are trained in pastoral and mystagogical matters and practice the sacrament of confession, spiritual direction is a specific ministry associated with a distinct pastoral role. Some priests or lay individuals specialize in spiritual direction or have a reputation for being spiritual directors. In identifying these samples, snowball sampling techniques are used as the participants are not explicitly identified.[21] Through chain referrals, spiritual directors and directees were identified from organizations that provide spiritual direction or teach it. Spiritual directors were recommended by their respective affiliations in an organization, and in turn, directors acted as gatekeepers for male directees.

Spiritual Director Sample

Training in spiritual direction is offered on various levels, either as priestly formation or a specialized course. All educational programs are open to

---

20. The study did not include inhabitants of Gozo, the second largest island of the archipelago.

21. When this research was conducted, there was no association in Malta for spiritual directors. *The Maltese Association for the Study of Spirituality and Spiritual Companionship* (MASC) was entered in the Register of Voluntary Organizations in Malta on the 30th of November 2019, see www.masc.org.mt.

laypeople. Table one outlines the educational institutions contacted with their respective courses and qualification levels.

Name of Organization	Level of Qualification
Faculty of Theology, University of Malta	Bachelor of Sacred Theology (MQF Level 6)
	Master of Arts in Spirituality (MQF Level 7)
	Master of Arts in Spiritual Companionship (MQF Level 7)
Centre for Ignatian Spirituality	Diploma in Spiritual Accompaniment (MQF Level 6)

Table 1—Maltese Educational Institutions teaching Spiritual Direction[22]

Institutions within the Catholic Church that provide spiritual direction as part of their pastoral ministry encompass diocesan priests, religious men and females within religious orders and lay organizations. Table two exhibits the organizations contacted for potential participants. All institutions were contacted for two purposes: to recommend members within their organizations who practice spiritual direction and to invite them to participate in the research. The first mode of contact with these institutions was through email. If no reply was received, the second mode of contact was through a phone call. However, once potential candidates reached a satisfactory level, some institutions were not followed up.

---

22. MQF stands for Malta Qualifications Framework.

Church Sector	Name of Institution	
Diocesan priests	Archbishop's Curia of the Archdiocese of Malta	
Religious Communities	Friars	Augustinians (OSA)
		Carmelites (O.Carm)
		De La Salle Brothers (FSC)
		Discalced Carmelites (OCD)
		Dominicans (OP)
		Franciscan Conventuals (OFM Conv)
		Friars Minor Capuchin (OFM Cap)
		Friars Minors (OFM)
		Missionary Society of St. Paul (MSSP)
		Salesians (SDB)
		Society of Jesus (SJ)
	Sisters	Augustinians (ASGM)
		Dominican Sisters (OP)
		Franciscan Missionaries of Mary (FMM)
		Franciscan Sisters of the Immaculate Heart (CIM)
		The Good Shepherd Sisters (RGS)
		The Sisters of St. Dorothy (SSD)
Lay Organizations	Society of Christian Doctrine (M.U.S.E.U.M)	
	Youth Fellowship	
	Centre for Ignatius Spirituality	
	Drachma	

Table 2—Spiritual Directors Gatekeepers[23]

Given the sensitivity of the subject under investigation, introductory meetings with every interested spiritual director were held to explain the purpose of the research and explore the possibility of accessing their directees. Out of the forty (40) potential candidates, thirty-eight (38) were male, and two (2) were female spiritual directors. Ten (10) spiritual directors were selected to participate in the study based on their experience and availability: eight (8) priests or friars, one (1) nun, and one (1) male lay spiritual director. The second female spiritual director was unable to participate in the research since she lived abroad.

23. The institutions listed in tables two do not reflect all the organisations that practise spiritual direction in Malta.

Spiritual Directee Sample

Spiritual directees were identified by their respective spiritual directors. Directors invited directees to participate in the research. The conditions determining the sample centered on two factors:

1. The first requirement is commitment. Not all Catholic men are devoted to the divine-human relationship. Some only subscribe to the faith in an external sense and stop there. Therefore, this research is oriented towards those men who are nurturing their spiritual journey. Most often, the commitment consciously to involve the divine in one's life brings with it the support of a mentor. This spiritual relationship is the first demarcation applied to distinguish the sample.

2. The second criterion considers the social context. As a blueprint, the circumstances of men are determined with the fifty-four forms outlined by Waaijman.[24] Five scenarios have been identified where the theoretical yield should be high:

    - Married straight fathers;
    - Unmarried straight men;
    - Separated straight men;
    - Single gay men; and,
    - Gay men in a relationship.

In total, the male participants' sample is made up of ten (10) men aged between thirty and forty-five. Each scenario has two male participants. In all cases, spiritual directors determined those candidates that met the requirements for the sample. This study opted as much as possible to conduct the in-depth interviews with those spiritual directors who did not provide potential directees for contact or whose directees were not chosen to form part of the interviewing sample. This was done to limit contamination and bias between spiritual directors and their directees.

---

24. Waaijman provides us with fifty-four forms of spiritualties systematized under three main categories: Lay Spirituality encompasses the lived spirituality of the family/household unit; Schools of Spirituality include traditional and well-established institutions of spiritual philosophies; and Counter Movement spiritualties which do not fit within the former forms but are located in the margins of society, see Waaijman, *Spirituality*, 9.

Data Gathering

Data about men's spiritual experiences are collected from two sources: spiritual narratives of directees and semi-structured interviews of spiritual directors. The goal is to illustrate men's spirituality by outlining the contours of the form, coming into terms with the form's contextual features, and analyzing the expressions employed within the form that signify the transformative relationship between the divine and men.[25]

Pre-scientific data from male directees were gathered through an adaptation of the Life-History method.[26] This study aligned the method to focus on spiritual history, qualifying it as an appropriate instrument closely related to the spiritual biography or *vita*, classically associated with the study of saints.[27] As a guide on the Life-History method, this study followed the methodology presented by Ken Plummer.[28] Unstructured interviews were held with participants. They were given the space to recount their spiritual story. Men could also bring any symbolic mementoes to substantiate their account. Priority was given to encouraging individuals to tell their spiritual stories with no interruptions. They provided rich testimonies revealing how the divine was involved in making sense of life.[29] Interviews also made it possible to hear how stories are being told. The interviews were considered both a source from which narrative detail might be extracted and a witness to participants' moods.

With spiritual directors, the focus was on their professional history. Although participants were also given the freedom to recount their story with no interruptions, specific themes about the triangular relationship of men, director and God were identified for discussion. The interviews touched on four parallel realities within the spiritual direction relationship:

1. the disposition of the male directee who, led by a desire to gain a clearer insight into his relationship with God, sought the presence of the spiritual director;

2. the approach taken by the spiritual director as a mentor on spirituality when supporting the directee;[30]

---

25. Waaijman, *Spirituality*, 600.
26. Plummer, *Documents of Life 2*; Atkinson, "Life Story Interview as a Mutually Equitable Relationship."
27. Waaijman, *Spirituality*, 602.
28. Plummer, *Documents of Life 2*.
29. Plummer, *Documents of Life 2*, 36.
30. Waaijman, *Spirituality*, 886.

3. the impact that is generated by spiritual direction in terms of progress, regression and challenges experienced; and,

4. the influence of social context in setting the stage for relationships and any issues encountered.

Interviews with directees were held first, and a preliminary analysis was undertaken. The interviews with spiritual directors followed. The key topics mentioned by directees were, therefore, able to be integrated into the interviews with spiritual directors.

Data Analysis

All interviews were recorded in audio and then transcribed.[31] *Atlas.ti* was used as a qualitative data analysis software for coding and thematic categorization.[32] At this stage, a reflective disposition towards the written transcriptions was vital. It involved an arduous exercise on the researcher's part to engage intuitively and creatively with the texts. The transcribed interviews were not viewed simply as stories but as unfinished (auto-) biographies.[33]

Each transcription was coded twice: first, a basic coding was used to create a chronology of events; then, an in-depth interpretive code was employed to look for trends and patterns. Memories, desires, present circumstances and future hopes of participants were connected in every story. The guiding principle was that narratives ought to bring forth an identity. The second exercise of coding used categories derived from the theology of John of the Cross, encompassing each aspect of the *dark night*.[34] Using a tabular approach, the *data corpus* from the transcripts was grouped into various *data sets* reflecting each aspect of the *dark night*.[35]

---

31. Plummer, *Documents of Life 2*, 149.

32. Software website http://atlasti.com/; Seale and Rivas, "Using Software to Analyze Qualitative Interviews"; Basit, "Manual or Electronic?," 2.

33. "One of the strengths of life story interviews is the strong emphasis on holism. Lives are seen as whole, the public and private cannot be separated, and lives are contextual and should be studied and understood this way." in Adriansen, "Timeline Interviews," 1:45; Plummer, *Documents of Life 2*, 78.

34. See Table 3—Map of the Dark Night.

35. Braun and Clarke, "Using Thematic Analysis in Psychology," 79; King, "Using Templates in the Thematic Analysis of Text," 257.

Ethical Considerations and Limitations

This type of research, like any other qualitative study, predicted a degree of depth and personal exposure from interviewees. Several ethical practices came into effect to protect participants from harm. The well-being of participants was of paramount importance. Therefore, a cautious and empathic approach was adopted with all contributors.

Consent forms detailing the nature of the project ensured that no participant was forced to contribute. Directees and directors took part voluntarily, free from influence and adequately informed of their rights and duties. Participants could withdraw from the study at any time, although none did. Anonymity and confidentiality were kept at all times throughout the whole research. Pseudonyms have been used in the narratives to protect the identity of participants, and audio data, once it was analyzed, was erased.

These basic ethical practices are now standard in qualitative research, but ownership and analytic power distribution still need clarification. This research considers ownership of the stories always in the hands of the interviewees. Participants had the power to decide what to share and what not to. At the point when the narratives were analyzed and interpreted through John of the Cross' spiritual framework, ownership shifted from the participants to the researcher. Compared to the directees, spiritual directors had an advantage in analytic power due to the sampling technique adopted. Spiritual directors acted as gatekeepers, identifying potential directees as participants. Their recommendations made the research possible, but there was a danger of favoritism. For example, directors' recommendations could have excluded a directee they deemed not to merit participation. Other limitations also transpired. Some develop from the approach itself and the social context:

1. Life-History carries an impression of suspicion from researchers underlining empirical objectivity; however, the strength of Life-History lies in exposing the richness of features behind narratives.[36] A problem of loss of control arises in front of the many variables that emerge. While Life-History methods expose diversity, it becomes impracticable to control or take note of every feature. Conducting further similar research with larger samples is the only way to confirm results.

2. Participation from female spiritual directors is lacking. This study was intended to include more significant female participation, especially because many women have taken specialized training in spiritual

---

36. See Freeman and Krantz, "Unfulfilled Promise of Life Histories," 1.

direction. However, it transpired that many of the trained women are not actively involved in spiritual direction. This might be because, in Malta, spiritual direction is still associated with priesthood, and the visibility of women offering spiritual direction in pastoral communities is still low.

Division of Chapters

The rationale outlined in the previous section is reflected in the structure of chapters. Chapter 1 explores the spiritual doctrine of John of the Cross. The process required that all his writings be critically examined to highlight the significant theological points in a comprehensible presentation. Chapter 2 introduces ten spiritual narratives of directees from five social realities: married straight fathers, single straight men, separated single men, single gay men and gay men in a relationship. It is a descriptive chapter in style and presents these narratives side by side. Chapters 3 and 4 proceed by connecting the spiritual framework of John of the Cross with the ten directees' narratives. These two chapters encompass three phases: the first phase systematically suggests how the ten participants fulfil the various levels of the *dark night*, and in phase two, eight observations hint towards a form of spirituality. Chapter 4 is dedicated solely to phase three of the analysis, and here interviews with spiritual directors are used to reflect on four themes: features of male directees, style of direction, fluctuations in spiritual development and the social context. While presenting the directors' contribution, this chapter also refers back to chapter 3's observations to further clarify the form of spirituality. Finally, the last chapter relates the data derived from the empirical study and its analysis to a selective theoretical corpus. In doing so, this study is situated in present research on three aspects: the human reality, how the divine reality reveals itself, and the mediated processes that bring out transformation. The resulting discussion is then aligned to John of the Cross' spiritual framework, and the chapter concludes by looking at the merits and responsibilities of spiritual direction with men.

Chapter 1

The Spiritual Doctrine of John of the Cross

This chapter introduces the spiritual model of Saint John of the Cross.[1] It acts as the *formal object* that examines men's spiritual narratives against one of the most profound analyses of Christian spiritual dynamics. John attempts to explain the spiritual relationship with God. His spiritual treasures remain relevant even during these times in bringing together psychological and spiritual dynamics together.

John's legacy includes four commentaries on four unique poems: *the Ascent of Mount Carmel, the Dark Night of the Soul, the Spiritual Canticle* and the *Living Flame of Love*. Being rich in imagery and symbolism, they all outline the path to perfection throughout our life. Through his poetry, John interprets his compositions to the reader. In doing so, he slowly reveals his spiritual doctrine. The drift behind John's writings is not constant. The *Ascent* and the *Dark Night* are more systematic and structured, while the *Canticle* and the *Flame of Love* tend towards poetic commentaries. All his writings are John's personal experiences. Through them, he reveals different theological aspects of the spiritual journey; aspects which many misinterpret or relate wrongly to them.[2] His other poems, personal letters and maxims concerning spirituality add to his major compositions.

---

1. For a biographical sketch on John of the Cross, see Kavanaugh and Rodriguez, *Collected Works of Saint John of the Cross*, 9; Herráiz, *Obras Completas*, 9; Dodd, "John of the Cross."

2. For a list of misinterpretations, see Chowning, "Free to Love."

This chapter aims to highlight all the fundamental theological points of John of the Cross in a comprehensible presentation.[3] From his spiritual journey, John's most salient points are elicited and are presented to those who desire a relationship with God. The *Ascent* and the *Dark Night* form the backbone of this arrangement. The chapter is divided into four sections dealing with the four facets of the *dark night*. However, as one proceeds, the *Canticle* and the *Flame of Love* intersect with their poetic elements.

THE ACTIVE NIGHT OF SENSE

In the first book of the *Ascent*, John recognizes the appetites as the primary obstacle the soul faces towards union with God. He elucidates their maneuvers and offers a remedy against them. He categorizes this engagement under the *active night of senses*. It is *active* since a person can participate when one is effecting a change, and it is *night* since the senses stop receiving delight.[4]

John's notions embody human desire. He is worried that gratification from worldly objects or creatures disrupts cohesion with God. Appetites are synonymous with passions, cravings, addictions, or attachments that one possesses. However, John does not speak against the capacity to desire. On the contrary, he is aware that the journey towards perfection is permeated with longings. He clarifies what one should yearn for and how one should act towards worldly attachments. As an example, John mentions David (Ps 88:15). Although David possessed many riches, his heart did not yearn for such wealth. Neither did he deceive himself. If one imagines David being deprived of all possessions, but his heart sought to attain value by owning them, he would still be in the wrong. In themselves, objects mean nothing. What dominates a person's worth is John's primary concern. As does David, John advocates alertness. Nothing is like God's love for a soul, so he emphasizes the need for a soul to be empty of all its desires, whether possessed or not.[5]

John distinguishes between *natural appetites* or biological instincts, which pose no hindrance to union with God, and *voluntary appetites*. Voluntary appetites can hinder as they interrupt the friendship with God owing to the grave act committed. Such acts carry full knowledge and deliberate consent of the person. Venial sin, although lesser in wickedness, still impinges in the union, especially habitual behaviors of the soul.

---

3. The quotations of John's poetry and prose are taken from *Collected Works of Saint John of the Cross*.
4. *Ascent*, Book 1, chs. 3–15.
5. *Ascent*, Book 1, ch. 3, no 4.

Often, they are appetites that the soul is not aware of and yet still participates in them.[6]

His teaching relies upon the idea that two opposite wills cannot cohabitate in a soul. The appetites' demands cannot mingle with the desire for union with God. The two are incongruent. When compared to God, all creatures and objects are hollow.[7] In God's sight, a person's attachments are pure darkness. Through the act of loving, the person attaches to the object and becomes equal to it. The likeness between the lover and the Beloved comes into effect, making the lover subject to the other. Hence a soul cannot attach to a created object and, at the same time, receive the fullness of God.[8]

> By the mere fact that a soul loves something, it becomes incapable of pure union and transformation in God; for the lowness of the creature is far less capable of the height of the Creator than is darkness of light.[9]

As a result, how love transforms a soul, John reveals his significant maxim comprising the whole doctrine: two contraries cannot coexist in the same subject. Next to God's love, all worldly entities offer fragmented love. Although God created all the mundane objects, there is a vast gulf between their worth and His. The only purpose that stands undivided and which properly values humanity is God's love. Anything else subjugates to Him.[10]

Taking the figure of a prisoner in a cell where the only provision of light is a small window, John considers the limitations of human perception. He does not state that humanity is a prison, but that humanity can only perceive in a limited way. One can seek what one can sense and act to possess that object that could give satisfaction. This mechanism is universal to all humanity. Trouble occurs when the senses become the predominant architects of

---

6. John lists the following examples of venial sins: "the common habit of being very talkative; a small attachment one never really desires to conquer, for example, to a person, to clothing, to a book or a cell, or to the way food is prepared, and to other trifling conversations and little satisfactions in tasting, knowing, and hearing things, and so on." *Ascent*, Book 1, ch. 11, no 2.

7. "When compared to God, these qualities are insignificant: the beauty of the world, the grace and elegance of creatures, the goodness offered by creatures, human abilities and knowledge, sovereignty and freedom of the world and the delight in things." *Ascent*, Book 1, ch. 4.

8. "For a better proof of this, it ought to be kept in mind that an attachment to a creature makes a person equal to that creature; the stronger the attachment, the closer is the likeness to the creature and the greater the equality, for love effects a likeness between the lover and the loved." *Ascent*, Book 1, ch. 4, no 3.

9. *Ascent*, Book 1, ch. 4, no 3.

10. *Ascent*, Book 1, ch. 11, no 3.

meaning. Clinging to perception without awareness of its limitations lead to injury.[11] John outlines six harms caused when pursuing appetites.[12]

1. **Weariness**: To satisfy the appetites involves a constant habit. As children are restless and difficult to please, so too are the appetites' demands. The person is left weary and stressed, and if the senses are satisfied, it is only temporary. Their fulfilment is like leaking cisterns, and their demands increase as a fever does. As time passes, their craves surge. A person who is subject to the appetites is left agitated. Rest at one place is hard, and the chase repeats itself until one comprehends that these objects give no inner peace. Even if temporary gratification follows, there is a constant unsettling feeling of emptiness.[13]

2. **Torment**: Appetites torment a person equal to the degree of their intensity. Since the need for satisfaction is powerful and extends over time, the soul toils by seeking its ending. One becomes a prisoner of one's own needs. John describes this torment as one being tortured on the rack, or like one who reclines nakedly on a bed of thorns and nails. The appetites wound, and their demands are burdensome. Relief ensues when one is free from captivity.[14]

3. **Blindness**: The way in which appetites blind the soul is by interrupting rationality. In themselves, they do not employ the intellect. They simply cry for attention and kindle the passions to seek what it craves. In this way, the mind is blind, decision making is blurred, and life lacks critical evaluation. Since both the will and memory relate to the intellect, they all become weak and dull. Like a moth that blindly seeks the beauty of light, it ends in the bonfire since it fails to consider the

---

11. *Ascent*, Book 1, ch. 3, no 3.

12. "...these appetites cause harm in two principal ways within those in whom they dwell: They deprive them of God's Spirit; and they weary, torment, darken, defile, and weaken them." *Ascent*, Book 1, ch. 6, no 1. "First these appetites weaken and blind, ... then they afflict and torment by chaining that person to the mill of concupiscence, for they are the chains by which a soul is bound." *Ascent*, Book 1, ch. 7, no 2. *Sayings*, no 113.

13. "The disturbances that appetites cause to the soul is like wind which disturb water (Isa. 57:20); the disappointments are like to a lover who misses his chance and is left alone and empty, or like one opening his mouth to receive food and instead eats air (Jer. 2:24); the demands of appetites are like a fire consuming wood, and as the fire dwindles it intensifies more." *Ascent*, Book 1, ch. 6, no 6 and 7.

14. John also engages with David from Ps 119:61 and Ps 118:12 to describe this torment in *Ascent*, Book 1, ch. 7.

surroundings and its safety. It is the same with humans. When blindly pursuing gratification, this could lead to dire situations.[15]

4. **Defilement**: John uses Jeremiah in Lamentations (4:7–8) to depict the beauty of the soul. The soul is whiter than snow, ruddier than ancient ivory and more beautiful than sapphire stone. But all is stained when the soul follows irrational inclinations. Adhering to the cravings is like clinging to dark pitch when gold or diamonds undergo refinement. According to John, all appetites need purification. Even if a little stain lingers, the soul would not be able to unite with God.[16]

> Inordinate appetites for the things of the world do all this damage to the beauty of the soul, and even more. So great is the harm that if we try to express how ugly and dirty is the imprint the appetites leave in the soul we find nothing comparable to it—neither a place full of cobwebs and lizards nor the unsightliness of a dead body nor the filthiest thing imaginable in this life.[17]

5. **Weakness**: Since the soul consumes its energies to the demands of the appetites, the practice of virtue declines. In this case, many cravings reign within and strength contracts as the battle for ratification would be against many opponents. John sees the soul's power going to waste like uncovered hot water slowly losing warmth or unwrapped aromatic spices losing their strong fragrance. Unbridled appetites end up consuming the soul unceasingly.[18]

6. **Depravation of God's Spirit**: While the first five harms are definite, this one is privative. Since a person toils to satisfy the appetites, his psychological attention would be channeled to seek only gratification. One is unable to know other perspectives until the expulsion of this hunger occurs. As God's spirit grants fullness, it cannot reside in a soul

---

15. *Ascent*, Book 1, ch. 8; "Appetites interfere with rationality like how vapor murk air and blocks sunshine; muddy water reflecting hazy images; cataracts on the eyes. Solomon is an example who in his old age was blinded by his passions and neglected to keep his appetites in check." *Ascent*, Book 1, ch. 8, no 6. About the risk of mistaking evil for good see *Ascent*, Book 1, ch. 8, no 7.

16. *Ascent*, Book 1, ch. 9.

17. *Ascent*, Book 1, ch. 9, no 3.

18. *Ascent*, Book 1, ch. 10.

who seeks crumbs.[19] The two are opposites and act against each other, and hence God's fullness is held back until the appetite is subdued.[20]

> What, then, has the hunger caused by creatures in common with the fullness caused by the Spirit of God? This uncreated fullness cannot enter a soul until this other hunger caused by the desires is expelled. Since hunger and fullness are contraries, they cannot coexist in the same person.[21]

Any harm deprives the soul of its powers and identity. They might not appear all at once, but gradually after the sweetness of gratification passes away, their bitter effects will be felt.[22] John's antidote is to mortify them. He values freedom and cherishes life's wealth beyond consumption. Failure to do so causes the soul to be captive in stressful, anxious and fearful existence. John encourages the soul to move forward in its quest for union with God and to cut all chords of attachments, even minor sins.[23]

> It makes little difference whether a bird is tied by a thin thread or by a cord. Even if it is tied by thread, the bird will be held bound just as surely as if it were tied by cord; that is, it will be impeded from flying as long as it does not break the thread. Admittedly the thread is easier to break, but no matter how easily this may be done, the bird will not fly away without first doing so. This is the lot of those who are attached to something: No matter how much virtue they have they will not reach the freedom of the divine union.[24]

The method leads to the nakedness of self. The soul wakes up to a new awareness about life that previously was taken for granted.[25] The soul

---

19. By examining Matt 15:26–27, John compares individuals wandering hungrily like dogs who are constantly dissatisfied. Through the dining imagery, holy food is held back from dogs in *Ascent*, Book 1, ch. 6, no 2.

20. *Ascent*, Book 1, ch. 6, no 1–5.

21. *Ascent*, Book 1, ch. 6, no 3 and 7.

22. *Ascent*, Book 1, ch. 11, no 5.

23. "What is worse, not only do they fail to advance, but they turn back because of their small attachment, losing what they gained on their journey at the cost of so much time and effort. Everyone knows that not to go forward on this road is to turn back, and not to gain ground is to lose," in *Ascent*, Book 1, ch. 11, no 5.

24. John also uses the metaphor of the remora, which prevents a ship laden with riches from reaching port in *Ascent*, Book 1, ch. 11, no 4; *Sayings*, no 18, 22, 23, 24, 25, 56, and 78.

25. In *Canticle*, Stanza 1, no 1, John outlines ten things that a person becomes aware of: obligation towards God for saving the soul, much of the soul's life has passed, that

works through correcting perspective through striving for authenticity. But John knows that when the senses undergo this discipline, they suffer. The pleasures from familiarities cease, and the sudden loss of meaning haunts the soul. Through perseverance, the object's clutches fail, and the soul's awareness expands. During this transition, the person suffers until one adapts to new knowledge. The deprivation of gratification is classified as *night* and becomes the *active night of sense*.[26]

> Hence, we call this nakedness a night for the soul, for we are not discussing the mere lack of things; this lack will not divest the soul if it craves for all these objects. We are dealing with the denudation of the soul's appetites and gratifications. This is what leaves it free and empty of all things, even though it possesses them. Since the things of the world cannot enter the soul, they are not in themselves an encumbrance or harm to it; rather, it is the will and appetite dwelling within that causes the damage when set on these things.[27]

Faced with the challenge of renunciation, John encourages his reader to heed the words of Christ in Matthew 11:28–29 and to find rest in Him.[28] The new awareness that the soul awakes to is described as a wound of love which creates in the soul a desire for God: *the longings of love*.[29] Since once's willpower is the answer to control the appetites, John directs the human being for a habit to study and imitate Christ. In doing so, one acts to direct satisfaction only for the honor and glory of God.[30] The restraint of appetites will cause resistance, but John reassures that God struggles with the soul through such purification and achieves more than if he had to create the soul from nothing since nothing does not resist back.[31]

During this *active night of the senses*, John instructs spiritual directors to be attentive to the undercurrents of the appetites that spiritual directees bring up to them. Directors are to encourage self-awareness and meditation

---

life is short, the path leading to salvation is constricted, the just are rarely saved, things of the world are vain and deceitful, everything fails and finishes, time is uncertain, heaven's accounting is strict, perdition is very easy.

26. *Ascent*, Book 1, ch. 3, no 1.
27. *Ascent*, Book 1, ch. 3, no 4.
28. *Ascent*, Book 1, ch. 7, no 3 and 4.
29. *Ascent*, Book 1, ch. 14, no 2; *Canticle*, Stanza 1, no 2; *Night*, Book 1, ch. 11, no 1.
30. *Ascent*, Book 1, ch. 13, no 3 and 4.
31. Ascent, Book 1, ch. 6, no 4.

so that directees can work upon themselves and own their spiritual lives. In the end, directors should stimulate freedom from the appetites' misery.[32]

THE ACTIVE NIGHT OF SPIRIT

John treats the *active night of spirit* in books two and three of the *Ascent*. While the night of sense is represented metaphorically at the start of the evening, midnight is the scene for the night of the spirit.

> The first night pertains to the lower, sensory part of human nature and is consequently more external. As a result the second night is darker. The second, darker night of faith belongs to the rational, superior part; it is darker and more interior because it deprives this part of its rational light, or better, blinds it. Accordingly, it is indeed comparable to midnight, the innermost and darkest period of night.[33]

This night focuses on a person's sense of self. In the night, one is sharing in the purification of three primary abilities: intellect, memory and will.[34] In book two, John evaluates the reflective properties of the intellect, while in the unfinished third book, John discusses memory and will. His doctrine relies upon the scholastic technique used at the time. Although John treats each faculty separately, they are a single psychological interface. Purification of the intellect brings about the same effects as to memory and to will. His aim in writing book two remains faithful to his original purpose:

> The discreet reader must always keep in mind my intention and goal in this book: to guide the soul in purity of faith through all its natural and supernatural apprehensions, in freedom from deception and every obstacle, to divine union with God.[35]

These three interior aptitudes which feed on the senses are the cultivators of a rational self. But moreover, they indicate and evaluate what is vital for the person. In every decision, they navigate the self towards its full realization. Furthermore, the soul uses the three faculties to find the manifestations of God's divine essence.[36] However, since they are of the world, their

---

32. *Ascent*, Book 1, ch. 12, no 6.
33. *Ascent*, Book 2, ch. 2, no 2.
34. *Ascent*, Book 2, ch. 6, no 6.
35. *Ascent*, Book 2, ch. 28, no 1.
36. *Canticle*, Stanza 1, no 3.

dimension of actualization is limited.[37] Nothing that what the three faculties produce in mind is capable of harnessing the totality of God, so the night of the spirit expands them. Slowly the soul must renounce all interior possessions to get acquainted with new functions. This loss is not purposeless, but it leads to wholeness and transformation.[38] Each ability must be cohesive in likeness to that of God and arrive at full fruition. The lesson is similar to the first night, but variations exist. Earlier, the objects needing mortification were the senses—external to the mind; now, it is reason itself. The areas where the self gets sustenance is wiped out. If the *longings of love* compelled the bride to seek the Beloved in the first night, the theological virtues now bid the soul adapt to God's character.

Although the theological virtues obscure their respective faculties, they likewise assist the self in transcending them. While obscuring intellect, faith affirms convictions. Even though what it claims cannot be fully understood, it inspires and shrouds God.[39] Hope reduces all gained possessions into insignificance but recalls what is fundamental and yet to be possessed.[40] Charity achieves willpower. First, the will negotiates between the divine and anything that the soul still clings to. Later charity impels the soul to be decisive with one's affections and elicits responsibility.[41]

> These virtues, as we said, void the faculties: Faith causes darkness and a void of understanding in the intellect, hope begets an emptiness of possessions in the memory, and charity produces the nakedness and emptiness of affection and joy in all that is not God.[42]

Faith, hope and charity are the soul's new garments. These are alien to rationality as they do not emerge from perception, but the soul employs them to reach nakedness and emptiness of self.[43] The trial is hard, but John

---

37. *Ascent*, Book 2, ch. 5, no 5.

38. For John union with God does not lead to the destruction of the soul but that the two become one in likeness and participation. He refers to Mark 8:34–35 in *Ascent*, Book 2, ch. 7, no 4; Matt 16:25 and Luke 9:24 in *Ascent*, Book 2, ch. 7, no 6. John clarifies that in this world, union can only reach a phase of likeness. A permanent union of the faculties to God in this life is impossible in *Ascent*, Book 2, ch. 5. John also uses the metaphor of the window receiving sunlight. Through the process of cleansing, the two become one through participation in *Ascent*, Book 2, ch. 6, no 6.

39. *Ascent*, Book 2, ch. 6, no 2.

40. *Ascent*, Book 2, ch. 6, no 3.

41. *Ascent*, Book 2, ch. 6, no 4.

42. *Ascent*, Book 2, ch. 6, no 2.

43. These three virtues are represented in John's accommodated use of the scripture as the three loaves in Luke 11:5 and as the six seraphs in Isa 6:2 in *Ascent*, Book 2, ch.

echoes Christ's instructions in Matthew 7:14: "For the gate is narrow and the road is hard that leads to life, and there are few who find it." John explain this figure in two manners: It is narrow since the soul must abandon dependency on worldly possessions, and it is constricting as many traps remain within the self.[44]

John's message points to those who call themselves friends of the Bridegroom. They have passed the beginners' stages and still drink from their interior spiritual possessions. In this divine relationship, routine devotion and comfort-seeking are not enough.[45] In truth, these interior objects become obstacles. Progression is hindered unless one abandons the need to control events. When all plans fall through, one does not only come to terms with life's limitations but is faced with the challenge to accord the *annihilation of self*. By annihilation, John understands a spiritual death in all things esteemed by the self.[46] While at the start, the person enjoys many spiritual delights, now the self must be decentralized. When the intellectual powers fail and hopelessness arises, the will is in a delicate position to live up to its desire. Failure to choose self-renunciation amounts to the spiritual journey going around in circles without getting anywhere.[47] In line with John's earlier advice to imitate Christ, here the perfect example is his crucifixion. Within that image, Christ displays the noblest level of self-annihilation. All darkens for Christ, even divine consolations.[48]

> ... at the moment of his death he was certainly annihilated in his soul, without any consolation or relief, since the Father had left him that way in innermost aridity in the lower part. He was thereby compelled to cry out: My God, My God, why have you forsaken me? [Matt 27:46]. This was the most extreme abandonment, sensitively, that he had suffered in his life. And by it he accomplished the most marvellous work of his whole life, surpassing all the works and deeds and miracles that he had ever performed on earth or in heaven. That is, he brought about the reconciliation and union of the human race with God through grace. The Lord achieved this, as I say, at the moment in which he was most annihilated in all things: in his reputation before people, since in watching him die they mocked him instead of esteeming him; in his human nature, by dying; and in spiritual

---

6, no 5.

44. *Ascent*, Book 2, ch. 7, no 1—3.
45. *Ascent*, Book 2, ch. 7, no 5; *Ascent*, Book 2, ch. 5, no 4 and 8.
46. *Ascent*, Book 2, ch. 7.
47. *Ascent*, Book 2, ch. 7, no 8.
48. *Ascent*, Book 2, ch. 7, no 7, 11.

help and consolation from his Father, for he was forsaken by his Father at that time, annihilated and reduced to nothing, so as to pay the debt fully and bring people to union with God. David says of him: Ad nihilum redactus sum et nescivi [Ps 73:22], that those who are truly spiritual might understand the mystery of the door and way (which is Christ) leading to union with God, and that they might realise that their union with God and the greatness of the work they accomplish will be measured by their annihilation of themselves for God in the sensory and spiritual parts of their souls. When they are reduced to nothing, the highest degree of humility, the spiritual union between their souls and God will be an accomplished fact. This union is the most noble and sublime state attainable in this life. The journey, then, does not consist in consolations, delights, and spiritual feelings, but in the living death of the cross, sensory and spiritual, exterior and interior.[49]

John views suffering for Christ as the remedy for the self. Harnessing the self keeps in check selfishness and encourages humility and prudence.[50] However, knowing that the human person still requires some object to lean on, John looks for some means of access that can bring clear communication and connection to God. He presents a long list of objects that the mind can produce, and one by one, he evaluates their reliability. Finally, he concludes that none are safe. Nothing of creation is a proximate mean to the divine. The surest instrument is faith.[51] Before examining how John of the Cross views faith, the properties of the intellect, memory and will be considered.

The Intellect

John names two impressions that the intellect can hold: the act of reflection that produces natural ideas, and supernatural knowledge received passively.[52] As regards natural ideas, John refers the reader to the *active night of senses*. He explains that when one clings inordinately to an object or creature, one does so first within the mind, and later through behavior. The mortification called for unto the appetites spread in the first degrees of rational thinking.[53]

---

49. *Ascent*, Book 2, ch. 7, no 7, 11.
50. *Ascent*, Book 2, ch. 6, no 7; ch. 7, no 5; *Sayings*, no 87, 92, and 95.
51. *Ascent*, Book 2, chs. 1–3 and 8–9.
52. *Ascent*, Book 2, ch. 10, no 2.
53. *Ascent*, Book 2, ch. 11, no 1.

In book two of the *Ascent*, John considers specifically supernatural knowledge. He distinguishes between two types: spiritual and corporeal. In the case of the corporeal, he looks at knowledge received from the external senses and the imagination. John focuses attention on the frequent habit of the imagination since beginners often experience its practice. It allows one to acquire a smattering of knowledge in mind through forms and figures and enjoy it through feelings into the senses. As for spiritual knowledge, John differentiates between two kinds: one conveys distinct insights, while the other unmasks vague and general knowledge. From the two, John finds assurance in the latter.[54]

Supernatural knowledge in the form of spiritual unctions (Corporeal)

John views spiritual unctions as the manifestations of inspiration which the soul comes to have without control. When the soul meets a meaningful occurrence, affection intensifies in the senses leading to creative expressions. These events are attractive and enhance enthusiasm for prayer, but John warns one not to pursue them for their stimulation. According to him, a person receiving these unctions runs the risk of gaining a gratified view of oneself. As pride increases, one errs in mixing spiritual matters with mere emotional arousals.[55]

Supernatural knowledge from the Imagination (Corporeal)

Within the imaginative power, John encompasses all the supernatural wonders that one receives in the forms of visualizations, sensations, fragrances and locutions. Often, they are a product of practicing discursive meditation. Rich imagery entices the soul to ponder over them. But, according to John, in the long run, they overwhelm the mind with their paradoxes.[56] Since imagination recycles what has already been known, it is an inadequate means for the union. In light of its limitations, he calls for its transcendence at the right time.[57]

The timing of renunciation is a sensitive matter. John agrees that it is a necessary tool that beginners use to relate to scripture and the life of the saints. Similar to a training ground, one begins to experiment with mental

---

54. *Ascent*, Book 2, ch. 10, no 4.
55. *Ascent*, Book 2, ch. 11, no 1—6.
56. *Ascent*, Book 2, ch. 11, no 4.
57. *Ascent*, Book 2, ch. 12, no 3.

recollection, the discipline of the appetites and a habitual posture towards God. However, such exercises are a means to a better end.

> Our Lord proves and elevates the soul by first bestowing graces that are exterior, lowly, and proportioned to the small capacity of sense. If the person reacts well by taking these first morsels with moderation for strength and nourishment, God will bestow a more abundant and higher quality of food. If individuals are victorious over the devil in the first degree, they will pass on to the second; and if so in the second, they will go to the third; and likewise through all the seven mansions (the seven degrees of love) until the Bridegroom puts them in the wine cellar of perfect charity [Sg. 2:4].[58]

John considers the exercises of the imagination as remote food for the union with God. As one makes way in the spiritual pedagogy, one would need to relinquish the earlier poles like climbing a ladder.[59] At the appropriate time, which the person cannot control, discursive meditation reaches its peak. Instead of fruitfulness, it starts yielding barrenness. For the person, praying is effortful, and entering in the meditative attitude feels cold. A disinclination to focus on the imagination on spiritual object begins, and instead of positive feelings, the person faces agitation and confusion.

According to John, when these signs appear, they signify that the road of meditation has been covered. One cannot go back and redo what was crossed. Rather than resisting or pushing towards the same method of prayer, spiritual directors are to encourage a soul to meet God with open regard, even if it appears as plain idleness.[60] This style of encounter is the adequate food that the soul is ready to consume. Pushing backwards makes the imagination an obstacle.[61] On this matter, John gives the following remedies:

1. Instead of forcing the imagination, one should slowly get accustomed to spiritual quietness;

2. Spiritual quietness prescribes one to learn how to equip one's vision with a general loving attentiveness to God; and,

---

58. *Ascent*, Book 2, ch. 11, no 9; ch. 12, no 5; ch. 17, no 2—5.

59. *Ascent*, Book 2, ch. 12, no 5.

60. *Ascent*, Book 2, ch. 12, no 6—9; The three signs that it is time to discharge this mode of communication are further discussed in *Ascent*, Book 2, chs. 13 and 14; *Flame*, Stanza 3.

61. *Ascent*, Book 2, ch. 14, no 3. John uses the metaphor of the *rind* in *Ascent*, Book 2, ch. 17, no 9.

3. If imagination resurfaces with forms and figures, one gently allows it to drift but with no excessive effort.

Abiding in this disposition allows the soul to receive God without conditions and hidden from human ways. Some arrive in a state of oblivion when they forget time and their intellect is abstracted from all forms.[62] However, according to John, this disposition cultivates a habit of contemplation which agrees with the merits of faith.[63] The object and aim of the spiritual person are to pass through all modes to attain contemplation. Now the soul is not elevated through fantastical and affective climaxes but through a loving simplicity withdrawn from all exterior and interior interruptions.[64]

> What the soul, therefore, was gradually acquiring through the labor of meditation on particular ideas has now, as we said, been converted into habitual and substantial, general loving knowledge. This knowledge is neither distinct nor particular, as was the previous knowledge. Accordingly the moment prayer begins, the soul, as one with a store of water, drinks peaceably without the labor and the need to fetch the water through the channels of past considerations, forms, and figures. The moment it recollects itself in the presence of God it enters into an act of general, loving, peaceful, and tranquil knowledge, drinking wisdom and love and delight.[65]

While before one could think that the journey to spiritual perfection is understanding particular ideas, now one awakes to the reality of love, that God wants to communicate with a person face to face.[66] According to God, it is at this moment that infused union commences. Once the soul expels all the interior vices within and remains in its pure and naked essence, God also encounters the soul in His pure essence.[67]

> What clearly follows is that when individuals have finished purifying and voiding themselves of all forms and apprehensible images, they will abide in this pure and simple light and

---

62. John uses the phrase *oblivion* to describe this happening in *Ascent*, Book 2, ch. 14, no 11 and 12.
63. *Ascent*, Book 2, ch. 11, no 6.
64. *Ascent*, Book 2, ch. 14, no 8 and 9.
65. *Ascent*, Book 2, ch. 14, no 2; ch. 16, no 5.
66. John views those persons who stick to the imagination as clinging to the ring of the spirit in *Ascent*, Book 2, ch. 14, no 4.
67. It is in this moment that the passive night of sense and spirit commences since the soul would have reached the limits of its own powers to purify itself in *Ascent*, Book 2, ch. 16, no 9, 11, and 12.

be perfectly transformed in it. This light is never lacking to the soul, but because of creature forms and veils that weigh on it and cover it, the light is never infused. If individuals would eliminate these impediments and veils and live in pure nakedness and poverty of spirit, as we will explain later, their soul in its simplicity and purity would then be immediately transformed into simple and pure wisdom, the Son of God. As soon as natural things are driven out of the enamored soul, the divine are naturally and supernaturally infused since there can be no void in nature.[68]

Distinct Spiritual Knowledge

When John discusses distinct spiritual knowledge, he attributes the qualities as "nobler, safer and more advantageous than the imaginative corporeal visions as they are already interior, purely spiritual and less exposed to the devil's meddling."[69] The soul receives them with no action on its part, but, like other apprehensions, they should not be the direct desire for the soul. John identifies four classes of such knowledge: visions, revelations, locutions and spiritual feelings.[70]

Visions

Visions are objects that the intellect receives in a manner resembling sight. Through divine light, some souls are granted the view of wonders of which they never had any apriori knowledge. According to John, human form can only receive visions about corporeal substances which divulge material things of heaven and earth. However, a soul would not be gifted to allow visions revealing incorporeal substance about God's glory. In front of such grandeur, the soul would depart the earthly body and pass to the next life. He writes:

> These visions cannot serve the intellect as a proximate means for union with God because they deal with creatures, which bear no proportion or essential conformity to God. Consequently, to advance by the proximate means, which is faith, a person should behave in a purely negative way as with the other visions we

---

68. *Ascent,* Book 2, ch. 16, no 4 and 10.
69. *Ascent*, Book 2, ch. 23, no 4.
70. *Ascent*, Book 2, ch. 23, no 1–5.

mentioned. Souls should not store up or treasure the forms of these visions impressed within, neither should they have the desire to cling to them. In doing so they would impede themselves by what dwells within them (those forms, images, and figures of persons), and they would not journey to God through the negation of all things. Though these forms remain impressed within the soul, they are not a great impediment if one is unwilling to pay heed to them. Even if the remembrance of these visions really does stir the soul to some contemplation and love of God, denudation, pure faith, and darkness regarding them will stir and elevate it much more, and without its knowing how or whence this elevation comes.[71]

Revelations

The manifestation of hidden truths or secret mysteries falls under the category of revelations.[72] John distinguishes between truths about creatures and truths about God. In both cases, a soul experiences delight. However, truths concerning God convey a deeper delight. Through contemplation, the soul sees in its core God's omnipotence, fortitude, and goodness. Often when the soul least expects, God bestows these touches on the soul. John views such communication as an aspect of the union with God. The devil cannot meddle or reproduce the knowledge, and the person finds it almost impossible to describe the encounter in plain language.[73]

> This sublime knowledge can be received only by a person who has arrived at union with God, for it is itself that very union. It consists in a certain touch of the divinity produced in the soul, and thus it is God himself who is experienced and tasted there. Although the touch of knowledge and delight that penetrates the substance of the soul is not manifest and clear, as in glory, it is so sublime and lofty that the devil is unable to meddle or produce anything similar (for there is no experience similar or comparable to it), or infuse a savor and delight like it. This knowledge tastes of the divine essence and of eternal life, and the devil cannot counterfeit anything so lofty.[74]

---

71. *Ascent*, Book 2, ch. 24, no 8.
72. *Ascent*, Book 2, ch. 26.
73. *Ascent*, Book 2, ch. 26, no 3 and 4.
74. *Ascent*, Book 2, ch. 26, no 5.

As a result of this encounter, the Supreme Principle imbues the soul with love. John looks upon this savoring encounter as a gift to the soul to remember and embrace. After the required refinement is complete, one receives this loving encounter.[75] When John speaks about the manifestation of secret mysteries, he refers to the gift of prophecy. Some souls who have journeyed along the path of purification develop a profound and sensitive awareness about the world. Through their perception, they can perceive something more about the world. John is adamant that souls should not heed such visions since they can distract, contradict, and mislead. Instead, he advises to mistrust this knowledge and to seek spiritual assistance.[76]

Locutions

John divides locutions into three categories: successive, formal, and substantial. A soul receives this knowledge in a form similar to hearing.[77] By successive locutions, a soul gives ear to what is communicated. Often it occurs during meditation. The danger associated with this knowledge is that the mind, by itself, can produce a dialogue where God is not partaking.[78]

> Manifestly, then, these successive locutions can originate in the intellect from any of three causes: the divine spirit, who moves and illumines the intellect; the natural light of the intellect; and the devil, who can speak to it through suggestion.[79]

Formal locutions are certain distinct words that the soul receives from another entity. These are like ideas passed to the spirit even when one is not meditating. Like successive locutions, the soul should not trust the given words or share its content with others even if they sound virtuous.[80]

Out of the three kinds, John values substantial locutions. They are words received by the soul in its substance which fulfils a great motivation towards charity. He finds these locutions safe since the words communicated are hidden and escape possession. Often, they are bestowed on to accomplish God's will.[81]

---

75. *Ascent*, Book 2, ch. 26, no 10.
76. *Ascent*, Book 2, ch. 26, no 11—18.
77. *Ascent*, Book 2, ch. 28—31.
78. *Ascent*, Book 2, ch. 28, no 5; *Ascent*, Book 2, ch. 29, no 5.
79. *Ascent*, Book 2, ch. 29, no 11.
80. *Ascent*, Book 2, ch. 30.
81. *Ascent*, Book 2, ch. 31.

> In this fashion he bestows substantial locutions on certain souls. These locutions are as important and valuable as are the life, virtue, and incomparable blessings they impart to the soul. A locution of this sort does more good for a person than a whole lifetime of deeds . . . As for these locutions, the soul has nothing to do, desire, refrain from desiring, reject, or fear. There is nothing to be done, because God never grants them for that purpose, but he bestows them in order to bring about what they express. For this reason they differ from the formal and successive locutions. And there is nothing for the soul to desire or refrain from desiring. A desire for these locutions is not necessary for God to grant them, nor would not wanting them hinder their effect. The soul should rather be resigned and humble about them.[82]

Spiritual Feelings

This kind of knowledge has to do with the sense of sensation, smell, or taste. John distinguishes two feelings: the ones that touch the affection of the will, and others that reside in the substance of the soul. Although these feelings are related to the faculty of the will, John places them in the intellect's classification since the mind can identify them.[83]

As regards touches to the affection of the will, John fails to describe them in detail even if he promised to do so in the third book of the *Ascent*. As to feelings that lie in the substance of the soul, John gives them the same properties as substantial locutions, which are a consequence of union. Although they bring sublime goodness, the soul receives them without desiring them. John admonishes the soul to remain humble and behave passively towards them.

> To avoid error as a result of these feelings, and any impediment to the profit coming from them, the intellect should do nothing about them other than behave passively and refrain from meddling through the use of its natural capacity. For as in the case of successive locutions, the intellect by its own activity easily disturbs and undoes that delicate knowledge, a delightful, supernatural knowing unattainable through one's natural capacity. Nor does the intellect by its own activity find this knowledge comprehensible but comprehends it only by receiving it.[84]

82. *Ascent*, Book 2, ch. 31, no 1 and 2.
83. *Ascent*, Book 2, ch. 32, no 2.
84. *Ascent*, Book 2, ch. 32, no 4.

The Memory

John treats the faculty of memory similarly to the way in which he classifies the intellect. He names three types of possessions that memory can hold: natural, imaginative, and spiritual objects. The same line of thought follows. As a person attains a strong footing in life and in spiritual matters, one would have acquired a prosperous memory in terms of experiences and objects. A process of unlearning and transcendence initiates for further progression. Through the act of emptying all possessions, memory expands and prepares to encounter God transparently.[85]

Hope is the theological virtue that obscures memory. The self transfers hope from the desire to possess material objects to God's. Nevertheless, even spiritual hope requires further purification since what is understood by it rests on what has been encountered and held in memory. The path of mortification and self-decentralization prolongs. As thoughts can distract the soul, so memories can elicit resistance. But, through the process of awareness and forgiveness, the memory reaches a proper stillness to receive the Holy Spirit.[86]

Forgetfulness of natural objects to the same degree as the first *active night of senses* achieves freedom from inordinate appetites. Positive results appear when a soul is undisturbed by memories about creatures that can give rise to annoyance, hatred, or agreeable views. When such matters do not manipulate the mind, nothing will strain the appetites.

> We experience this all the time. We observe that as often as people begin to think about some matter, they are moved and aroused over it, little or much, according to the kind of apprehension. If the apprehension is bothersome and annoying, they feel sadness or hatred, and so on; if agreeable, they experience desire and joy, and so on. Accordingly, when the apprehension is changed agitation necessarily results. Thus they will sometimes be joyful, at other times sad, now they will feel hatred, now love. And they are unable to persevere in equanimity, the effect of moral tranquility, unless they endeavor to forget all things. Evidently, then, this knowledge is a serious impediment to possession of the moral virtues.[87]

---

85. *Ascent*, Book 3, ch. 2, no 1 and 2.

86. Here, John gives us two examples of how this moving by the holy spirit looks like in *Ascent*, Book 3, ch. 2, no 9–12.

87. *Ascent*, Book 3, ch. 5, no 1–3.

With the intellect, memory has the power to store all the supernatural forms that pass through the imagination. Their markings imprint within, and often the intellect is led to recollect and reflect upon memories. John lists the following tribulations when one is stubbornly clinging for further clarity.[88]

1. Often natural nuances are confused like supernatural ones. Clarity of thought and rationality fall through. One would waste time discerning the apprehensions in the hope of finding harmony. However, the truth about these phenomena is often hazy;[89]

2. If one persistently attempts to unravel the truth in imaginative apprehensions, then many occasions of presumption, pride, and stubbornness increase. Virtue works inversely. Not only it humbles the self in prudence, but it also nurtures poverty in possessing these figures. According to John, in most cases, fantastical events inflate the self;[90]

3. Presumption brings about a shallow judgement against life and God. Instead of finding a haven in the concealment of faith, God is condensed to a set of needs or wounds;[91]

4. Matters worsen for a soul if in the unceasing indulgence on imaginative possessions, demonic deception develops. False ideas appear as good, and the mind fails to choose the right path;[92] and,

5. Instead of uniting hope in God, one affixes it to artificial wonders which continuously dissatisfy the soul.[93]

John urges negation of the memory. In doing so, a soul is free from any form which calls for attention and distraction. If one suspends the evaluation of such apprehensions, then one does not waste time and proceeds quickly to God. Referring to contemplation, John desires spiritual persons to focus on remembering the loving knowledge and movements that God imparts to the soul. Such knowledge is the safest means for the union.[94] These spiritual gifts flee appropriation either in figures or plain language. However, although elusive, the soul is conscious of them in the substance of its being. They are spiritual marvels overflowing into awareness, but the

88. *Ascent*, Book 3, ch. 7.
89. *Ascent*, Book 3, ch. 8.
90. *Ascent*, Book 3, ch. 9.
91. *Ascent*, Book 3, ch. 12.
92. *Ascent*, Book 3, ch. 10.
93. *Ascent*, Book 3, ch. 11.
94. *Ascent*, Book 3, ch. 13.

faculties fail to comprehend their essence. John identifies spiritual feelings and touches as safe memories that the soul should recall since in doing so, the spirit is further inflamed by love. They are sensible recollections because their bestowal rests upon living poverty of spirit successfully. God, in His perfect judgment, chooses to yield the fruits of contemplation to the soul.[95]

The Will

At the end of the *active night of sense,* John admonishes the soul to acquire two mental possessions: imitating Christ and seeking God's honor and glory in every circumstance. Faith bears the most excellent imitation to that of Christ, while utter love for God reveals the strength of the will.

> You shall love the Lord your God with all your heart, and with all your soul, and with all your might.[96]

This verse summarizes John's doctrine about the purification of the will. A divided will signify the soul's internal struggle to love God over others. One repeatedly confronts the lingering sin of idolatry within the self. John mentions joy, fear, hope and sorrow as the four passions that guide the will. Whenever the soul accedes to one of these affections, the other three follow. They seek to preserve the self in possessing that which is valued and satisfying. However, nothing in the world truly lasts. Often these passions are yearnful and restless. Until the soul learns that God is the most reliable preservation for its existence, the passions will never give rest since they feed on creatures and the world's possessions.

> The less strongly the will is fixed for God and the more dependant it is on creatures, the more these four passions combat the soul and reign in it.[97]

For John, the strength of the will is not the perfect ability to escape sin, but the capacity to recognize weakness and transcend it. On its own, moral perfection does not bring humility and risks nurturing pride. The strength of the will is not visible through the soul's affections towards external objects, but by observing how its interior aptitudes bend towards glorifying God.[98] John describes joy as the corporeal passion, which finds pleasure in

---

95. *Ascent,* Book 3, ch. 14.
96. Deut 6:5.
97. *Ascent,* Book 3, ch. 16, no 4.
98. "The principle is: the will should rejoice only in what is for the honor and glory of God, and the greatest honor we can give him is to serve him according to evangelical

internal and external objects. He distinguishes between active and passive joy.[99] The former delight which the soul is aware of, while the latter is unrecognized. He outlines six kinds of objects where delight takes root. These will be briefly presented.

Temporal Goods

Temporal goods comprise material riches, status, children, and marriage that one possesses oneself of momentarily in this world.[100] Many people work incessantly and laboriously to possess them. Even though they are not bad in themselves, they often intensify vanity. According to John, to possess temporal goods often brings on idleness, superficiality, and forgetfulness of God. These render a person to feel shielded from misfortune. When these riches offend the soul and the ensuing suffering leads one to reconsider life genuinely, it is then that the moment for growth arises. John lists four harms, one worse than the other.[101]

1. First harm: when a person is engrossed in the joy of creatures, a person becomes surfeited and blunt in mind towards God;
2. Second harm: once the soul permeates in freedom and delight in created things, a feeling of dissatisfaction ensues about spiritual exercises. Instead of approaching God intimately, prayer becomes a routine formality;
3. Third harm: when a person is distant from God, the mind is remiss of God's loving law and runs the risk of acting immorally; and,
4. Fourth harm: when a person completely forgets God in all one's thoughts and actions, the will becomes corrupt, and the person willingly violates the moral good.

John admonishes a soul to possess temporal goods but within the limits of *liberality*.[102] Creatures and objects are to be kept with a wideness of heart and without inner detachment. By doing so, the soul is free from

---

perfection; anything unincluded in such service is without value to human beings." *Ascent*, Book 3, ch. 17, no 2.

99. Abruptly, John ends the third book of the *Ascent* and fails to continue with passive joy and the other three passions. Later in his other writings, one recognizes that the origins of passive joy are the divine operations within the soul.

100. *Ascent*, Book 3, ch. 18.

101. *Ascent*, Book 3, ch. 19.

102. *Ascent*, Book 3, ch. 20, no 1.

delusions. Possessions are to be of service to others. Delight is permissible, but objects are held within the clarity of reason.

Natural Goods

Natural goods embrace beauty, elegance, body constitution and talents. John observes how excessive attachment to these goods often brings about mental distraction, delusion, and emotional sorrow. The soul can admire their beauty, but one should be vigilant about excessive import. As such goods are earthly bound, John reminds that with the passage of time they easily vanish.[103] He outlines five harms and links their causes to the sin of fornication.[104]

1. First harm: possessing these natural goods often creates a vain self, and other people are regarded and viewed inferior;
2. Second harm: since these objects flourish in the senses, lust can dominate the appetites and consequently mislead judgement;
3. Third harm: often, these natural goods draw compliments from others. One can easily be deluded in forming one's sense of worth through praise and false validation;
4. Fourth harm: if one seeks sophistication in all, then decision making and judgement of spirit veers into dullness;
5. Fifth harm: what is truly vital in life and in spiritual progression is overlooked, with the result that the mind proceeds in its distractions and illusions; and,
6. Sixth harm: as the required purification for union with God is challenging, the will develops a weak character when it is facing spiritual pressures.

When one is cautious about the lustful effects of natural goods, one will prepare the soul to esteem neighbor's kindness and love beyond appearances. It is a step towards valuing self-denial instead of self-centeredness. Moreover, one is strengthened against the temptations stemming from sensuality and lust.

---

103. *Ascent,* Book 3, ch. 21.
104. *Ascent,* Book 3, ch. 22.

Sensory Goods.

In this category, John groups all objects that give delight to the senses. These include melodies, food, sensations, and imagination. Since the senses are mundane, they can only lure and give delight appropriate to their earthly parameters. John advises caution and prudence. Although they satisfy and intensify feelings, they can lead to superficiality. Like the previous goods, delight through the senses is to be elevated only to God. The will should not evade these sentiments but must be wary not to reduce prayer to entertainment.[105] By observing souls who are dependent on these goods, John outlines four harms:

1. First harm: failure to deny excessive joy in sensory goods leads to a vain and sensual spirit. This behavior also affects the relationship with God and results in distraction, indecency and discomposure;

2. Second harm: immoderate attachment to the pleasure to listen to what others narrate induces occasions of gossip, envy, and wrong influences;

3. Third harm: excessive pleasure in food leads to gluttony and drunkenness and consequently clarity of mind is obstructed; and,

4. Forth harm: obsessions regarding the sensual and intimate sensations lead to covetousness and boastfulness.[106]

Moral Goods

Under this category, one finds the exercise of virtues, adherence to God's law and political prudence. John acknowledges that such interior properties are worthier than external possessions. While these goods bring on tranquility, peace, and order, one should direct their merits to the glory of God.[107] Failure to transcend them and align them with God can conduce to a variety of harms:[108]

1. First harm: when one acquires these moral goods, these can lead to pride. As a result, a subtle arrogance ensues towards others for holding different lifestyles, values or principles;

---

105. *Ascent,* Book 3, ch. 24.
106. *Ascent,* Book 3, ch. 25.
107. *Ascent,* Book 3, ch. 27.
108. *Ascent,* Book 3, ch. 28.

2. Second harm: when these goods do not show any regard for the glory of God, their main object is for their gratification rather than for the common good. Instead of shielding one's works, attention-seeking and admiration is pursued;

3. Third harm: failure to proceed along the path of perfection occurs because when consolation ceases, the soul is deterred and attributes the lack of perseverance to one's weaknesses;

4. Fourth harm: if satisfaction is the persistent condition for one to apply moral goods, then mortification of the self and suffering for Christ is loathed; and,

5. Fifth harm: owing to pride and a sense of entitlement a soul who is accustomed to receive positive opinions would object to diverging opinions which brings on embarrassment to the self.

It then follows that when one does not value the reception of satisfaction from moral goods, one cultivates a meeker personality. Service for the common good is rendered for the glory of God and any feeling of fear or tribulation becomes less intense. Furthermore, a humble soul is admired by the people around without any initiative on one's part.

Supernatural Goods

John here discusses all the supernatural goods that a soul receives from God. He identifies two kinds: supernatural exercises and spiritual goods. Whereas supernatural activities are at the service of others, like the healing of the sick and the expulsion of devils, spiritual goods comprise delights derived from the secret knowledge of God's love which the substance of the soul receives. On considering the two kinds, John admonishes one to rejoice in spiritual goods.[109] According to John, if one attaches importance to the wonder of supernatural exercises, one risks the following harms:

1. First harm: discernment of supernatural phenomena becomes complex. The soul is exposed to the danger of being deceived as supernatural exercises coming from God are associated with witchcraft and sorcery;

2. Second harm: since one attached more importance to the wonders of supernatural exercises, faith deteriorates. One finds it difficult to trust God unless signs emerge; and,

---

109. *Ascent*, Book 3, ch. 30.

3. Third harm: persons who crave for extraordinary manifestations incorrectly believe that God is inclined towards miracle works. They miss the point. God does miracles only out of necessity rather than desire.[110]

Spiritual Objects

In this category, John discusses spiritual objects that invite prayer, reflection, and knowledge. He mentions some devotional and motivational objects like statues, paintings, sacred music, and spiritual places. His message is constant. All these objects serve as instruments to encounter God, and the soul's delight should not rely simply on their artistic or emotional properties.[111] Although John mentions three other passions governing the will, he only deals with joy. He ends the third book of the *Ascent* but fails to amplify further on fear, hope and sorrow.

Having now illustrated the various possessions that the three faculties offer to the self, John of the Cross proceeds by explaining how discerning the origins of experiences is a constant challenge in spiritual life. For the faithful soul, it is a constant predicament that brings rumination, fear, and confusion. What is lost is interior stillness, which is so essential in the encounter with God.[112] John pleads the soul to dissipate its apprehensions since no clear answer will be received. A favor becomes a barrier as one devotes assiduity towards it. John outlines three reasons why seeking clarity of such experiences is in vain:

1. Often these incidents contain figures and forms which are a product of the material world. Their message is tainted by matters other than the spiritual. So, the certainty of their divine origins is questionable;

2. Although God is the creator of all goods, His love is superior. The three faculties cannot contain Him. Instead, communication ensues secretly in the substance of the soul; and,

3. Adhering to the distresses of apprehensions leads to captivity. The over spilt effects in the faculties partly manifest spiritual love and often bring about misunderstandings. Moreover, the devil can conjure similar properties leading to further deception.[113]

110. *Ascent,* Book 3, ch. 31.
111. *Ascent,* Book 3, ch. 33.
112. *Ascent,* Book 2, ch. 11, no 7.
113. John uses the metaphor of the market or a seaport to depict how the soul seeks

John reassures that rejection of these apprehensions, beautiful as they may appear, does not offend God. True healing is placed perfectly in the person itself, and God desires that the soul encounters him in spiritual nakedness through faith.[114] John describes faith as the secret ladder to God. It is secret since it reveals matters which are foreign to the world but unique to the soul. It is a ladder that depicts the spatial distance between God and the world. In choosing faith, one becomes equally disguised both from one's self and others. The journey resumes without detection and disturbances, but the soul suffers by leaving senses, imagination, and spiritual experiences aside so as not to be betrayed. Now one is not misled by either selfish expectations or any tricks of the devil.[115]

Faith is like the brightest light that dazzles all, including the light emitted by a person's abilities. It overwhelms everything as the sun's intensity blinds the eyes. It has a dual quality: blinding and illuminating all at once. It surpasses every hand-created and imagined object and leads to a state of unknowing; from many means to no means.

> Faith, the theologians say, is a certain and obscure habit of soul. It is an obscure habit because it brings us to believe divinely revealed truths that transcend every natural light and infinitely exceed all human understanding. As a result the excessive light of faith bestowed on a soul is darkness for it; a brighter light will eclipse and suppress a dimmer one. The sun so obscures all other lights that they do not seem to be lights at all when it is shining, and instead of affording vision to the eyes, it overwhelms, blinds, and deprives them of vision since its light is excessive and unproportioned to the visual faculty. Similarly, the light of faith in its abundance suppresses and overwhelms that of the intellect. For the intellect, by its own power, extends only to natural knowledge, though it has the potency to be raised to a supernatural act whenever our Lord wishes.[116]

For John remaining in faith is holy ground. It demarcates the presence of God.[117] He advocates the soul to wear the same garments as God's and take faith as a guide. Faith becomes the only article in this world that is in

---

comfort and understanding in *Ascent*, Book 2, ch. 16, no 4.

114. *Ascent*, Book 2, ch. 17, no 7 and 8.

115. *Ascent*, Book 2, ch. 1, no 1.

116. *Ascent*, Book 2, ch. 3, no 1.

117. In scripture, God, is wrapped in this dual quality: the dark cloud that illuminates the path for the Israelites to cross the Red Sea; the cloud filling the temple; God communicates in darkness to Moses and Job; darkness is his hiding place (Ps 18:10–11) in *Canticle*, Stanza 1, no 3–12.

harmony with God. Union in likeness starts through this act of imitation. Resistance to faith exposes one's stubbornness. However, the *passive night of sense* is required for faith to become the nobles' instrument for the soul.

THE PASSIVE NIGHT OF SENSE

In the former treatise, as John outlines the self-denial from appetites, he urges the reader to direct all energy towards self-authenticity. If one succeeds to keep oneself away from inordinate attachments, tribulations diminish.[118] However, for John, spirituality is not a solitary adventure. Although a person devises an itinerary and builds an identity, eventually, it fails. In spite of the fact that human desire can be honest, it is imperfect as the self tends to reduce God to a device for achievement. As the roots of appetites are far-reaching, the soul acting on its own is not enough. Some are so deeply rooted that the soul, unaware, still fails to resist them out of temperament. The soul is incapable of casting them aside, while others who see through these defects do not have the power of means to bring on healing.

In the *Dark Night*, John explains the path to the union from its relational aspect. God has a significant role to play. He was and has the ultimate power to perform what others cannot do and is conscious of the soul more than anyone else. If a person genuinely desires union, then one must turn to Him. In the *Dark Night*, God elevates the soul to His dignity and so communication transpires superiorly. It is then that one realizes how the holy journey was God's desire in the first place. An internal struggle is provoked when one fails to cede one's tendencies and inclination to control one's life.

When John refers to the passive aspect of the night, he signifies God's role towards the soul. Our attention is drawn to how John's division of the *dark night* does not follow a linear progression. The four spheres indicated in the *Ascent* and the *Dark Night* operate simultaneously and do not proceed from one level to another.

Unintentional Selfishness

The *dark night* assumes that a person made way in the spiritual journey when the soul chose God and achieved many valuable things. While engaging in the practice of spiritual meditation, delight is received, virtue is nurtured, and a sense of command in life is acquired. At this point, one

---

118. In speaking about the passive night of sense, John of the Cross assumes that the soul is actively practicing virtue, exercising mortification and meditation in *Canticle*, Stanza 3, no 4 and 5.

reaches a plateau. In John's assessment, these results are consistent with the grand plan. However, the objective is still remote as the self is still rooted in a selfish disposition, even if one acts out of goodwill. It is unintentional selfishness since the soul is not conscious of it, yet it affects one's conduct towards others and God.[119]

According to John, beginners often have an intense enthusiasm for spiritual matters and are overconfident. They suggest pride by giving lessons to others and by seeking to win attention unto them.[120] Envy gets the upper hand. If they receive constructive criticism, they object to it with resentment. Often, they find another spiritual director with whom they feel more esteemed since a sound reputation is their primary concern. Anger and arrogance feature too.[121] These people quickly get upset and discontented with others' opinions.

Contrary to beginners, the proficient adopts a humbler attitude. Since the *dark night* discredits all expectations, they feel at ease with their little needs. The achievements of others are admired, and praise becomes a strange thing to them. The night brings forth a finer charity since a meeker person finds it more comfortable listening and adapting to others.

Moreover, beginners indulge excessively in many spiritual possessions. Rather than being pleased with the presence of God, they seek many experiences for their consolations. The person hardly concerns themselves about self-mortification, and instead, they pass from one experience to another. They are always searching for refined food either through strict penances, reading books, or attending retreats, among others. The night blinds all these sources from affording satisfaction and compels one to remain in spiritual poverty. But slowly, they find out how God's hiding place lies within them and thus learn to approach him with an uncomplicated loving attention.[122]

Beginners are also sensitive in their sensuality. When one receives spiritual delight, physical arousal sometimes responds. At other times, it disturbs recollection through the act of remembering.[123] John shares how part of the healing of the passive night is its power to reorder these senses towards a better love for God.[124] Lastly, John also reveals how beginners inevitably reduce God to an object in the midst of their worldly possessions. Although they made progress, they are reluctant to move further in

---

119. *Night*, Book 1, ch. 8, no 3.
120. *Night*, Book 1, chs. 2 and 12, no 7 and 8.
121. *Night*, Book 1, ch. 5.
122. *Night*, Book 1, chs. 3, 6, and 13, no 1.
123. *Night*, Book 1, ch. 4.
124. *Night*, Book 1, ch. 4.

the relationship as now they feel comfortable in their little created world. As the spark of desire becomes less intense, they shun discipline.

> It is enough to have referred to the many imperfections of those who live in this beginner's state to see their need for God to put them into the state of proficients. He does this by introducing them into the dark night, of which we will now speak. There, through pure dryness and interior darkness, he weans them from the breasts of these gratifications and delights, takes away all these trivialities and childish ways, and makes them acquire the virtues by very different means. No matter how earnestly beginners in all their actions and passions practice the mortification of self, they will never be able to do so entirely—far from it—until God accomplishes it in them passively by means of the purgation of this night.[125]

When a person has acquired some strength to endure what is in store and not renounce the cause, the *dark night* of the senses commences. It is at this moment when the sun is shining brightly and the soul is receiving many spiritual delights that the door of gratification is suddenly closed. Affection attributed to God's love ceases, and the old methods of seeking Him become dry. The sun loses its brightness. Although God consumes the mind of the soul, one finds no respite. He feels remote and unreachable. John views this particular form of sorrow as a sign that the soul is thirsty for that satisfaction that came to one's knowledge through meditation. As a person assesses progress in accordance with what gives delight to one's life, now everything is misty. All progress seems in vain. Many doubts haunt the mind as it conjures thoughts of betrayal and foolishness for believing in love. If anger was voiced when others instructed the soul, now all the rage is directed to God. John makes it clear that the sorrow that the soul faces is not bestowed by God. However, since God's love is shifting from being visibly communicated to infused secretly in the substance of the soul, the self jumps in protest.[126] As indicated in the *Ascent*, one's senses will not consume objects of pleasure, and thus the interior faculties will become obscured to comprehend. The soul enters into an existential crisis since that identity, constructed on previous modes, appears abandoned. Suddenly everything is operating in reverse. The ascent that the soul toiled so much to climb becomes the most profound fall. As one reaches the edge, pity, bitterness, and grief haunt the soul. Engulfed in such lifeless conditions, the soul believes that misery will be its destiny forever.

125. *Night*, Book 1, ch. 7, no 5.
126. *Night*, Book 1, ch. 10.

As a remedy to the soul's current events, John proposes that consolation is not to be derived from discursive meditation but to wait for God's presence quietly. Even if the stillness appears unproductive, patiently, the interior turbulence will abate. As the last thing, what the soul wants is the delay in reconciling with God as a result of possessing a disturbed spirit. At long last, the soul grows in endurance and through infused contemplation, the soul becomes stronger in the love and trust towards God.[127]

John uses the metaphor of a mother nursing a child to describe the present dynamics.[128] Like a child who has spent enough time suckling at the breast, the mother withholds her bosoms. So, the child develops through the consumption of solid food. Contemplation is the new spiritual food. As God withholds his delights from the soul, one grows in relation to Him beyond human senses. However, at first, the soul does not recognize this new nourishment and instead tastes its own bitterness. Like a mother, the timing of denying such enjoyment is in His hands. According to John, those who attain this threshold become adept in spiritual life in Christ. They slowly adapt to contemplation and are transformed into a new joy and love towards God. John marks this accomplishment as their *spiritual betrothal* to God.[129]

John also addresses spiritual directors, as their assistance on this night is essential. Often people passing through the *dark night* would not have support from friends since nobody can console or understand their agony. According to John, a spiritual director should accompany those who are being purified and be able to distinguish the signs from other ailments. Since the effects of the *dark night* resemble other mental health symptoms, primarily clinical depression, John outlines three signs to distinguish the properties of the *dark night*:[130]

1. The first sign: one does not derive satisfaction from any spiritual or material object. The person feels confused since no reason can be identified for this sudden change of events;

2. The second sign: one is so continuously concerned about God, that the soul suffers for believing that God has forsaken the person. Consequently, a person would look at the future as predestined to be a failure. Until God is discovered again, motivation to carry out the daily

---

127. *Night,* Book 1, ch. 11, no 11.
128. *Night,* Book 1, ch. 1, no 2.
129. *Night,* Book 1, ch. 1, no 2.

130. Melancholia is the term that John uses to describe one who has a mental condition characterized by extreme sadness and a bitter will. Melancholia was the term that preceded modern medical diagnosis for clinical depression see *Night,* Book 1, ch. 9.

routine diminishes. Even if the soul utters anger towards God, it only signifies an urgent thirst for Him to satisfy;[131] and,

3. The third sign: linked to the second sign are all the soul's failures to meditate and understand. Old spiritual exercises no longer have meaning, and the soul is in a state of powerlessness as it cannot solve or put aside the crisis.

The Benefits Received from the Dark Night

Even though the soul passes through extensive suffering, John mentions the benefits which the soul receives. Due to the night, a person's sense of self-awareness enhances.[132] Whereas in a time of prosperity, the mind was engrossed in success and managing life, now it was touched by spiritual death, exposing the fragility of being human. In times of satisfaction, the soul was more tactless towards God, but after these events, the soul becomes humbler and more prudent. If in the past, the gratification was put down to God's approval, now nothing lulls towards presumption. The soul mistrusts everything. Instead, one remains aware of one's vulnerability and, at the same time, regularly remembers Him. Knowing how fragile life is and how nothing of the world can genuinely satisfy, one only trusts God. This brings forth freedom of spirit, and vulnerability turns into a source of strength. The soul relates and interacts with everything in the world but with a detached attitude. Nothing will preclude the soul from turning to the Beloved. If in the past, the soul boasted and desired to be seen, now a calm presence prevails. One trusts that God can achieve more than any behavior the soul can perform. Now the soul can engage with others in the world, and with God without the vices associated with beginners.[133]

Moreover, the soul awakens to a new knowledge of God that rests in the soul's substance.[134] Slowly, as one becomes inured to this state, the soul succeeds to know God not through many activities, feelings, or experiences but through an interior disposition. John speaks of infused contemplation. God finds a new pasture where he uninterruptedly communicates to the soul. Now that the soul has reached interior calmness, John prepares the reader for the last aspect of the passive night.

131. *Night*, Book 1, ch. 11.
132. *Night*, Book 1, ch. 12.
133. When John speaks of the faults associated with beginners, he takes up the seven capital sins in *Night*, Book 1, chs. 2–7.
134. *Flame*, Stanza 1, No 9.

THE PASSIVE NIGHT OF SPIRIT

As the soul now passed through the *passive night of sense*, the union is not so remote, but the timing has not yet arrived for *spiritual marriage*. John shares how the *passive night*, "serves more for the accommodation of the senses to the spirit than for the union of the spirit with God."[135] Now one has a proper rule to follow, and the battle between senses and spirit is over. Every part of the soul is calibrated.

Since the soul hides further within the cover of faith, and everything has been vanquished, what becomes the only obstacle left to overcome is faith. As indicated in the *active night of the spirit*, one is more attuned to how God communicates. Contemplation replaces reliance on the three interior faculties.[136] In this state, proficients receive many spiritual delights, but if the effects filter into the senses, this indicates that the night of the spirit is necessary. According to John, the *passive night of sense* already reduces external impacts since now God communicates to the soul through infused contemplation. However, given that the soul's senses are attuned and do not hinder the soul, the spirit is further fortified.

In the *Canticle*, John describes how the soul arrives in the *passive night of the spirit*. The soul first seeks the Beloved by retrieving various traces of His love.[137] But such knowledge intensifies the wound of love for Him.[138] The soul moves from knowledge of creation to knowledge of rational creatures. All impart inspiration about the Beloved. They draw a sketch of the Beloved in the soul, but in turn, augment the sorrow since it is not complete. The soul turns to faith as its last remedy. Through it, the sketch is refined as it is infused rather than grasped by the soul, but again it is not perfect.[139] Hence the soul's desires are not yet satisfied.[140] The remaining step is for the spirit to move beyond faith and be endued with qualities for the actual divine encounter.

However, two kinds of imperfections in proficients linger: habitual and actual. Habitual detriments escape the spiritual purgation of sense like old stains which linger in the spirit.[141] On the other hand, actual imperfec-

---

135. *Night*, Book 2, ch. 2, no 1; *Canticle*, Stanza 18–21; *Flame*, Stanza 1, no 18–24.

136. *Canticle*, Stanza 2, no 6.

137. *Canticle*, Stanza 25.

138. All the knowledge of God she gains from the world, John names it as *stammering* knowledge in *Canticle*, Stanza 4–7.

139. *Canticle*, Stanza 12, no 8.

140. *Canticle*, Stanza 13.

141. John uses the metaphor of the *herd* to explain that there will always be some little object that the soul keeps attached to in the world in *Canticle*, Stanza 26.

tions are a result of original sin, which every person has inherited from the fall of Adam and Eve.

> These proficients also have the *hebetudo mentis*, the natural dullness everyone contracts through sin, and a distracted and inattentive spirit. The spirit must be illumined, clarified, and recollected by means of the hardships and conflicts of this night. All those who have not passed beyond the state of proficients possess these habitual imperfections that cannot, as we said, coexist with the perfect state of the union of love.[142]

The *passive night of the spirit* perfects the soul by instilling a new divine consciousness; love and knowledge of God, which positions the soul in a perfect and unchanging status. Sometimes it grants mystical knowledge, while at other times, it inflames the spirit with God's love. Light and heat are the two metaphors that John employs to describe the effects of the *dark night*.

Like the former phases, the light emitted torments the soul in this night.[143] It blinds understanding, empties memory and distresses the will. John states:

> To prove the first reason, we must presuppose a certain principle of the Philosopher: that the clearer and more obvious divine things are in themselves, the darker and more hidden they are to the soul naturally. The brighter the light, the more the owl is blinded; and the more one looks at the brilliant sun, the more the sun darkens the faculty of sight, deprives and overwhelms it in its weakness.[144]

Since the spirit lingers on possessiveness, this dark light is not treated calmly. Two contraries do not coexist in the same subject, and the soul passes through an internal struggle. The soul rejects the light since it sees the end of its life approaching, and its essence is on the verge of death. The mind is burdened with desperation, and the will is too weak to dispel it. When the dark light intersects humanity, the substance of the soul feels like being torn apart.[145] Like the crucified Christ, as death approaches, the soul feels utterly abandoned by God.

> When this purgative contemplation oppresses a soul, it feels very vividly indeed the shadow of death, the sighs of death, and the

---

142. *Night,* Book 2, ch. 2, no 2.
143. *Night,* Book 2, chs. 5 and 6.
144. *Night,* Book 2, ch. 5, no 3; Ps 18:11–12.
145. John also describes the pulling apart as melting away, undone by a cruel spiritual death and swallowed by a beast.

sorrows of hell, all of which reflect the feeling of God's absence, of being chastised and rejected by him, and of being unworthy of him, as well as the object of his anger. The soul experiences all this and even more, for now it seems that this affliction will last forever.[146]

The soul is imprisoned in its poverty and misery. No sense of meaning is accessed, and one penetrates a void of no perception. Prayer seems unheeded, and the soul is "like hanging in mid-air, unable to breath" and finds no respite from friends or God.[147] In such a situation, people accompanying the soul must have deep empathy. For even though this night, in the end, will be beneficial, in the present moment, everything for the soul is miserable.

> This war or combat is profound because the peace awaiting the soul must be exceedingly profound; and the spiritual suffering is intimate and penetrating because the love to be possessed by the soul will also be intimate and refined. The more intimate and highly finished the work must be, so the more intimate, careful, and pure must the labor be; and commensurate with the solidity of the edifice is the energy involved in the work.[148]

John calls this refinement a *happy night* since the soul's sufferings are not in vain. Through it, the soul is elevated and receives knowledge about earthly and heavenly objects.[149] John employs the element of heat to exhibit a secondary effect of the *dark night*.[150] While light enters the intellect, heat exalts the will. While the *passive night of sense* imparts feelings of fervors and solicitude for God, here, the soul experiences a deeper degree of love. The spirit is enkindled with the wound of divine love.[151] Like wood being consumed by fire, heat penetrates the wood and unites the two elements together.[152] John describes this love as a foretaste of God, but it is still incomplete as the soul has not departed the world. It is a passionate love between two lovers.

---

146. *Night*, Book 2, ch. 6, no. 2.
147. Ezek 24:10–11; Wis 3:6; Ps 69:1–3; Lam 3:1–20; Job 16:12–16.
148. *Night*, Book 2, ch. 9, no 9.
149. *Night*, Book 2, ch. 9.
150. *Night*, Book 2, ch. 11.
151. The enkindling love is the loftiest love the soul can achieve in this world in *Flame*, Stanza 1, no 17.
152. For John, the metaphor of wood burning in a flame symbolizes transformation in *Flame*, Stanza 1, no 3–5.

> The soul is purged and prepared for union with the divine light just as the wood is prepared for transformation into the fire. Fire, when applied to wood, first dehumidifies it, dispelling all moisture and making it give off any water it contains. Then it gradually turns the wood black, makes it dark and ugly, and even causes it to emit a bad odor. By drying out the wood, the fire brings to light and expels all those ugly and dark accidents that are contrary to fire. Finally, by heating and enkindling it from without, the fire transforms the wood into itself and makes it as beautiful as it is itself. Once transformed, the wood no longer has any activity or passivity of its own, except for its weight and its quantity that is denser than the fire. It possesses the properties and performs the actions of fire: It is dry and it dries; it is hot and it gives off heat; it is brilliant and it illumines; it is also much lighter in weight than before. It is the fire that produces all these properties in the wood.[153]

For John, all the spiritual touches and divine wounds conferred on the soul come together under this love. Now the soul is aligned correctly to the first commandment as one harmonious being and receives many blessings.[154] The soul learns to rely only on this enkindling of love. Nothing of the world substitutes the strength the soul receives from it.[155]

As much as the divine wounds give delight, they intensify the pain of not being one with God.[156] Now a thin veil separates the soul from God. While the soul foretastes something of Him, yet the thirst remains. God remains uncaptured. This impediment creates a new sorrow within the soul. Previously the person suffered the effects of purification, but now the anxiety for love haunts the soul. Although the soul is now secure and fortified, the spirit is impatient for the journey to end. It desires that faith is torn apart, so the union is affected totally and immediately. The soul is so inebriated by the love of God that it becomes bold. A sign of new courage is instilled.[157]

> The reason is that since love now imparts a force by which the soul loves authentically, and since it is the nature of love to seek to be united, joined, equaled, and assimilated to the loved object in order to be perfected in the good of love, the soul hungers and thirsts for this union or perfection of love still unattained.

153. *Night*, Book 2, ch. 10, no 1.
154. *Canticle*, Stanza 25.
155. *Night*, Book 2, ch. 11, no 5.
156. *Canticle*, Stanza 1, no 14–20; *Canticle*, Stanza 8–11.
157. *Night*, Book 2, ch. 13, no 5; *Canticle*, Stanza 12, no 7, Stanza 25; *Flame*, Stanza 1, no 1 and 29.

And the strength now bestowed by love, and by which the will has become impassioned, makes this inflamed will daring. Yet since the intellect is not illumined but in darkness, the soul feels unworthy and knows that it is miserable.[158]

John throws sight on three properties attributed to faith. Two of them pertain to the nature of this night, while the other concerns the soul. This serves as a summary of his whole method. The first property attributed to the *dark night* is its secretive knowledge.[159] It is too lofty for the human intellect to discover. The Holy Spirit instead infuses this knowledge to the spirit. At the same time, it remains imperceptible. As contemplation grants clarity, it is beyond full comprehension. A secondary effect of its secretive nature is that while it provides clarity, it hides the soul in an abyss of wisdom. It is an in-depth perspective far removed from every created knowledge which grants the soul a keener awareness of self, life, and human dynamics. However, more importantly, in this dark womb, the soul gains knowledge about the science of love.

For John, the second property of faith is that the science of love is a ladder.[160] Like a thief, one ascends this fortress of knowledge to plunder and possess the goods and treasures of heaven. The *dark night* transforms the thief into a lover. A spiritual paradox comes into effect since the ascent is a descent. For the contemplation to exalt the spirit, old and imperfect ways of the self are darkened and chastened. According to John, one ascends further as much as the self is led down. Through life's events, John imagines the soul going up and down the ladder over time until it balances everything into a regular habit. However, movement is continuous. One realizes how knowledge of self and knowledge of God are two interconnected devices. John summarizes the science of love with different steps.

1. First step: the soul is longing for love. One comes to terms with the world's inability to fulfil one's being. The appetite for mundane things fails to satisfy, and a new search commences. Dissatisfaction is the beginning of the ladder of contemplation.[161]

2. Second step: while one searches for God, one does not pay heed to anything else until one finds God. A solicitous perspective gradually

---

158. *Night*, Book 2, ch. 13, no 9.
159. *Night*, Book 2, ch. 17.
160. *Night*, Book 2, chs. 18 and 19.
161. Song 5:8.

develops, and the mind is quickly turned to Him. At the same time, the soul develops a subtle but anxious longing for love.[162]

3. Third step: here, the soul performs many works of love. The fervor of love inspires the will to act and perform. To the person, the effort might be seen small, but it signifies that the fire of love is slowly kindling. The soul's virtues augment and learn to be humble and prudent.

4. Fourth step: once the soul transcends spiritual satisfaction, the fire of love yields a habitual desire to suffer for the beloved. The demands of the self are stilled, and the soul is not deficient in consolations. Much has already been bestowed from God, who compels the soul to suffer for His sake.[163]

5. Fifth step: the delay for union haunts the soul. The thirst for God intensifies, and even the slightest distance between the two annoys the soul. Every time such desire for union is interrupted, the soul faints in miserable longings,[164]

6. Sixth step: the soul learns to proceed towards God swiftly. Since now the required purification is almost complete, the soul receives many spiritual touches and delights from God.[165]

7. Seventh step: Love is further enkindled within the spirit, and it produces an ardent boldness to conquer the distance. The soul reacts with a holy impatience, and it does not shy out to declare it.[166]

8. Eighth step: love impels the soul to find out and lays hold of the Beloved. A subtle union is reached, but at the same time, it is not lived continually.[167]

9. Ninth step: since the union of likeness has been established, love causes the soul to burn gently. Similarly, when the apostles received the flame of love, the Holy Spirit produces much delightful zeal in the spirit.

10. Tenth step: the soul is entirely assimilated in the love of God. Actual union with the Beloved is complete, and the soul departs from the body. Now the soul receives a clear possession of God.

---

162. Song 3:1–4.
163. Song 8:6.
164. Ps 84:2.
165. Ps 42:1.
166. 1 Cor 13:7.
167. Song 3:4.

Lastly, John describes the soul as if it were departing for the spiritual journey in disguise.[168] Like wearing an invisible garb, the soul is not recognized or caught. Nothing distracts the soul from the goal. By hiding, souls are more secure against the world, the devil and even their own selves. Faith, hope, and charity are the new garments appropriate for the way. Due to these qualities, love of self and love of the world do not find their way into the soul.

Spiritual Marriage

This chapter concludes by briefly describing the state of *spiritual marriage*. It occurs when the *passive night of spirit* reaches its desired objective. God elevates the soul to the state of union and transforms the soul in likeness to His nature. What remains for the soul to receive is total clarity and consummation of divine love. A thin separator remains, and once God tears it, the soul enters his inner cellar.[169]

In such a union, the soul receives much communication from the Beloved. The soul has earned its place near Him, and since true love does not know how to keep secrets away from the lover, God reveals divine mysteries to the soul. A new name is given to the soul and receives knowledge about the incarnation and the redemption of the human race.[170] Communication between the lovers happens on the bed of the soul; within the substance of the soul. There through the soul's act of total surrender to God, gains the capacity to recognize the graces he imparts, the omnipotence surrounding him and the perfect love and peace he bestows.[171] Moreover, the person is awakened to one's beauty. All the divine virtues are perfectly preserved within the soul.[172]

Looking back to the spiritual journey, the soul recognizes how God never abandoned the cause. From the onset, God desired the soul. Like a dove, it returned home since no rest was found. Those moments of spiritual pain and suffering become synonymous with God's gaze which was directed upon the soul. He acceded to the soul's plea for further union. Nevertheless, it is God that concludes the final matter. Without Him, the soul was powerless. God concludes the work by purifying the soul and strengthening

---

168. *Night*, Book 2, ch. 21.

169. The inner cellar is the last and most intimate degree of love in this life see *Canticle*, Stanza 26.

170. *Canticle*, Stanza 23 and 24.

171. *Canticle*, Stanza 24.

172. On the garland of virtues, see *Canticle*, Stanza 30.

it in both sensory and spiritual aspects. Two features emerge from this relationship:

1. While the soul recognizes God's omnipotence, it is now fully conscious that He desires that every soul is united with Him; and,

2. As the soul acted together with God for its perfection now in his presence, its efforts are directed towards the kingdom of love. Human love is transformed, and like a bee, the extracted sweetness from all things is used only for God's love.[173]

However, in the union of likeness, the soul is still not satisfied. That last thin veil remains an obstacle in the way. The soul's last and most supreme desire is the fulfilment of the beatific union. All obstacles are to be removed and pleads with God to tear it apart so that perfect enjoyment in eternal life is achieved.[174] Interestingly the soul desires to be dissolved and bond with Christ. These were the same effects of the *passive night* when it produced a feeling of gnawing in the spirit. However, now the soul is well fortified and prepared.

In the *Flame of Love*, John ventures to pronounce the indescribable. He exhibits some aspects of how the actual union would look. Expanding on the metaphor of the log being consumed by fire, John notes that at one point, the flame annihilates the wood and transforms into a single fervent flame. Similarly, the soul is predestined to follow this metaphor. The attributes surrounding God will be endowed by the soul too, and one would participate in an everlasting fire of love wounding and emitting an unending consummation of love.[175]

The last image that John leaves to the reader is the soul united with the everlasting fire that is always wounding and loving. At this point, the spiritual model of John of the Cross ends and thus, this chapter concludes its purpose. Here a concise presentation of the Saint's module was outlined. In chapter 3, the doctrine will serve as the yardstick for assessing men's spiritual experiences, but not before introducing the male participants' contribution in chapter 2.

---

173. *Canticle*, Stanza 27.

174. *Canticle*, Stanza 36; *Sayings*, no 26; Also see John's poem *Stanza of the soul that suffers with longing to see God*.

175. John calls this continuous emission of love the arts and games of love in *Flame*, Stanza 1, no 8.

Chapter 2

Ten Spiritual Narratives of Men

While chapter 1 introduces the objective paradigm for this study, this chapter seeks to find out, *how do men live spirituality?* Ten spiritual stories portraying the experiences, sometimes emotionally disturbing of ten men are presented as examples. Each man narrates in detail his own story how it unravels itself until the spiritual aspect prevails. These stories provide us with an account of spiritual transformative processes which arise from lived experience.

The ten stories are divided into five categories mirroring five social roles: married straight fathers, single straight men, separated straight men, single gay men and gay men in a relationship.[1] Participants shared their experiences freely, without any intervention on the part of the investigator. These persons spoke in Maltese or English, but sometimes both languages were employed. All Maltese quotations were translated into English. Care was taken to remain true and faithful to the original version and to project, as much as possible, the same feeling as that transmitted by the persons involved. Translated Maltese intervention have their original extracts as footnotes.[2]

---

1. Details about the criteria of the sample composition are found in the introduction of this study, see Methodology.
2. Pseudonyms are being used to protect the identity of participants.

MARRIED STRAIGHT FATHERS

The Story of Peter

Peter, who is in his forties, is married to Sarah and has two young children. Both hold a tertiary degree; Peter in engineering and Sarah in management and education. Their future is a journey marked by evidence of faith, new discoveries about God and their spiritual responsibility.

Looking back at his childhood, Peter recalls the parable of the sower to describe his family environment as "good and fertile soil."[3] He was brought up in a conventional Catholic Maltese family and succeeded in life, thanks to his parents' constant care and guidance.

> They are very good people. Using the Parable of the Sower, I can say I am one of the seeds which fell in good soil. And thank God for that, but obviously that also brings about responsibility.[4]

Today his parents look up to him, but although he is very grateful to them, he has perceived their faith as being "based on very little rational understanding" since he was young. Thus, he felt dissatisfied about this matter despite their unconditional love towards him. As is the practice in Malta, when he was young, he attended *Mużew*.[5] Through catechism, he learned about faith up to the age of sixteen. Also, he attended recreational events organized by the society. While being present at these classes, he observed the exercise of faith of three *soċi*:[6]

> It was socially a lot of fun, and it was also a good basis for learning and [gaining] knowledge. More importantly, receiving their witness. I have a lot of respect towards these three people, who are now married. They inspired me. It's very hard; I don't remember what they taught me. If you ask me what I remember, the thing I remember most is that these three youngsters were

---

3. A parable of Jesus found in the three Synoptic Gospels in Matt 13:1–23, Mark 4:1–20, and Luke 8:4–15.

4. "Nies tajbin ħafna. Jien wieħed minn dawk li nista' ngħid, jekk nuża' l-parabbola tal-ħamrija u ż-żerriegħa, li jien waqajt f'ħamrija tajba. And thank God for that, but obviously iġġib responsabilità."

5. *Mużew* or MUSEUM is the Maltese term used by people to refer to the Society of Christian Doctrine, a lay society made up of men and women who voluntarily teach catechism to children and adults. See www.sdcmuseum.org/. It is the usual practice that children attend their local *Mużew* until the age of sixteen, which parallels when the sacrament of confirmation was administered.

6. *Soċi* is the term used to identify the members of the Society of Christian Doctrine.

extremely generous. That is what I remember, with their money and time. MUSEUM had an important impact on me.[7]

Later, he attended another Christian community. It was during these years that he experienced a deep sense of curiosity, confusion, and misgivings. Biological and psychological changes were part of the reason. What was most important was a desire to answer the not simple questions about God and life.

> I was always full of questions and often full of doubt about God, and anything [regarding] God . . . but I didn't use to find much consolation. I remember saying, "Prayer is always dry."[8]

His school subjects led him to enroll for an engineering degree, which whetted his inquisitiveness. He viewed this search as a stumbling block as no answers were forthcoming, but rather distancing him from his faith. Nevertheless, he persisted in practicing the customary religious services. Neither the Christian community of which he formed part, nor his school subjects satisfied his curiosity. No space was offered to communicate and deepen his relationship with God. Instead, they laid much stress on community building and skills development.

> The experience is [one which strengthens a sense of] community. Even though I haven't seen the friends I made there in ten years, if we sit down together [now], there would instantly be a lot of intimacy. And that has a lot of value. However, at the same time, at least from my experience, this community was also lacking in certain aspects. I learnt many things on spirituality after I left this community. A lot of attention [was given to] being-with, respecting the other, being a community. However, the challenging element, that of delving deeper into the relationship with God, was excluded.[9]

---

7. "It was a lot of fun soċjali, imma it made a very good basis ta' tagħlim u knowledge. More importantly receiving their witness. Dawn it-tlieta min-nies, illum miżżewġin, imma għandi ħafna rispett lejhom. Ispirawni. It's very hard, jien ma niftakarx x'għallmuni. Jekk tgħidli x'tiftakar, l-iktar li niftakar li dawn it-tliet żgħażagħ kienu ġeneruzi b'mod estrem. That is what I remember. Bi flushom u ħinhom. Il-Mużew kellu impatt importanti fuqi."

8. "I was always full of questions and often full of doubt about God, and anything about God . . . imma ma tantx kien ikolli ħafna konsolazzjoni. Niftakar ngħid, 'prayer is always dry.'"

9. "Hija esperjenza ta' very strong on community. Il-ħbieb li għamilt hemmhekk even though ilni ma narahom għaxar snin, jekk inpoġġu bilqegħda mil-ewwel ikun hemm ħafna intimacy. And that has a lot of value, imma fl-istess ħin, għall-inqas naħseb jien fl-esperjenza tiegħi, din il-komunità, kienet lacking minn ċertu aspetti

His aspiration was fulfilled when he entered university. The course taught him "to be a logical thinker, to solve problems, be a doer, and go ahead and find solutions where others might find it daunting." However, this approach did not work with human relationships. He was deemed emotionless and intellectually insulated. At this stage, his wife played a crucial role. Through their relations, she brought forth a complementary aspect of life. Peter called it the feminine aspect. Sarah was endowed with artistic qualities that elicit attention to feelings. Being his witness, she urged him on to explore his affections. His knowledge of God contributed to self-growth and human relationships. The exploration of the affective not only yielded self-knowledge but also offered a new challenge; a conflict between his inner self and his promotion at work.

> There was something I never thought much about. When I used to meet friends [who asked me] how I was doing, I always used to grumble about work. There were many things I didn't like, but one of the most important was that I was growing older. I started experiencing a disharmony between the value system of my workplace and my interior one. Adding to that, I also had to work long hours. I started realizing that my children were growing [and] they barely saw me.[10]

Changing careers was not an easy feat. He heard about a post within one of the local church organizations. Following discernment and some "sleepless nights," he risked the job. His salary was lower, but now he could enjoy more quality time with his children. Moreover, his wife could return to her profession. Spiritually, he met other people seeking God daily. This also yielded satisfaction and accountability towards God since he was now directly "working in his field." He enrolled in a theological course to gain new insights into his line of work.

> On one of those days when I feel dead inside, [when] I can't find God, I have a very easy way out. I simply watch the people around me, and they are witnesses to me.[11]

---

wkoll. Ħafna mill-affarijiet fuq l-ispiritwalità tgħallimthom wara li tlaqt din il-komunità. Ħafna attenzjoni on being-with, of respecting the other, of being community, but the challenging element, delving deeper fir-relazzjoni m'Alla was excluded."

10. "Kien hemm xi ħaġa li qatt ma ffittjajt fiha u meta kont niltaqa' mal-ħbieb, "Kif sejjer?" I was always grumbling fuq ix-xogħol. Hemm ħafna affarijiet li ma kinux qed jogħġbuni imma waħda mill-iktar importanti kienet li I was growing older. Bdejt inħoss li l-value system ta' fejn kont qed naħdem u tiegħi interjorament kienu wisq in disharmony u plus il-fatt illi kelli naħdem sigħat twal ħafna u bdejt ngħid jien it-tfal qed jikbru . . . bil-kemm jarawni."

11. "Meta jkolli xi ġurnata li nkun xi ftit deaden inside, ma nkunx nista' nsib lil Alla,

What inspired him most was witnessing others living their faith. Also, while praying, Peter uses his imagination during meditation. Such exercises made his faith stronger by imaging how biblical characters used to react to their emotions.

Becoming a father was not easy for Peter. His marriage was marked by two miscarriages causing the couple a lot of stress and pain. It was a time of extreme pain. His prayers turned into lamentations. Peter divulged how marginalized and angry he felt, especially when he saw other children. Sarah proposed the idea of adoption, which Peter initially refused, but finally accepted. Adoption brought about new life adjustments. In these circumstances, the couple lacked the preparations needed for such a change. Suddenly, two young strangers shared their home. Another problem was their children's attachment. On being deprived of his familiarities, the son was deeply traumatized. On several occasions, he threw tantrums and displayed learning difficulties. All these struggles called for a commitment by the couple. Feelings of failure and rejection also ensued.

> Our son came to us very badly traumatized. I remember feeling shocked [and] after a week I told Sarah, "If things don't change, he can't stay with us." The situation was very bad. I remember calling my friend and crying. I felt like I had ruined my life.[12]

Peter adopted the parable of the prodigal son as his experience.[13] He swapped himself into the figure of the Father on the roof, waiting patiently like him for his son to respond at his own pace. When moments of doubt arose, he recognized them as part of a person's need to control and did not allow his vulnerability to block him.

> I feel that sometimes I want to say, "Our Father, who is waiting on the roof" because there is so much meaning to that. There are many experiences that I've lived [through] that [are based] on this statement. It has a lot of meaning. If I had to choose one factor that helped [me] understand the nature of God the most, [it would be that of] being a father. Not because I am supernatural, but because I [am experiencing] our relationship, what I feel for him, what he does for me, and the unconditional love that I experience. I realize it is unconditional when I'm faced

---

I have a very easy way out. I simply watch the people around me, and they witness to me."

12. "It-tifel ġie għandna very badly traumatised. Niftakarni tkexkixt. Niftakar wara ġimgħa lil Sarah kont għadtilha, "If things don't change, ma jistax jibqa' magħna." Is-sitwazzjoni kienet gravi. Niftakar inċempel lil ħabib tiegħi u nibki. Ħassejtni li fottejt ħajti."

13. A parable by Jesus found in Luke 15:11–32.

with a challenge. I feel like this very often, though, this feeling of wanting a world of good for my son and my daughter. This teaches me how God regards me. Words fail me to explain better [than this].[14]

Now an element of deep intimacy exists between Peter and God. The act of exchanging himself into the figure of the Father on the roof signifies that God is always gazing upon him in real-time. Paternal responsibility gave access to God. But what is more important is that God's gaze meant intimacy and accompaniment. God is closer beyond his comprehension. These struggles became the frameworks that revealed his spiritual identity.

> I am ready to say that if there is one reason why [God] placed me in this world, it is because of this boy. It's still very hard to be his father, [both] on a human and on a spiritual level. Even when I experience spiritual direction, my son always features. [This is because] he is at the very center of what God asked me to be and to do in this world. And it's not always easy.[15]

The Story of Paul

Paul, who is in his late thirties, is a businessman married to Helen and has four children. His upbringing was subject to his parents' contrasting personalities, with an assertive mother and a meek father. As a family, they participated in Catholic activities and services. As a child, he sometimes served as an altar boy.

Although they are Maltese and acquainted with the Maltese language, Paul's family speaks in English.[16] Consequently, he attended church schools

14. "Inhossni li xi drabi nkun irrid nghid, 'Missierna li qed tistenna fuq il-bejt' because there is so much meaning to that. There are many experiences that I lived that stand on this statement. It has a lot of meaning. If I had to choose one factor that helped most understand in-natura t'Alla hu li nkun missier. Not because I am supernatural, but because of seeing how the relationship goes, what I feel for him, and what he does for me, and the unconditional love that I experience. I know it is unconditional because then ninduna meta jkolli xi challenge. Imma hafna drabi nhossni hekk, this feeling of wanting a world of good to my son and to my daughter. Din tghallimni kif Alla jhares lejja. Words fail me to explain better."

15. "Nasal biex nghid li jekk hemm raġuni waħda għaliex poġġieni fid-dinja hu minhabba dan it-tifel. It's still very hard to be his father, on a human level anka fuq livell spiritwali. Anka meta jkolli spiritual direction, my son dejjem jifficerja. Ghax he is at the very centre of what God asked me to be and to do in this world. And, it's not always easy going."

16. In Malta, there is a perceived distinction between those who choose to speak in

rather than state ones. However, during the transition from primary to secondary education, he enrolled in a different school. This separated him from his friends.[17] This decision brought about challenging encounters. Apart from the shock of being with unfamiliar people, he faced bullying due to his accent. Confronted with this form of intimidation, Paul fought back.

> In my teenage years I rebelled quite a bit. I had a group of friends. I always sought friends who are the cooler friends, so each group, from cool to cooler to coolest. In my time, that is what I thought. And that entailed a lot of drugs, so at the age of twelve or thirteen, I smoked my first joint and from there to another group where I started ecstasy; starting from half a tablet to one for a couple of years until the age of . . . I started at the age of fifteen or sixteen with ecstasy until twenty-five.

Despite the dangers of substance abuse and drug dealing, Paul was highly esteemed and admired by his companions. Not only did he impress his friends with the number of drugs he consumed, but he also engaged in drug trafficking. Now, he was a member of the cool tribe. Eventually, Paul gave up his drug-taking habit and was no longer addicted. Unfortunately, two problems still "plague" him: the tendency to please others and to watch pornography. Paul became curious about pornography at the tender age of ten. He had found his brother's hidden videos and watched them when he was alone at home.

> My brother had a big impact on me, and little did he know what I was doing. At the time, he was fifteen years. Later, my mother started working in the morning. So, when she was out, especially during exam time when I would be home, I would see his videos. I remember masturbating without getting the sperm—it must have been prepuberty.

Such a lifestyle of drugs and promiscuity persisted through his early twenties, and his dependence on such bad habits increased every year. Then a major twist occurred: his spiritual conversion. He began to experience internal confusion and became dissatisfied with life. Other friends noticed his anguish and encouraged him to attend Christian retreats and services.

Maltese or in English. The latter is known as *tal-pepè*. This distinction marks political and social class stereotypes. Children from families known as *tal-pepè* tend to attend church or private schools rather than state ones.

17. At the time, the Maltese educational system still used the Common Entrance Examination (CE) system. Paul passed the exams and had the opportunity to enroll in one of the church schools. See Evolution of the Common Entrance examination: www.timesofmalta.com/articles/view/evolution-of-the-common-entrance-examination.320414.

After several refusals, he decided to accede to their proposal. Beneath his tepidity, Paul admitted that "there was something. Searching, curious for something that [he] I liked. Something attracted [him] me." He recounts:

> This guy came up to me at the end of the mass, "There is this retreat next weekend. You should come." I said thank you but not for me. Three weeks passed, and I went home very late at night or very early morning. At around half twelve in the afternoon, they called me, and they told me, "The applications are closing. Are you still interested?" I was in a state of drugs the night before, so I told them yes, that I will come. It sounded good. I am a pleaser, and I stick to my words a lot, so that is my character. I had to go. I went alone. I knew no one.

He took his drugs with him, and by Friday evening, he "corrupted" all his roommates in smoking dope. He felt uncomfortable, and his uneasiness turned into anger. He could not understand what others were experiencing or feeling during this retreat.

> Saturday, I had a lot of anger. A lot of anger! I don't know from where it stemmed, but I wanted to shoot them all. I think it was frustration because there was a lot of spirituality which for me was, I don't get it. "I don't know why you are doing this, and I don't get it." But I was seeing something that I still wanted. But I couldn't. I wasn't thinking like this at the time, now I know.

Faced with this anger, he took a friend's advice and spoke with one of the coordinators. This encounter proved to be crucial. He opened up to him but anticipated what was coming. While he was attracted by the spirituality presented to him, he was afraid that if he chose God, he would have to renounce his lifestyle, including his friends. There was no compromise between these two entities. He had to decide.

> If I had to bring something, I would bring this quote, "Don't worry. One would remove a cloak with force either by wind or by heat, and you would want to remove it." And that is how God works. He does not force you into anything, but it is up to you to decide. And, somehow, I relaxed because that chat made me relax.[18]

After having spoken to the coordinator, Paul felt understood and reinvigorated. He left the retreat with a fervor to pray and was directed to relate with Jesus's parables. A week later, he faced his first test. He was invited to

---

18. The quotation Paul refers to is taken from Aesop's Fable entitled "The North Wind and the Sun."

meet two groups of friends simultaneously. He was in a state of conflict as he had to choose between his old and new friends. He did not want to disappoint anyone. Deep down, he wanted to be with his new friends, as "I [he] was the newcomer, they took care of me [him] and so on, and I [he] received the attention from girls and guys." The need for validation was still persistent. Change was slow, but one day while meditating on the Parable of the Sower, its figurative warning struck a chord. He saw his life cast like a seed upon a rock. Mindful of the consequences, he made a choice.

From that point, Paul looked for a praxis to rebuild his life. He sought assistance and guidance from the coordinator of the retreat, and a relation of spiritual nature was established. His director met him every week, sometimes twice or three times a week. His style was firm, laying stress on prayer and discipline. The spiritual relationship went beyond direction. Paul involved himself within the community that his director led. He engaged in opportunities of mission, evangelization, travelling and voluntary work. This was a spiritual honeymoon. He would get "high on his new drug [prayer]" and felt important among community participants. This involvement was all about status and power, but it did not last long. It developed into an unhealthy dependency which left Paul feeling suffocated.

> He is still a lovely man and did great things in my life, especially when it comes to discipline, but at the time, I remember wanting him dead, honestly. I couldn't see a way out but see him dead. I remember thinking it daily. "Let see, maybe another twenty years for this guy to die." I was like in prison. And, I ended up going up to his spiritual director and asking him for advice. And, the one thing he told me is to amputate.

Amputation was not easy. It meant leaving the community which had become so central in his life. He had to, but slowly. The conflict also affected his spirituality. He questioned how much he projected his spiritual director's image on God and how little he knew God. He began to doubt everything.

Later, he built up other relations. He got to know his wife, and his commitment towards her was the final step to detaching from the community entirely. These struggles also brought about self-exploration. Paul sensed a recurring need to attach to influential male figures and wondered if such undercurrents were associated with his father. While his mother was the household leader, his father identified as a delicate and quiet type. From a business point of view, his father was weak, and Paul often ended up correcting him.

Due to these issues, Paul felt that his relationship with God has deteriorated. Pornography and swearing have resurfaced. Prayer used to keep him in check, and when he ceased, the old self emerged. He wished to realign spiritually towards God, and this time correctly.

> With time, my relationship with God got a big hit. So, my relationship is now inexistent, to be honest. I have my spiritual director and my Sunday mass, and that's it, and I am not even praying, which for me it is the fulcrum of spiritual life. I feel that if I am not connected, I lost it. At the moment, I do not feel connected. I don't feel there's any excuse. It's a matter of priorities. I am well versed in my business, I have four children, but it's not an excuse. It's priorities. So, I go from work to home, home to work, and nothing else.

Besides this boring routine, another concern was for his marriage. Raising four children was no easy feat. Being mindful of the responsibilities that marriage demands requires consistency. With the help of his new spiritual director, Paul hopes to recover his relationship with God. Now it is proper direction since, with his previous director, it had come to a point where he knew which buttons to press to get positive responses.

> For me, freedom is what I carry: truth and freedom. The truth will set me free. If you had to ask me who is God for you? I wouldn't say God is love, I would say God is truth. That's the main feature that comes out for me from my personal experience. And it remained with me. In fact, God is love, I don't know if I ever experienced love, the love of God, which is another facet that I need to explore. I wish to experience it.

SINGLE STRAIGHT MEN

The Story of James

James is a single man in his late forties and owns a business in catering and hospitality. As a young boy, he was labelled as indifferent to schooling. He displayed challenging behavior and was disciplined continuously for it. School was tedious, and he experienced difficulties in comprehending his school subjects. By today's rules, he would be diagnosed with attention deficit hyperactivity disorder (ADHD). His parents tackled his lack of interest through exhortations, but all was in vain. James found school to be a waste of time and ignored much of its value. According to him, everybody failed to notice what really interested him.

> What was lacking from their end was the fact that they never recognized what I loved for them to encourage me towards that. They wanted to shift their own ideals onto me. They did not see the abilities God gave me, but [only] what they wished to impose on me. In good faith. It was not done with bad intentions towards me.[19]

By the age of sixteen, he left school and began to work in a factory. Starting from a basic position, he was eventually promoted to a more technical position. James's younger years were marked by deep-seated anxiety. He felt awkward with his friends, unable to interact or appreciate the activities typically associated with teenagers. He constantly felt as a misfit and his only refuge was music, mainly Bob Marley. James was attracted to the lifestyle the singer promoted and eventually experimented with drugs. Between the ages of seven and eleven, he complained of hair loss. At first, the barber was held responsible, but it turned out to be a case of sudden shock that caused this condition.[20] Neither James nor any family members could remember the source. Later, his sexuality was another daunting matter for him. James always felt sexually attracted to the opposite sex, yet he constantly questioned his sexual orientation. Simultaneously, he entertained a lot of doubts about religion.

> At the age of twenty, I was faced with another important question regarding my sexuality. I never felt attracted towards men, but I had many psychological doubts. Such doubts weighed so heavily on my mind that I fell deeper into my depression. So, I [pondered about] the question, "Who is God?," which was not easy to answer. It is not a question one can answer immediately. And then there was this other [dilemma], "Who am I attracted to?" And when I tried to reason it out, I could not find a reason. And various other things, [such as] "Where is all this sadness coming from?"[21]

19. "Min-naħa tagħhom in-nuqqas kien li qatt ma raw x'ħabbejt biex jippuxxjawni fuqha. L-ideal tagħhom xtaqu jpoġġuh fuqi. Mhux jaraw x'kapaċitajiet tani l-Mulej, imma xi xtaqu huma jpoġġu fuqi. Bit-tjubija kollha tagħhom. Bla ebda nuqqas lejja ma kienet."

20. The medical condition James is referring to might be *Alopecia Areata*.

21. "Ta' twenty, inħolqot mistoqsija kbira oħra ġo fija rigward l-orjentament sesswali tiegħi. Ġibdiet lejn ġuvintur qatt ma kelli biss f'mod psikoloġiku kelli ħafna dubji. Li dawn id-dubji tant saru tqal ġo rasi li komplejt naqa' ġod-depression. Mela kien hemm il-mistoqsija "Min kien Alla?" li kienet daqsxejn antipatka biex issolviha. Mhux li tista' tirrispondiha boom boom. Imbagħad kien hemm din il-ħaġa 'Jien lejn min miġbud?' U meta tipprova tirraġuna ma kienx hemm raġuni fuqha. U diversi affarijiet oħra, 'Dawn id-dwejjaq minn fejn ġejjin?'"

"Who is God?" I never really believed the concept that everything just started to exist; nothing comes about on its own. I wanted to know. [Thus, even though] with limitations, I started my own research in music and books, [while also] asking around. And I reached a point [where I believed that] God existed. I don't know what He looks like and I don't want to accept that I am susceptible to the country I was born in. If I were born in Libya, I would be Muslim and Jesus wouldn't be my master. [The fact] that Jesus is my master did not make sense to me. So, I reached my own conclusions, that God is up there, He created everything and everyone does what he can to survive.[22]

Apart from this matter, his wish was to own a business. After many failures, he took over a band club in a local village. This endeavor brought approval from his family. "He is a good-for-nothing" used to be his father's mantra. Now he was well-regarded. Success followed, but it enhanced his drinking and drug consumption.

And from that [little] boy who was incapable of much . . . at home I was quite mocked by my father. It always felt like nothing I did was ever good [enough] for him. Instead of encouraging and helping me, he always used to scold me; he never helped me. He ruined my self-esteem. That was another issue that I took quite long to deal with. I worked at a band club, where I got caught up in drugs. I had a girlfriend at the time too, but I still had thoughts about my sexuality in mind. "What am I? Straight? Gay? Bisexual?"[23]

James admitted that deep down, he was searching for meaning, for his questions to be answered and for the emptiness within him to be satisfied. Thus, having a reason to live. Amidst the confusion, he believed in God that

22. "'Min hu Alla?' Għax kont ngħid, il-kunċett li sar kollox waħdu qatt ma daqqli, għax xejn ma jsir waħdu. Ridt inkun naf. U qbadt ngħmel ir-riċerka tiegħi fil-limitazzjonijiet tiegħi bil-mużika u naqra xi ktieb. Dak iż-żmien ma kienx hawn aċċess għall-internet. Tiltaqa' ma' bniedem u ssaqsih. U wasalt f'punt li jeżisti Alla. Ma nafx kif inhu u ma rridx naċċetta li jien suxxettibli għall-pajjiż li tweldit fih. Kieku jien tweldit il-Libja kieku jien Musulman u Ġesù mhux sidi. Li Ġesù hu sidi ma kinitx tagħmel sens għalija. U ħriġt bit-teorija tiegħi li Alla qiegħed hemm fuq, ħalaq kollox u kulħadd jagħmel li jista' biex jisservajvja."

23. "U filli minn dak it-tifel li mhu kapaċi jagħmel xejn, għax id-dar kont immaqdar ħafna minn missieri. Qisek tagħmel x'tagħmel, qatt ma ġġibha żewġ miegħu, u flok jippuxxjak u jgħinek, dejjem iċanfrek, ma jgħinekx. Is-self-esteem ikissirhulek. Dik kienet issue oħra li domt ħafna biex nittekiljha. Naħdem il-każin, hemmhekk iktar inqbadt mad-droga. Kelli tfajla dak iż-żmien ukoll, biss b'dan il-ħsieb tal-orjentament sesswali ġo moħħi. 'Jien x'jien? Straight? Gay? Bisesswali?'"

guided everything. While he was free to choose, the way events began to unfold was a result of grace. Before leading us to his spiritual conversion, James highlighted that at the time, he was extremely hostile towards the Catholic Church. He argues how the church thrives upon its riches was not compatible with the ideals set by Christ. This made him livid.

> I also had a lot of anger towards the church. I hate injustice. I used to feel there was injustice surrounding Jesus. And I still feel this. That there is injustice surrounding Jesus; how can someone be born in poverty and then you have whatever you have? I used to notice these contradictions which pushed me further away from the church. And I used to challenge every priest I met. [I was full of] anger.[24]

One day at around midnight, a priest together with two friends entered his social club. They asked for tea, but James took the opportunity to challenge them. Upon confronting them about the reason for their visit, the priest replied, "I was praying, and I felt the need to come down here and enter the first bar, which is open." James was not impressed but agreed to attend a prayer meeting that the priest organized just because he enjoyed the dialogue. The experience turned sour. Upon seeing the decorations, he felt repulsed. He left and never returned.

As the days passed, his sadness intensified. Although making a profit from his business, his desperation reached a point of no return. His anxiety reached its climax. He felt hopeless and engulfed in depression. Drugs were the only relief amidst this alienation, but rather than giving him rest, they exasperated his tribulations. He began to harbor suicidal thoughts, and though he lacked the courage to take his life, he was counting the days when his life would end. When he could not resist anymore, he contacted the priest whom he came to know. Their meeting lasted two hours, and after listening to him, the priest invited him to pray together in front of the Blessed Sacrament. During adoration, James's feelings intensified:

> At that moment, I experienced Satan. Satan told me, "Ignore him. Don't believe in Him. He's a hypocrite." And I persisted in prayer, and at that moment, something happened which I cannot describe in words. I thought I was in Heaven. Everything stopped. Time stopped. I experienced a sense of peace

---

24. "U kelli rabja kbira lejn il-Knisja. Jien idejquni l-inġustizzji. Jien kont inhoss li hemm inġustizzja ma' Ġesù. U għadni nhossha. Li hemm inġustizzji ma' Ġesù fuq il-livell li kif tista' qed turini bniedem li twieled fil-faqar u mbagħad għandek dak li int għandek? Kont nara dawn il-kontradizzjonijiet li begħduni mill-Knisja. U ma kontx nara qassis li ma mmurx niċċelinġjah. Rabja kbira."

at a rhythm which doesn't exist. I can't explain the happiness; ecstasy.[25]

He left without saying a word. Upon arriving at his home, he burnt all his drugs. This event brought a sense of peace like never before. Acceding to the priest's advice, now his spiritual director, he sought places of solitude to cultivate this new encounter. He stated that what he experienced was not a product of his mind, and whenever he sought God, he received affection. James chose the biblical quote, "Come to me, all you that are weary and are carrying heavy burdens, and I will give you rest"[26] that best captured his situation at the time. This was a new adventure, and change was already noticeable, so much so that his friends remarked, "How could it be that he used to indulge in drugs and now he wants to say the rosary. He was against the church and now with the rosary beads in his pocket?" His anxiety remained, and slowly, James learnt prayer comforted him. He could not pretend that God fixed him. He stopped demanding miracles and sorely recognized his responsibility.

> My life was a dark alley. This experience lit up [my life]. Somehow, I have direction. If I did not know where to go, even though the light is far away, I know I must get to that point. But the confusion remained. The Lord wanted to teach me, "Whatever has to happen on a human level, will happen."[27]

He proactively accounted for this. If, in the past, he rebelled with drugs, now he could not use prayer as a form of escapism. Slowly, with constant dialogue with his spiritual director, James started attending psychotherapy with the aim of confronting his anxiety. Therapy helped to conceptualize his issues, identify their cause and most importantly to differentiate between those thoughts he could do something about, and others that were compulsive and beyond his reach. Both his spiritual director and psychologist were suspicious that he could have obsessive-compulsive disorder (OCD), and so they referred him to a psychiatrist. The diagnosis turned positive, and he was prescribed medication.

---

25. "Dak il-ħin esperjenzajt ix-xitan. Ix-xitan beda jgħidli, 'Tagħtix kasu. Temminx fih. Dak ipokrita.' U komplejt nitlob u dak il-ħin ġara xi ħaġa li ma nistax niddeskriviha bil-kliem. Għedt li kont il-ġenna. Waqaf kollox. Il-ħin waqaf. Dħalt f'paċi u f'ritmu li hawn ma jeżistix. Ferħ ma ngħidlekx, ecstasy."

26. Matt 11:28–30.

27. "Ħajti kienet triq mudlama. B'din l-esperjenza xegħel dawl. B'xi mod għandi direzzjoni. Jekk jien ma kontx naf fejn ser immur, għalkemm id-dawl qiegħed 'il boghod, naf li rrid nasal hemm. Imma d-diżordni hemm baqgħet. Il-Mulej ried jgħallimni, 'Li għandu jsir fuq livell uman għandu jsir.'"

> I couldn't disobey anymore. After that [experience], I healed. I was relieved. Can you imagine carrying twenty kilos in your head? All of a sudden, I got rid of them. I started living fully. Before, there was spiritual harassment, but then I [experienced] a complete [recovery].[28]

Assuming responsibility and building up confidence formed part of the success of the therapy. His frequent adventurous travelling became his canvas for self-exploration and conversation with God. Travelling around the world broadened his perspective. He had never travelled alone, but now it became an expression of his freedom. It also compelled him to be mindful of his temperament. Anger often surfaced but being unaccompanied taught him to cope.

> My relationship with God strengthened as I had a lot of free time in which I did nothing. I learnt that [everyone] needs time spent doing nothing. The Maltese mentality [states that]—my father's—time spent doing nothing is wasted time. In reality, in order to work on oneself, one needs some time doing nothing. I had entered a system where I had to be productive. Travelling helped. I used to read the Bible while travelling. Today I help drug addicts whom I meet on the streets.[29]

Before, James did travel but was unable to appreciate the beauty places offered due to his tribulations. After his spiritual awakening, he went to Calcutta for missioning. There he came face to face with human misery. He then travelled to Nepal, Thailand, Peru, Serbia, and the Philippines, among others. Every journey inspired in him a spiritual lesson, either the appreciation of God through creation and culture or human resilience amidst poverty and post-war conflict.

> Following all these experiences, the Lord gave me courage and direction. I know who I am, and I know my life's goal. This is all

---

28. "Ma stajtx ma nobdix iktar. Imbagħad, minn hemm, fiqt. Ħadt ir-ruħ. Timmaġina ġġorr għoxrin kilo ġo rasek? F'daqqa waħda ħlist minnhom. Bdejt ngħix to the full. L-ewwel kien hemm harassment spiritwali, imma mbagħad sibt healing b'mod komplet."

29. "Kbirt fir-relazzjoni ma' Ġesù għax kien ikolli ħafna ħin ma nagħmel xejn. Tgħallimt li għandek bżonn ħin li ma tagħmel xejn. Fil-mentalità tagħna Maltija—ta' missieri—li ma tagħmel xejn hu ħin mitluf. Fil-verità biex taħdem fuqek innifsek trid ikollok ħin li ma tagħmel xejn. Kont dħalt f'sistema li bilfors trid tkun produttiv. It-travelling għeni. Kont naqra l-Bibbja waqt li qed nittrevilja. Illum ngħin drug addicts li niltaqa' magħhom fit-triq."

thanks to my spiritual director, who always led me step by step. Always [a small step] ahead of me. I try to obey him.[30]

For James, spiritual direction became a reference point. He would bring up questions concerning God and life in the hope that he would have a clearer understanding. He identifies trust and the ability to be challenged as two values that are a part of the direction he receives. He is urged for further maturity with God; one which moves beyond "good feelings, or what I am getting from him, but trust." Through assistance, he was steered to flourishment, but sometimes weaknesses were neglected. Temptations to dabble in drugs remain, but this makes him more credible. The "prison, which once confined me [him]" became the meeting place for others who are depressed, lost, or addicted to drugs.

The Story of Nathaniel

Nathaniel, who is in his forties, left the priesthood and the monastic community he formed part of in his mid-thirties. At present, he is a single man involved in academia and culture. Nathaniel is still coming to terms with the uncertainties of his decision. Leaving the priesthood and religious life remained an inner wound.

> I grieved my priesthood; I was passing through the different phases of a bereavement process. I was in a depressive phase, [and I experienced] solitude, uncertainty, and a sense of void towards the future. I remember I had sent a message to my spiritual director, and I told him, "Today is the anniversary of my ordination. I don't know if I should be happy. I don't know if I should regard it as a curse. I don't know how I should look at this experience. Right now, I'm [only] sure that it has weighed me down, and I am still carrying the consequences of this."[31]

The journey to the priesthood began when Nathaniel was a teenager. During the summer holidays, he attended a set of religious sessions about

---

30. "Wara dawn l-esperjenzi kollha l-Mulej tani kuraġġ u direzzjoni. Naf min jiena, u naf l-iskop ta' hajti. Dawn grazzi għad-direttur spiritwali tiegħi li dejjem mexxieni pass pass. Dejjem biċċa qabli. Nipprova nobdih."

31. "I grieved my priesthood, but I was passing from those different phases tal-bereavement process. Kont għaddej minn depressive episode, solitudni, l-inċertezza u l-bahh quddiemek. U niftakar bgħatt messaġġ lid-direttur spiritwali tiegħi u għadtlu, 'Illum hu l-anniversarju tal-ordinazzjoni tiegħi. Ma nafx jekk għandix inkun kuntent. Ma nafx jekk għandix inħares lejha bħala sehta. Ma nafx kif ser naqbad inħares lejha din l-esperjenza. Bħalissa naf żgur li taqqlitni u għadni qed inġorr il-konsegwenzi tagħha.'"

vocations. He held mixed feelings about the sessions, but instead of stopping, he kept moving on. Once, he witnessed the ordination of a priest and felt his calling.

> God makes use of such episodes to determine a person's [life] story. This I am convinced of. Whatever that moment was, God guided me to where I am today. I am who I am today because I used to be a priest. I wouldn't be able to love the way I do, [if it weren't for that]. I would still be cynical, alone in my room.[32]

From admission to the priory until his ordination, Nathaniel observed positive results. Being immersed in various social circumstances as part of his novitiate enriched his leadership and social skills. He was mentored towards character building, and many academic opportunities emerged. Nathaniel was considered by the friars as a "highly motivated person," and they encouraged him to study further. He completed his studies and did his ordination as if he were "running a race; one success after another."

> When I joined the monastery, I was cynical and very pessimistic. Gradually, I became an optimist. I started viewing life in an adventurous way. It was God's way of [helping me] come to terms with myself, discovering the new me. No, not the new me, but who I [really] was.[33]

It was noted that while studying abroad, he perceived that matters were not going the way he thought. While the priory was described as "an extension of the maternal womb," abroad, everything became cold. Many expectations were imposed on him, and his opinion was not considered. At university, he further isolated himself and deep down, he wished to return home. He sought counsel in the hope of comprehending his dilemma, but few were empathic. Some superiors blamed him for having such feelings. Only one friend offered a listening ear. Nathaniel opted to repress his feelings and complete his studies. All the repression brewed into anger. Once he finished his studies abroad, he returned to Malta, but his inner battles persisted. His only solace was participation within two local non-governmental organizations. Such involvement was not part of his ministry. Rather, they were recreational activities that he enjoyed. But such refuge did not last

---

32. "Alla jinqeda b'dawn l-episodji biex jikteb l-istorja tal-persuna. Dik konvint minnha. Kien x'kien dak il-mument, Alla ċaqlaqni biex iwassalni fejn jien illum. Jien fejn jien illum għax kont saċerdot. Kieku ma nkunx kapaċi nħobb kif inħobb illum. Kieku għadni ċiniku, magħluq ġo kamarti."

33. "Meta dħalt il-kunvent jien kont ċiniku u ħafna negattiv. Bil-mod il-mod sirt bniedem pożittiv. Sirt nara l-ħajja b'mod avventuruż. So, it was God's way to make me come to terms with myself, discovering the new me. No not the new me, but who I was."

long. Many projects were assigned to him, and he ended up renouncing his interests due to a lack of time. This made him suffer from burnout. Another indicator was the number of times he visited his parents' home. From weekends he ended up visiting every day. As days passed, his anger intensified. People started noticing it, and one day he received an e-mail from a fellow friar concerned about his temperament. Nathaniel was livid by the message, but later, he confronted the truth. "Why am I reacting like this? This divulges everything about me. He touched a nerve." Although the signs were numerous, Nathaniel kept resisting until an encounter swept him away. He fell in love with a woman.

> [The battle within] was a terrible issue as I always felt extremely sinful, ashamed and guilty. I had so much shame and guilt that I could not discuss it during confession. And so, I entered a very dark and ugly alley. I was leading a religious life, and I never [brought myself to] confess this issue; [I kept it to myself] up to when I became a novice. I was in hell. After that, given I had established a friendship with the priest, I discussed it. It was very liberating, but I still had major issues with my sexuality. So, when I fell in love, it was affective, emotive, and even physical ... I felt extremely ashamed and guilty. Even the simple fact that I had fallen in love. Then [once] she told me bluntly, "Nathaniel, I do not care, I love you." At that moment, I cried a lot because it was the first time I had heard those words from someone who was not family. It was the first time I felt loved. It was the first time I felt that I loved this person.[34]

Although he loved her, he felt there were manipulative connotations. She did not respect boundaries, and once she invited him to be intimate with her. When he refused, she disappeared. This was devastating for Nathaniel. He had experienced love immediately followed by rejection. Shame and guilt overwhelmed him, and he began contemplating suicide. Due to his desperation, he thought of ending his life three times until a friend helped

---

34. "Mieghi nnifsi kienet issue terribbli għaliex I always felt extremely sinful, shameful and guilty. U tant kemm kelli shame and guilt li lanqas kont kapaċi nitkellimha fil-qrar. Allura jien dħalt ġo sqaq ikrah hafna. Jien kont fil-ħajja reliġjuża u sannovizzjat kont qatt ma qerrejt din l-issue. I was in hell. Minn hemm għax bnejt ħbiberija mal-patrijiet iddiskutejtha. It was very liberating, but still I had major issues with my sexuality. Allura, meta I fell in love it was the affective, emotive and even the physical ... I felt extremely shameful and guilty. Even the simple fact of feeling that I fell in love. Then she told me point blank, "Nathaniel, I do not care, I love you." Dak il-mument bkejt fuq li bkejt because it was the first time I heard those words from someone who is not family. It was the first time I felt loved. It was the first time I felt that I loved this person."

him out. Nathaniel compared his journey of awakening with a gay man who would describe his coming out experience. His friend could comprehend him perfectly as he was a father of a gay son. He recognized the signs which empowered him to seek professional help. Nathaniel stopped procrastinating and sought psychological support.

Inevitably the link between sexuality and priesthood were faced. Nathaniel's upbringing viewed sex or the sensual as taboo. Through therapy, he confronted his pent-up feelings and acted towards wholeness. Later, he requested leave of absence from the provincial to find the meaning of his future, but it was rejected outright. He was precluded from administrating the sacraments. Rather than being given assistance and support, he was met with rejection again. Furthermore, when he requested to celebrate Mass for a planned wedding of a friend, the provincial did not accede to this request.

> He told me, "You went back on the word you gave God, will you find it difficult to go back on the word you gave him [his friend]?"[35]

Although financial assistance was offered in the form of remuneration, what Nathaniel sought was emotional assistance to come to reconcile himself with his decision and to integrate back into society. On this level, the ecclesiastical institutions did not provide any assistance.

One of the factors intensifying insecurity was the dispensation issue which, according to canon law, is granted after forty years. However, exceptions are granted in cases where children are involved, or when former priests enter civil marriage. While he understood the restrictions imposed by the regulation, he felt that it generalizes and did not specify those who discerned their path and came to a decision with the backing of a spiritual director and other specialists.

An obstacle that blocked Nathaniel from beholding his reality was his fear of what people would say about him. He was anxious that friends, colleagues, and the community he had ministered would judge him. He perceived the disappointment of those couples he had led to the sacrament of marriage. When going through their photo albums, they would now remember him as one that forsaken his post. He anticipated shame and guilt. Consequently, he began to muster the courage to face the matter. Another obstacle had to do with his family. He was brought up in a conservative family and taking such a decision would cause a lot of stress to his elderly parents. He referred to the allegory of the chariot by Plato to describe how

---

35. "Qalli, 'Tajt kelma lil Alla u ħa terġa' lura minnha, ħa ssib diffikultà biex terġa' lura mill-kelma li għadt lil dan?'"

fear and shame were the two motives driving his reactions. He ended up repressing everything and instead engaged in relentless work. For Nathaniel, priesthood became a means of production with constant activity either in the form of academic pursuits or pastoral ministry. In the end, he ignored his well-being just to please others.

> And when I made my decision to stop, the priests were disappointed. I always mention this, [the] shame and [the] guilt as well as the downward spiral of pleasing others. Most importantly, it reflects love, as I realized that my emotional life had flourished in my late thirties. Before that, I was very much loved, but I did not love myself. Which is fine, but very painful. When I realized [all this] I cried a lot during my session with my psychologist.[36]

Much of therapy's merit had to do with Nathaniel identifying the origin of his actions. Self-awareness led to the recognition of how much anxiety was transmitted to him by his mother due to complications when she was pregnant with him. It was a high-risk pregnancy since she had several miscarriages. Yet his mother made a leap of faith. She ended up bedbound due to complications, "and that was the key; the anxiety. I absorbed the anxiety of my mother biologically and emotionally." Previously unaware, Nathaniel also realized that this anxiety was part of his childhood. He has very faint memories of it, but he remembered that as a child he preferred to keep to himself. Teachers noticed the pattern, and whenever he was approached, he would feel threatened and throw tantrums. Attachment trauma continued through the years, even in his adult life. Nathaniel described his father as a "mysterious box," distant and with a sense of bitterness towards life. There were a series of failures in his life that molded him into a pessimist. Although finding it difficult to show affection, Nathaniel described his father as a "tuning fork; soundless but deeply resonating."

As a priest, he always felt distant from God. Even during Mass, while there was an intimate atmosphere, a layering of disconnection persisted. His behavior amounted to disorientation. That spark and feeling in his teenage years had faded away. It was most likely a result of his own needs. He could not know any better, and yet he was still angry at himself. Following his departure from the priesthood, he was pitchforked into a position to consider the humanity of Christ. While briefly alluded to it in the past, after his own

---

36. "U meta għamilt id-deċiżjoni li nieqaf kien hemm id-diżappunt mill-patrijiet. Dejjem ngħidha, shame and guilt and the downwards spiral of pleasing others. And most important it reflects to as love, għaliex jien irrealizzajt li my emotional life opened up in my late thirties. Before I was very much loved, but I did not love myself. Which is fine but very painful. Meta rrealizzajt bkejt ħafna quddiem il-psikologu."

hard scrutiny, he found that Christ's humanity was surer and nearer. Even other biblical figures became paradigms of psychological and spiritual value. Like them, he could never again dismiss his humanity. Rather, he had to befriend it and explore his nature together with Christ. Such profoundness was not practiced as a priest. Looking back at his priestly role, he described it as a "tiger locked in a small cage." Nathaniel described the two years leading to his departure as "a living hell." He felt isolated and abandoned by God. His prayers were ones of lamentation which brought to his mind how Christ felt when He was crucified. Only after the tribulation dissipated, he was able to realize that he never was alone in the first place.

> Nowadays, I am on a more confident path. I had a very close and intimate encounter with Christ, much more [intimate] than my encounters with him during my religious life, and even in the administration of sacraments. This may also be because I've been through hell in the past two years, [as] I felt that God was not present. My question was, "Where are you?" and "Why?"; Jesus's questions on the cross. In this, I see the depth of the psychology of our Lord Jesus Christ. And after, like Moses, I looked back, and I saw that God had passed [from there]. And I think that every human being experiences such a thing. While you're passing through moments filled with problems, you don't see Him.[37]

SEPARATED STRAIGHT MEN

The Story of Thomas

Thomas, who is in his early forties, is a manager. At the beginning of the interview, he shared his "first curiosity about God." One day, he overheard his friends talking about God: "Do you know how you see Jesus? Look at the bulb, close your eyes, the light that you see is God." He was only six years old, but that statement disappointed him. He bore this innocent memory throughout the years, and today he defines spirituality as "my [his] greatest desire to know God."

37. "Illum ninsab f'mixja iktar kunfidenti. Kelli laqgħa profonda ma' Kristu iktar milli ltqajt miegħu fil-ħajja reliġjuża, u kemm fl-amministrazzjoni tas-sagramenti. Forsi anka għal-fatt li f'sentejn għaddejt mill-infern ta' ħajti, imma ħassejt li Alla ma kienx preżenti. Il-mistoqsija tiegħi kienet 'Fejn int?' u 'Għaliex?'; mistoqsijiet ta' Ġesù fuq is-salib. Hemm nara l-psikoloġija fil-milja tagħha ta' sidna Ġesù Kristu. U wara, bħal Mosè ħarist lura u rajt li Alla għadda. U naħseb din hi esperjenza ta' kull bniedem. Sakemm tkun għaddej mill-problemi ma taraħx."

Until the Sacrament of Confirmation, Thomas practiced religion according to his mother's instructions. After he satisfied the customary religious requirements, he no longer found faith important. He stopped attending Mass and put aside all religious objects. Thomas "lived life to the full. The typical attitude of a Maltese Christian," where one lays heavy emphasis on pleasure and disregards religion. By the age of twenty-three, he was getting married. This became a significant event that would shape his life.

Thomas admitted that part of the reason why his first marriage dragged into complications was also his fault. Since he was timid, Thomas repressed his desires. As a couple, they had intimacy issues, but rather than working to solve them, they both hid in work. Another warning was his wife's father, who had shown signs of control and abuse. At college, he sought a second opinion by a priest, but he dismissed Thomas's concerns as regular matters.

> Regardless of all these things, we proceeded with [our plans]. Surely enough, certain issues resurfaced after marriage. I used to talk to her [about them] a lot. This thing about intimacy is very important to me. I cannot live with my sister. It's important [to me] that things fall into place. She never agreed as, in her opinion, a good wife is someone who cooks, and does this and that. "This is all in your head," she used to tell me. To cut a very long story short, at a certain point, after about a year and half/two years, I gave up on the situation, and I started focusing on work, [on my] studies.[38]

Concentrating on education and work, he had several promotions. But the distance between the couple augmented. Both lived on the same premises but led separate lives. Then, an extramarital affair developed. He got to know a woman, and sexual attraction ensued. She "was very challenging and thrilling because she was extremely intelligent." He ended up "head over heels in love with her. Intimacy followed, and he felt euphoric. It was 'a new world I [he] never lived.'"

> Nowadays, I believe the [Holy] Spirit was allowing my heart to beat in various ways. In the meantime, my attraction towards this girl increased and my relationship with my wife started to

38. "Fost dawn l-affarijiet kollha we proceeded with everything. Surely enough, ċertu affarijiet baqgħu joħorġu wara ż-żwieġ. Kont inkellimha ħafna. Din il-biċċa tax-xogħol tal-intimità importanti ħafna għalija. Jien ma nistax ngħix ma' oħti. Importanti li l-affarijiet iridu jitranġaw. Hi qatt ma qablet għax għaliha a good wife hi li issajjar, tagħmel hekk u tagħmel hekk. 'Dan kollu kummiedji f'moħħok kienet tgħidli.' To cut a very long story short, at a certain stage wara xi sena u nofs, sentejn, qtajt qalbi mis-sitwazzjoni and I started really focusing on work, studies."

deteriorate, [becoming] much worse than it was before. After I completed my Masters [degree], I naturally had more time on my hands. [Due to this] I had more interaction with my wife, and I found myself sharing a room with someone I didn't know. It was an internal shock. In reality, I wanted to be with this other new person, but I couldn't, but I know I am married, so my confrontational issues resurfaced even faster.[39]

The spirit was calling for his attention in several ways, and on one occasion, Thomas was reading a newspaper magazine. He came across a Christian prayer group advert and was drawn to it. After some days, he got in touch with them.

I knew I was passing through a very tough time, and I heard that, in suffering, some people resort to these things, and something really struck me deep down. I had the email address of a Christian entity; this was a huge issue [for me]. It was unusual. I wrote an email. I moved it to my drafts [folder] and left it there. I was torn between wanting to send it and not wanting to do so. It remained in my drafts [folder] for seven days. Finally, I wrote a big disclaimer that, "I wished to attend, but [with the understanding that] I would be allowed to flee if I felt uncomfortable with the situation."[40]

Thomas attended the prayer group meeting and felt at ease. "It's a very relaxed way how to tackle faith; ideal for nonbelievers or non-church goers." Thomas was reintroduced to the Catholic Catechism, but he noticed how nobody corrected others in group sharing sessions. There was an atmosphere of genuine acceptance that led him to assess his behavior.

I suddenly started to realize that I was in the wrong. I was in the wrong, not only morally, but I was also in bad shape. My conscious beat even stronger. An important fact; some months

39. "Illum nemmen l-ispirtu beda jħabbat il-qalb tiegħi b'diversi modi. In the meantime, jien komplejt ninġibed lejn din it-tfajla u r-relazzjoni tiegħi mal-mara bdiet tiżżarma ħafna iktar milli kienet qabel. Wara li spiċċajt il-masters awtomatikament ilħin li ġie f'idejja kelli iktar interaction mal-mara u spiċċajt fl-istess kamra ma' persuna li lanqas nafha. It was an internal shock. Fir-realtà ridt inkun ma' din il-persuna l-ġdida, però ma stajtx, però naf li jien miżżewweġ, allura my confrontational issues iktar bdew joħorġu."

40. "Kont naf li għaddej minn ħafna tbatija u kont nisma' illi fit-tbatija hemm min idur lejn dawn l-affarijiet and something really struck me deep down. A Christian entity illi kellha email address kienet xi ħaġa kbira. Dawn qisu mhux tas-soltu. Ktibt email. Ħallejtha fid-drafts. Bejn ħa nibgħatha u bejn ma rridx. Sebat ijiem għamlet fid-drafts. Fl-aħħar ktibt big disclaimer li, 'Nixtieq niġi imma jekk ma jogħġobnix ix-xogħol intir 'il barra.'"

earlier, I felt my conscious bringing to my attention something I was doing [wrong]. At a certain stage, I decided to shut it down. Like, "you shut up and let me do whatever I want to do." It was vulgar. From that day onwards, a time span of a year and a half, I started [my journey] downhill.[41]

Thomas' life was in a "mess." He consumed drugs, and their side effects had a negative impact on his job performance. He abandoned friends who advised him otherwise and instead started frequenting "high-profile people." His work involved many travelling trips. While abroad, he participated in drug parties and attended strip clubs.

I suddenly realized that these were all bad. Not just thieving is wrong. If the measure was such, in reality, the measurement was much longer and bigger, of the things one needs to do to be . . . , or the things that one doesn't have to do to be Christian.[42]

His life was on the "fast lane," and it started to malfunction. Once, during meditation, he randomly flipped the Scriptures, and his eyes fell upon the word, "adultery." Since he knew what the word meant, it touched a nerve. He could not resist anymore, and he sought assistance from a priest involved in the group he attended.

He told me, "If you're passing through all this suffering, if you're experiencing this thirst for love, if you're going out of your way to be liked and loved, it's quite obvious that you behave like that." He told me, "Don't you dare stop [meeting] the other person because you'll go crazy." I was astounded.[43]

Thomas found reassurance. He started embarking on his journey of truth and complemented spiritual direction with psychological and psychiatric support.

41. "F'daqqa waħda bdejt nirrealizza li I am in the wrong. I am in the wrong not only morally but qiegħed vera fil-ħażin. Il-kuxjenza bdiet tħabbat iktar b'saħħitha. Punt importanti ħafna, ftit xhur qabel jien kont inħoss li l-kuxjenza kienet qed tiġbidli l-attenzjoni meta nagħmel xi ħaġa. At a certain stage, I have decided to shut it down. Like, 'You shut up and let me do whatever I want to do.' Kienet vulgari. Minn dak inhar 'l hemm, perjodu ta' sena u nofs, vera qbadt in-niżla."

42. "F'daqqa waħda bdejt nirrealizza li dawn kollha ħżiena. Mhux sempliċiment li tisraq hu ħażin. Jekk il-kejl kien daqshekk, fil-verità l-kejl kien ħafna itwal u ikbar, tal-affarijiet li għandek tagħmel biex tkun, jew l-affarijiet li ma tridx tagħmel biex tkun Kristjan."

43. "Qalli, 'Jekk inti għaddej minn dik it-tbatija kollha, jekk inti għaddej minn dak l-għatx għall-imħabba, jekk inti qiegħed tagħmel minn kollox biex tingħoġob u tinħabb, mhux ovvja tagħmel hekk.' Qalli, 'Ara ma jfettillekx tieqaf mill-persuna l-oħra għax tiġġennen.' U bellahni!"

> I have always been successful in life. I have always got what I wanted, be it work, sports or tournaments. Whatever it was, I always faced whatever I embarked on with determination. Perseverance, right? I always got to where I wanted. But in marriage, I couldn't manage. And my frustration because of that used to drive me crazy as it was not in my control.[44]

Thomas attempted to make sense of his marriage—that unsuccessful area in his life which he could not control—by eliminating those objects which obscured his vision. He stopped taking drugs and attending certain nightclubs. He found relief by saying the Rosary. Prayer became his new outlet for good feelings. He changed this attitude of separation even with the extramarital woman who gave him affection. The plan, which was supported by his spiritual director, was to discern the reality of his marriage. He could not simply quit and move in with a new woman without first solving the problem, as other problems would recur. He chose to take the longer route and discern if his marriage truly existed. If not, he would file for annulment. This was his greatest renunciation: to "know the truth about his marriage." Through prayer and fasting—his "two wings"—he faced the challenge. He resisted and pleaded, "I will leave her, but you [God] have to replace her."

> And I remember, up to this day I [still] don't know, if it was a psychological issue or if the [Holy] Spirit truly manifested itself. Referring to the moment I'm talking about, I prayed so hard, I felt a hug, a physical manifestation. I used to feel it only under the effect of ecstasy, or anything that used to raise me high. My heart wanted to explode. So, I am not sure if it is a mental thing or a true manifestation of the [Holy] Spirit.[45]

This sign became a "turning point," leading Thomas to distance himself from the other woman completely. Communication was eventually discontinued, and all souvenirs were thrown away. Now he focused his full attention on his marriage, but the relationship deteriorated even further.

---

44. "Jien kont successful f'ħajti. Kull ħaġa li ridt dejjem ħadtha, jekk ix-xogħol, jekk sports jew tournaments. Hi x'inhi, jekk ħa nidħol għaliha ser nidħol bis-saħħa. Perseverance sew. Dejjem wasalt fejn ridt. Imma fiż-żwieġ qatt ma stajt nasal. U l-frustrazzjoni minħabba dik, kienet iġġenninni għax it was not in my control."

45. "U niftakar, sal-lum għadni ma nafx, jekk ma kinitx xi ħaġa psikoloġika jew l-ispirtu vera mmanifesta ruħu. Imma mal-mument li qiegħed ngħid hekk, tant tlabt, inħoss tgħanniqa, a physical manifestation. Kont inħossha biss, meta kont bl-ecstasy jew xi ħaġa li kienet itellagħni high. My heart wanted to explode. So, I am not sure if it is a mental thing or a true manifestation of the spirit."

What was happening? Every time we used to meet with someone [to work on our problems] when we started digging into [our] problems, she used to shut down and escape the issue. The more I met with psychologists and read up on self-development [and] personal growth, the more I matured and grew, both spiritually and psychologically. I grew further away from her, as she used to live in her own bubble.[46]

She used to tell me, "We are at a point of no return. I don't trust you anymore. Whatever you did, forget it. This is my life. If you want to join me, do so. I am not going to change and move towards what you want."[47]

Rather than deciding to separate, Thomas focused his energy on voluntary work. Through this activity, he got to know another woman and risked repeating the same cycle. His spiritual director challenged him and asked:

The issue is that I spent three days in this person's company. Nothing wrong, but [I] had the time of [my] life. Whereas with my wife, I had been struggling for so long, and [the relationship] was so boring and dull, even though [I was] trying so much. "Thomas, are you sure you're on the right track with your wife?"[48]

Thomas recognized the roots of the problem. Being a non-confrontational person goes back to his childhood, and that was his greatest obstacle. Fear was the problem. He took the decision to separate, even if that meant upsetting his wife, his mother and other people in the community. He was confronted by his spiritual director, "Imagine if you were to die right now and find yourself before God, would you still think what you are thinking? Would you still say these words?" There, he recognized his marriage was truly void.

---

46. "X'beda jiġri? Kull darba li konna morru għand xi ħadd, when we started digging into the problems, she used to shut down and she used to run away from the issue. Iktar ma bdejt nara psychologists u naqra fuq self-development, personal growth, iktar bdejt nimmatura u nikber kemm spiritwalment u psikoloġikament. Iktar bdejt niddistakka minnha għax kienet imbagħad tgħix in her own bubble."

47. "Hi kienet tgħidli, 'We are in a point of no return. Jien lilek ma nafdakx iktar. Għamilt x'għamilt, forget it, this is my life. If you want to join me, join me. I am not going to change and come towards what you want.'"

48. "The issue is li għamilt tlett ijiem tiġri ma din il-persuna. Nothing wrong, but you had the time of your life. Mentri mal-mara ilek tipprova dan iż-żmien kollu and it is so boring and dull, even though you are trying so much. 'Thomas are you sure you are on the right track with your wife?'"

> I became more aware that all this was happening because of my childhood. My upbringing; I had always been the black sheep of the family. My mother very much preferred my older siblings, so I always used to go out of my way to please her. I always felt I could not disappoint. Consequently, all my decisions were [always] made based on keeping the peace.[49]
>
> From then onwards, I decided [to proceed towards] annulment. It was a painful phase. I still remember seeing her cry and packing [her things], I remember leaving the house I had built myself. It was a point of separation. I went to live alone. It was soon Easter time, and it was one of the [most] painful Easters of my life.[50]

Thomas filed for an annulment. Even though his wife wished to reconcile, he rejected the proposal. After the annulment was granted to the couple, he entered a new relationship. He also got involved in pastoral ministry and shares his story with the youth who attend the community he forms part of.

The Story of Jude

For Jude, spirituality is universal. The merging of the physical with the spiritual is an invitation that is open for everyone. The idea is not what creed one follows but how authentic a person is. This understanding of spirituality is the fruit of Jude's life events. He is disappointed when he meets people who just subscribe to a faith and "speak like parrots." They talk, and yet, they are shallow.

> Personally, nowadays, I view spirituality from a basic human perspective. We are [both] human and spiritual beings. The spiritual and the physical aspects [coexist] holistically, which is also a universal level. One doesn't have to be Christian. I know people who aren't Christian but live a spiritual life, often much more than Christians. But then, as Christians, spirituality [also]

---

49. "Sirt iktar self-aware li dan kollu beda jiġri minħabba t-tfulija tiegħi. L-upbringing tiegħi, I was always the black sheep of the family. Ommi kellha preferenzi kbar ma' ħuti, allura kont nagħmel minn kollox biex ningħoġob ma' ommi. Dejjem kont inħoss li ma nistax niddiżappunta lil xi ħadd. Allura d-deċiżjonijiet tiegħi kienu jkunu kollha bbażati biex ma niksirx il-paċi."

50. "Minn hemm 'il quddiem iddeċidejt li ser nagħmel l-annullament. It was a painful phase. Qed nara lilha tibki u tippakkja, qed nara lili nitlaq id-dar li bnejt jien. It was a point of separation. Mort ngħix waħdi. Ġie l-Easter u kien one of the painful Easters of my life."

means accepting Jesus in my life, and I allow Him to restore the man [in me].[51]

"The acceptance of Jesus as the one who restores life" is his personal spirituality, but he admits that living the call is hard. Theorizing about such matters is easy, but there is always some form of personal resistance. He admits from the very start that he is currently seeking authenticity. He qualifies this search by distinguishing between the "actual self" and the "ideal self." For many years he chased ideals that he thought would make him happy, but instead they produced pain, anger, and confusion.

Jude shared that the way society acts is complicated. He feels withdrawn from it. He obeys a set of rules imposed on him, but like an animal circus, he feels life is artificial. "We created our own circus, and the system oppresses us." For him, there is no freedom. He observes how people chase dreams, and in spite of the fact that they possess so many riches, they have empty lives.

> I don't think it makes sense. We are forcing violence onto our humanity in order to live. In fact, we are ruining our own selves. Even if one takes a look around, "I do not fit in." Man has everything but is empty [within]. Everyone is depressed. We've created our own circus. We are not fully responsible. The system imposes on us ways to live on a human level.[52]

Jude's childhood was filled with loneliness. He does not blame his parents but recognized that they had limited caring skills. As he grew up, he constantly felt alone. Low self-esteem increased, and he felt no sense of safety. He created many "shields" to guard himself. When he reached the age of sixteen, he felt he missed much of life. During this phase, Jude also enquired about God whom he wished to belong to and put amend to the confusion and loneliness he bore. He felt there was an interior battle between the good and evil spirit, i.e., God and Satan. He could not remain

---

51. "Spiritwalità, għalija personali, illum il-ġurnata naraha mil-aspett bażiku uman. Aħna esseri umani u esseri spiritwali wkoll. Hemm l-aspett spiritwali ma' dak fiżiku bħala livell ħolistiku, li hu wkoll livell universali. M'hemmx għalfejn inkun Nisrani. Naf persuni li mhux Insara u jgħixu l-ħajja spiritwali, ħafna drabi iktar mill-Insara. Imma bħala Nsara mbagħad, l-ispirtwalità hija l-aċċettazjoni ta' Ġesù f'ħajti u li nħallih jirrestawra l-bniedem."

52. "Ma narahiex li tagħmel sens. Qegħdin nisfurzaw il-vjolenza fuq in-natura tagħna biex ngħixu. Fil-fatt qegħdin infottu lilna nfusna. Tara anka madwarek, 'I do not fit in.' Il-persuna għandha kollox imma vojta. Kulħadd bid-depression. Ħloqna ċirku għalina stess. We are not fully responsible. Is-sistema timponi fuqna kif għandna ngħixu fuq livell uman."

indifferent and was urged to choose. After spending days ruminating about life, he consecrated his life to Satan.

Jude admitted that his parents' lack of love and care pushed him on that path. They always discouraged him. The constant message he received from them was that he was "not good enough." As he progressed in his Satanic lifestyle, he practiced black magic and swayed others to follow his path. In hindsight, Jude acknowledged that everything was a deception. He thought he entered a "palace," but it was a "prison cell where darkness and confusion reign." He felt manipulated, but the urge to be good resurfaced. Later, he spoke to "a white magic witch." This man gave him a Bible to read.

As he examined the Bible closely, he felt positive. He sought solitary places for reflection and began attending Mass. Gradually, he recognized that practicing magic was not compatible with God's loving message. This drove him to seek an exorcist and to hand over his Satanic items. Since Jude wished to walk the path of Christianity, he regularly attended Mass and the Sacrament of Reconciliation. He called this phase his conversion, and at one point, he desired to try the life of a friar.

> I had a word with someone who is responsible for vocational callings. I called and visited. I had long hair [at the time], and he was shocked when he saw me. We started chatting, and he showed me around the monastery. The first thing he asked me was whether I had any O-Levels. To me, it was scandalous that I was discerning my vocation, and he asked me about my O-Levels. It would have been better had he spoken to me about Jesus. I did not care about O-Levels.[53]

Living with the friars, he felt uncomfortable. Prayer was "dry," and he did not feel at home. He bitterly left the monastery and sought the hermitic life. But after two years, he considered such life as "unbalanced."

> I had spent two years in solitude. But I became aware of the imbalance. Even though I appreciated silence and solitude as values, that didn't mean I had to give up my life as a way of life. There are moments where I need silence and other moments. I came back.[54]

---

53. "Kellimt lil wieħed li kien jieħu ħsieb il-vokazzjonijiet. Ċempiltlu u mort. Jien kelli xagħri twila u ħa qatgħa meta rani. Beda jkellimni u jdawwarni l-kunvent. L-ewwel ħaġa li saqsa kien jekk għandix O levels. Jien għalija kien skandlu li qiegħed niddixxerni vokazzjoni u saqsieni x'O levels għandi. Aħjar għadtli xi ħaġa fuq Ġesù. X'jimpurtani mill-O levels."

54. "Kont għamilt sentejn eremita. Imma rajt li ma kienx hemm bilanċ. Għalkemm kont napprezza s-silenzju u s-solitudni bħala valur, però ma jfissirx li għandi naghti ħajti bħala forma ta' ħajja. Hemm mumenti fejn irrid is-silenzju u hemm mumenti

When he returned to Malta, he found employment. However, Jude stated that life was still meaningless. He had no place to live at, and during this period, his father died of cancer. During this sensitive time, he encountered his spiritual director. Through the sessions, he felt empowered and came to desire to study theology.

> I wished to do a course in theology, and I completed a diploma. I enrolled for a diploma. I was satisfied with my performance in the first exam, and I [then] read a degree. I spent three years out of work, and I focused on it. And at the same time, [I kept] searching.[55]

After finishing the degree, Jude entered into a relationship with a woman. They married shortly after. He hoped to build a family based on Christian values as no other role was suited for him. However, it was a calamity that would generate anguish and anger. Before marrying, signs of incompatibility with his future wife were already evident, yet he moved forward.

> Marriage, we could not find common ground, not even on a human level. For instance, my friends and I, there are certain qualities we share. In their absence, we wouldn't be friends. With her, there was nothing. I always hoped we would one day get there—a lame idea.[56]

She was distant from the church. After introducing her to Fr Shaun, who was his friend, she felt comfortable and started to attend church service. Jude hoped that the priest would guide them as a couple and stimulate her in the need of faith. He was optimistic, but their relationship did not improve.

> She was always ambiguous. She escaped me. She never spoke to me about her feelings or about what she was going through. I used to text her to talk, and she used to reply, "There is nothing to talk about." When you love someone, there doesn't have to be

---

oħrajn. Ġejt lura."

55. "Kelli xewqa nagħmel kors fit-teoloġija u għamilt diploma. Dħalt nagħmel diploma. Wara l-ewwel eżami rajt li mort tajjeb. U għamilt degree. Għamilt tliet snin ma naħdimx u iffokajt fuqu. U fl-istess ħin infittex."

56. "Iż-żwieġ, lanqas fuq livell uman ma konna wasalna. Per eżempju jien u l-ħbieb hemm ċertu kwalitajiet bejnietna. Li kieku m'humiex hemm kieku ma nkunux ħbieb. Magħha ma kien hemm xejn. Dejjem kont nittama li tasal—idea fażulla."

a reason to talk. If necessary, we speak nonsense [together]. But it's still time [well] spent with someone you love.[57]

While Fr Shaun was in the picture, Jude stopped spiritual direction with his priest. Instead, he shared his concerns with Fr Shaun. He would often advise Jude to give her space. But, as the months passed, Jude felt suspicious. He noticed her spending many hours chatting with Fr Shaun rather than him. The chats were mainly brief at first but later took longer throughout the night. What augmented his suspicion was when Jude invited Fr Shaun to be the confessor of his fiancée, but Fr Shaun refused, stating it would have been inappropriate. Being conversant in Canon Law, Jude knew that priests would be automatically excommunicated if they administered the Sacrament of Reconciliation to a person with whom they had sexual encounters. Evidence that her contact with Fr Shaun was not only limited to spiritual guidance emerged when Jude read the chat history between his fiancée and Fr Shaun. The content comprised sexually explicit messages, including the sharing of pictures. Jude felt betrayed by his fiancée and abused by the priest. He confronted them but was convinced by Fr Shaun to seek forgiveness and to persist with the relationship. Jude complied and deleted his evidence.

> I'm weak. I'm telling you. And I'm working on it. I'm foolish. I carry responsibility because I forgave. I think this was the mistake. Yes, I had to forgive, but now I have to go. "You have your life; I have mine." I forgave them at my expense. I forgave them but not myself. They persisted in their manipulation. I suffered the consequences of this as he was a priest.[58]

They did not break up, but they proceeded with the wedding. Jude felt conditioned to comply. Fr Shaun encouraged the couple to the sacrament of marriage in the hope that Jude would not expose him.

> Marrying would mean I forgave her and forgiving her [meant] forgiving him too. I accepted it all. And when he answered me,

---

57. "Hi kollox vag. Taħrab minni. Jekk ikollha xi ħaġa ma tkellimnix. U jien kont nibagħtilha ejja nitkellmu u hi kienet tgħidli, 'M'hemmx fuq xiex nitkellmu.' Meta thobb lil xi ħadd ma jridx ikun hemm raġuni għala titkellem. Jekk hemm bżonn ngħidu ċ-ċuċati. Imma hin ikkunsmat ma' xi ħadd li thobb."

58. "Jien pastizz. Qed ngħidlek jiena. U fuq din qed naħdem fuqha. Jien iblah. Nieħu r-responsabilità għax ħfirt. Jien naħseb l-iżball hu dak. Iva, kelli naħfer, imma issa jien ser immur. 'Inti għandek hajtek; jien għandi hajti.' Jien ħfirtilhom b'dannu għalija. Ħfirtilhom u ma ħfirtx lili nnifsi. Huma komplew jimmanipulaw. Ħaġa illi batejt minnha għax hu kien saċerdot."

he used to ask me whether I would be more aware. "Love forgives. Be tender."⁵⁹

Immediately after the marriage, the cycle repeated itself. His wife gave him no affection. Infidelity with Fr Shaun resumed. This time he left the matrimonial home. Jude was devastated. He shared how easy it was for him to spiritualize everything that was occurring in his life. He felt guilty and angry. But he does not nurture any ill-feeling against the whole institution because of the manipulation of one priest. He still loves the church, as Christ does so.

Jude went back to his previous spiritual director for guidance. Through the sessions, he recognized that their marriage never truly existed. He then filed for an annulment. Jude feels that whatever he tries in life, he always fails. He sees life as a continuous struggle to survive rather than to enjoy it. When people ask about his situation, he feels they perceive him as a victim. They quickly break off since, in his view, they prefer meeting positive people.

> What is my purpose? Why should I live? Living on means more suffering. I think I would fail even in committing suicide. I've had a life [full] of failures. My life has always been survival. It's too much.⁶⁰

SINGLE GAY MEN

The Story of Philip

Philip is a teacher in his early thirties. For the interview, he presented extracts from his spiritual journals, which are a record of his journey of faith as well as the struggles he faced to know himself. For Philip, praying and writing are intertwined. During moments of prayer, he often allows his thoughts to freely flow into sentences. But on other occasions, he records valuable experiences which become significant mementoes. Philip identifies himself as a gay man, and in many aspects, his spirituality includes those efforts to embrace his sexuality.

---

59. "Niżżewweġ tfisser li jien ħfirtila, u jekk ħfirt lilha, ħfirt lilu ukoll. Aċċettajt kollox. U kif kien jirrispondini kien jgħidli imma issa ser teħodha b'aktar awareness. 'L-imħabba taf taħfer. Be tender.'"

60. "Jien xi skop għandi? Għala nibqa' ħaj? Għalija iktar tbatija nibqa' ngħix. Jien naħseb li jekk nagħmel suwiċidju naħseb ifallili wkoll. I've had a life of many failures. Ħajti surviving dejjem. It's too much."

He recounted how as a young boy he frequented the sacraments and later joined the choir. "God was always sought out in his activities." He was instructed to always adhere to the moral instructions set by the church. As a teenager, he attended a charismatic group but felt ill at ease with their style of prayer. "I will tell the truth. I never felt that it was my spirituality. My aim was to make friends." Little did he know that this feeling of peculiarity would predominantly characterize his spirituality.

Later, he entered seminary since he thought that the priesthood was an ideal lifestyle. He was introduced to spiritual direction and was encouraged to find a priest to accompany him. The ones he found were "highly intelligent and religious" but felt they did not quite understand him well. He moved from one director to another but always felt tensed.

> He [his spiritual director] was spiritual but what I felt in him was that he didn't have much life experience. He had never worked in a parish. I remember my father had passed away when I was at the seminary, and I used to feel that, in reality, he did not understand me. I always felt I hadn't found my spirituality yet, neither when I was at the parish, nor when I [joined] the charismatic group, nor when I entered the seminary. It felt like, deep down, I had never really found my spirituality.[61]

He desired self-knowledge, a place that he could call home. Life continued, and while abroad, as part of his training, he heard about Ignatian spirituality. He was inspired by its merits and attempted to attend an Ignatian retreat.

> I felt the need to experience an Ignatian retreat. When I was there, I had no money. Even though I worked in a school, I also had a lot of expenses. The money I earned I used to spend on food, [and] to live with the Father; I didn't have a lot of money.[62]

Providentially, Philip still managed to attend as a friend defrayed the expenses involved as a gift. At the retreat, he meditated about life and confirmed his calling for the priesthood. He was filled with enthusiasm.

---

61. "Kien spiritwali imma li kont inħoss fih hija li ma tantx kellu esperjenza talħajja. Qatt ma ħadem f'parroċċa. Niftakar missieri kien miet meta kont is-seminarju u kont inħossu li ma kienx jifhmni fil-verità. Kont dejjem inħoss li għadni ma sibtx l-ispiritwalità tiegħi. La meta kont fil-parroċċa, la meta kont għand il-kariżmatiċi, la meta dħalt is-seminarju. Qisu deep down l-ispiritwalità tiegħi ma kontx qisni fil-verità sibtha."

62. "Kelli x-xewqa nagħmel irtir Injazjan. Meta kont hemm ma kellix flus. Għalkemm kont naħdem ġo skola, imbagħad kelli ħafna spejjeż. Il-flus li kont naqla' kont nonfoqhom biex niekol, biex ngħix mal-Fr, u ma kellix ħafna flus."

> I used to visit a big cemetery to meditate [about] death. It was a powerful experience. What my priest told me, "When you leave, you will experience the grace of God, which will also be accessible for you to touch." I had had this fixation of becoming a priest since forever, as a priest's life is a very beautiful one.[63]

Returning to Malta, he was met with disappointment. He failed the seminary psychological screening, which was "a big blow" for him. His road towards priesthood was suspended, and he felt disoriented and abandoned. Philip described himself as a resilient individual. He kept asking for guidance until a friend recommended that counsel be sought from Fr Elijah. Not only was he in demand by many persons, but he has assisted many persons who failed the screening for the priesthood. But once again, Philip found a closed door. His invitation for spiritual direction was not accepted. Fr Elijah had too many requests for consultation. But he referred him to another colleague. But, again, Philip did not click with him. He again approached Fr Elijah, who, when he saw him in such a severe state, he accepted Philip as his spiritual directee.

> When I had met Fr Elijah, I remember thinking it would have been ideal to have him. I genuinely did not feel like the other priest was suitable for me. He either didn't speak or spoke too much. Fr Elijah was very talkative [and was] continuously narrating stories. It was a big grace [to have him] as I was reserved, anti-gay, studying at the Faculty of Theology, [and] with hundreds of books at home. I was reserved and dull—suffocated. Fr Elijah helped me a lot. He was open-minded. Firstly, [with regard to] spiritual direction, he followed the principles of St Thomas, "Deus natura non destruit set perfecit." God does not destroy nature but develops it further. If I'm good at literature, God will use that as a basis to develop. If I'm gay, he will [do the same].[64]

---

63. "Kien hemm ċimiterju kbir fejn kont nimmedita l-mewt. It was a powerful experience. Li kien qalli l-Fr, 'Issa kif toħroġ, il-grazzja t'Alla taraha u tmissha b'idejk.' Jien minn dejjem kelli din il-manija li nsir qassis għax il-ħajja ta' saċerdot hi ħajja sabiħa ħafna."

64. "Jien meta ltqajt ma Fr Elija għadt dan ikun ideal li jkolli lilu. Mal-qassis l-ieħor jien ġenwinament ma ħassejtux tajjeb għalija. Jew ma jitkellem xejn, jew jitkellem ħafna. Fr Elija kien talkative ħafna, jirrakkonta l-istejjer. It was a big grace għax jien kont magħluq, anti-gay, fil-Fakultà tat-Teoloġija, nistudja, b'mijiet ta' kotba d-dar. Naqra magħluq u mdallam—suffocated. Fr. Elija lili għeni ħafna. Kien open-minded. L-ewwel ħaġa, spiritual direction, kellu l-prinċipju ta' San Tumas: 'Deus natura non destruit set perfecit.' Alla ma jkissirx in-natura imma jibni fuqha. Jekk jien tajjeb fil-letteratura, Alla ħa jibni fuq dik. Jekk jien gay, ħa jibni fuqha."

Fr Elijah's first advice to Philip was to "stop studying at the Faculty of Theology and change the course." Through this change, he would neither become bitter nor envious when he saw his companions succeeding in their studies. Philip followed his lead and found himself in an uncharted world. Philip started to engage in the secular world. Everything brought about self-reflection, and he experimented with freedom. Gradually he developed a lifestyle that he could call his own. Fr Elijah foresaw those areas that Philip had to work on, from self-care to belongingness. Fr Elijah was a step ahead, prompting Philip forward. Philip joined a lay Christian community and was "exposed informally to Ignatian spirituality" while he built his circle of friends. But that was not enough. Fr Elijah could perceive Philip's sexual repression.

> Fr Elijah used to pass subtle comments, "Don't you like her? And her?" Referring to girls. Although I prayed, had friends and had settled down, I still felt like something was wrong. I had [thus] buried myself deep into my studies.[65]

Philip always felt different from others. Something was hidden inside him, but he could not identify it. He noted some indications of this hidden issue when he would become emotionally attached to certain male friends. Afterwards, he would manifest physical symptoms.

> There was a good friend of mine, and I strongly clung to him. And Fr Elijah used to tell me, "You are clinging too much with him." I think this affects many gays before they come out."
>
> I literally became sick. I got panic attacks. I couldn't get better. I had to stop driving. On the [hidden date], I lost consciousness and [was taken] to hospital. The doctor told me, "Do you have some serious trouble?," [to which] I replied, "No, I don't have any troubles. On the contrary, I've just found employment." He told me, "You need to speak to a psychologist as soon as possible." I don't recall ever feeling anything [bad]. But to the doctor it was clear. I went to speak to Fr Elijah about it. I didn't trust them. He told me he would ask around for a good psychologist, and he gave me Henri Nouwen's biography. After that, I started working towards my coming out experience.[66]

---

65. "Fr Elija kien jitfagħli l-botti, 'Din ma togħġbokx? U din?' Għat-tfajliet. Jiena mbagħad kont inħossni għalkemm nitlob, kelli ħbieb u kont isettiljajt, kont inħoss li però kelli xi ħaġa ħażina. Kont head on, b'mod intensiv qawwi ħafna nistudja."

66. "Letteralment imradt. Qabduni panic attacks. Ma nistax nieħu ruħ. Kont insuq kelli nieqaf. Fil-[hidden date], kont instabatt ma l-art u mort l-isptar. It-tabib kien qalli, 'Inti għandek xi nkwiet gravi?' Għadtlu, 'Le m'għandix inkwiet. Anzi għadni kif sibt

Therapy and reading the biography of Henri Nouwen helped Philip to probe unexplored areas inside him. Gradually, he realized that he was gay.

> Touching it was very difficult, but somehow I managed. My sexual life was inexistent, totally inexistent. I don't watch pornography, I don't masturbate, nothing. Inexistent. It was completely dead. Sexuality within the church, even at the seminary, sexuality was very . . . even at home—nowadays through psychological therapy—it was always a taboo subject. Sexuality was always [regarded] as dull and dirty. If you look at the history of the church, sexuality was taboo. What happened . . . touching it was difficult, but then I started dealing with the fact that I am homosexual.[67]

During this period of inner turmoil coupled with new revelations, Philip remained steadfast in prayer. His prayer was one beseeching, "God to really enlighten me [him]." He realized that Henri Nouwen was most probably a gay person too. Although he did not disclose it in his writings, the way he behaved exposed him. Philip revealed that although there were many similarities, he went a step further.

> While I was undergoing therapy, and while I was reading his [Henri Nouwen] biography, I realized I would end up just like him if I didn't come out. He did a lot of good deeds, but he [also] went through useless suffering. Once I was praying and I said to myself, "Is it worth suffering?" I look at my group. Even though they went to church, gays were all accepted. So why should I be the one to be suppressed? Shouldn't I talk?[68]

---

job.' Qalli, 'You need to speak to a psychologist as soon as possible.' Issa jien ma kont inhoss xejn. Imma għalih kien ċar. Jien mort inkellem lil Fr Elija fuqha. Ma tantx kont nafdahom. Qalli ħalli nsaqsilek għal psychologist tajjeb u tani l-bijografija ta' Henri Nouwen. U minn hemm bdejt naħdem fuq il-coming out experience."

67. "Touching it was very difficult, but somehow I managed. Jien il-ħajja sesswali tiegħi, ma kinitx teżisti, kompletament ineżistenti. Jien la nara pornografija, la nimmasturba, xejn. Ineżistenti. It was completely death. Is-sesswalità fil-Knisja, anka s-seminarju bħala ambjent, is-sesswalità kienet ħafna . . . anka l-ambjent tagħna tad-dar—illum through psychological therapy—minn dejjem kienet taboo subject. Is-sesswalità dejjem kienet dark u maħmuġa. Jekk tara l-istorja tal-Knisja, is-sesswalità kienet tabù. Li ġara, touching it was difficult, but then I started dealing with the fact that I am a homosexual."

68. "Waqt li qed nagħmel it-terapija, u waqt li qed naqra il-bijografija tiegħu, jien ħassejtni li jekk I am not going to come out ħa nispiċċa bħalu. Għamel ħafna ġid, but he went through useless suffering. Darba I was praying u bdejt ngħid, 'Is it worth suffering?' Jien nara l-grupp tiegħi. Għalkemm kienu jmorru l-knisja, il-gays kienu accepted kollha. Allura jien ħa noqgħod suppressed? Ma nitkellimx?"

The first person he informed that he was gay was Fr Elijah. He felt obliged to tell him, and the response was one of genuine acceptance. "God loves you. He is walking with you. He is with you, and it is not an issue for him." Such words were much appreciated by Philip, and in fact, they motivated him not to despair. Henceforth, he embraced his identity and came out to other close friends and eventually to his family. His prayer suddenly intensified. He was led to consider a new question, "I had a very big question mark. 'Am I to enter into a relationship or not?'" Philip tried to discern this new dilemma by attending a retreat, reading books Fr Elijah suggested and waiting for God to illuminate his mind.

At present, Philip is at peace with his sexual orientation, and at the same time, he is trying to put into practice the principles of living the single life. He divulged this decision with only a few persons, as most people, gay or straight, find it rather odd. Even though at times, he gives the impression that he is convinced about God's mandate for him, doubts and fears still persist. An area he is afraid of is loneliness. Since his father passed away, he is frightened that he will be alone if he loses his mother.

> Am I happy? I believe it is a good decision. Am I happy? I am happy but I am still coming to terms with my solitude. These thoughts help me a great deal and I feel the need to pray as these thoughts intensify. I believe God was asking me to make this decision. I believe in Ignatian spirituality. I need a sign to make a difficult decision. I felt God was saying, "No!" For instance, the seminary: "No!" And they weren't my decisions [to make]. They'd be external decisions. Relationships: "No!" I struggled a lot. Decision taken. I've made my decision. I hope God will help me. It is not an easy decision.[69]

The Story of Matthew

Matthew is in his late twenties. He was raised in a religious family, and from a young age, he was exposed to the catechism of the Catholic Church and

---

69. "Am I happy? I believe it is a good decision. Am I happy? I am happy but I am still coming in terms with my solitude. Huma ħsibijiet li juġġħuni ħafna. U inkun irrid nitlob għax dawn il-ħsibijiet jintensifikaw. Kienet deċiżjoni nemmen li Alla kien qed jitlobhieli. Jien nemmen fl-ispiritwalità Injazjana. Jekk ikolli nieħu deċiżjoni iebsa nkun irrid sinjal. Jien ħassejt lil Alla jgħidli, 'Le!' Eżempju, is-seminarju, 'Le!' U ma jkunux deċiżjonijiet tiegħi. Ikunu deċiżjonijiet mill-estern. Relazzjoni: 'Le!' I struggled a lot. Decision taken. Jiena min-naħa tiegħi id-deċiżjoni ħadtha. Nittama li Alla jgħini wkoll. It is not an easy decision."

the sacraments. He described spirituality as his persistent desire to connect with someone superior to him.

> I think that my idea of spirituality is trying to connect as a result of my experience with God in every possible way. My talents, time, relationships, as well challenges, struggles from various situations marked my life. I think they are all related to my image of God, which has changed throughout my journey. The image of God that I have today is that of a God who accompanies, guides, who yearns to relate with every other person and me. It is an image that is the result of my past experiences. Spirituality occupies a special place in my life.

This all began when he watched a film titled *Brother Sun, Sister Moon*.[70] He was fascinated by the image of Saint Francis of Assisi. At that time, he was only twelve years old and was attracted to the simplicity, poverty, and fraternity that the Saint depicted. He got in touch with the friars and began to attend vocational meetings and other pastoral activities aimed at youths. "It was thanks to these encounters which helped me to develop a spiritual relationship with God." However, looking back, life was so occupied by the monastery that he lacked any involvement in the secular world.

> I think at that age . . . I was channeled towards religious life from a young age. Obviously, [this] did not allow me much time to explore other areas in my life; the secular world. My friends [all] attended vocational meetings. And that was a flaw that would remain along the way.[71]

He enrolled at secondary school and contact with the friars remained. He felt that his calling was to become a friar, and so he commenced the process of entering the novitiate. Everything was new to him. "[It] was a struggle on personal issues but enriching on the spiritual side."

> I'm an only child. I don't have siblings. It was already something new. I found myself living with another person in a community. It's already quite difficult living with your own siblings, let alone with other people who have characters, backgrounds and ideas different to your own. The first two years were, in a way, a shock.

---

70. A 1972 film directed by Franco Zeffirelli.

71. "I think at that age, I was channelled for the religious life from a young age. Obviously, ma tatnix ic-cans nesplora areas ohrajn f'hajti; the secular world. Il-hbieb tiegħi kienu dawk li jattendu l-laqgħat vokazzjonali. And that would be a flaw that would remain along the way."

Trying to find my place in this new environment, albeit it was familiar. But living there is a different matter.[72]

Despite the challenges which community life bring on, prayer was enriching. Matthew kept a daily prayer routine and later began to adapt a deeper engagement with the Word of God. Pastoral initiatives continued and all in all Matthew coped. However, a storm was impending. While at university, his mother was diagnosed with cancer, and suddenly he had to juggle with studies, family matters and the novitiate. It was a demanding time. His mother's illness brought him face to face with uncertainty, vulnerability, and powerlessness, but in the end, his mother recovered.

> Personally, this experience helped me mature. I became more autonomous. I became better at housework. At the same time, I am at the monastery. Encouraging mum and sustaining dad. I felt more responsible for them. I intentionally did not let go. It's hard. At the same time, there were [some] events and circumstances I had no control over. I just had to wait and see how things progressed. And it was part of a spiritual experience. To wait, to trust, to be patient, and to let go in some way [or other].[73]

Matthew managed to complete his studies and resumed his journey for the religious life. Part of his novitiate involved living abroad. The place where he lived elicited serenity, and so he spent many moments of solitary prayer.

> I succeeded in becoming more attentive to what I was personally receiving from the Word of God. Through the daily readings, seminars, retreats, [and] reflections. I gradually started to appreciate the Word of God more. I became more receptive to what God was personally trying to tell me, and I could live the liturgical life more intensively.[74]

72. "Jien tifel waħdi d-dar. M'għandix aħwa. Diġà it was something new. Sibt ruħi f'komunità ngħix ma persuni oħra. Diġà diffiċli tgħix mal-istess aħwa tal-familja, aħseb u ara ma' persuni oħra b'karattri, backgrounds u ideat differenti. These first two years where in a way a shock. Trying to find my place in this new environment minkejja li I was familiar. But living there is a different matter."

73. "Din l-esperjenza lili kabbritni fis-sens fuq l-at personali. Sirt iktar awtonomu. Sirt naf nieħu ħsieb iktar l-affarijiet tad-dar. At the same time, I am at the monastery. Naghmel kuraġġ lill-mamà u sustaining dad. I felt more responsible for them. I did not let go intentionally. It's hard. At the same time, there were events and circumstances which I had no control. I just had to wait and see how things go. And it was part of a spiritual experience. To wait, to trust and to be patient and to let go in some way."

74. "Irnexxieli nkun iktar attent għal dak li jingħata lili personali mill-Kelma t'Alla.

Nevertheless, the life of fraternity remained a challenge. Matthew was confronted by the same problems he had in Malta involving a person in the same community with whom he affectionately attached. He tried to earn his attention, but fear steered him to suppress all his emotions and transferred his thoughts to work.

> This is an area that will tarnish my name for many years, even today. The area of sexuality was a blemish on me and still is at present.

Matthew never uttered a word with the friars about this problem. But according to him, signs were evident. The only person to whom he had hinted that he had unresolved affective issues was the spiritual director he had at that time. He had advised him to seek a psychologist when he would return to Malta. Matthew linked his struggles to a history of sexual repression. At the time, he did not identify as a gay man, but everything was pointing in that direction. Matthew felt convinced that the religious life was his path, but he realized that the issues of fraternity impacted his ability to decide well. He did not trust himself, and he was surprised that the friars did not act. In hindsight, everything was so evident. He travelled for the second time, but this time the city he lived in was "a total anti-climax." It was a busy and noisy city, and he could not adapt to this new environment. Simultaneously the craving for intimacy haunted him. During his stay, and for the third time, he was attracted to a man. The cycle recurred.

> Even this year, I met another person with whom I felt comfortable. The same feelings I had with the other two persons resurfaced. It sets you thinking. This is the third time. At first, we were friends, and then at a certain stage, I became very possessive and very demanding. But he did not reciprocate—the third time.

At this point, Matthew raised his concerns with a new spiritual director and a meeting with the provincial was arranged. As a result of that meeting, a psychologist was identified.

> The psychologist tried to understand what was happening. I was honest with her. She knew that there were certain attractions towards men. She did not view them as signs of homosexuality, [though]. Instead, she used the term, "a buried heterosexual." I don't know if it makes sense, but what she meant to say was: because I was denied relationships with girls, my relationship

---

Permezz tal-qari ta' kuljum, seminars, irtiri, riflessjonijiet. Sirt napprezza l-kelma t'Alla. Sirt noqgħod attent għal dak li Alla qiegħed jgħidli b'mod personali u stajt ngħix iktar intensive l-ħajja liturġika."

> with my father was not so good, and [adding] the fact that I was living with men in a religious community, it seemed like my only outlet was that of being attracted to men.[75]

The psychologist's interpretation was not convincing. Eventually, Matthew decided to leave the monastery. He felt that it was not the ideal place where he could tackle such issues. Moreover, some friars felt uncomfortable. Matthew described his entry into a secular world as passing "from one desert to another." Everything revolved around the monastery. He had no friends, and he was unemployed.

> I felt confused and lost. I was angry and frustrated. Angry at myself, I had this feeling of disappointment and failure. What I mean is, how could my attraction towards St Francis and all that ideal suddenly [change because] you find yourself out. Nowadays, again [through the] benefits of hindsight, I believe I did not complete a proper discernment. I hadn't taken into consideration myself as a whole. And I took the commitment, when I left the monastery, to somehow find an answer, to explore this area further. What was this darkness? I want to give it a name. I want to truly know who I am—the true person.[76]

Matthew sought answers by looking for a Christian community that discussed sexuality in the realm of spirituality. He attended prayer meetings of different groups, but his search failed. He felt apprehensive. Either he met with conservatives who thought about sexuality in a narrow way or with straight couples who would not discuss the subject of sexuality in all its aspects. However, during this period, he knew of a friend who also had the same journey as his. This friend turned into a role model. Seeing how he dealt with the same issues, at one point, Matthew plucked up the courage to seek psychological advice.

---

75. "The psychologist tried seeing what was happening. Ftaħt magħha. She knew that there were certain attractions towards men. Ma kinitx tarahom bħala sinjali ta' omosesswalità. Rather the term she used was 'a buried heterosexual.' I don't know if it makes sense, imma li riedet tgħid huwa: li minħabba li kont imċaħħad minn relazzjonijiet mat-tfajliet, u r-relazzjoni mal-papà ma kinitx daqsekk tajba, u l-fatt li kont qed ngħix ma' irġiel f'kommnità reliġjuża qisu the only outlet was that of being attracted to men."

76. "I left confused and lost. I was angry and frustrated. Angry at myself, I had this feeling of disappointment and failure. Fis-sens, filli hemm din l-attrazzjoni lejn San Franġisk u l-ideal kollu, u f'salt wieħed you find yourself out. Today, again benefits of hindsight, I believe I did not do a proper discernment. I didn't take in consideration il-fatt tal-persuna tiegħi kollha kemm hi. And I took the commitment, when I left the monastery, to somehow find an answer, nara din l-area x'inhi. Din is-swidija x'inhi. I want to give it a name. I want to truly know who I am—the true person."

> He [the psychologist] was an ex-priest, and I was told to go to him. He [his friend] had helped him explore this area. We had similar dynamics and resistances. And I thought I could give it a try too. And that was another blessing as well. He helped me. He is very direct. He doesn't beat around the bush, he asks you [questions] point blank. Maybe that is what I needed. Very direct. And I started this walk with him. I remember I had always felt I was gay, but I reached a point during [our] sessions when I had to admit to myself that I was gay; after that, I started accepting it. I started to acknowledge it.[77]

Acceptance generated positive results. His relationship with God became more transparent. He stopped hiding and instead started to "name it [his sexuality], including the feelings I [he] had in prayer." At present, he forms part of a community that examines the phenomena between sexuality and spirituality. But Matthew admitted that he is still at the early stages of the coming out process.

> Even in the eyes of God, I can freely be myself. The community I found was another blessing in this transition stage. Time will tell because I still feel I am in transition. This group is providing me with space to live my faith with other persons. It did help me, and it helped me with my sexuality. The difference between the [name hidden] experience and the experience within this community is that my sexuality and my spirituality are slowly merging.[78]

---

77. "Kien qassis u mbagħad ħareġ, u qalli mur għandu. Kien għenu biex jesplora din l-area. Kellna similar dynamics and resistances. U għadt ħa nipprova mmur għandu jien ukoll. And that was another blessing as well. Għeni. Hu tip dirett ħafna. Ma jdurx mal-lewża, jaqbad u jsaqsik mill-ewwel. Maybe that is what I needed. Skjett ħafna. U bdejt din il-mixja miegħu. Niftakar, I always felt that I am gay, imma wasalt f'punt fis-sessions li I had to tell it to myself that I am a gay person and from there I started accepting it. I started acknowledging it."

78. "Anka quddiem Alla, I can be freely myself. Il-komunità li sibt kienet another blessing in this transition stage. Time will tell għax I still feel I am in transition stage. Dan il-grupp qed jipprovdili spazju, biex ngħix il-fidi ma' persuni oħra. It did help me, and it helped me with my sexuality. The difference between l-esperjenza [name hidden] u l-esperjenza f'din il-komunità hi li sexuality and spirituality are slowly merging."

GAY MEN IN A RELATIONSHIP

The Story of Luke

Luke, who is in his late thirties, is a gay person. He works as a policeman, and in his free time, he engages in voluntary work with religious and non-governmental organizations. Community work has always been part of his character. "I enjoy being involved. I am not a passive person who will just stay put." Family members were involved at the local parish, and naturally, he was led towards social engagement.

He was affiliated with the Society of Christian Doctrine (MUSEUM). He taught Catholic catechism to children but later left the Society. While a member, he lived according to the commitments that the Society stood for but faced with his sexual dilemmas, celibacy became a problematic obligation. Either due to a lack of assistance or due to his inability to fulfil the commitment, he left. It was a difficult decision as his life revolved around the Society.

Luke's coming out process was also not a straightforward matter. Fear that he would be deemed negatively led him to resist acknowledging he was gay. He also knew individuals who had been expelled from their parents' households. Apart from these fears, Luke experienced the loss of his mother, and he was greatly grieved. Later his fear intensified when he learned that his father prepared his will and had allowed Luke to remain at the matrimonial home until he got married. He was terrified as nobody knew he was gay.

> My father told me, "I want to write my will in front of you." I replied, "Are you already thinking about it?" He said, "You can't tell what will happen." True. My mother's [passing] came unexpectedly. I had met with my siblings; I still used to live with my dad, and he wrote, "Until Luke is ready to marry, the house remains his, and he has the right to live in it, even if I die." And I felt terrified. I knew I would never marry.[79]

To deal with his dilemmas, Luke kept meeting with his spiritual director. Later, he also sought psychological assistance. Luke resisted therapy, but he slowly recognized and admitted his new identity. Eventually, Luke accepted himself as gay but dreaded revealing it to his father. Not much affection was between them, and so he decided to safely reveal his identity from a

---

79. "Missieri qalli, 'Irrid naghmel it-testment quddiemkom.' Għadtlu, 'Diġà qed taħsibha?' Qalli, 'Ma tistax taf x'jiġri.' Veru. Tal-mamà ġiet mingħajr ma stennejnieha. U ltqajna l-aħwa u jien kont għadni ngħix ma' missieri d-dar, u kiteb, 'Luke, sakemm jiġi biex jiżżewweġ, id-dar tibqa' tiegħu, u għandu dritt jibqa' jgħix fiha anka jekk jien niġi nieqes.' U jien twerwirt. Kont naf li jien mhux ser niżżewweġ."

distance through a letter. His father held no bitterness towards him, so Luke summoned up his courage to disclose his identity to his siblings and other family members. Luke regarded the way his coming out progressed as proof that prayer truly functioned. As he received positive reactions, he felt loved.

> It was the first time that I had spoken to dad about such matters. I had never spoken to him about work, let alone about something so personal and intimate. Gradually, my cousins, aunts and uncles, and then my friends found out. My fear faded away and that's where I knew that prayers are effective. I imagined there were people who were less fortunate than me. Some people had hung themselves because their parents would not accept them [for who they were]. Others ended up on the streets. There are still some who do not accept me [as I am], but that is not my problem. I want to proceed with my life. I kept up my meetings with my spiritual director, [even though] our encounters were less frequent, as I [gradually] found my feet.[80]

During the transitional phase, he met a person who would later become his husband. Recently they got married after eleven years together.[81] However, reaching the decision to marry was morally conflicting. Luke was aware that the Catholic catechism prohibited this lifestyle. Marrying would be public knowledge which would draw possible backlash. Eventually, after examining his conscience, he acceded to the proposal. At times, he would feel guilt rising. However, when he joined a Drachma, he found reassurance.[82] It was a space where he could freely reflect on his worries with others. When he left the Society, he disregarded all forms of religious expression. By attending the session of this new community, his commitment to prayer was readjusted. He felt reassured that he was not alone in his quest to unite sexuality with spirituality. The tensions developed his spirituality, and consequently, he convinced his husband to attend the sessions as well. This brought further joy to Luke.

80. "Kienet l-ewwel darba li tkellimt ma' missieri fuq dawn l-affarijiet. Jien lanqas qatt ma kont nitkellem miegħu fuq ix-xogħol, aħseb u ara fuq affarijiet daqshekk personali u intimi. Bil-mod il-mod saru jafu l-kuġini, iz-zijiet u mbagħad il-ħbieb. Il-biża' li kelli sfumat fix-xejn u hemmhekk iktar għadt li t-talb jaħdem. Immaġinajt li hemm min hu iktar sfortunat minni. Hawn min tgħallaq għax ma aċċettawhx il-ġenituri. Hemm min spiċċa barra. Hemm min ma jaċċettanix, imma mhux problema tiegħi. Jien irrid nibqa' għaddej bil-ħajja tiegħi. Bqajt niltaqa' mad-direttur spiritwali tiegħi, naqqast il-frekwenza, għax bdejt naqbad art."

81. Same-sex marriage in Malta has been legal since September 1, 2017. In April 2014 Malta allowed civil unions for both same-sex and opposite-sex couples.

82. Drachma is a Maltese lay LGBTIQ+ Christian community. See www.drachmalgbt.blogspot.com.

> As soon as I found out that retreats were being organized, I was glad, as retreats were only organized annually at MUSEUM. Three in silence. It used to feel like a booster. And I miss it. We will attend [one] next month. [We are] looking forward.[83]
>
> Nowadays I look forward to every meeting. We go together. There is encouragement. I have to admit that while I still attended MUSEUM, I had always attended the daily mass. I used to follow prayers prescribed by the society [I was in]. I was a spiritual person. Since then, [however] I've changed a little. I had literally stopped [attending mass] on Sunday, and I stopped saying the rosary. I didn't want to pray. However, I still feel I sinned. It lasted for about a year until I found my feet, and then I started again. Not as much as before, but given I have the time, I do attend mass. Furthermore, I still seek time alone with God.[84]

Marriage generated different reactions from friends. There were those who genuinely acknowledged his status, but others reprimanded him. At first, he fought back, particularly on social media, but later, he stopped defending his cause.

> Various priests, who are also my friends, and who know me well, accept me for who I am. That helps. I'm not saying that they never bring [my wrongdoings] to my attention, but it's not a closed door. I've also encountered some people who have closed the door on me. I don't blame them. I've kept myself updated on Church doctrines, teachings and what the Church is going through. I'm often very tempted to answer people's comments on Facebook, but I hold back. There are some [who regard] the Church negatively, always, whatever it does, and this is a known fact. The Church is always to blame; there are some people who think the Church never does anything right, only bad. I've sometimes entered discussions that lead to nowhere, and then I said, "Why? It's not worth the hassle."[85]

---

83. "Malli sirt naf li jorganizzaw irtir ħadt pjaċir, għax irtir darba fis-sena l-Mużew konna nagħmluh. U tlieta fis-silenzju. Kien ikun il-booster. U nimmisjah. Issa ħa nattendu x-xahar id-diehel. Looking forward."

84. "Illum looking forward għal kull laqgħa. Immorru flimkien. Backing hemm. Ikolli nammenti li sakemm kont il-Mużew quddiesa kuljum qatt ma kont nitlifha. Ittalb kont ngħidu preskritt mis-soċjetà. Kont bniedem spiritwali. Minn dak inhar 'l hawn thalltet ftit is-sistema. Il-Ħadd kont waqaft letteralment, rużarju xejn. Talb ma rridx naf bih. Imma xorta ġo fija nħoss li nqast. Qisu dik is-sena li għamilt hekk, sakemm qbadt art, u mbagħad qisu rġajt. Mhux daqs qabel, imma jekk ikolli ċans quddies nismagħha. Apparti dan, xorta nfittex hinijiet li nkun waħdi m'Alla."

85. "Diversi saċerdoti u patrijiet ħbieb tiegħi, li jafu x'jien, jaċċettawni kif jien.

I remember that after we got married, I don't usually upload many photos on Facebook, my husband did as he's the chatty one. We were at a feast, as I attend various feasts in summer, and there were some priests [who told me], "Congratulations!" Some [of these priests] I had never spoken to. I appreciated [their well wishes]. There were [also] some who blocked me and cut me off after that day. There were some who were happy for me, others who weren't. Pope Francis has now offered some opportunity. Maltese leadership too.[86]

Luke also mentioned the friars that he, together with his husband, came to know through their voluntary work. The relationship with the friars is healthy, and for him, it signifies genuine acceptance. They are aware of the union, and on the wedding day, the prior attended the celebrations. But he chose not to attend the civil ceremony owing to the guidelines set by the Curia. Luke appreciated the prior's presence at the after-celebrations.

The parish priest was invited to our civil union, and he did attend. He also attended the party, the second part. I told him, "If you come, even if for fifteen minutes, it's enough. Your presence, the fact that you're there, is already good." But he came [and] he had fun.[87]

Luke admitted that he felt hurt by those who rejected his lifestyle. Often, they expressed their opinion directly to him. According to him, such persons do not distinguish what is truly vital in life from the irrelevant. It is impossible to alter their perspective, and so he gave up persuading. Such rejection came from all quarters—the monastery, colleagues and lay friends.

Dik tgħin. Mhux qed ngħid li ma jiġbdulix widnejja, imma mhux bieb magħluq. Iltqajt ma' min għalaqli l-bieb ukoll però. Ma neħodhiex kontrihom. Bqajt inżomm ruħi aġġornat x'tgħid il-Knisja, x'tgħallem u minn xiex tgħaddi. Ikolli seba' mitt sena aptit nirrispondi n-nies fuq Facebook, imma nitfa' pass lura. Hemm min il-Knisja dejjem ħażina. Tagħmel x'tagħmel, u dik nafuha. Dejjem taqlagħha, imma hemm ċertu nies li qatt ma tagħmel tajjeb, ħażin biss. Għamilt xi darbtejn nidħol f'diskussjonijiet li ma jwasslu għal imkien u mbagħad għadt, 'Għalfejn? Lanqas ħaqq il-kedda.'"

86. "Niftakar wara li żżewwiġna, fuq il-Facebook jiena ma ntellax ħafna ritratti, ir-raġel tella' għax hu jgħid. Jien noqgħod aktar lura. Konna xi festa, għax indur il-festi fis-sajf, u kien hemm diversi qassisin, 'Awguri ta!' Kien hemm xi wħud li qatt ma kellimthom. Apprezzajt. Kien hemm min minn dak inhar 'l hawn ibblukkjani u qatagħni. Hemm min ħa pjaċir, u hemm min le. Issa, il-Papa Franġisku fetaħ naqra l-bieb. It-tmexxija f'Malta wkoll."

87. "Il-kappillan kien mistieden għas-civil union tagħna u ġie wkoll. Ġie għall-party, għat-tieni parti. Għadtlu, 'Anka jekk tiġi għal kwarta, biżżejjed. Jien il-preżenza tiegħek, li qiegħed hemm diġà, hi tajba.' Però ġie. Ħa pjaċir."

Then I've got other [friends] who are more straight to the point. Friends of mine, who, however, do not accept that I am in a relationship, that I live with this person, whom I'm also married to—[a] civil union, not that there is much difference. Then I say [to myself], "Isn't this better than a person who wanders around? Isn't it better that we live together in a house, that everyone knows about us, and that I answer the door to a house blessing or to anyone, and that I help everyone?" Some men have abandoned their wives or are violent towards their children. I consider them for who they are. They are still my friends, and I speak to them when I can. Then there is another group who have given up hope on me completely. My place is in hell and that's it.[88]

Today, Luke feels at peace with his life, particularly before God. What matters to him is being authentic and genuine, not only being reconciled with his sexuality but having the courage to go beyond and consider other life matters. Even though the church does not endorse his lifestyle, he still attends Mass. For him, gay or straight does not really matter, since at long last, everyone is "sick," and God is the true "doctor" of the soul.

Nowadays, I've accepted the situation completely. I'm happy with my partner, [with] our life, my job, with God, everything. After I left the MUSEUM, even entering a church was a struggle. However, "I did not come to call the righteous, but sinners." I do have a place inside the church [community]. If the sinner is told not to go to church, it's like telling the sick not to go to hospital. I've tried to explain this. "They receive the eucharist and then they gossip on people." [If one] visits the doctor who prescribes some pills, won't that person take them? Aren't you doing the same thing? Receiving the eucharist doesn't mean you became a saint.[89]

---

88. "Imbagħad għandi oħrajn li huma iktar straight to the point. Ħbieb tiegħi, però ma jaċċettawx li jien qiegħed ma xi ħadd u li ngħix f'relazzjoni u miżżewweġ—civil union, ma hemmx xi differenza. Imbagħad jien ngħid, 'Mhux aħjar hekk milli bniedem li jiġri? Mhux aħjar hekk ngħixu ġo dar u taf bina, u niftaħ il-bieb għat-tberik u għal kulħadd u ngħin lil kulħadd?' Hemm min mhux qiegħed mal-mara jew isawwat it-tfal. Imbagħad neħodhom ta' li huma. Inżommhom bħala ħbieb tiegħi, inkellimhom fejn nista'. Imbagħad hemm dak il-grupp li m'hemmx ċans. Posti l-infern u daqshekk."

89. "Illum aċċettajt is-sitwazzjoni to the full. Kuntent mal-partner, il-ħajja tagħna, ix-xogħol u m'Alla wkoll. Meta tlaqt mill-Mużew anka li nidħol il-knisja kienet qisha gwerra. Però, 'Jien ma ġejtx biex infejjaq li min hu mfejjaq.' Jiġifieri l-knisja hu posti. Jekk qed tgħid lill-midneb tmurx il-knisja, qisek qed tgħid lill-marid ma jmurx l-isptar. L-istess ħaġa. Jien din ġieli nispjegha. 'Imorru jitqarbnu u imbagħad jgħidu fuq in-nies.' Mela mur għand it-tabib, jgħidlek ħu kors pinnoli, u ma teħodhomx. Mhux l-istess qed

Luke mentioned two spiritual figures that guided him in his journey. They inspired him, and he followed their lead. These were Saint Anthony of Padova and Pope Saint John XXIII. Both manifested a humble persona, and he was attracted to their virtues. When he was younger, he used to think that saints were perfect and blameless humans. Their defects, issues and mistakes were not mentioned but concealed in catechism classes. After coming out, he noticed how he held false concepts about them. They were humans too, and like him, they struggled with how to act. People have perceptions and make judgments about them, especially by those who challenge the status quo.

> Sometimes I laugh when I think about all the readings about the life of saints when I was still part of the MUSEUM. Sometimes we depict [saints] as heroes and not humans. And I used to say [to myself], "Goodness me, have these people never grumbled? Have they never had any difficulties?" Nowadays, I look back and I say to myself, I'm grateful I read about them because I like to project them into my own life.[90]

At work, colleagues are aware of his status. As the environment is rough, foul language is often the "language" uttered by colleagues. But since Luke behaves differently, they regard him as a person who has moral principles. In moments of anxiety or when faced with personal troubles, they turn to him for moral advice. He finds this view rather odd as he is conscious of his flaws and defects.

> Police know well that swearing is part of our culture. They never heard me [swear]. I don't swear, I barely use foul language, [even though] I'm quite impatient and very much a perfectionist. But when there is an issue at the police station, and something happens where some element of spirituality is involved, I have no idea why but I'm the one they refer to for such matters. I'm not the ideal person because I know my background. I know my reality. But they see something in me. Maybe they know I go to church.[91]

---

taghmel? Ma jfissirx li mort titqarben sirt qaddis."

90. "Xi kultant nibda nidħaq għax ngħid, meta kont il-Mużew konna naqraw ħafna fuq il-ħajja tal-qaddisin u minhiex għaddew. U xi kultant inpinġuhom qishom xi eroj u mhux bnedmin. U kont ngħid, 'Marija santa, dawn qatt ma jgergru? Qatt ma kellhom diffikultajiet?' Illum il-ġurnata nħares lura u nibda ngħid, imnalla qrajt fuqhom għax inhobb inpoġġihom fil-ħajja tiegħi."

91. "Il-pulizija magħrufin li d-dagħa huwa l-lingwaġġ tagħna. Jiena qatt ma semgħuni. Jien ma nidgħix, bil-kemm nitkellem ħażin. Issa jien nervuż għax inkun irrid l-affarijiet eżatti. Imma meta jkun hemm xi kwistjoni l-għassa u tiġri xi ħaġa li jkun

He recounted how one of his seniors said that a policeman must be "hard-headed and cruel." Luke disagreed. Although his line of work involves handling criminality or misbehavior, in the end, he tries his best to respect the dignity of human beings.

> I told him, "Definitely not! Do you mean to say that policemen are bad and cruel?" Trying to be proactive is one thing. Being cruel is another. Even if I have to arrest someone who is giving me a hard time, I use some force, but once I've cuffed him, I stop, as he would have stopped [too]. If he's cuffed, [there's no need to] kick him, don't throw him on the ground, as in that case, you're the one who's in the wrong.[92]

Luke stated that his own personal spiritual journey showed him that spirituality is not a gift reserved for a few. He considers spirituality, as Saint George Preca described it, like water in which fish live. While he looks at it as a lifestyle, it permeates every feature of himself, including his sexuality.

> You can be a spiritual person without being closed up in a monastery, without being a hermit. You can be a very active person, who goes to the gym, is part of organizations and keeps fit. But spirituality has to be part of that too. If a glass is full of pebbles, water would still seep in and fill [all the crevices]. As Saint George Preca used to say, "Spirituality resembles a fish in water." That's why I referred to it as a lifestyle. One can decide not to be spiritual. In that case, I feel that there is an important missing part.[93]

---

hemm bżonn ta' idea naqra iktar spiritwali, ma nafx għalfejn, jgħidu lili. Jien m'iniex il-persuna ideali għax naf il-background tiegħi. Naf is-sitwazzjoni tiegħi. Imma huma jaraw xi ħaġa fija. Forsi jaraw li nkun il-knisja."

92. "Għadtlu, 'Le ta! Jiġiferi il-pulizija ħżiena u kattivi?' Taħseb b'mod ħażin biex it-tajjeb ma jonqosx mod, u tkun kattiv mod ieħor. Jien anka jekk ġejt biex narresta lil xi ħadd, u qed jagħtini hard time. Tagħmel forza imma once li mmanettjajtu nieqaf għax hu waqaf. La mmanettjatu ttihx bis-sieq, titfgħux ma l-art għax imbagħad inti li qed tkun il-ħażin."

93. "Issa tista' tkun spiritwali mingħajr ma tkun magħluq ġo monasteru, mingħajr ma tkun eremita. Tista' tkun bniedem attiv f'kollox u tmur il-gym, u tmur f'organizzazzjonijiet u żżomm ruħek fit. Però l-ispiritwalità tidħol hemm ukoll. Bħal meta jkollok tazza biċ-ċagħaq, l-ilma kullimkien jimla. Kif kien iħobb jgħid Dun Ġorġ, 'L-ispiritwalità hi bħall-ħuta fl-ilma.' Għalhekk għadtilha lifestyle. Tista' tiddeċiedi li ma tridx tkun spiritwali. Hemmhekk inħoss li jkun hemm xi ħaġa importanti nieqsa."

The Story of Andrew

Andrew is in his early forties and works in the medical sector. From a young age, he felt different from other boys. Throughout his life, he grappled with the awareness that he was a gay man. In his late teens, Andrew moved abroad where he suppressed his sexual desires and instead focused on his career. Academic success rewarded him financially, but he paid an emotional price. He did not reconcile with his sexuality and felt wrecked.

> I felt I wasn't the same as others in terms of sexuality. For many years, but many years, it was hard to accept it [being gay], because I thought that either I was going through a phase, and that phase was so long, or there is something wrong with me because this is wrong, this is unnatural.

Returning to Malta, Andrew was unable to keep his issue dormant anymore. He felt tormented. Abroad he had two sexual encounters, which caused guilt, so he could no longer avoid his reality.

> I had like two encounters in seven years because I felt so guilty. I came back. For the first year, I did not accept it, but a year after, I returned and I said, "I can't continue living like this."

He felt empowered when he became aware that several friends and family members were also gays. For a brief period, he went "to the other extreme." He explored his sexuality and disregarded the moral rules which governed his ideas about homosexuality and religion. But this manner of living did not yield any serenity.

> So, for a short while, I went to the other extreme. For a period, I put away all notions of gays, all notions of what I am doing is wrong because God's law says clear what it is. That, for me, in the long term, does not work. So, what I was before in some ways worked, I was a bit more at peace, but then I felt I am living a lie because I never accepted it. On the other hand, when I briefly accepted it and I journeyed out into the gay subculture, it was just nothing left.

Andrew grappled with finding the middle ground. He searched for a way how he could live his sexuality in the light of Christian faith and in conformity with the Catechism of the Catholic Church. He looked outside the gay subculture. One day he met a priest who would later become his spiritual director. Andrew not only felt understood by his spiritual director but was counselled not to view homosexuality as a malice. It was a part of his life, and he had to learn how to cope with it. Through the sessions, he learned what is the real issue in the light of Christian values. Thanks to his spiritual director, he moved away from disowning it and started delving deeper into acceptance and self-responsibility. Gradually, he reclaimed it as his own. But he was still internally confused on how he should exercise his sexuality.

> It is hard because I try to live the teachings of the Church because I believe in the Church but being gay is hard. It is very hard, and if I do not and follow my own inclinations, they can take me anywhere. Today it's like this. Tomorrow it's like that. So, for me having guidance, having rules, for me, works. Although in the short term I suffer a bit, I believe in the long term I will relish God. I see it like this. My inclinations are to go and have sex with someone, but my thoughts, my inner being, says that that is wrong, not because it is gay, but because it is not within a stable relationship. It is not as God planned. And that gave me a lot of guilt. I realize, as well, that most of the people I used to hang around with, for them, to have a good time, used to do drugs consistently. I tried it. On a physical level, it did nothing. I didn't even take anything from that. And then I felt guilty. But if you do not do it, then you are cast out.

Andrew finds that the gay subculture to be immersed in superficiality. He neither partakes in it nor believes in the values it promotes. His way of life is based on the teachings of the church. But at the same time, he faces isolation. Andrew views himself as a minority within a minority, and all these dynamics are exemplified as the "cross he has to bear."

> People say, "Christ yes, but the Church no." But they do it because it suits them. I pick the good things and throw the bad things away. You either take the whole plate or nothing. If Christ said that I am Truth, the Way, and the Life, then that is it, take it or leave it. Do not pick what suits you and leave the rest behind. This is where I come from.

The moral values which Andrew adopted for his life were arduous as he included his partner in the story. Although they live together, their relationship is not sexual. He practices the vow of chastity, and his partner acceded to this.

> I don't have sex with him. No, I don't because those are the rules of the Church. It's hard with him and with others. It isn't that I say no to him and yes to others. I don't. But it is hard, it is extremely hard, and I chose it because I believe that's what Christ

> wants from me. If you become a priest or a friar, are they not supposed to be chaste? What have I got special? It's hard for him and for me. Because the culture is what it is. The culture is—not all—but most of the people I know have an app. It's called *Grindr* on their phone, and the *Grindr* will tell you, I do not have it myself, but I have seen it being used. It will tell you, "Joe is fifty meters away and wants to meet you," and they do it all the time. You go with him, and him, and him, and him, and then realize from the medical feedback why certain diseases are so prevalent. I am sorry to say, the gay subculture, in general, encourages it. I have difficulty with gay pride. Is there a straight pride? No, so why the gay pride? To celebrate equality. Yes, but it doesn't mean that you can do what you like. So, I find myself a little bit of a minority in the minority. And it is quite painful because you feel alone. On a human level, you feel alone.

At present, Andrew is experiencing turmoil in his relationship. It came to his knowledge that his partner was abusing drugs and having multiple sexual encounters. All these revelations amounted to betrayal, which overwhelmed him.

> Recently, I found out certain things about him. It came out all at once. His addiction to cocaine, his meeting with other people on *Grindr*. I've let him live a life of comfort because, for me, money is not a problem. I put on blinkers—if I don't see, I don't know. And [it] all came out this Christmas, and I said I couldn't live this life anymore. "Either you see the same things from my page or else I can't." It's very painful. I went to see my spiritual director, and I realized, partly, it was my fault. I was blind to it, and I let it go. I never confronted it. I do not like confrontation. So, it was all comfortable for me not seeing, but it led to this. And I have come to realize as well that with all the good intentions of the world, unless the person, your best friend, your partner, your husband, whoever sees life with the same lenses that you have, it is hard because the fundamentals wouldn't be there.

He discussed the problem with his spiritual director, who directed him to face his partner. Instead of blaming, Andrew used his anger to challenge him.

> But then I said, it is time to tell him, and I asked him. So now I am going through this crisis, and I felt sorry initially, but I realize that maybe through pain and through the darkness of the world, the mess of the world, maybe God will touch and change him. We'll see. I mean, I was told to chuck him out, but I cannot.

> He has nowhere to go. It is hard trying to be the one keeping everything together. I find myself between him and my parents, between him and my brother, between him and his parents, and between him and pleasing God. Because I feel God has given this. "You stick with this. And don't compromise not for yourself or others." I have myself caught in between choosing, and I always try to compromise. And compromise, I think, gets you nowhere in these things.

Andrew is at a crossroads. These revelations jeopardize his life. Now he is forced to face the dilemma of either stopping the relationship or compromising and remain where he is. On the one hand, he believes that his circumstances were permitted by God to test his endurance, and, on the other hand, he is confused and puzzled about how to follow God's will.

> I want to do God's will, but I do not know what it is. I don't know at this point. Is it to continue with the life I have now being in a relationship according to his will? Or is it forgetting all about that and doing something else? And what I am going to do? There is no way I think I could live in a community of men being a gay man. And with reason. Do I become a hermit? I don't know. I know the way I live, the choices I made led me to this. But it hasn't brought me closer to happiness. Actually, it made things worse because I have more problems all over the place.

> My spiritual director told me to kick him out. "People don't change." I disagree with him. I think people can change. Do they do it often? "No." Is it easy? "No." But I think they can change because God changes them.

Confronted with his current problem, Andrew plans to go abroad for a retreat to reflect and reach a decision on his future. Amidst all the upheaval, he interprets the revelations with a sense of relief since now he knows the truth about his partner and their relationship.

> I am glad this whole issue with my partner came out. Despite all the pain, shouting and crying, I say, "God, thank you!" Had it not happened, I would have gone on covering up inside—layers upon layers. Closing my eyes to what I know, or feel is happening—getting frustrated with everyone, including God. So, I am glad it happened. Because finally, it came out.

With this last story by Andrew, this chapter fulfils its objective by introducing ten stories of men, which will act as the *material object* of our investigation. By reading the stories, one already notices how the human person has many psychosocial connections and complexities. Therefore, this study will move into its analysis phase to elucidate all these fields of tension. The subsequent two chapters juxtapose John of the Cross' spiritual doctrine with the ten spiritual stories and bring in the contribution shared by spiritual directors.

Chapter 3

Strangers of the *Dark Night*

While chapter one gives a resume of John of the Cross' spiritual doctrine, and chapter two provides a presentation of the ten participants' narratives, this chapter proceeds to connect the *material object* with the *formal*. The ultimate aim is to delineate a form of spirituality consisting of performances, obstacles and motifs.

The objective is reached in three phases. Phase one presents the outcomes by observing how the ten participants, here referred to as directees, satisfy the different criteria in John of the Cross' scheme. In doing so, they position themselves into various clusters of the *dark night*. Phase two deals with the recurring patterns in each cluster and the benefits received by the participants to attain spiritual maturity. Lastly, in phase three, the views of spiritual directors are introduced either to substantiate or give a different viewpoint from the directees. In this chapter, phases one and two are presented, while the third phase will be discussed in chapter four.

Throughout chapters three and four, quotations from participants will be introduced to substantiate a particular theme, but only a few quotes will be referred to in the main text due to space constraints.

MAPPING THE DARK NIGHT

To facilitate the interpretation of John of the Cross' doctrine, it was expressed in a terse way on a table made up of four columns and four rows. The columns show the difference among the four aspects of the night, while the rows focus on four variables: the obstacles, the warnings or signs, the remedy, and the outcomes. John of the Cross' salient arguments are summarized in each intersection. Although the scheme helps in its analysis, it was not utilized in a rigid manner. No story fits perfectly in any intersection since the four aspects of the *dark night* operate simultaneously. Although in the *Ascent* and the *Dark Night,* John organizes each night in a chronological way, one following another, in the *Canticle,* the four facets of the night operate instantaneously. Hence, the table functions as a sensing device; as each participant's story progresses, different areas are discovered.

The Active Night of Sense

Obstacles and Warnings

According to John of the Cross, the first obstacle one confronts in the path towards union are the appetites, which include all the inordinate external attachments to which a soul, whether intentionally or unintentionally, clings. Relying on these attachments produces habits and lifestyles which yield satisfaction, approval and consistency. Warnings that life is flawed appear when interior emptiness bypasses the gratification derived from giving way to these attachments, and the person feels pressure to satisfy it.

MARRIED STRAIGHT FATHERS

In Peter's narrative, no mention was made of any specific external attachment. He spoke about the importance of understanding how matters of this world evolve. His approach to life was intellectual, and he viewed the world mechanically, with problems to fix. His most reliable method of interaction became the engineering perspective. However, he discovered that such capacity was not enough.

> The world of engineering was not enough . . . It took me many years after university to appreciate what I have gained through engineering, but [I had] to go beyond [what I had learnt] and not apply those set of rules to my relationships.

His need for deeper meaning persisted even after he enrolled in a youth group. Although community building was emphasized, his inner desire to learn to develop a relationship with God was not emphasized adequately. At University, the engineering program became such a major stumbling block that he considered many times whether to change this course.

	A	B	C	D
	Active Night of Sense	**Active Night of Spirit**	**Passive Night of Sense**	**Passive Night of Spirit**
Obstacles				
1	The **appetites** include all the inordinate interior and external attachments to which one, intentionally and unintentionally, clings.	How the **intellect, memory** and **will** are engaged to secure a sense of meaning and identity.	The soul accomplishes spiritual progress, but the blemish of interior and external attachments remain. The soul is unaware of their meddling. God gently heals the soul's **unintentional resistances** towards Him.	As the soul hides further within the cover of faith and overcomes all impediments, **faith** becomes the only obstacle left to remove.
Warnings			*Signs*	
2	Warnings that attachments hold the self is seen by observing the mechanics of **consumption** and the **gratification** one receives. In the long run, a variety of **harms** emerge, which lead one to seek a remedy.	Warnings emerge from the **prosperity** achieved in spiritual life. The intellect, memory and will are rich with interior possessions which yield **enthusiasm**. However, unpredicted events lead to **failure, loss of meaning** and an **unapproachable God**.	The rise of **spiritual poverty** darkens all that the soul possesses. God is experienced as **distant, neutral,** and **unapproachable**, and the soul enters into an existential crisis. A **greater presentiment** for God ensues, but the struggle to let go of control remains.	The self arrives at proper **synchronisation of sense and spirit**. All traces of self-possession is removed, and many spiritual touches are received in the substance of the soul. All signs lead one to the **readiness to receive the Beloved,** and until such union is realised, a great desire for it be completed wounds the soul.

	Remedy				
3	Mortification and **denudation** are the remedies that encourage one to distance oneself from that which limits.	**Transcendence** and **renunciation** of interior possessions are the remedies that lead one to step outside of comfort zones.	When all means fail, the soul is led to **wait quietly, trust,** and **attend** to God **Contemplation**).	In its waiting for the veil of faith to be torn apart and to receive the Beloved, the soul is led to **self-annihilation.**
	Outcome				
4	One arrives at **authenticity** and **nakedness of self**. Temporary perplexity and discrepancy of existential meaning are experienced until one adapts to a **new awareness** beyond the limited and accustomed perceptions that one formerly possessed—the desire for God, the **longings of love**, increases.	One encounters the reality of the **theological virtues** and slowly begins to adapt to God's character. The mind widens, memories are appeased, and new freedom is relished.	Through the merits of contemplation, a **new strength** is infused in the substance of the soul. **Transformation** of desire and character restoration slowly comes to be, and a new awareness of God's love increases (**Spiritual Betrothal**).	God elevates the soul to the state of union and transforms the soul in likeness to His nature. A **new name** is given to the soul as it partakes in the **consummation** and **outpouring** of divine love. (Spiritual Marriage)

Table 3—Map of the Dark Night

Although he acknowledges the beauty of mathematics and how it forms a perspective that identifies what others take for granted, he realized that applying the same rules to relationships was unsatisfactory. The affective element was lacking. In exploring it, he encountered disapproval from immediate relatives and friends. Mistrusting his emotions, Peter focused only on obtaining academic qualifications. Meeting these expectations returned esteem, but at a price. His affectivity was still restrained. As an example, when Peter spoke about his career with friends, he always ended up grumbling. Moreover, he felt bitter. The lack of harmony between his values and those of the company rendered him unhappy.

Paul names three external attachments: drugs, status, and pornography. The reason why he indulged in drugs was the rejection he experienced from his school friends. While engaged in drug trafficking, he earned admiration. Even if these drugs could lead to premature death, as happened to his friend, he reached a stage when to please others and to satisfy his need was critical. To impress, he used to take a greater dose than that taken by others. He always tried to excel others and thus be superior to them.

> I do not want to belittle it because it was hard, but I didn't feel it was hard at the time because my surroundings were like that. It's ten times worse nowadays, and people still tell me, although I don't know many people who still smoke. But people who are in it say that everyone smokes dope; everyone does. But I am so out of it now. But I know what they mean, and everyone had sex, everyone had drugs, and I took a bit more because I took ten, others would take five. I used to deal a bit. I used to buy for my friends, but I used to call it buying, but it was dealing. So yes, drugs were part of my life.

Later on, Paul gave up drugs, but the desire to hold a prestigious status persisted. The place of drugs was taken by other objects and activities appropriate to the environment he was in. At the workplace, he attained an executive position, while in his religious community, he quickly formed part of the leading team. To attain status, he did his level best to ingratiate himself with men who hold power, be it the teacher, the community leader, or the boss; thus, encouraging them to prefer him over others. In their presence, Paul held power, and others venerated him. However, in the long run, Paul realized that such tactics ended up in dire situations. The indulgences he experienced were temporary. As the relations evolved, a lot was expected from him, with the result that he felt suffocated. His identity became so merged with the male leadership figures that he felt alienated. Breaking away brought conflict, and sorrow left him empty. Pornography eased the aridity. It generated temporary ecstatic feelings; however, at the same time, it was a cause of guilt.

Straight Single Men

James' predominant attachment was drugs. Following the reggae lifestyle, he began to use such substances. It was a rebellious sign against the world, which he experienced as having discredited him. James' parents tried to urge and encourage him to make way in education. However, since he did not make any progress at school and was not interested in matters concerning his home, he disappointed his parents. To his parents, he was viewed as a mischievous son, and his talents were ignored. What provided him with an outlet was the life of a hippie where he could entertain positive feelings and belong to a community of his liking. Many of his questions about life were partially answered by Bob Marley's philosophy of life.

> When I was growing older, [at the age of] fourteen or fifteen, I asked myself certain questions, while slowly discovering music too. I was quite influenced by the singer, Bob Marley. Other artists ridiculed God, while feeling that they themselves were gods, in some way [or other]. And this nurtured the question, "Why is he different from the rest?" Between [the ages of] seven and eleven, my hair started to fall out. I obviously blamed the hairdresser, poor chap. When I grew older and did some research, I found out it wasn't the barber's fault for being dirty, but something which can be brought about by shock.[1]

When he ran a restaurant, the use of drugs added to his difficulties. James also complained of anxiety and of compulsive thoughts, which caused confusion and misery. He gained the respect of his family when he founded a catering business. But this was a short duration. His addiction intensified, and thus life became meaningless. Sadness increased, and James descended into misery, even considering suicide.

To be productive, be it in academia or in ministry, is Nathaniel's external attachment. He earned admiration for his many talents, but the industry in which he was employed became a significant hindrance.

> And my love for books started here, a love which wasn't there before. Becoming a novice was a very positive experience. It was a year spent away from books, even though I still somehow experienced academic life. Sometimes I used to read some books about spirituality. Thus, it was a race [against time]. My formation was rushed. One academic achievement followed another, and I was always regarded as a highly motivated person.[2]

---

1. "Waqt li qed nikber, fourteen or fifteen, taqbad issaqsi ċertu mistoqsijiet, u taqbad u tisma' diski wkoll. Qisni kien impressjonani kantant, Bob Marley, għax artisti oħra kienu jirridikulaw lil Alla u kienu jħossu li huma allat b'xi mod. U nħolqitli mistoqsija, 'Imma kif dan hekk u oħrajn hekk? X'hemm?' Bejn seven u eleven bdiet taqagħli xagħri. Ovvjament weħel il-barbier miskin, li meta qbadt nikber u għamilt ir-riċerka fuqha din mhux għax il-barbier kien maħmuġ imma din tiġri minħabba xi xokk."

2. "U bdejt dan il-proċess fejn nirrelata iktar minn qatt qabel mal-kotba. Meta tlajt għan-novizzjat kienet esperjenza pożittiva ħafna. Kelli sena ngħixha 'l bogħod mill-kotba. Biss, b'xi mod jew ieħor, il-ħajja akkademika kont ngħixha. Xi drabi kont naqra xi ktieb fuq l-ispiritwalità. Allura kienet ġirja. Il-formazzjoni kienet ġirja. Riżultat akkademiku wieħed wara l-ieħor and they always saw a highly motivated person."

Working towards its goals resulted in a purposeless life like a car driving to no destination. Expectations became burdens, as guilt precluded him from finding a solution. No attention was paid to his emotions, but instead, he enrolled in two voluntary organizations. His sermons earned him the admiration of the community, while voluntary work created friendships. These two areas made up for the lack of fraternity in the religious community of which he was part. But this relief was only temporary. As more responsibilities were devolved on him, he lost his interest. Unfortunately, the worst elements in his character started to emerge. He isolated himself and snapped angrily for trivial matters. His immediate relatives noticed this change of behavior, but he was afraid to face the real issue. The constant repression of his desires tipped him into depression, and he entertained negative thoughts, including ending his life. He felt like a bird or a tiger confined in a small cage.

Separated Straight Men

Thomas was attached to his industry. He aspired to obtain a degree and thus excel in his career. Another attachment was the voluntary work in which he was involved. Besides this attachment, he sought euphoric feelings through drug-taking, consumerism and two extramarital affairs. At a later stage, he took to praying. However, he engaged in all these activities while not paying attention to his failed marriage. It was the real inordinate attachment that Thomas struggled to resolve. After marrying at the age of twenty-three, he had always felt uncomfortable with his wife on account of their evident incompatibility. He believed that if things did not work out, he would continue living as a bachelor.

> I always felt that this person wasn't right for me. However, I was [also] a non-confrontational type of person. I used to do anything to please, to see everyone happy and at peace. [A] peacemaker. Occasionally I used to tell her, "It's best to stay together so as not to create all that fuss, hysteria and screaming." I used to feel overwhelmed and say, "No, it's best to stay together." That was how mature and self-disciplined I was. To the extent that I [even] used to say, "Worst case [scenario], I get married and then I'll become a bachelor, or live like a bachelor."[3]

3. "Dejjem kont inhoss that this person is not the right person for me. Però dejjem kont a non-confrontational type of person. Bhala persuna kont nagħmel minn kollox biex nikkuntenta 'l dak li jkun, biex nara lil kulħadd kuntent, kulħadd fil-paċi. Peacemaker. Ġieli kont ngħidilha, 'Isma aħjar nibqgħu flimkien għax ma tagħmilx sens dak l-istorbju, hysteria u ħafna tweżiq.' Nixxokkja ruħi, u ngħid: 'Le, aħjar nibqgħu flimkien.' Daqshekk kienet il-maturità u d-dixxiplina li għandi miegħu nnifsi. To the extent li kont

Lack of intimacy and improper communication persisted. Instead of taking the bull by the horns, Thomas engaged in various activities in the hope that he would derive some satisfaction. But in point of fact, he led a double life with extramarital relationships. For Thomas, this was an outlet that produced elated feelings, but he also felt guilty, and at some point, he restrained this feeling. In short, his life became a mess. In this state, he turned to a religious community for help.

Jude resorted to the occult to gain power and importance for his existence. Lack of care marked his childhood. His parents did not expect much from him. As a result, he had no direction or self-esteem. What he desired was a father who could empower him to live life courageously. First, he experimented with black magic and white magic.

> I had a lonely childhood; I grew up alone. My parents did their utmost to offer me a good upbringing; I have no doubt that they did all they could, but with their limitations. I don't blame them at all, but I feel I grew up alone, and that left its toll on me. Low self-esteem [and] lack of security. Due to this, I developed my own shields. I identified myself with these shields, even though that wasn't me but the shields.[4]

> [A] sense of belonging. I felt the need for someone to be my father. Someone who could provide me with a [sense of] identity and power. Not to feel weak all the time, due to the low self-esteem I had. And in some instances, I had received and obviously it was all a mirage, something you try to touch but it vanishes.[5]

Later Jude adhered to the church's instructions. He mixed objects and rituals from incompatible sources and hoped that powerful spirits would grant him strength. The Satanic lifestyle only caused him interior oppression. On relinquishing it, he wished to do good in life. Jude's spiritualized style persisted. When he took part in the sacraments, he was obsessed with rigid rituals. He joined various religious communities in the hope of finding the right environment: one where spirituality was taken seriously. But his attempt proved futile. His next goal was the ideal of marriage. Although

---

nghid, 'Worst case, niżżewweġ u mbagħad nibqa' bachelor jew nghix ta' bachelor.'"

4. "Tfulija li nara li trabbejt waħdi. Anke jekk kelli l-ġenituri u għamlu ħilithom biex irabbuni sew, m'għandix dubju li għamlu li setgħu, imma kellhom il-limiti tagħhom. Ma nagħtihom l-ebda tort, imma mmarkatni għax ħassejtni kbirt waħdi. Low self-esteem, nuqqas ta' sigurtà. Minħabba f'hekk ħloqt ħafna tarki. Iktar identifikajt lili nnifsi ma' dawn it-tarki, imma dak mhux jien imma t-tarki."

5. "Sense of belonging. Jien kelli nuqqas u ridt xi ħadd li jista' jkun missieri. Xi ħadd li jagħtini identità u poter. Ma nħossnix dejjem dgħajjef. Tirrifletti l-low self-esteem li kelli. U f'ċerti perjodi kont irċivejt u ovvjament ikun kollox tlellix, tmissha u tinfaqa'."

the relationship was strained, he still married. He then found out that his wife was engaging in virtual sexual encounters with the priest who was their mentor. Consequently, he filed for an annulment. All his efforts and attempts were in vain. He felt desolate and went back to square one.

Single Gay Men

Matthew and Philip experienced similar attachments. From a young age, their lives revolved around either the parish or a religious congregation. The figure of Saint Francis of Assisi attracted Matthew, while the priesthood was admired by Philip. Both worked very hard to attain their ideals but, at the same time, distanced themselves from the secular world.

Within the religious community, Matthew grew in many aspects. However, from the onset, fraternity was challenging to him. Clashes ensued. Matthew was greatly affected by intense fondness for another member of the congregation. This was not a one-off case but repeated with three different friends. In each case, he became possessive, with the result that friendship with the other members of the community was severed. Matthew felt embarrassed and feared that these incidents could jeopardize his dream. Subconsciously he suspected he was gay, but this thought terrified him.

> There was that part of my life, the need for affection and a more intimate relationship, [a need] which used to haunt me along the way. I was so scared to face this [need for] affection and an intimate relationship, for fear of things going terribly wrong, and in some way, my life project would fail.[6]

Subduing his feelings was ineffective, and the pattern recurred. As satisfaction from other activities started to dwindle, fraternity could not be ignored. This was no longer a matter of concealment as it became a problem for the other members of the community. Sharing his feelings discreetly, under cover of fraternity, with his spiritual director, Matthew knew that the director suspected that it was a matter of sexuality. He was advised to find a psychologist, but he ignored the advice.

> Sexuality, in general, wasn't mentioned. To be fair, the first time I had some hints was because of my spiritual director. I think he was the first to understand, that I was probably feeling

---

6. "Kien hemm dik l-area f'hajti, il-bżonn ghall-affett u ghal relazzjoni iktar intima li used to haunt me along the way. Kien hemm hafna biża' li jekk ser naffronta din il-haġa tal-affett u ghar-relazzjoni iktar intima kienet ħa tmur kontra kollox u, b'xi mod, ser ifallili l-proġett ta' hajti."

attracted towards men. He tried to help me see and understand. He didn't push. He understood this from what I used to tell him. I was very open with him, [at least] until I was equipped to be open. I used to speak to him a lot about this attraction I had for someone within the community. There was this person. [It was] a recurrent thing, [and] it happened in different ways, with different persons, which confirms what I actually felt. But there was this person, just as there was another person in Malta, who I felt more comfortable [with]. I tried to attract his attention. I gave it my all. I tried to please him, and the other person did not reciprocate. Otherwise, things would have gone . . . Then my relationship with this person took a turn for the worse, as I was frustrated, and he too became frustrated seeing me become more possessive.[7]

Moreover, his mentors were not empathetic to him. As his internal conflict evolved, Matthew was led to raise the matter with the provincial. This matter filled him with shame. A psychologist was assigned to him. Since he had no siblings and his father was not supportive, she concluded that, in her opinion, he was a suppressed heterosexual. Matthew felt misled and decided to leave. He believed that the monastery was not the ideal place to tackle his sexuality.

As Philip worked diligently to become a priest, he was not conscious of how inadequate his perspective of life was. Only after he progressed in self-awareness did he realize how stifled he had been back then. Philip paid much attention to studying and to exploring different practices of faith as inspired by others. After attending an Ignatian retreat, he convinced himself that the life of priesthood would be his aspiration. Everything seems to be going well and as he intended until he failed the screening exam for the priesthood.

---

7. "Sexuality in general ma kinitx imsemmija. To be fair, the first time li kelli ċertu hints kien minħabba d-direttur spiritwali tiegħi. Hu naħseb kien l-ewwel wieħed li fehem, li seta' kien hemm din l-attrazzjoni lejn l-irġiel. Ipprova jgħinni nara u nifhimha. He wasn't pushing. He used to see it from what I used to tell him. I was very open with him, open sakemm kont equipped li nkun open. Jien kont inkellmu ħafna fuq din l-attrazzjoni li kelli għall-persuna fil-komunità. There was this person. A recurrent thing, it happened in different ways, with different persons, which confirms what I actually felt. But there was this person, just as there was another person in Malta which I felt more comfortable. I tried to nakkwista l-attenzjoni tiegħu. I gave it my all. I tried to please him, and the other person did not use to reciprocate. Otherwise things would have gone . . . Imbagħad ir-relazzjoni tiegħi ma' din il-persuna spiċċat mit-tajjeb għall-ħażin. Għax jiena kont frustrated, and he became also more frustrated seeing me becoming more possessive."

> It was, at the time . . . nowadays I believe it was a big grace. At the time, when I was faced with it so suddenly without warning, it was a big blow. I had noticed I had become very institutionalized. I don't know, for example, how to prepare a CV. It's very normal as everything is done for you when at the seminary. When summer is close, [for example], your placement is chosen for you. If you need to send an application to university, it is taken for you; we were institutionalized. Something which hurt me a lot at the time was that no one offered to help. In the beginning, no one offered to help. I left, and no one met with me. I felt really abandoned, very much [so]. Let me be clear. Like gays, many who do not find help spread all over the place. People like me felt completely lost. You begin to understand why some people blame institutions.⁸

Gay Men in a Relationship

Similarly to Matthew and Philip, Luke's attachments revolve around the parish life. From a young age, he was always involved in activities and later joined a lay religious congregation. In the evenings, he was responsible for teaching catechism to children and during the day, he worked in a school run by the same society. He sought to lead a life according to the values prescribed by the society of which he formed part. He regularly participated in all religious activities. For many years, this lifestyle provided him with stability and a sense of purpose. Following such a lifestyle meant distancing himself from the secular world.

> After I left the MUSEUM, there was a time when I started experiencing new things. It was like someone who used to live in a monastery and left. And I had never really paid much attention to what was happening outside. I didn't have friends outside MUSEUM.⁹

---

8. "It was, dak iż-żmien, illum ngħid li kienet grazzja kbira. Dak iż-żmien, meta ġiet fuqi mingħajr l-iċken indikazzjoni, it was a big blow. Jien kont innotajt li I became very institutionalised. Lanqas naf pereżempju kif nagħmel CV. Hi normali ħafna, li tkun is-seminarju, kollox jagħmlulek huma. Kif jiġi s-sajf, il-placement jagħżluhulek huma. Jekk inti tapplika l-università jieħdu l-applikazzjoni huma; konna institucionalised. U ħaġa li weġġgħatni ħafna dak iż-żmien kienet illi ma sibtx għajnuna. Fil-bidu ma sibt għajnuna mingħand ħadd. Ħriġt u ħadd ma ltaqa' miegħi. I really felt abandoned; very much. Ħa nkellmek ċar. Dan bħall-gays, ħafna li jsibux għajnuna u they spread all over the space. Nies bħali they felt completely lost. Imbagħad jeħduha kontra l-istituzzjoni u tibda tifhimhom."

9. "Wara li tlaqt mill-mużew kien hemm żmien fejn bdejt nesperjenza ħafna

After the death of his mother, Luke encountered difficulties in meeting the obligation to live a celibate life, thus he decided to leave.

Hard work and purchasing power are the two evident attachments in Andrew's narrative. He has achieved many academic qualifications and is financially prosperous. He also experimented with drugs, but he did not become an addict as they failed to give him pleasure. His two habits distracted his attention from his interior problems. His mind would be focused on achieving new goals and enjoying luxury. The first life issue was his sexuality. As a young boy, he felt different from others, but for many years he viewed his feelings as something wrong and unnatural. Later, he explored the gay subculture but was disappointed by its level of superficiality. He refused to accept his sexuality and instead focused on his career.

> I never really accepted it, never, because I felt it was wrong and that there are ways how to overcome it. So, I invested all my energies, sometimes it is a blessing, sometimes not, into other things, in my profession, my career, and my studies. These things proved to be fruitful because materially I have a good profession, I have a beautiful house, all the material in the world, I have it.

Nevertheless, Andrew developed a relationship with a man. To this day, they live together, but the relationship is non-sexual. Both consented to this form of partnership, but Andrew discovered that his partner used his money for drugs and to meet other men. This is his current dilemma. Andrew had thought for many years that something was going on, but he initially decided not to pay any attention. Now that everything is out in the open, it has developed into an urgent issue. One can argue that his partner is an attachment to Andrew.

Remedy and Outcomes

Mortification or denudation is the remedy to the *active night of sense*. John of the Cross encourages one to distance oneself from any attachments from which one needs to sever oneself. The aim is to discover a new awareness of self that is more authentic and transparent. Although renunciation brings out perplexity, this is only temporary. One finds new knowledge beyond the limited and accustomed perspective that one formerly possessed. Moreover, the desire for God intensifies.

---

affarijiet ġodda. Dan qisu xi ħadd kien jgħix ġo kunvent u joħroġ. U jien qisni ma tantx kont nagħti kas x'kien qed jiġri barra. Ħbieb barra mill-mużew ma kellix."

Married Straight Fathers

Peter had instances when a poem or friends brought sentiment, but he did not nurture it. At University, he attended spiritual direction regarding his life's calling. His wife was instrumental in nourishing intimacy. Since she was a painter, expressing feelings was her domain. Through her example, Peter explored what he termed as his feminine side. It appears that as a couple, they complimented each other's qualities. Indulging in affections to his wife was what one expected from him. Thus, Peter was not only relying on his intellect. As the story evolves, one observes how Peter could risk distancing himself from his expectations. In fact, he pursued a course leading to a master's degree in management in order not to remain in a technical role. Tapping into the affective yielded positive results.

> For a big part of my life, I was incapable of being in touch with my feelings. I'm simplifying [things] now, but my inner capacity to be in touch with my feelings has definitely grown. Hence the possibility of having more meaningful and intimate relationships. And by becoming a better father, or a better husband, or a better son, the more I come to know God.[10]

His perception widened, and in doing so, he learnt to trust moments of inspiration. Being in touch with his feelings resulted in meaningful relationships and consequently opened up his relationship with God. His account of this process suggests that he became attuned to his personhood, grew in empathy and discovered self-meaning. Furthermore, Peter approached God not only through questioning but also through feelings. With his acquired identity, Peter achieved harmony.

Deprived of the three attachments, Paul did not solve all his problems. He managed to give up drugs, but he is still clinging to other attachments. He terminated his relationship with his girlfriend. Drugs were what brought them together, but suddenly he felt unsatisfied with his lifestyle. A friend convinced him to join a Christian community. He attended Lenten sessions, a weekly Sunday mass followed by a weekend retreat. He succeeded in renouncing drugs when he was meditating on the parable of the sower and comprehended the implications of his lifestyle.[11]

---

10. "There was a lot of time in my life where I was not able to be in touch with my feelings. Issa qiegħed nissemplifika imma for sure kibret ħafna fija l-kapaċità to be in touch with my feelings. U allura possibilità ta' relazzjonijiet iktar meaningful, iktar intimi. And by becoming a better father, or a better husband, or a better son, the more I come to know God."

11. Matt 13: 1–9, 18–23.

> I saw my seed on a rock, and I consciously felt and was fully convinced something happened there. I ended up praising God for three hours straight. It was my conversion, and that is where I have to go back to every time. Now fifteen years later, when I stumble, I always go to that moment.

Paul viewed that event as a turning point. Henceforth, he began spiritual direction with the leader of the community. Being under the wing of the leader, he acquired a new image. He was admired and thus felt important. Moreover, he would spend hours in front of the blessed sacrament in awe. Paul described prayer as his new drug and climbed the hierarchy of the community in a short time.

> I was in awe, it was something new, new people, new image, but I felt the heat. I felt the heat, and I wanted it. I was with the leader. I wanted more. I was always picking him up, always next to him, and he used to carry me, really take me . . . It was, wow. Newcomer, two months later, he is going out with the leader.

Boundaries between spiritual direction and friendship became distorted, and all of a sudden, the honeymoon period turned into a prison. He felt captive. What hurt him most were the conflict and hard feelings. The same pattern occurred at his workplace. His boss at work and the community leader shared the same traits, and Paul found himself in the same cycle. Many months had to pass before Paul could disengage from this situation. He set up his business and focused on family, but spiritually he felt numb. Paul was gripped by loneliness. Today he receives guidance from a friar. Boundaries are secure. He has realized that status, in the end, proved futile. He found that spiritual guidance was now edifying, whereas before, he only knew how to manipulate the sessions. Paul's prayers are confined. The only place where he was able to pray was in front of the blessed sacrament. Due to pressure of work and other commitments, he was not always able to visit the chapel. However, when he feels disconnected, he still indulges in pornography and disregards his wife. His knowledge of God revolves around his experience of how truth can set him free from unhealthy situations, but he desires to experience God's love beyond emotions, a love that transforms his mind.

Straight Single Men

James' turning point in life occurred when he struck up a friendship with a friar. Although the first experience at a prayer meeting was not to James' liking, when he was at the brink of collapse, he sought the friar's aid. After listening to his story, the friar counselled James to pray in front of the blessed sacrament. It was here that James found true peace, which he had never experienced before.

> And at that moment I realized that everything I had done in my life was for such a moment. Drugs, sex, everything for such a moment. The following day I woke up [and] sat near the sea. When I opened the door, I realized that I had risen from the dead. I cried in happiness for more than an hour. I started to hear the sea and the birds again. I had been dead. I cried for a long time in happiness and when I stopped, I called the priest.[12]

His first reaction was the destruction of his drugs. This encounter stimulated vivacity. He began to attend spiritual direction to acquaint himself more with God. This resulted in psychological healing and spiritual enthusiasm, but this change did not occur immediately. A beacon of light appeared in James' life. Not understanding this change of behavior, some of his friends, including his girlfriend, left him. Nevertheless, James kept the restaurant. The compulsive questions remained as well. After some hesitation, James sought the help of a psychologist and later of a psychiatrist. He was diagnosed with obsessive-compulsive disorder, but he views himself as having been cured. Putting to rest these compulsive questions brought freedom. He began to travel on his own, participating in voluntary work or spending time alone meditating. The sense of adventure still persisted. As James faced all his previous fears, in turn, he matured in self-knowledge and creativity. The friar introduced him to a lay community, and new friendships ensued. Despite several positive results, his addiction to drugs persists. Despite his efforts to restrain the temptation, he at times indulges in drugs in the company of his friends. However, when he does, his conscience pricks him, and he feels guilty for being distant from the source of life, the eucharist.

On many occasions, Nathaniel had the opportunity to reflect on his needs, but he procrastinated. Subconsciously he realized that doubting his emotions would impact his vocation. While he was abroad, he was on the verge of collapse. Being sad, he confided with a fellow student who was a psychologist. He was advised to be assertive. This counsel encouraged him,

---

12. "U dak il-ħin irrealizzajt li dak kollu li għamilt f'ħajti kien għall-mument hekk. Id-droga, is-sess, kollox għall-mument hekk. L-għada qomt, inżilt ħdejn il-baħar. Kif niftaħ il-bieb irrealizzajt li jien kont mejjet u rxuxtajt. Infqajt nibki bil-ferħ. Għamilt fuq siegħa nibki. Erġajt bdejt nisma' l-baħar u l-għasafar. Jien kont mejjet. Bikja twila bil-ferħ u kif waqaft ċempilt lill-qassis."

but Nathaniel kept procrastinating. His emotions started to get out of control. Either he burst out in anger, or he cried unexpectedly. When Nathaniel summoned up the courage to speak to his superiors, they reacted in a harsh way. Not only did they lack compassion, but they blamed him for his attitude. Nathaniel had expected mercy as exercised in the confessional. The last straw occurred during a pilgrimage when he fell head over heels in love with a woman. His repressed sexual feelings so embarrassed him that he even thought about suicide. Noting his state of mind, his friends urged him to seek professional help. After requesting leave of absence from his priestly role, Nathaniel left the religious community. Being distant from his formal community brought about uncertainty, but at the same time, it gave him an opportunity to evaluate his life.

> There was a time when I regarded my priestly ordination as a curse, not a blessing. It felt like a rope round my neck. There were [other] moments when it felt like a blessing. Obviously, when you're ordained [a priest], it feels like the blessing of blessings. I have now totally reconciled with my past. I look back and say it was a blessing, a big blessing.[13]

Now he is leading a new life and delved into the roots of shame and guilt without any shackles and devoid of the esteem that priesthood inevitably held. With God, Nathaniel discovered a new inner resonance. In his past role, God had felt distant to him even when he administered the sacraments; a barrier had precluded him from accessing God.

Separated Straight Men

Being in the company of members of a lay religious community led Thomas to start spiritual direction. Unlike other friars, his director did not judge him. Thus, Thomas was emboldened to seek the truth about his marriage. It was a ray of hope. What Thomas wished was to bring order to his life by renouncing particular immoral activity, to attend to his wife and hope that compromise be reached.

> I was both shocked and embarrassed and I literally burst out crying. [It was] the first time in my life that someone was interested in who I really am, and how I feel, rather than in what

---

13. "Kien hemm mumenti fejn l-ordinazzjoni saċerdotali tiegħi rajtha bhala sehta, mhux barka. Rajtha bhala mażżra ma' għonqi. Kien hemm mumenti fejn rajtha bhala barka. Ovvjament meta tiġi ordnat thossha barka fuq il-barkiet. Illum qiegħed f'punt rikonċiljat b'mod sħiħ mal-passat tiegħi. Inhares lura u ngħid kienet barka, barka kbira."

> the law states. And I think that was the moment when I started a proper conversion process. Rather than a point of conversion, [it was] a point of hope.[14]

Thomas succeeded in forsaking drugs, strip clubs and the extramarital relationship. He also sought psychological assistance to discover the truth. Thomas was resilient in his quest. However, matters with the wife did not improve. In this circumstance, Thomas had to make a decision. As matters became difficult, he engaged vigorously in charitable work. But he struck up an acquaintance with a woman. Many of his friends warned him about his improper behavior, but Thomas was afraid to confront his wife. On becoming aware of the situation, she requested that Thomas leaves their home, and an annulment was filed. His wife later changed her mind, but he did not. Through therapy, Thomas became conscious that a need to please others controlled his actions. He found the roots of his conduct in the fact that he was not his mother's favorite and constantly had to work hard to please her.

On reading the Bible for the first time, Jude was inspired to distance himself from the occult. A light went on for him. His profane objects were all destroyed. He acted in accordance with Christian practice and attended the sacraments.

> That was the first Bible I ever had. And I started reading. I started from the Book of Genesis. I thought it was just one book, but I discovered various ones. While I was reading, I felt something, like a light penetrate through me, and I saw a different me.[15]

The sacrament of reconciliation led him to befriend a spiritual director. Through this reconciliation, Jude discovered his aptitudes. He succeeded in finding employment, made friends and obtained some academic qualifications. The fundamentals of his humanity were attained through spiritual guidance and direction. Attaining self-esteem, in a gradual way, led him to graduate in theology. But Jude sought more. He desired God to show him his vocation. Realizing that the religious life was not to his liking, he sought the ideal of marriage.

---

14. "U bejn inħsadt u bejn inblajt u infqajt nibki litteralment. L-ewwel darba f'ħajti li xi ħadd interessah min hu jien, u kif qed inħossni jien, milli l-liġi x'tgħid. And I think that was the moment that I started a proper conversion process. Milli point of conversion, a point of hope."

15. "Dik kienet l-ewwel Bibbja li kelli. U bdejt naqra jiena. Bdejt mill-Ġenesi. Jien ħsibt li kienet ktieb wieħed imma kien hemm diversi kotba. Waqt li bdejt naqraha nħoss xi ħaġa, qisu dawl jidħol ġo fija, u bdejt nara differenti lili nnifsi."

Single Gay Men

Matthew considered failure when he left the monastery. Once he settled, he had new commitments. But his problems were of a sexual nature, and he did not seek any help. He only harbored these thoughts, and discreetly he looked for a lay community where sexuality and spirituality were discussed. A change came over him when he met a friend who had the same problem. When his friend openly declared to Matthew his sexuality, he felt pushed to imitate him.

> He hadn't come out at the time. [He was still] closeted, as I was. It was me and three other people from there. We used to meet every weekend, on a Sunday or Saturday, to go for a walk. We used to talk. He had done his walk and at some point, he started coming out. He came out at the same time I did. We have very similar stories. While I was listening, I had mixed reactions. I was torn between admiration towards him for something I was going through as well, and the lack of understanding as to why I could not follow his example. I was at liberty to do so. Couldn't I find the courage? It didn't happen at the time.[16]

He began therapy. Self-acceptance is the primary step. Through the help of the psychologist, who was direct but empathetic, Matthew started to accept his sexuality, but he had not attained full acceptance. Matthew began coming out to his friends, but the biggest challenge was to face his parents. Practicing his faith is now authentic. At the monastery, he was only focusing on a commitment as he liked the friars. But now, the spiritual aim is to live up to his faith.

Philip expressed mortification in two stages. The first one is a result of a decision that others took about his dream. This caused anger and confusion. Subsequently, he sought guidance from his religious circles. But his pleas fell on deaf ears for many months. However, entire mortification calls for consent by the person. This led to the second stage of his denunciation. Following the advice of his spiritual director, he changed course and gave up studying theology. This involved him in moving to a different institution

---

16. "Dak iż-żmien ma kienx out. Closeted as I am. Minn hemm konna jien u tliet persuni oħra. Konna niltaqgħu every weekend, on a Sunday or Saturday, għal xi mixja. Konna nitkellmu. Hu għamel il-mixja tiegħu and at some point beda ħiereġ. Kien għamel il-coming out miegħi. Niftakar jien u hu għandna storja simili ħafna. Jien u nisma' kelli mixed reactions. Bejn ammirajtu li ħareġ b'xi ħaġa li anke jien għaddej minnha u bejn bdejt ngħid, allura għaliex ma nagħmilhiex jien. Kelli l-libertà li nagħmilha. Ma nsibx il-kuraġġ jien? Ma seħħitx dak iż-żmien."

where ideas held by his companions were not in line with his previous perspective.

> "Don't pursue Theology [because] you'll indirectly be limiting yourself to the same structure as the seminary. You'll see your friends achieve certain things, and you wouldn't have achieved anything. You will grow bitter." He told me to allow my wound to heal [and] to distance myself. I had no friends when I left the seminary. Changing faculty was a good decision. [I witnessed] some who spoke about what they had done with their girl the night before, others who were against the church, and an atheist professor . . . This was [both] an [eye] opener and a shock. [These situations and people] helped build my character.[17]

The relationship with his spiritual director was crucial to Philip, for whom his director became his most trusted person. Through his director's intervention, Philip built a circle of friends, joined a lay religious community and took care of his outward appearance. Philip was very conservative in demeanor, but he gradually came out. He graduated as a teacher, but as he attained some stability, a new problem emerged: his sexuality was not expressed. On one occasion, Philip was attracted in a fond way to a friend, but Philip overlooked these feelings. Cunningly his spiritual director probed him, but this matter was so neglected in Philip that he developed panic attacks. Unaware of their cause, he started attending therapy and discovered he was gay. His acceptance was quite rapid. He made progress in this intimate matter when his spiritual director acknowledged him and told him how much God loved him and will nurture this quality.

Gay Men in a Relationship

Luke felt perplexed and confused when he left the lay congregation. However, later on, he enrolled as a policeman. The one matter which remained unresolved was his sexuality. He still attended spiritual guidance, and later psychological therapy was sought. Luke had the courage to probe sexuality discreetly and, in the process, encountered his partner. He harbored no ill feelings about being gay, but guilt haunted him. This was not an easy matter

---

17. "'Tkomplix teoloġija, tibqa' fl-istess struttura indirettament tas-seminarju. Tara li sħabek hadu hekk, u int ma tieħu xejn. You will grow bitter.' Qalli l-ferita ħalliha tingħalaq, tbiegħed. Ħriġt mis-seminarju u ma kellix ħbieb. Bdilt il-fakultà u kienet grazzja kbira. Min jirrakkonta x'għamel mat-tfajla filgħaxija, u min għax ma jaqbilx mal-Knisja, u l-professur ateu . . . Din kienet apertura u xokk. Bdew jibnuli l-karattru."

for him. What he feared most was how others would judge him and be rejected, particularly by members of his family.

> I made the good decision of keeping up my meetings with my spiritual director. He was very patient with me, as patient as Job, [and] sometimes he used to tell me, "Holy Mary, how long is it going to take you to understand?" And I used to reply, "Be patient. Imagine you're talking to a priest who left the monastery." The concept is simple, but I didn't want to accept reality. It's not that I couldn't understand, but I was scared of being guilty of something or other. Slowly, with prayer and patience, and I sometimes met with him three times a week. My mother's death had left its toll on me, something which I didn't take care of. In fact, I needed to visit a psychologist. So, it was a pile up of things. My mum's death, I had left the MUSEUM, this [new] way of life, and my dad was going to do that blessed testament. A pile up of things. So, I had both spiritual and psychological help, and I somehow pulled through.[18]

When his mother died, his father decided to draw up a new will — leaving the house to Luke until he got married. This decision terrified him as he feared that his siblings would turn against him. Through therapy, he resolved these thoughts, and he declared openly that he was gay to his father. His partner was also accepted as a member of the family, and they entered a civil partnership. What was uppermost in his mind was how friends and acquaintances would react to the civil partnership. He received both positive and negative reactions. However, Luke has a strong character. He was conscious that other gay people faced rejection and decided to get involved and bring a change in society's mentality. Despite attaching importance to live up to the merits of spirituality as prescribed by the church by attending Sunday mass or retreats, the personal encounter with God was side-lined.

Although Andrew was successful in his career and owned many possessions, this did not allow him to attain self-realization. He engaged in more activities like buying a second house or enrolling in another academic

---

18. "Li għamilt tajjeb hu li żammejt xorta direttur spiritwali. U miskin ħa paċenzja ta' Ġob miegħi għax xi kultant kien jgħidli, 'Marija santa, kemm ser iddum biex tifhem?' U kont ngħidlu, 'hu paċenzja. Immaġina qisek qed titkellem ma' patri u telaq mill-kunvent.' Il-kunċett hu ħafif u sempliċi imma jien qisni ma ridtx naċċetta l-biċċa tax-xogħol. Mhux ma bdejtx nifhimha imma bdejt nibża' li ser inkun ħati ta' xi ħaġa. Bil-mod il-mod, bit-talb u bil-paċenzja, u ġieli tliet darbiet f'ġimgħa iltqajt miegħu. Il-mewt t'ommi affettwatni u ma ħadtx ħsiebha. Infatti kelli bżonn immur għand psychologist. Allura, kollox ma' kollox, il-mewt tal-mamà, tlaqt mill-mużew, u mbagħad dan l-istil ta' ħajja u missieri ser jagħmel dan l-imbierek testment. Kollox ma' kollox. Allura, kelli l-għajnuna kemm spiritwali u psikoloġika u b'xi mod wasalna."

course to avoid reality, but full denunciation from this pattern has not transpired. Regarding his sexuality, through the intervention of his spiritual director, he realized that denial was causing only harm. However, he seems not fully to have settled this matter.

> There was Mass, and I went. He [spiritual director] was there and was administering confession. And I went, and I told him, "Father, I am gay," and he told me "So?" For me, it was a big deal. And there it started, and I've come and learned denial is useless, but I have come to see that the majority of people who live their gayness fully are very shallow. It is very superficial. It is based on having a good time, on drugs, on promiscuity, on what I own, what I buy, how I look, and so it is very fake. There is more to life, more to oneself than this. There is mind, body and spirit. And from the three, I believe that the spirit is the one that lives forever because it was made by God in his image.

As to his partner, Andrew is currently at a critical point: he must either sever or maintain the relationship. Although his spiritual director advised him to terminate it, Andrew believes God could change his partner's mentality. Since Andrew is currently deeply involved in the struggles of mortification, it is too early for clear outcomes. He has reached a stage in his life at which he cannot escape or delay a decision any longer. One option to remedy this difficult situation would be to go abroad and spend some time away from all the commitments he has in Malta. He hopes God will illuminate his mind and reach a decision.

The Active Night of Spirit

Obstacles and Warnings

In the *active night of spirit*, John of the Cross' considerations are the obstacles regarding the inner faculties. Through one's intellect, memory and will, one secures a purposeful identity and acquires control and serenity. God is wrapped in knowledge that complements and, at the same time, is submissive to one's achieved identity. The intellect gains knowledge, memory is vivid with experiences, and the will is strengthened. From such fruition, warning signs emerge as well. In the long run, their worth is exhausted, leading to unpredicted events, bringing unexplainable failure and obscuring God's presence.

Married Straight Fathers

From his experience of the *active night of sense*, Peter attained balance in utilizing the two aspects of his personhood. Tranquility resulted in marriage. As a couple, they enjoyed a five-year extended honeymoon period. Peter satisfied his parents' expectations, and thus they admired him. Since he fulfilled their expectations, he was determined to accomplish more. In other words, his will was confirmed. Through God's help, matters seemed to be pleasant. Peter approached God with confidence and was inspired by the actions of others.

> It became a very important spiritual journey. It was a very, very important milestone in my relationship with God, and I feel it was a very enriching experience. I witnessed, for instance, lectures, some of which I still hold at heart. Witnessing someone speak with so much certainty and others who were on a pedestal but then expressed their doubts. And, also, witnessing my companions. It was a very enriching experience.[19]

In Peter's narrative, receiving the witness of others was a constant theme, and he desired to be a source of inspiration too. This actually happened, but not according to his plans. Infertility became a cause of great anxiety, which was a challenge to him. His wife had two miscarriages, and his desire to be a father was not fulfilled.

Renouncing drugs and entering the lay community, Paul gained new knowledge and a disciplined attitude towards spirituality. His director had a real impact on him. Paul was consoled, but tension arose between him and the leader of the community. He reached the point that whatever the leader advised, Paul only disapproved, and consequently, anger towards the leader ensued. His separation from this community came at an emotional cost. At present, Paul is unable to understand why attachment to men in power occurred.

> In fact, there was someone else in my childhood years, a teacher who was quite powerful but different. [It] seems like I cling to these figures. I kind of lead them to attach to me because I like

---

19. "It became a very important spiritual journey. Kienet a very, very important milestone fir-relazzjoni tiegħi m'Alla u nħossni tgħallimt ħafna fuq livell esperjenzjali. Tgħallimt pereżempju the witnessing of lecturers illi xi wħud minnhom baqgħu f'qalbi. Tara lil xi ħadd jitkellem b'ċertu konvinzjoni u nies li kienu fuq pedestall imbagħad jesprimu d-dubji. And, also, witnessing my companions. It was a very enriching experience."

their attention. I am seeking that, I will be seeking that attention. I go to the top.

He had sought therapy as he indulged in pornography, but these dynamics remained unexplored. Paul described his father as too humble and a failure. He never respected him, and they often quarreled. However, on observing how his children esteem their grandfather and relate to him, he realized the gentleness his father was endowed with. It seems that his father's character is courting him to explore himself.

Single Straight Men

As a teenager, James held many questions about God. Unfortunately, his childhood was marked by constant discouragement. He was antagonistic. God was impersonal and distant. He was of the opinion that life was a struggle to survive. However, following his conversion, his perspective to life changed to an adventurous one and marked a celebratory phase in his spirituality.

> I sought moments of prayer, alone. I didn't use to travel; I first used to see places, and then travel to understand myself better. The Father suggested I should find time alone. "Go and do the things you enjoy doing; go for walks." I shared an experience with two friends. It helped me a lot. I experienced prayer more, and even life in the community. I used to go for walks alone in the countryside. I had never done it before. I wanted to challenge myself further. I started travelling alone. I grabbed a backpack and went to India. Alone. I slowly left my fears behind. There were many of them. I had been oppressed.[20]

Firstly, enthusiasm filled his spiritual style. Instead of drugs, he said the rosary, travelled, meditated on scripture, and engaged in voluntary activities. Secondly, what he had missed in childhood could now be relegated to the past as change occurred. While James's natural father was sparing in his attention towards him, his spiritual director accorded paternal love. Through the friar's help, James regained self-determination and meditated

---

20. "Kont insib mumenti ta' talb waħdi. Ma kontx nittrevilja, l-ewwel nara l-postijiet, imma mbagħad nittrevilja biex ngħarbel lili nnifsi ahjar. Il-Father issuġġerieli nsib ħin għalija waħdi. 'Mur agħmel dak li thobb, imxi.' Għamilt esperjenza ma' żewġt iħbieb. Għenitni ħafna. Dħalt iktar fit-talb u fil-ħajja komunitarja. Kont immur mixjiet fil-kampanja waħdi. Qabel ma kontx nagħmilha. Ridt inkompli niċċelingja lili nnifsi. Qbadt nittrevilja waħdi. Qbadt backpack u mort l-Indja. Waħdi. Bdejt noħroġ minn dawk il-biżgħat. Kien hemm ħafna minnhom. Kont bniedem oppressed."

upon God. The third characteristic is James' approach to God in an intimate manner. In his prayers, James received comfort and substituted the happiness that drugs offered. Although his conversion brought about healing, his compulsive thoughts persisted. James did not seek help from professionals and instead believed that God would change him without any action on his part. However, James became conscious of self-responsibility. His current challenge is to find a balance between being responsible and, at the same time, being receptive to God's direction. His relationship with the divine has been transformed from one of consolation to one based on trust.

Through focusing on therapy, Nathaniel confronted many interior feelings and thoughts. Making sense of them is his present situation. Bereavement is the term that Nathaniel used to qualify his healing. His mother's response to her difficult pregnancy was the primary source of anxiety, and this impacted the way he coped with feelings. In describing the dynamics regarding his birth, he assumed greater responsibility to protect and not bring shame to his parents. His departure from priesthood caused his parents much apprehension. Reflecting on these memories, Nathaniel also felt distressed about his priesthood. He compared his experience to the coming out process of gay people. This helped him to cease feeling resentful towards himself and to realize that firstly he had to have mercy on himself. As he made sense of his past, he realized how much he ignored his affective aspect, which also led him to his repressed sexuality.

> I started the session with my psychologist. He was very understanding. I narrated to him my story, and then he told me, "I do not think, and I do not believe that this city is the problem. Let me ask you a simple question about an experience that every bishop and every pope passed through. When were you head over heels in love?" It was liberating. "Right now!" And it was the issue.

All these inner diggings showed the character of the real Nathaniel. This also manifested itself in his prayer. While in the past, his prayer was mechanical, now he approaches God with his whole self. Through his struggles, he discovered how Christ is truly the culmination of humanity.

Separated Straight Men

In order not to endure shame and confrontation, and out of fear of making a decision, Thomas stuck with his marriage. Even after dismissing everything that could cloud his judgment, his efforts were directed at proving that he was morally in the right direction and that God would take it upon himself to fix the marriage. One could note that Thomas never found the courage to decide and expected his wife to take the initiative. In the meantime, Thomas engaged in intense prayers and fasting in the hope that if he performed these sacrifices, God would intervene and help him to settle his marriage issues. His spiritual director invited him to attend an event where the appearance of Saint Mary occurred to a man. During this event, he received a special message from her desiring his conversion. These events enhanced his dedication, and he managed to distance himself from all attachments. But a problem arose when he tried to sever his extramarital relationship with a woman who provided him with intimacy. In this case, he was not successful.

> I couldn't persist in fixing and seeking the truth in my marriage when there was someone else involved. However, it was rooted so deep in my heart, like a very old tree, that it felt like trying to uproot something. It was very painful. It was the most profound spiritual moment for me.[21]

> "I'm ready to give her to you. I'm ready to entrust her in your hands but don't let me suffer so much. Don't let me cry." I got a nosebleed from all the crying. I think it was the deepest pain I had ever felt in my life. I don't think I had ever been so deeply hurt before.[22]

Thomas thought that God wanted him to give up this relationship. Thus, he pleaded with God that he would comply provided that this relation be substituted for something else. Thomas received a sign, a physical manifestation in the form of an embrace. He felt ecstatic. Following his decision, he realized that it was a turning point. Spiritual enthusiasm was imbued in him. He engaged in so much voluntary work that he forgot the issue at home. However, on encountering another woman, he became fully aware that he had been ignoring his predicament. He had no one else to turn to, but Thomas still resisted the need to decide. Matters unfolded in such a way that his wife unexpectedly had a change of heart and asked Thomas to

---

21. "Ma stajtx inkompli nirranġa u nsib il-verità fiż-żwieġ tiegħi waqt li hemm xi ħadd ieħor fin-nofs. Imma tant kien hemm għeruq ġo qalbi, like a very old tree, li kont inħossni qed naqla' xi ħaġa. It was very painful. Kienet l-iktar punt ta' profondità fl-ispiritwalità tiegħi."

22. 'Lest li nagħtihielek, lest li nħalliha f'idejk, imma tħallinix inbati din it-tbatija kollha. Tħallinix nibki.' Tant kemm kont bkejt li kont infraġt. U nibki, I think it was the deepest pain I ever felt in my life. Naħseb qatt ma weġġajt f'ħajti."

leave the matrimonial home. Thomas once again believed this was God's intervention.

Jude was influenced in two ways, relating to how he perceived himself and how he interacted with the world. The first concerns upbringing. He always kept in the background, and his lack of confidence haunted him. The second is spiritualizing all events. Occult practices and meditation enhanced the skills of discipline in prayer. Although he realized how Satanism and Christianity do not coexist, his style of prayer did not change. This increased mental tranquility, but he ventured into fantasy. Not only did he distance himself from others, but he also rented a garage to use for meditation. This mode of living kept repeating, and he ignored other critical human qualities. The impulse he felt to live perfectly the Christian ideals was so commanding that he took rushed decisions. Marriage was the latest of these. Jude did not evaluate his circumstances based on reality but through the ideals he desired to possess, thinking that God would be pleased.

> Moments of anger. Be thankful for the bad things in life, as they open your eyes to the good things you weren't paying attention to before. From my experience, I've regarded the good things life has offered me as bad. Even forgiveness backfired. In prayer, not to blame God, but I used to pray to the Lord, "Lord, I believe in you." I kind of expected Him to do something, which He didn't. I had put responsibility on God, when God had entrusted me with the reigns to my own life, when He had given me reason and free will. I didn't use them. I threw all responsibility back unto Him. Very sad. I almost feel like I [was trying to] control [Him]. Even going to work seemed like an effort.[23]

His inner feelings were continuously signaling caution, but this had no effect. Being abused, Jude chose to forgive. He thought that if he were to forgive, God would take responsibility for everything and miraculously bring change. However, it never happened.

---

23. "Mumenti ta' rabja. Kull deni ħudu b'ġid. Jiena l-esperjenza wrietni, kull ġid ħadtu b'deni. Sal-istess maħfra daret kontrija. Kont immur fit-talb, not to blame God, imma kont nitlob lill-Mulej, 'Mulej nemmen fik.' Qisu ppretendejt li hu ser jagħmel xi ħaġa u hu m'għamel xejn. Jien kont qed naghti responsabbiltà lil Alla meta Alla tani l-ħajja f'idejja għax tani r-raġuni u r-rieda. Ma użajthomx. Tfajt kollox fuqu. Very sad. U kważi qed inħossni li pprovajt nikkontrollah. Anke mmur ix-xogħol inkaxkar saqajja."

Single Gay Men

What dominated Matthew's inner faculties was his dream of becoming like Saint Francis of Assisi. He aspired not to the universal image of Saint Francis but to the one depicted in *Brother Sun, Sister Moon*. One could argue that his profound attraction to the figure of the Saint also involved his sexuality. If one temporarily puts aside that aspect, one cannot ignore the fact that in many ways, Matthew thrived on spiritual knowledge and practice. Although the issue of fraternity haunted him, he received many splendid benefits in prayer, enhanced by his biblical knowledge. What he succeeded in achieving helped him to approach reality. However, the sexual issue threatened this path. Each time he was carried away by affections, fear exposed failure. In these circumstances, his answer was to focus his will by exerting more repression. Unfortunately, the monastery was not receptive to his development.

> When the psychologist saw the state I was in, and all the dynamics, and when the provincial saw that the attraction for the other person was becoming too much, even for the community, due to conflict, I decided, "Ok, best stop here." I think it was—leaving was a good decision, in the end. Things weren't going to get better. The monastery was not the right environment to explore sexuality, and neither was being in a religious life. In my opinion, there is no place for being open in a monastery. It wasn't the right place to discover myself. I had to leave. I had to free myself from all these commitments of the profession, to be freer.[24]

Even when his mother was diagnosed with cancer, from his narrative, one concludes that the friars were more interested in him meeting the deadlines of the novitiate than attending to his feelings. Regarding his sexuality, Matthew contended that his sexual predicament was very evident, and thus he wondered how his mentors, who were trained psychologists, did not recognize this. The possessive elements in his character alone were adequate signals. Following his novitiate, Matthew kept repeating the same central

---

24. "When the psychologist saw the state I was in and all the dynamics, and when the provincial saw that the attraction for the other person was becoming too much even for the community, due to conflict, I decided, 'Ok, best to stop here.' I think it was—it was a good decision at the end to leave. L-affarijiet ma kinux ser jitjiebu minn dak il-lat. It wasn't the right environment, in a monastery, to explore sexuality within the religious life. Nahseb kif narah jiena, m'hemmx dan il-ftuh fil-kunvent. It wasn't the right place to discover myself. I had to leave. I had to free myself from all these commitments of the profession to be freer."

issue. Even the psychologist appointed by the monastery caused more confusion than healing.

Philip's predominant inner inclination was his desire to become a priest, followed by many other possessions, which were a result of how Philip aligned himself with the prevailing norm. This included hostility towards secular society and negation of anything concerning sexuality. Philip felt comfortable with Ignatian spirituality. For him, this was the instrument that shaped his prayer. In every step he took, Philip wanted to seek God's will. He attended retreats twice a year, read spiritual books and meditated on scripture. To confirm his ideas in life events, Philip expected a sign either through consolation or through thoughts that his mind apprehended in his reflections. His relationship with his spiritual director is pivotal. Philip lost his father, and the spiritual director acted as his father in most aspects. All difficulties were discussed with him, and his counsel was superior to anyone's opinions. Through their interaction, Philip acquired more self-determination. Despite his initial deep disappointment when he failed the screening for the priesthood, he made great strides forward.

Growth in all three interior faculties resulted. In suppressing his sexuality, Philip realized the consequences as manifested in the life of Henri Nouwen. He regarded Nouwen's repression as useless suffering, and this pushed him forward to self-acceptance. Although his love for God intensified, Philip faced challenges when his spiritual director died and in exploring how he would live his sexuality. He missed his director, who has been a fundamental source of clarity. He even desired to be in a relationship, but Philip concluded that God would not approve of this step. At a retreat, the phrase "what seems to me white, I will believe black if the hierarchical Church so defines" by Saint Ignatian of Loyola surprised him.[25]

> Deep down I felt that God was calling me, that He doesn't wish me to start a relationship. Deep down He did not desire it. My spiritual life is marked by this, "What I deeply desire, God seems to disapprove of." Ordination was one of them. It was an issue. However, I had this deep certainty that I shouldn't start a relationship. That God did not want me to. It was something He was asking of me. I shivered so hard during the retreat that the cleaner asked me, "Is something the matter? Why are you shivering so much?" I woke up at night, I opened the book on an excerpt from Saint Ignatius, "If the wall is white and the church is

---

25. Actual quotation is "What seems to me white, I will believe black if the hierarchical Church so defines."

saying it's black, you have to say it's black." I was certain God did not want me to start a relationship. It wasn't a question of sin.[26]

Philip interpreted it as a sign from God. But he admits that loneliness could ensue when leading a celibate life. To assuage the anxiety, he is exploring the value of aloneness and devoting more time to prayer.

Gay Men in a Relationship

What directed Luke's actions were the ideals as he interpreted them through his involvement in the religious society. However, reconciling himself with sexuality and being accepted by his family led Luke to evaluate his spirituality. He maintained that if one is committed to spirituality, then positive results will ensue. His story confirms the assertion. However, he realized the gulf between the ideals presented to him and his actual life. This was possible by focusing on his humanity and on questioning the perception that Saints were perfect humans and were never prone to err.

> When someone writes about the lives of saints, nothing is included about when these saints get angry, [or] when these saints experienced solitude. The only saint I know of who spoke clearly was Mother Teresa. When [she spoke about] the years she spent praying and couldn't hear answers. As if it was a dark time [in her life]. And that's when I realized, "They experience something similar too."[27]

What remained an inspirational figure to him was Pope John the XXIII for his humble attitude. Luke aims and seeks to practice those same values at the workplace and with others. However, Luke's style of prayer remained formulaic. Although during the transitional year he abandoned prayer, he

---

26. "Deep down I felt that God was calling me that he doesn't wish me to enter in a relationship. Deep down he did not desire it. My spiritual life is marked by this, 'What I deeply desire God seems to disapprove of.' Ordination was one of them. It was an issue. Imma kelli ċertezza kbira li m'għandix nidħol f'relazzjoni. Li Alla ma ridnix nidħol f'relazzjoni. It was something he was asking from me. Tant bdejt nirtogħod waqt l-irtir li kien hawn dan li jnaddaf u qalli, 'Ġralek xi ħaġa? Kemm qed tirtogħod?' Qomt billejl, ftaħt il-ktieb u ġiet is-silta ta' San Injazju, 'Jekk il-ħajt hu abjad u l-Knisja qed tgħid li hu iswed, inti trid tgħid li hu iswed.' Kelli ċertezza illi lili Alla ma ridnix inkun f'relazzjoni. Mhux kwistjoni ta' dnub."

27. "Li għandek f'dawn il-ħajjiet qisu ma jkun hemm ħadd li jikteb meta dawn il-qaddisin jirrabjaw. Meta dawn il-qaddisin sabu ruħom waħedhom. L-unika qaddisa li naf li tkellmet b'mod ċar hi Madre Tereża. Meta għamlet dak il-perjodu ta' snin titlob u ma tisma' xejn. Qisu dak iż-żmien mudlam. U ħemmhekk li qisni irrealizzajt, 'Mela jgħaddu minnha dawn.'"

now desired to regain some of its merits. Through his involvement with an LGBTIQ+ religious community, in the company of his husband, he started again to pray regularly. When asked how all these characteristics influenced his encounter with God, Luke admitted that at times he felt guilty for not being consonant with the Catechism of the Church but affirmed that his vow to his husband was his final decision.

The way Andrew's family dealt with problems was by sweeping them under the carpet. A pervasive mode of perfection and stability endowed with luxury reigned in their way of life. This had an impact on how Andrew coped with life. What Andrew viewed as the safest and reliable instrument was the church teachings that should govern his life. As a result, he did not confide in himself on account of his propensities and the values of the gay subculture. Andrew tried to explore a religious group where sexual and spiritual integration were discussed. Being perplexed by their teachings, he was left feeling that he forms part of a minority within a minority. The feeling of loneliness disturbs him. He often depicted his sexuality and his current relationship with his partner as the cross that God has given him to carry in the hope that all his suffering would be rewarded in heaven.

> I learned to build a treasure in heaven because I believe in it. I build this for myself in living God's will, whatever that is. I have no idea what God's will is for me in my life. I try to live the faith. Not just saying things but living, which is hard because it means going against one's inclinations. My defects, my inclination to take the easy path. I think ultimately that what brings merit in front of the Lord, for me—guarding against myself for Him. I believe He died for us on the cross. He became a man. He didn't have to. He could have left it at any point, but He didn't. He suffered. He had lots of doubt, He asked God to take the chalice away, but He did it for us. Can't I do this small thing for him? And I hope in the long term, when I am with Him face to face, I will be a good servant, that's all. And compared to what He did for us, it is nothing. He is my God of the Scripture. It's hard.

Since his relationship with his partner was open, Andrew feels stuck. He is contemplating how to proceed: should he meet the expectations of his relatives or continue to carry the cross by staying with his partner? Failure and judgment are looming, causing Andrew to plead with God to change his partner's mind by accepting the merits of abiding in His law and all the sacrifices endured.

Remedy and Outcomes

When the self is decentralized and experiencing tribulations, John of the Cross advises remaining in faithful stillness towards God and cooperating in the slow work of self-renunciation. When the interior faculties are obscured, the self receives a new perspective. Faith tempers presumption but, at the same time, adapts the soul to God's loving and mysterious character. Hope prioritizes love as that expectation above all else the soul desires, and finally, love strikes with a new passion that is truly unique to the person and synchronized with God. From the experience of marginality, one expands into new freedom.

Married Straight Fathers

When Peter became eager to know more about the issue of adoption, a remedy arose gradually. Even if this involved some problems, the process was gradual. His wife was again instrumental in helping him to overcome his initial objection to this idea. He attended an introductory course about adoption and embarked on psychological therapy. Eventually, they adopted two children. Learning how to nurture them brought about further responsibilities and self-awareness. Peter often spoke about unconditional love and how his parents, in their simplicity, loved him. He also commented on the numerous instances of generosity by catechists he met as a child and how saints dedicated themselves to love. He felt being in the same scenario.

> I truly appreciate what my parents passed on to me. My parents set me on a path, but [then] our paths diverged quite a bit, as I do not perceive God in the same way they do . . . I can say quite confidently, and this is not something I've recently discovered, [that] my parents gave me the capacity to understand unconditional love.[28]

At first, the children displayed attachment problems—particularly the boy who rejected Peter and his wife outright and had many tantrums. Peter was apprehensive but was consistent in showing love towards the children. Progress was made gradually. Unconditional love is Peter's new aim. Due to this new responsibility, Peter quit his previous employment. He started working in a retreat house which allowed him to be more present at home

---

28. "Napprezza hafna x'tawni l-ġenituri. Il-ġenituri tiegħi set me on a path but our paths diverged quite a bit għax I do not resonate with the way they perceive God . . . Jien nista' ngħid, b'wiċċi minn quddiem, u din mhux illum skoprejtha, missieri u ommi l-ewwel ħaġa li tawni hi l-kapaċità li nifhem x'jiġifieri tħobb bla kundizzjoni."

and to support his wife in her career. This enhanced his spirituality so much that he enrolled in a course about spiritual direction. Peter explained that adoption did not answer completely his inner emptiness of not having his own children, but it met many of the characteristics of parenthood. Although adoption was, to some extent, one of his desires, he still felt unfulfilled internally. However, he transcended his expectations to have control over everything.

At present, Paul is finding it difficult to focus his attention on God. However, the unexplored image of both his father and the new spiritual director might be two instances that could influence him in this regard. Self-awareness remains fragmentary.

Single Straight Men

Although Nathaniel seems mature, the dispensation of priests from celibacy is a source of anxiety to him. In line with the Maltese ecclesial law, dispensation to priests is not granted before forty years. Exceptions exist, but the rule safeguards those who leave and change their minds and return. However, Nathaniel has struck up a relationship with a woman. Thus, the ecclesiastical law places him in a state of direct disobedience to the vow of chastity. Although he complies with the rules, one suggests that he struggles to dismiss the notion of being perfect. Moreover, Nathaniel manifested dissatisfaction that he had not comprehended his feelings earlier. He also expressed concern that his past would be a shadow that would accompany him forever, and others might also judge him. Total self-acceptance appears not to be fully completed. How others perceive him remains a concern. Even though he learnt that perception and reality do not always coincide, Nathaniel still made every effort to overcome his misconceptions about being a perfectionist.

Separated Single Men

With hindsight, Thomas considered whether the signs he received were authentic. The person who alleged that the blessed virgin appeared to him was exposed as a fraudster. His spiritual director often appealed to him not to attach much importance to the manifestations he received but was advised to listen to his conscience.

> I was hooked at the time as [these things] used to add a certain thrill to my life. I used to see these things as amazing. To me

they were so real. Nowadays, if someone comes up to me and tells me, "I can pray and witness things happening that instant," my mature side would say, "Poor chap, it's not the case." But the truth is that it's real and important to him. For him it's an important stepping stone towards maturity. So first I removed drugs, then some friends, some business, some travelling with rich clients. Then I started to realize I could not lead a double life.[29]

Following his annulment, Thomas did not divulge the way he was praying. He only stated that no matter what was the outcome of the decision by the ecclesiastical board, he would still remain in a relationship with his new partner even if this was in conflict with the rules of the church.

Gripped by much desolation, Jude gradually came to terms with reality. Everything about faith was spiritualized. As a result, he ignored his responsibilities. He did not even employ his intellect to examine his affairs wisely. He pursued only the ideals he had created. This way of operating is what he has learnt, but inner emptiness still remains. He only prayed so that God would have mercy on him as he gave up hope.

It's not easy and I [often] feel like giving up. [I'm] vulnerable and it seems like nothing works. Now that I'm trying to find the right path. I'm forty years old with nothing saved. I can't buy anything. I have no support. My mother tells me to go live with her. But I'm scared I'll fall ill. Now I hope that the bishops will be patient enough and willing to help me.[30]

The only person supporting him is his spiritual director, and he feels he has to rebuild his life from scratch. Expecting the verdict of his request for annulment was the only way forward as no clear direction was in sight.

---

29. "Dak iż-żmien I was hooked għax kienu jimlew ċertu thrill f'ħajti. Kien hemm dak l-element li kont nara dawn l-affarijiet so amazing. Għalija kienu tant reali. Meta llum jiġi xi ħadd u jgħidli, 'Naf nitlob u dak il-ħin jiġri xi ħaġa,' mil-lat matur tiegħi ngħid, 'Jaħasra mhux il-każ.' Imma l-verità hi li għalih hi vera u importanti. Għalih dan importanti għax hi stepping stone li wieħed irid jgħaddi minnha biex jimmatura. Allura, l-ewwel neħħejt id-drogi, imbagħad neħħejt ċertu ħbieb, ċertu business, ċertu safar ma' klijenti b'ħafna flus. Imbagħad jien bdejt nirrealizza li ma stajtx ngħix double life."

30. "Mhux faċli, u naqta' qalbi. Vulnerabbli u qisu nothing worked. Issa li qed nipprova nsib art tajba. Jien għandi erbgħin sena. Ma faddalt xejn. Ma nista nixtri xejn. M'għandi l-ebda sapport. Ommi tgħidli mmur ngħix magħha. Imma nibża' li nimrad. Issa nispera li l-isqfijiet ikollhom il-paċenzja u l-volontà li jgħinuni."

Single Gay Men

The greatest act of renunciation in Matthew is his departure from the monastery. The ideal lifestyle that he sought to adopt was over. He was overtaken by confusion and desolation. He had no choice but to explore the secular world, create new goals and find an answer to his sexual dilemma. Undoubtedly the most significant outcome throughout Matthew's journey is that he gradually succeeded in respecting himself. All aspects of his self, including the sexual, are in total awareness, but Matthew still struggles to accept himself.

> I am a gay person, I accepted it, and I am trying to integrate it into my life. But somehow, I needed something else which could help me bring order, which would help me understand the purpose of my life, which could help me integrate this aspect of sexuality with the rest of my life.

Being different, he still finds it rather difficult to receive God's love. A problem that has arisen is his desire to know how to serve God as a gay person. While he is befriending his sexuality, he desires to know his vocation. This is a sign that suggests that theological virtues are slowly molding his vision.

The Passive Night of Sense

In this aspect of the night, God's acts of love toward the soul subtly become visible. John of the Cross has realized that the advancement in spirituality signifies a relationship between God and the person. In the case of the active night, progress is in the hands of a person's sense of necessity, but here attention is given to God's initiative. Contrary to the dynamics of the active night, one cannot be too sure when God indeed acts towards the soul. His ways and plans are in the substance of the soul.

Trying to identify elements of the *passive night of sense* in the participants' narratives did not yield many results. For the most part, expressions revolved around the first two phases of the night. Most participants are either striving in their self-denial of their attachments or have not realized how insecure their inner faculties are with God. What they strive to acquire or protect is an identity that interprets God's will towards them. Such signs indicate the need for the *passive night of sense* which, according to John, purifies the soul's grip to control the divine relationship. Although in the narratives, much was attributed to God, by John's criteria, it could be otherwise. Only Peter mentioned the virtue of contemplation, which is an essential feature here.

Obstacles and Signs

The *active night of sense and spirit* brought out much spiritual empowerment in Peter. However, many doubts still linger. Unanswered questions persist, relating to his role as a parent and to how to put principles of social justice into practice. These doubts can be associated with the soul's unintentional resistance, which still mistrusts God.

The primary sign that revealed God's intent to meet the soul without any intermediaries excluding faith was the rise of spiritual poverty. Everything that Peter possessed, externally and interiorly, became insufficient instruments in communication. He had no one to turn to who would assure him. Even God seemed to disappear. Until he perceived the new ways, God seemed distant and unapproachable. His experience of infertility can be linked to his desperate state when anger and resentment emerged.

> I never imagined how great the wish for children can be, and how difficult it is to witness such a frustrating wish. The experience of praying with such desire [and] earnest, and it seems like God remains silent.[31]

The image of the Jews in the desert corresponded to his experience. When he saw other families, he felt hurt by envy. He was rather angry with God when he could not understand why God seemed to abandon him. In the face of his earnest desire, God's silence pierced him further. As he could not find any consolation, he concluded that his life was ruined and that his despair would never come to an end.

Remedy and Outcome

In such case, John of the Cross' remedy is to be patient, to confine in God and to let Him approach the person subtly. As one strives to understand, John's advice was not to worry but to approach and trust God through the merits of contemplation. A new strength is infused in the substance of the soul, and this leads to the transformation of desire and restoration of character. John of the Cross describes this space as the *spiritual betrothal* between the soul and God.

When he looked back, Peter concluded that God remained faithful to him, but at the time, he could not comprehend how. Peter found being a

---

31. "Qas kont nimmaġina kemm tista' tkun kbira din ix-xewqa għall-ulied u kemm hi iebsa tara x-xewqa frustrata. The experience of praying with such desire, earnest u donnu Alla jibqa' kwiet."

father to his adoptive children rather difficult. Although their welfare was central to what God expected from him, gaining their trust was not easy. Peter witnessed the slow dynamics of love. He concluded that to gain love, one had to be patient, be available to others and trust in the goodness of the other. His predominant desire was to love and care for them, but this did not depend only on him. Through this process, desires and temperament were transformed, and new strength developed. On asking Peter to speak specifically about his witness of God, he uttered these words:

> One important revelation was experiencing infertility. Did I see God there? I saw God as bigger than me, sometimes hard to understand, but in some strange way, He is always faithful. Nowadays, my heart is full with all the children I have, in a way I never imagined. That's one example; another is the way my parents loved me and their simplicity. It seemed like [we were] a normal family, but looking back, I learnt [the meaning of] unlimited and unconditional love. As I had witnessed, my parents live in this manner.[32]

Peter described how the parable of the prodigal son,[33] especially the image of the father waiting on the roof, applied to him: not only in the way he was living with his children but his relationship with God. The same dynamics he faces today as a father suddenly were analogous to the relationship between him and God. In his role as a father, Peter assumed the attributes and aspects of God—fatherhood. All the dynamics of the relationship, how the son responded, what he felt for his son, all led to greater intimacy and responsibility: unconditional love. Peter's continuous prayer was devoted to this new connection which was a result of the virtue of contemplation. God is felt nearer in mysterious ways, which Peter was unable to decipher and describe fully. Like his son, God expects Peter to respond gently. However, Peter is not yet assured and convinced about this way. Thus, as he slowly adapts to dark faith, he seeks spiritual direction to appraise God's presence in his life.

---

32. "One important block of revelation was experiencing infertility. Have I seen God there? I have seen God as being bigger than me, sometimes hard to understand, but in some strange way he is always faithful. Illum il-ġurnata qalbi mimlija bit-tfal li għandi b'mod li qatt ma immaġinajt. Dak eżempju wieħed, ieħor il-mod kif ħabbewni, is-sempliċità t'ommi u ta' missieri. Kienet tidher normal family, imma meta llum inħares lura tgħallimt inħobb mingħajr expectation, without stopping. Għax rajt lil missieri u lil ommi jgħixuha."

33. Luke 15:11–32.

The Passive Night of Spirit

When considering all the criteria governing the last phase of the *dark night*, it appears that none of the participants met the criteria. Faith is not yet their sole instrument of communion with God. Even Peter, although dedicated to contemplation and passed through the purification of selfishness, it was too early for him to mention faith as the safest and most secure means to approach God. At the same time, one appreciates that all the deepest desires of the participants are directed towards this night. Specifically, they all desire to achieve complete synchronization of self where spirit and sense operate in harmony. Their desire was to fulfil God's will, even if they misunderstood it. Carrying out a social role is not enough, as it only articulates a strong longing to be part of God's flock. The men expressed their love and commitment towards God through their activities. Although such desires are imbued with self-preservation, one cannot ignore the desire to work for the kingdom.

The lack of results in this phase could also be attributed to the class of participants in this research. Although all the merits of John of the Cross' doctrine were adequately outlined in the scheme, in the case of the participants' sample, there were limitations. Since the last phase of the *dark night* is so specific and intimate to the person, and as John states, the use of plain language becomes redundant to describe it, it makes sense that men who are in this phase would not agree to participate in such research. The reason for adopting this attitude could be various:

1. Fear that nobody would comprehend them when they relate their experiences;
2. Concern that they would be judged, and their experiences considered meaningless and nonsensical; and,
3. Disquiet that sharing their experiences might lead them to feel proud of being favored by God, and communication with God would be severed.

Sketching Men's Spiritual Form

While phase one related the life narratives of participants with John of the Cross' spiritual trajectory, in phase two, several characteristics mold the form of spirituality. These observations are interpretations and thus depart from the participants' specific viewpoint. Each one is coded as OB with a number associated with it, so in phase three, all observations are related to the spiritual directors' input. Primarily these observations focus on the expectations participants hold for themselves and their lives and how, in the end, they are transposed unto God.

OB1. The Origins of Attachments

From the previous analysis, one notes how all attachments are originally neutral objects among others in the world. They become attachments when the soul perceives them as essential and relies on them for its survival. A closer look shows that the place where values were learnt and acquired was in childhood. The family is the primary source. Relatives, especially parents, instilled a set of moral codes that the son had to live up to. While principles engender conduct, goals evolve into expectations. While meeting these expectations bring about consolation, failure gives rise to shame and sadness.

OB2. The Consumption of Attachments

Expectations one holds are part of the interior possession about which John of the Cross speaks in the *active night of spirit*. From the narratives, one notes such expectations, which include academic achievement, social status, and reputation. These expectations are the parents' ideals for their sons. On the other hand, attachments are regarded as external possessions that either point towards dedication to reach the ideal or function like garments that the soul puts on to show off its achievements. Other sources that influence and may accentuate these attachments and expectations are mental disorders, extraordinary family circumstances, secondary socialization, media, societal and cultural ideals at the time.

However, one finds two contrasting reactions in men that were interviewed: those who meet the expectations of their parents and those who disappoint them through their failure. Those who assent to their parents' expectations adopt them as their desires. Objects such as books, religious activities, or academic merit that parents would influence one to engage with develop into attachments for the soul. The soul would not know anything else except that which the parents provided. The soul not only does its utmost to flourish in these objects, but it protects them since in protecting them, it protects itself and the satisfaction they impart. One notes that many of the participants made their parents happy through participating in these objects, even in adulthood. Consequently, the sons remain an extension of the parents.

In contrast, those who disappoint their parents meet their disapproval. In such cases, the parents seek to guide their sons, resulting in diminished self-esteem. Parents and sons may not be on the same wavelength with the result that the sons seek other outlets beyond the family unit. Labelled as rebellious, one notes how some participants indulged in drugs, alcohol, pornography and satanism. They remain an extension of their parents but through disagreement.

OB3. The Father's Recognition

The previous observation can be further refined. As to their parents, one notes that the participants do not regard their mothers and fathers the same way. A marked difference in their attitudes towards their parents prevails. Only Jude and James say that their father took a tough line with them. The other participants either did not mention how their father influenced their life or had a poor opinion of their father. Often the relationship between son and father is not clear, and amongst the interviewees, the father's influence was ignored. Even when invited to share more about their fathers, participants either did so quickly or changed the subject.

When the father disapproves of the son's behavior, the relationship can result in rejection by both parties, as if the sons subtly and internally declare that they do not wish to resemble their fathers. Thus, the constant position of the father is not clear, or distant or in direct conflict. What remains is the father's gaze upon the son. How their father looks at them either signifies strong disapproval or a complete lack of affection. A barrier is created. The father becomes the son's most fearful hindrance but must also be won over.

On the other hand, the mother figure is at the forefront of attention. She is approachable, intimate and forgiving to the son. She urges and encourages the son to conform to the ideals. In the case of Peter, she admonishes him not to abandon the engineering degree, while in Paul's case, his mother was instrumental in his pursuit of a business career. In some cases, one also notes how the mother camouflages the father. However, when the mother is also distant towards the son, as in the case of Thomas and Jude, matters take a turn for the worse as the son must face two challenges. Overall, five observations can be outlined:

1. the sons become aware of the differences in their parents' attitude early in childhood;
2. the mother is preferred as she is more approachable than the father, and so the delight she offers takes precedent;

3. fathers often keep themselves at a distance and thus are feared or ignored;

4. although the mother is much more in their thoughts, this does not mean that the father did not influence the participants in any way or that participants hold no regard for their father. The distance produces a greater struggle to discover what the father expects from them and how to bridge the differences to earn his love. Often the son gets the impression that he has to prove his worth with his father to merit his affection. However, some fathers are never satisfied with their son's performance; and,

5. different attachments reflect what the son receives from the parents. Often what the mother encourages takes precedent due to better affinity with the sons. On the other hand, other attachments may develop to replace the shortcomings or deficiencies of the father. These attachments often would be external to the family environment.

Where each participant falls on this spectrum depends on the relationship they hold with the parents. Also, the family culture has an impact on the sons.

OB4. The Formation of Identity

As the son faces the challenges of adulthood, their identity sets in. Their expectations are so ingrained that participants treat them as their desires. Mundane matters are all unconsciously directed to attain this desire which includes values, conduct and even their likings. Self-determination is present, but it is exclusive to those boundaries. Philip, Nathaniel, Luke, and Matthew exercised their free will and desired to enter a religious form of living, but at the same time, their freedom was limited. In the case of Peter, when he decided to change the course, he was pursuing, his mother strongly disapproved and was so concerned about his decision that he decided not to go ahead with his desire. The boundaries are very much in control of the parents since the expectations were theirs, to begin with. Even those who sought validation from outside the home, particularly James, Jude and in some ways Paul, created an identity made of values, conducts and possessions which confirmed their identity, which was contrary to what the family tried to mold in them.

In both scenarios, the man's identity adopts in a strong way everything that corresponds to the ideal but discards anything unrelated to it. Philip, Nathaniel, Andrew, Luke and Matthew abandoned the secular world. Influenced by the values at that time, mingling in the secular world while aspiring to become a priest was unacceptable. Similarly, James and Jude manifested the same pattern. Creating their deviant identities, they renounced the existing state of affairs, including the religious aspect. From these dynamics, two remarks can be made:

1. Identity enhances judgement on values not only on immediate objects, which are the soul's attachments but also on the broader context. Judgment is binary and submissive to the ideal that the soul desires to attain; and,

2. The soul thinks that by avoiding all enemies and obstacles that can menace the path towards the ideal, everything will be under control and succeed in life.

OB5. The Appearance of Failure

Change in participants' lives occurs when their attachments fail to grant fulfilment. From the narratives, one encounters two ways how this came about:

1. gradual inner emptiness and incompleteness disturb the soul. The more the soul tries to fill it by consuming the familiar attachments, the more it disrupts mental stability; and,

2. sudden events beyond the soul's control block the ability to engage with the attachments. Progress towards the ideal comes to an end.

The invitation to mortify attachments begins when the soul is subtly alerted by inner signs and feelings that matters are not functioning well in their life. However, since perspective is restricted and the soul knows nothing else but the dynamics of engaging with their attachments, they would resist and protect them even more. While in attachments, one finds comfort, security, and delight, in depriving them confusion and loss reigns. Attachments engulf a soul in a protective and sustaining shell, but at some point, cracks start to appear. Resistance against mortification appears in various ways:

1. disregard of the pricking of the conscience;

2. procrastinating action or finding excuses not to confront reality;

3. intensification of the dose when consuming familiar attachments, be it drugs, pornography, or workload;

4. directly trying to suppress the emptiness by exercising in severe self-discipline; and,

5. ecstatic feelings are sought from different sources to mitigate the state of misery or unhappiness.

John of the Cross indicated that the damage caused by attachment appear vividly when the soul fights back by employing various methods of resistances. The protective wall often gives way to some unfortunate event or when the soul cannot function reasonably due to melancholy. When resistance reaches its limits, a decision must be made by the soul: either to sink in misery or to seek help. The next act of mortification is to seek assistance since the soul ventures beyond its perception and no longer relies on itself. At this stage, the soul adopts a process of introspection as it searches for existential meaning. Nonetheless, resistance often keeps surfacing as the soul would be trying to confer with each attachment it possesses in a bid to determine the roots of these expectations and thus alleviate the shame, guilt, and fear in not reaching its goal. When mortification occurs and how long it takes is subject to the temperament of the soul. All participants have, to varying degrees, passed through this path.

Professionals and mentors have a critical role in the dynamics of mortification. Often the participants affirmed that spiritual directors, psychologists, and mentors contributed either to enhance self-awareness and self-love or complicated matters through their insensitivity or misinformation. Progress was noted when participants found a non-judgmental space to air their views. On the other hand, blame only augmented confusion and guilt.

A significant relationship has developed between each participant and their spiritual director. One can conclude that the professional relationship retrieved elements that were in a paternal relation. Often participants remarked indirectly how their spiritual directors acted towards them like a father, which their natural father failed to do. They valued the way that spiritual directors were approachable and empathetic to them. This resulted in empowerment to improve their lives.

OB6. The Continuous Reconfiguration of Identity

The process of mortification reconfigures identity as the soul distinguishes between what was inherited and its uniqueness, limitations, and desires. However, this is not a one-time process. The soul learns that introspection is a vital key to life and that the process of mortification is a continuous process throughout a lifetime. According to John of the Cross, it is impossible to renounce all external and internal possessions at one attempt. The depth of introspection and dissection is subjective to the soul's life story. However, with every act of mortification, identity expands. Paradoxically as the soul humbles itself, it ascends in new aspects. All participants are in this phase. The only differences lie in their degree of introspection and renunciation. Since the process of mortification is spiral, bringing further growth with every cycle, other features can be noticed that regulate the whole process. These are:

1. A soul's attachment becomes inordinate when the soul relies on it too greatly. Like an oil lamp, the soul will rely on the satisfaction from attachments until the oil lasts. Nobody knows the timing when an attachment would give way. However, in becoming aware, the soul realizes how other fundamental aspects of the dignity of being human were ignored. This can be seen from the interviewing exercise itself. A critical factor that stood out and influenced participants' life narratives was their mood. For instance, Andrew and Jude appeared heartbroken at experiencing such a challenging time. Their main focus was a particular recent matter in their life that provoked shock and confusion. Otherwise, the participants' mood was calmer. Despite narrating other difficult situations, during the interview, their approach was more serene;

2. At the time of renunciation, the soul resists surrendering. However, since every soul is unique, the degrees of resistance are subjective to temperament and how daring the soul is. Once again, nobody knows precisely how much a soul can oppose change nor the sources of strength that could compel progress.

3. The consolation and desolation that emerge from attachments affect the soul in different ways. Desolation, rejection, and failure impel the soul to move out of its comfort zone and flourish in other unperceived areas, while consolation and satisfaction make permanent the skills it acquires. Breaking away from old habits leads the soul to discover new freedom. The acquired consolation, in turn, further encourages the soul to continue relying on instruments like discursive meditation for self-awareness. However, the soul is not in control when these techniques will give way;

4. When the inner emptiness develops again, it is the right time for the soul to revisit itself by exploring new areas. The lingering sense of

emptiness demarcates incompleteness, and the limits of time in resolving some aspects of the newly acquired identity are again questioned;

5. Freedom inevitably includes grief. If the process of transformation impels the soul to examine what it inherited or acquired and forsake in varying degrees many of its interior possessions, then grieving what was or how things could have been is part of healing too. In this process, the source of power controlling identity is distilled. As self-determination and responsibility increase, the soul takes a contented stance and allows others to be disappointed over its unique way of existing without feeling shamed.

OB7. The Uncontained God

The element of God was intentionally omitted in the previous observations to show that the process of mortification and so, the dynamics of the *active night of sense and spirit*, fall under the domain of psychology rather than theology. Although participants mentioned their search for God to find the meaning of life, the theory of John of the Cross that possessions do not provide access to God is valid. One can argue that in many ways, God is put in an inferior position when compared to the ideals that participants held even when they followed religious practices such as discursive meditation. When the exercise of appropriation resulted in consolation, the soul affiliated them to God, but when no result ensued, God was perceived as silent or distant. One can argue that the fluctuations in the soul are not associated with God but are a result of the consequences of subscribing to an identity that returns to the same feelings that the soul experienced when it received gratification or disapproval from others, especially parents. Identity has been considered as a canister of possessions that the soul selectively chooses to build the self. Neither the successes nor the failures of identity can be attributed to God. Inevitably the question that arises: *How does God act?*

OB8. A Progressive Refinement of Perception

One can note how God accompanied participants when they modified their ideas and ways to access Him. The following fluctuations can be observed in participants:

1. Often participants adhered to a formulaic way of religious expression. As children, they had received religious teachings at catechism classes

and engaged in different practices reflecting the family's style. Later in life, these customs were either absorbed as essential values to live up to or rejected outright. Their decision depends on how as sons either conform to the expectations of others or not.

2. In both scenarios, participants continued to practice their methods as they provided some form of gratification, either through religious practices or secular ones. It is as if they declare that by adhering to the ways of their parents, God will favor them, or by rejecting him, nothing is truly lost. However, in the two scenarios, different outcomes ensued.

3. When what they depended on failed to sustain stability, both groups entered crisis. Through therapy and spiritual direction, one notices how the two groups change places. Those who conformed, faced dryness, and began to explore other non-religious aspects of being human. On the other hand, the rebellious, often through an ecstatic emotional experience, started to engage with religious practices. In both cases, participants began to regain what had been rejected earlier on in life. In exploring the other side, gradually, all human dimensions are left unturned, and the soul begins to question what they relied on in the past that defined them. The merit here is that the soul starts to judge God's nearness by its reflective capacity rather than relying on others.

4. Transparency towards God is subject to the level of self-awareness that the soul achieves and the merits of self-acceptance and self-love. For the most part, all participants are immersed in these processes. God is perceived as one that really loves the soul for its uniqueness, with the result that the soul slowly begins to often seek more of Him. New spiritual practices emerge. Most prominently, discursive meditation begins to appear through engaging in biblical reflection, active meditation often through the spiritual exercises of Saint Ignatius, attending retreats, spiritual lectures, and voluntary work, among others. All these practices lead to the following:

    a. Jesus becomes the new role model, which leads to a slow transformation of previously held ideals;

    b. a new expectation which can be described as the quest for the truth emerges; and,

    c. the newly derived knowledge produces consolations, and the soul feels favored by God.

5. Since dependencies are deeply rooted within the soul, becoming free of them necessitates a long process. Often the consolations derived from discursive meditation produces a dangerous perception. Most participants were of the opinion that by engaging in prayer and by doing so much for God, He would settle their life problems without any action on their part. As some participants learnt, they had to assume responsibility in their life and use their human skills when dealing with worldly matters. The soul realizes that it cannot rely heavily on the newly acquired means and in the consolation it derives from them, but must discern in a better way.

6. The only narrative that gives us more elements than the ones listed above is that of Peter. Nothing is taken for granted but how he describes his relationship with God denotes a mature spiritual perception as stated in the following observations:

   a. His ability to discern is clear. The participant was able to discern between what others expect of him and what he assents to assume. Nothing is attributed to God. As in the case of deciding to adopt, one can argue that today more methods are available as options, but the very fact that whatever he decided was not interpreted as God's will is important. What God stands for is ultimately distant from his responsibility;

   b. Following on point a, God's will is still sought, but it is received as something clear and at the same time vague. The participant was unable to describe in plain language what he receives, but ultimately it pushed him towards the theological virtues. Faith begins to emerge as a means of communication, and most of his actions settle in waiting for God; and,

   c. The dynamics in point b suggest an act of contemplation. It is not one of appropriation. Although the temptation to understand and control remains when Peter seeks answers from God, he instead receives accompaniment. God appears as one who is present with the participant amidst all the challenges as a father rather than one who settles his pending matters or provide the answers.

> I feel that sometimes I want to say, "Our Father, who is waiting on the roof," because there is so much meaning to that. There are many experiences that I've lived [through] that [are based] on this statement. It has a lot of meaning. If I had to choose one

factor that helped [me] understand the nature of God the most, [it would be that of] being a father. Not because I am supernatural, but because I [am experiencing] our relationship, what I feel for him, what he does for me, and the unconditional love that I experience. I realize it is unconditional when I'm faced with a challenge. I feel like this very often, though, this feeling of wanting a world of good for my son and my daughter. This teaches me how God regards me. Words fail me to explain better [than this].[34]

If God's preferred appearance is one that accompanies the soul with His presence rather than one who resolves matters, then one can revisit all narratives from this perspective. However, this research will now continue by associating these observations with the information derived from spiritual directors who have men as their directees.

---

34. "Inhossni li xi drabi nkun irrid nghid, 'Missierna li qed tistenna fuq il-bejt' because there is so much meaning to that. There are many experiences that I lived that stand on this statement. It has a lot of meaning. If I had to choose one factor that helped most understand in-natura t'Alla hu li nkun missier. Not because I am supernatural but because of seeing how the relationship goes, what I feel for him, and what he does for me, and the unconditional love that I experience. I know it is unconditional because then ninduna meta jkolli xi challenge. Imma ħafna drabi nħossni hekk, this feeling of wanting a world of good to my son and to my daughter. Din tgħallimni kif Alla jħares lejja. Words fail me to explain better."

Chapter 4

Companions of the *Dark Night*

Progressing from the previous phases in chapter three, this chapter introduces the views of spiritual directors. Spiritual directors offered a broad perspective of what goes on during spiritual direction and revealed different issues directees bring to their attention. Each director discussed four fields of tension: the characteristics that they identify in their male directees, their style of spiritual direction, the dynamics of transformation and how the social context can influence men. Presentation of the data will follow these four areas.[1]

FEATURES OF MALE SPIRITUAL DIRECTEES

Men approach spiritual directors, and they have reasons for doing so. The first area of inquiry was to explore the intentions of men. What the directors observed was men's desire to deepen the relationship with God as the primary motive of directees. However, as what directees understand by the word deepening might be subjective, directors were invited to qualify this statement. Following analysis, the different interpretations were grouped under five arguments:

1. Primarily directees desired to learn how to pray and access the divine in a better way. Through consultation with spiritual directors, they sought a space to speak about their personal experience of faith freely and expected to receive wise accompaniment.

---

1. Pseudonyms are being used when quoting spiritual directors to protect their identity.

2. Some directees were inspired to explore spirituality after listening to a homily, attending a seminar or following a conversation on social media. They would approach spiritual direction to satisfy the curiosity about this human ability.

3. Driven by an aspiration to be authentic, directees would seek spiritual direction to integrate all aspects of their lives, primarily those that bring about anxiety. They would bring questions about identity, vocation, and desires. Their primary motive would be to enhance their good qualities in their lives and align themselves with God. They would hope that by owning a heart attuned to God, a greater good is achieved. Spiritual directors mentioned two areas: men's desire to know God's will for them and to remain focused on their vocation in their everyday life.

4. Associated with the third point is men's desire to manage, in the light of the Christian faith, particular issues which cause anxiety, such as dissatisfaction with their careers, identity formation, sexuality, complex relations, disappointments, and conflict within communities. One spiritual director even mentioned politicians who sought discernment on ethical issues like artificial intelligence and the divorce bill.

5. Directees who made way in spirituality would approach spiritual direction to look for greater intimacy with God. Often they would be blocked or experiencing spiritual dryness.[2]

Although these five scenarios are evident across the ten directors, two spiritual directors observed that directees are not always so clear in their intentions. Some would not know what spiritual direction involves, but men's desire for authenticity clarifies as they open up. Within these five areas, one can also note two persisting elements: discernment and continuity. Discernment requires uncertainty, and evidently, men approach directors as they are in a not-knowing position. Furthermore, dedication to the quest for truth is equally visible. This dedication is often expressed by regularly meeting spiritual directors and by involving in spiritual and religious practices like retreats, voluntary work, liturgy, and evangelization. Discernment and continuity are the two vital prerequisites for men seeking spiritual directors. If directees are satisfied with their answers and are not engaged with the quest for truth, they would not bother about exploring spirituality. Moreover, it rests upon the director to identify men's intents and distinguish the task of spiritual direction from counselling, catechism, formation or pastoral care.

2. Apart from these five scenarios, one spiritual director mentioned that some would seek direction as a requirement for a course in spirituality that they have registered.

> Moses: One would have to see why a man comes for spiritual direction. What led him to come? Would someone like that know what is involved in spiritual direction? Some people don't know what spiritual direction entails. Some come because they would like to have a relationship with God. Others come because they would have gone through a very bad patch. And so, they come till they get over it.³

These observations are congruent with how the ten directees behaved with their quest for truth. Not only did they seek spiritual direction to deepen their relationship to God, but they sought it at a specific time when they willfully arose to its importance and understood that on their own, they would fail. Moreover, they were committed to searching for truth beyond the structures of direction by engaging in activities to enhance their perspective. In the past, they would not have thought of enrolling in a course on spirituality or frequenting a Christian group of friends or spending hours meditating on scripture.

However, six out of the ten spiritual directors mentioned another scenario. Some men approach spiritual directors when they are facing an existential crisis that demands an urgent call for help since these men would feel stuck in life and gripped by deep melancholy. Men would encounter a problem that leads them to perceive life as meaningless. While questioning their reality, managing the hopelessness becomes a pressing matter. Being in such a vulnerable state, they would be seeking some way to recover self-meaning. In such circumstances, reaching out to a spiritual director would be their ultimate act of courage, with some directees discontinuing spiritual direction once the crisis is resolved.

> Joshua: These are the three areas. There are those who feel crushed, and so they come at the last minute. "I'm in the dark. I feel I'm in an abyss. I don't have any other way out and so this is my last shot." Then there are those who have progressed, but at a certain point, they seem to falter, and so they want to continue on their way. [Lastly] I meet several of these cases: they want to deepen their experience and those who are still searching.⁴

---

3. "Jiddependi għalfejn raġel jiġi għad-direzzjoni spiritwali. X'qanqlu li jiġi? Min jiġi jaf x'jiġifieri direzzjoni spiritwali? Hemm min ma jafx x'inhi direzzjoni spiritwali. Hemm min jiġi għax irid relazzjoni m'Alla. Irid jikber. Hemm min jiġi għax qala' xi daqqa tajba. Allura jiġi sakemm joħroġ minnha."

4. "Dawn huma t-tliet areas. Mela min hu mkisser, allura, jiġi fl-aħħar minuta. 'Jiena fid-dlam, jiena fl-abbiss u m'għandix triq oħra u din l-aħħar għażla.' Hemm min mexa imma f'ċertu punt qisu waqaf u jkun irid jimxi aktar u minn dawn għandi diversi li jiġu: li jridu japprofondixxu, u oħrajn li qed ifittxu."

These observations by spiritual directors are also echoed within the ten directees' interviews. Some, like James, Nathaniel, and Jude, reached out to a spiritual direction at a point when they had met with an unsurmountable problem and felt estranged from life. After the crisis was resolved, they kept frequenting spiritual direction, but as Andrew shared, meeting his spiritual director diminished once he recovered meaning. Since this study rested upon spiritual directors to identify potential directees to act as participants in the interviewing process, this study does not have access to men who discontinued spiritual direction. However, the assertion that spiritual directees discontinue direction once they resolve their crisis is plausible.

After discussing the directees' intentions, spiritual directors were invited to outline features that they notice that directees bring during the sessions. Often these features were explicated through comparison to female directees. However, before proceeding with this path, this study noticed other contextual variables which regulate the directors' field of vision. These variables are only evident when all the separate transcripts are put together.

DEMOGRAPHICS

a. <u>Gender</u>: As a general observation, all spiritual directors, barring one, noted that more women than men attend spiritual direction. One lay director is an exception to this pattern, with all his clients being men.[5]

b. <u>Social class</u>: Not all spiritual directors have access to directees from all areas of society. Only six spiritual directors, who often have been engaged in spiritual direction for many years, appear to have a wider pool of men from different social strata. One spiritual director highlighted that his directees come from all areas of life. Some do not even attend the sacraments, and so they cannot be labelled as the typical middle-class Christian men and women who conform blindly to what the church says. The other four spiritual directors not only have a smaller pool of directees, but often their directees would have a tertiary degree or would be familiar with the basic concepts of spirituality. However, some directors noted that through retreats, they would be exposed to other social contexts.

---

5. This director could not explain why all his clients were men. However, throughout the interview, he shared that other spiritual directors referred him male directees to explore spirituality and the single life. As a result, this director developed a sort of specialization and reputation among spiritual directors.

CONTEXT OF DIRECTEES

What was noted were three contexts that distinguish the type of men who seek spiritual direction. The first subgroup includes men who educated in Jesuit institutions tend to seek directors who are either Jesuits or trained in Ignatian spirituality. This group is distinct from the others since they would have been nurtured in an exclusive culture. The second subgroup is made up of men involved in religious communities, but no distinct spiritual culture influenced their identity. While being familiar with different spiritual concepts, they would have picked insights from different contexts. In the third subgroup, one finds men who are not involved in any religious community. They might be aware of the different Christian lay communities, but one can describe these men as deviant in that their perspective places them outside of the prevailing religious consensus. No school of spirituality would have influenced them, and some might not be as committed to the practice of sacraments.

As noted in point b, not all spiritual directors are involved with these three subgroups in similar ways. Although all spiritual directors have contact with straight and gay men, only a handful have contact with gay couples or men who have separated or divorced from their marriages.

Although spiritual directors are aware that a spectrum of characteristics prevails among men and women, they still identified particular patterns. Their exposition points to one fundamental desire governing men's lives: *a deep desire to be loved by God*. Often this yearning is understood as the pursuit to be perfect, happy, successful, and ultimately good in front of God and others.

> Joshua: The common element which I see is that every person thirsts to feel comfortable before God. To be able to believe in him. It might be a subjective idea of God, even a false one, but in that erroneous idea, there will still be, just the same, an element of truth. There is also a spark of the life of the spirit. This is something one finds in everyone.[6]

This principle motive of men, which spiritual directors reveal, is not the distinctive characteristic between men and women. Both sexes share this deep desire of being good and loved by God. Being male or female does not matter in spirituality, as both have the same yearning. According to spiritual directors, the differences lie in their attitudes. This study will now comment

---

6. "Il-ħaġa komuni li nara hi li f'kull bniedem hemm l-għatx biex iħossu tajjeb quddiem Alla. Li jemmen fih. Issa tista' tkun idea t'Alla skont il-qies tiegħu, falza, imma xorta waħda f'dik l-idea falza hemm element ta' verità. Hemm element tal-ħajja tal-ispirtu wkoll. F'kulħadd komuni din."

on the several observations on men's attitudes mentioned by spiritual directors.

A Temperament that Values Self-Sufficiency

The general observation was that when men seek direction, they often already possess an energetic disposition towards life. They already own an individuality that accomplishes their masculinity through their personal goals, personality and other achievements. Men were described as self-determined, but they tend to rely heavily on their capabilities, predominantly on planning, investigation, and problem-solving skills. Often, the purpose of approaching spiritual direction would be to integrate issues that men's analytical aptitudes fail to resolve. When men's accustomed ways fail to attain a deep feeling of security, they would have no other option but to seek help. This feeling of disheartening occurs gradually or, in some cases, suddenly and then develops into a crisis.

> Samuel: In the case of a woman, it's a different question. Women seek help at a much earlier stage. But men seem to want to go the way of "doing it yourself"; then, when they don't manage, they seek help. This is what I see when I compare the two, and I see this difference even in the case of the women I guide.[7]

One spiritual director further clarified that sexual orientation does not affect this pattern. As a general observation, men, no matter if straight or gay, are self-determined and rely on themselves to find answers. Thus, they tend to approach spiritual direction much later than women.

> Moses: I have to draw a distinction between men and women. Men are very independent. When they come to you, they seem very independent. In other words, men typically take more control of their life. Other men who come for spiritual direction are usually successful in many aspects of life. Successful in the sense that they manage to live their life normally. They will go through ups and downs, they will experience failures and successes, but there you are. The masculinity comes through. In the sense that one can see the driving force of the man who takes the reins in his hands because he's the man. And what is interesting here is

---

7. "Naraha differenti minn nisa. In-nisa jfittxuha hafna qabel. L-irġiel donnhom, do it yourself, then when you cannot, seek help. Hekk nipprova nqabbilha, u anke man-nisa li nsegwi naraha din id-differenza."

that this does not depend on sexual orientation. It doesn't make a difference.[8]

Women seek assistance much earlier. Primarily, they seek a space to express their feelings and to be empowered in life. Directors described women as holding a broader and multi-layered perspective of life. What often drives them is their sensitivity and affectivity, which accomplish a better ability to form relations. Men tend to be confused about their affective domain and attach less importance to relationships. Spiritual directors noted that much of their intervention focuses on facilitating men to relate and make sense of their feelings.

A Linear Understanding of God's Will

How men consider the will of God is closely linked with the temperament of self-reliance. The spiritual directors interviewed repeatedly contended that men hold many misconceptions about how to discover what God wills for them. Often, they deem it a task that needs to be unraveled through their performance and good conduct. They do not consider the quest as a path to confront the self, which ultimately leads to a celebration of life, but would contain much waiting, sacrifice, and suffering.

> Jeremiah: Perhaps the dominant form is people talking about the will of God, and perhaps this stands from the fact that most of the people who have come to me for direction, and I, come from the background of Ignatian spirituality and have long standings with the Jesuits. It is a concept that people have many misconceptions about, and it is often the source of distress or difficulty in direction. The idea of finding the will of God for me. As though the will of God is something enclosed in Pandora's box and one learns about it at one's peril. This also applies to the people who come as clients. It was, especially in the early part of my life, where I came from, and it took me a while to understand more deeply what the will of God is, which is, essentially, my flourishing. Not an imposition. Not something to be guessed

---

8. "Ikolli naghmel distinzjoni bejn l-irġiel u n-nisa. Mela l-irġiel huma very independent. Meta jiġu jidhru li huma very independent. Typical men, jiġifieri, jieħdu l-hajja f'idejhom. L-irġiel l-oħra li jkolli u jiġu għal direzzjoni spiritwali ġeneralment huma rġiel li they are successful in many aspects of life. Successful in the sense of li they manage well in life fin-normalità. Ikun hemm ups and downs, ikun hemm failures u mhux failures, imma it is there. Il-masculinity tidher. Fis-sens, dik id-drive tar-raġel li jieħu r-riedni f'idejh u li he is the man. U hawnhekk, jiġifieri, li hu interessanti li ma jiddependix mill-orjentazzjoni sesswali. Ma tagħmilx differenza."

about. Not necessarily, again, a common misperception, something to be acted on, or not something involving mission, tasks and work. But essentially an invitation to a relationship; with God, particularly.

One director connects this attitude with how the Maltese psyche is modelled. According to him, since in Malta, celebration as a way of life is not accentuated, spirituality is reduced to something that needs to be performed through participation in events and missions.

An Emphasis on Conduct

Spiritual directors also argued that men are more concerned about their conduct than women. Being preoccupied with how good and perfect they appear, they lay much emphasis on their image. On the one hand, they want to be faithful to God, but on the other hand, they wish to remain relevant in the presence of others. Particular emphasis is laid on sexual sins like masturbation and, in some cases, watching pornography. Often sexual expression arouses feelings of guilt and anguish, especially in men who keep engaging in this behavior even after maturing in spirituality.

> Samuel: The relationship with God, which I see is characteristically expressed by men in terms of morals. Morals in the sense "Am I doing the right thing, am I making the right choices?" Specifically in relation to the family and to work. These are the two specific areas. I am a Christian, and I need light and guidance and somebody to reassure me that I am making the right choices.[9]
>
> . . . I see that certain men tend to give their spiritual life a more moralistic angle, and this comes out in guidance, "Am I doing the right choices? Am I giving a good example to my family?" and even prayer tends to be concentrated around this theme. I think that every person lives a reality through which they perceive everything. I see this tendency mostly in men.[10]

---

9. "Ohrajn nara li r-relazzjoni m'Alla, il-lingwaġġ, il-karatteristika fl-irġiel hija l-morali. Il-morali fis-sens, 'am I doing the right thing and the right choices?' B'mod speċifiku fil-familja u x-xogħol. Dawk iż-żewg areas b'mod speċifiku. Jiena Nisrani u għandi bżonn dawl u guidance u akkumpanjament illi qed nagħmel the right choices."

10. ". . .ċerti rġiel narahom illi l-ħajja spiritwali jagħtuha iktar xejra moralistika u allura l-akkumpanjament, 'am I doing the right choices? Qiegħed inkun ta' eżempju tajjeb għall-familja tiegħi?' Anke t-talb idur ma' din il-ħaġa. Jiena nara illi kull persuna għandha realtà li minnha tara kollox. Dawn l-iktar li narahom fl-irġiel."

> Daniel: But obviously, with men, there is also areas of sexuality with the usual things, part of what being male means, and the area usually brings a lot of anguish, masturbation, for example. Not always, but sometimes they do. It would be a concern. It's about the whole personality, one's maleness.

Directors noted that men's sense of transgression immobilizes them as they perceive God's condemnation over them and thus, become discouraged. They fixate on self-pity even though they know that God is merciful. Purification of guilt and working for integration would take much attention in spiritual direction. Directors attribute these dynamics to a history of indoctrination that men had concerning sexuality which further engenders insensitivity and deficiency in affectivity. They mentioned how some religious groups adopt and promote a rigid attitude against sexuality. Often grey areas are ignored, and sexual expression develops into a taboo. Much of the work of spiritual directors focuses on undoing the rigid misconceptions and helping directees view sexuality as a positive human quality.

Resistance to Surrender Control

How the distance between the soul and God is bridged is always a source of struggle. In front of God's mystery, men would feel anxious that what they own in terms of meaning might be taken away. Spiritual directors noted that men act in this way since they would not have decentralized themselves. Only after they pass through purification do they realize how they are always at the receiving end with God. God's nearness is often qualified as disempowerment since matters would not be fully in their control. Men wrestling with God is the predominant figure in their spirituality. Women lament when God is perceived as silent or distant. They not only desire to be led but unite with the suffering of Christ much more easily. Directors described women as better disposed to stay with suffering even for a long time to bring reconciliation and goodness in the relationship. Instead of surrendering, men choose to show affection through commitments and acts of love. Rather than staying with grief, they would want to minimize it to bring out goodness.

> Joshua: On a somewhat less deep level, a man finds it very difficult to let go, whereas a woman is more open to abandon herself to the mystery. A man finds it difficult to let go because he is still attached to his point of reference. Because in his heart of hearts, a man realizes he is not a man, but he is always at the receiving end, always. And one of the challenges I meet in the

spiritual direction of men is precisely this, that a man often is not accepting—although there is a whole spectrum of possibilities—he doesn't want to be on the receiving end. He wants to be God himself.[11]

However, directors noted that although these acts are to be admired, men engage in such a way to retain control and indirectly to keep God at bay. Even their language exposes this. The servant motif is the predominant figure of speech used to describe their relationship with God. They would want to be good disciples by acting towards the kingdom but considering the divine relationship as spousal would be challenging for men to relate.

> Moses: I know that God is there. I have a good relationship with him. I am in control. Please leave me in control even if I have to ruin things, but I am in control. And when finally the situation gets out of hand, and then I am no longer in control, then I will go to him (for direction). It seems there is this dimension, it's as if it's a question of a friend, or my elder brother, or my father. Here is the contradiction. Close, but at a distance. And when I mess things up, then, surely enough, I come to you. This is why I put it as a matter of losing control. On the other hand, if I had to mention one characteristic in the case of women, I would put it like this: "Why is he so far away?" It's as if I caused you some offence. But in the case of men, as long as God is at a distance, "thank you. When I need your help, I'll let you know. You don't have to come close. I will tell you myself when I need you." This is the dynamic. But in my experience, the feeling of being distant troubles women.[12]

---

11. "Fuq livell, biex nghidu hekk, inqas profond, ir-raġel isib diffikultà kbira biex jintelaq, filwaqt li l-mara hi miftuħa aktar għat-telqien tal-misteru. Biss isib biex diffikultà għax ikun għadu ma nsiehx iċ-ċentru. Għax fiċ-ċentru r-raġel jagħraf illi hu mhux raġel. Imma hu always in the receiving end, always. U fid-direzzjoni spiritwali waħda miċ-challenges li nsib f'dik li hi d-direzzjoni tal-irġiel hi din; li r-raġel ma jridx jaċċetta ħafna drabi, mhux dejjem ta, spectrum, ma jridx li he is on the receiving end. He wants to be God himself."

12. "Naf li Alla qiegħed hemm. Għandi relazzjoni tajba miegħu. I am in control. Please leave me in control anke jekk infattarha, imma I am in control. Meta mbagħad taħrab is-sitwazzjoni minn idejja, u mbagħad I am not in control, imbagħad immur għandu. Hemm qisu din id-dimensjoni, qisu ħabib; my elder brother, my father. Hemm qiegħda, contradiction. Close but at a distance. Imma mbagħad meta propju nfattarha, e come una puttana, niġi għandek. Għalhekk qed ngħid losing control. Mentri l-mara, jekk ikolli nieħu karatteristika hi, 'għaliex qiegħed 'il bogħod? Qisu għamiltlek xi ħaġa.' Mentri raġel, sakemm Alla qiegħed 'il bogħod—'Thank you. Meta għandi bżonnok ngħidlek. M'għandekx għalfejn tersaq. Meta għandi bżonnok ħa ngħidlek jien.' This is the dynamic. Mentri mara, mill-esperjenza tiegħi, 'il bogħod idejjaqhom."

A contradiction is noted. Although men would consider themselves as friends of God, they do so as long as the distance remains. Whenever they feel that God has favored them, men tend not to be regular in prayer. While being aware that God is present, they take this relationship for granted. They recognize that if matters suddenly take a turn to the worse, they can seek God anytime. As one spiritual director noted, God becomes more of a prostitute than a friend.

Men and the Trinity

One spiritual director discussed how men relate to the persons of the Trinity. According to him, Jesus is often the predominant figure. They would be looking for a visible figure on whom to model their lives. Later, through spiritual direction, men are led to relate with the Holy Spirit and the gifts imparted to the soul. This spiritual director noted that God the father used to be the predominant person in men's minds, but according to him, tables have turned. Often, men's issues with their fathers were transposed onto God and would have been a subject dealt in spiritual direction, but nowadays, they are becoming even more remote in their sons' lives. Directees would hold a fragmented image of God the Father. According to this director, there is a new phenomenon of the absent mother in the child's formative years and questions who is replacing these imperative images in children's minds. However, this spiritual director is also aware that often men transpose unto him the father image. Without realizing it, directees seem to be developing a bond and idealizing him like a father they never had. Other spiritual directors noted that God, the father, is the primary person of the Trinity that men often relate to while women tend to relate mainly with the image of Jesus.

> Abraham: I do not find in my spiritual direction people that are mainly concerned with the father figure or God the father. I do not think so. It would be there, obviously, but it wouldn't be what they are coming with themselves. I might identify it and see it if they have a problem with the father figure transferred onto God, but when that happens, it happens. But it is not the main thrust of men, I find. What they are seeking is a relationship with Jesus: to understand him, to have him in their life, to please him and to walk with him and to encounter him.
>
> Sometimes I have to be very careful, especially when it comes to vocational discernment. I have to be so careful because without young men realizing, he would be developing a bond with me, as a priest as a Jesuit, also idealize me who would be a father

to him possibly a father he never really have. As young people often idealize their father, I have found they idealize me, and that can so easily become "I have a vocation." They would not say "like me," but as I used to hear, "my father is a doctor, so I want to become a doctor."

> Moses: As a man and as a woman, they obviously relate in different ways. Women relate more to Jesus. A man talks more about God. I have never gone into this. A woman is more engaged with Jesus, whereas a man is turned more to God. One is invisible, and the other is visible, tangible, a human being, a man. The other is God.[13]

Distinct Characteristics owning to Social Identity

One aim of this research is to explore specific features among single, separated, or married men or gay men in a relationship. The data derived for this specific inquiry is sketchy since only a small number of spiritual directors have access to this information under investigation. However, the general agreement is that in all scenarios, the spiritual path would be identical. The soul must come to love one self through purification and slowly proceed to offer oneself anew.

Married Straight Fathers

The general issue in straight married couples is that often the spouses take each other for granted. Men tend to give much attention to their wives during spiritual direction, but the tension would be one of misunderstandings and miscommunication. One spiritual director also attributed abuse as a barrier between married couples. He encountered situations when directees would have a history of abuse which consequently disrupted the marriage. Through spiritual direction, he would lead the person to greater awareness about the source of conflict and empower the directee to reveal it to their spouse.

> Moses: As far as relationships are concerned, in a heterosexual couple in which the man is straight, the woman takes him for

---

13. "Obviously, bħala raġel u bħala mara, jirrelataw b'modi differenti. In-nisa iktar jirrelataw ma' Ġesù. Raġel iktar jitkellem fuq Alla. Qatt ma dħalt fiha hekk. Mara iktar fuq Ġesù, raġel iktar Alla. Wieħed inviżibbli u l-ieħor viżibbli, tanġibbli, bniedem, raġel. L-ieħor Alla."

> granted. However, women do this too on a different level. OK they quarrel, and there will be tension between them, but the problem is that one does not understand the other and vice versa. Women think in a certain way and men in another.[14]
>
> Daniel: For example, even men and women in the context of counselling; the effort of men trying to understand women because the mechanism is very different and I always suggest this book, "Man are from Mars, Women are from Venus" because it is true because there are contexts when men do make an effort.

When considering the wife's role in the interviews of the directees, one notes a difference. Peter's wife was a prominent person he referred to in his narrative. He accentuated his wife's artistic perspective, which completed his logical perception. From his account, it appears that they complemented each other. Tension between the couple can be subtly observed in Peter's narrative when he spoke about the resistance he held to the idea of adopting. The wife first came up with the idea, and Peter had to make sense of the option. Thus, the content of spiritual direction for Peter would inevitably include discussing the wife's option.

On the other hand, Paul accentuated how he is aware of how often he takes for granted his wife and how she gently probes him to give attention to their marriage. Throughout his interview, Paul gave much more importance to the dynamics with his previous spiritual direction and began to speak of his marriage when probed to do so. This might indicate that Paul still has not resolved the wound of those events, and although abuse might be a punitive term to describe those events, one can notice how the past can block one from giving appropriate attention to their marriage.

Moreover, two spiritual directors noted a shift in perspective by men they accompanied through the sacrament of marriage. As men become fathers, their perspective of life transforms. In the past, they sought God as sons filled with a desire to impress and do for him, but as fathers, they are more conscious of responsibility. Even the relationship with God focuses more on the paternal aspect.

> Samuel: I have found that in some cases, certain men have a sense of sonship. A sense of God as a father, and this, so to speak, has an almost very human basis, as if it was their own fatherhood. In some cases, I have found that this applies in a special way to

---

14. "Fejn jidħlu relationships qisu in a heterosexual couple, straight men, il-mara tieħdu for granted. Anke n-nisa, imma on a different level. It's okay, iġġieldu u jkun hemm tension imma l-kwistjoni tkun wieħed ma jifhimx lill-oħra. U l-oħra ma tifhimx lill-iehor. Mara taħseb mod u raġel jaħseb mod ieħor."

those whom I would have accompanied previously and had now become parents. As soon as they become parents, they begin to discover more and more God's fatherhood. Some of these cases involve persons I would previously have accompanied before they got married, and their outlook would have undergone a transformation.[15]

Single Straight Men

Spiritual directors differentiated between three types of single men they encounter in their ministry. Each bringing specific needs:

One spiritual director noted that some single men never risk doing something radical about their life. They always resist, and at the same time, they grumble about their life. They remain immobile with no purpose. Years pass with no transformation. Such men pose a considerable challenge to spiritual directors since with God, one also has to risk loving.

> Joshua: Now, in my experience of single men, there are some who have never found their way, they never decide on their way, because sometimes it happens that they are cowards: if I follow this path there's a risk, if I follow the other, I will also be at risk . . . one cannot move forward with people like this. I am being blunt, but one cannot go forward because they are the kind of people who present me with the greatest challenge. They come for direction, yet they do not have an aim in life, and they don't want to find one. They don't want to commit themselves to a certain style of life. These are the more complex cases, those involving single men. They come at the age of thirty or thirty-four, or even going to forty, and still, one cannot register any progress. They are still rooted to the same spot they were on when I last saw them ten years before. They cannot take a decision and so one cannot do anything with people like this. Even if one proposes to them a sacrifice in the footsteps of Jesus Christ, it would be futile because of the risk involved. In the long run, such people stop coming after a certain number of years.[16]

15. "Fi whud sibt li ċertu rġiel għandhom sens ta' wlied. Is-sens of God, the father li huwa, biex ngħidu hekk, għandu bażi kważi ħafna umana, kważi l-fatherhood tagħhom. Xi whud minnhom sibt li b'mod speċjali anke dawk li tkun akkompanjajthom qabel u wara li saru ġenituri. Kif isiru ġenituri jibdew jiskopru iktar din il-paternità ta' Alla. Ftit minnhom dawn akkumpanjajthom qabel u żżewġu, u l-perspettiva tkun inbidlet."

16. "Issa, l-esperjenza tiegħi ta' single men: hemm single men li ma sabu qatt triqithom. Li waslu li ma ddeċiedu qatt fuq triqithom għax xi kultant ikunu beżżiegħa; għax

Two spiritual directors noted that some single men have consciously chosen to live a celibate life. They consider their single status as a mission and attend spiritual direction to discuss their chosen lifestyle.

> Jeremiah: And then another category would be celibate men. I mean, celibate not necessarily identifying as straight or as gay but fundamentally identifying as celibate. So, the big questions about the single life, the spiritual value of this, the relational challenges that come from it. I can think of two people in the past with whom I have conversations about this.

> Joshua: And then there are those who are single by choice. And it is a very specific choice. One could have someone choosing to be single in order to really offer oneself as a layman in some field. Yes, certainly. I have in mind people like those who join the MUSEUM they would have decided to adopt a missionary life but on their own. Very often, they already have a prayer life and they would be striving for union with Jesus Christ.[17]

Lastly, directors noted that some single men desire a relationship and yet fail in their intentions. Their failure would cause much suffering as they evaluate their life. These men tend to have an identity crisis since they feel incomplete for failing to have a relationship and a family.

> Joshua: Then there are single people by imposition, so to say. And in such cases, one finds a great sense of failure, a sense of not having succeeded. Their numbers are increasing. And then there are single people because of suffering or trauma, and in such cases too, this is an imposition. There are different kinds.[18]

---

naghmel hekk riskju, jekk naghmel hekk niehu riskju . . . ma' dawn in-nies ma tistax timxi. Qed inkun goff, għax ma tistax timxi għax huma l-iktar nies li jipprezentawli challenge. Jiġu għad-direzzjoni però m'għandhomx skop u ma jridux isibu skop. Ma jridux commitment, stil ta' ħajja. Nithassarhom fl-istess ħin. Dawn huma l-aktar tip difficli ta' single men. Jiġi ta' tletin, ta' erbgħa u tletin, iż-żmien għaddej, erbgħin, u fejn inti għadek. Fuq l-istess maduma li ħallejtek għaxar snin ilu. Deċiżjoni ta' xejn u allura ma' dawn ma tistax. Għax anke jekk tipproponilhom sagrifiċċju ta' Ġesù Kristu, imma għax hemm riskju. Fl-aħħar mill-aħħar dawn in-nies jispiċċaw biex jaqtgħu wara snin."

17. "Imbagħad hemm dawk li huma single b'għażla. U għażla speċifika. Jista' jkollok single għax verament irid joffri lilu nnifsu bhala lajk xi mkien. Iva u żgur. Qed ngħidlek bhal tal-mużew, iddeċieda fuq hajja ta' missjoni, però waħdu. Hafna drabi jkollhom hajja ta' talb u jimxu lejn l-għaqda ma' Ġesù Kristu."

18. "Single b'impożizzjoni, biex ngħidu hekk. Anke dawk, allura hemm ikun hemm sens kbir ta' falliment, sens ta' 'ma rnexxejtx.' Qed jiżdiedu dawn. Imbagħad ikollok singles għaliex minħabba sofferenzi fil-ħajja, trawma fil-ħajja, u dik ukoll hi imposta. Hemm diversi."

When considering the two participants who fall in this subgroup, James and Nathaniel, one notices that their contribution does not fit quite well within these three categories outlined by spiritual directors. The need to be in a relationship did not feature prominently in James' interview. He shared that although he is available for a relationship, it does not indicate that he is passing through an identity crisis for failing to be in one. James shared that he is honest in his intentions when meeting someone new but does not hold back to reject offers for a relationship if the other person does not hold a similar perspective of life as his.

As for Nathaniel, since he was a priest and, at present, in a relationship, he also does not fit in the subgroups outlined by spiritual directors. His narrative revolved around his experience of priesthood and how he made sense of the grief he faced. It can be argued that Nathaniel's story would form part of the experience that priests bring to spiritual directors, but this area is beyond this study's scope.

Separated Straight Men

According to two spiritual directors, these men also tend to have an identity crisis. Their failed marriage would lead to many doubts about their masculinity and future, especially for failing to meet others' expectations. As a general observation, directors noted that men long for a family, but they consider it as an extension and enhancement of their masculinity. These two directors stressed that they consider men's conscience the ultimate source of truth and do not oppose these men's behavior if they begin to explore other relationships. Often these men reach a better resolution of what occurred in their first marriage through other relationships. However, not all spiritual directors feel comfortable with this attitude. Some would not accept these men as directees and prefer to refer them to others.

> Moses: Separated or divorced, even single gay men. A crisis in masculinity. "Why? Why am I a man?" Again, losing ground, losing control, losing, that's the issue. It is said that usually women get married because they want children, and a man marries because he wants the woman, but it's not so clear cut. Which means, a man gets married because he wants a family. It's like when a woman marries and wants [children]. [For] women it is different, the perspective is different. A woman wants a family, and she is primarily moved because she needs a man to have children. After she has children, he [loses importance]. A man gets married because he wants a family and ironically what he

searches for in [his woman] is to enhance his masculinity, [approval] and also to show off his masculinity. She becomes his extension. A woman marries to have children, and then the husband [moves down to] third or fourth class.[19]

Thomas and Jude are the two directees that fall in this category. In both cases, the observations done by spiritual directors can be noticed. Marriage failure brought upheaval for both men, but the point of difference is their nature of expectations. While Thomas was afraid to decide and be in conflict with his mother's expectations, Jude held no expectations from others but created his own out of his need to fit in an ideal lifestyle according to his understanding of Christianity. In the case of Jude, the crisis is more evident as the wound is fresh. However, congruent with the spiritual directors' observations, Thomas resolved his crisis by working on himself and entering into a new relationship, leading him to compare the relationships. Thomas indicated that his spiritual director did not insist that he renounces the extramarital relationship he had developed as it was the only source of affection he was experiencing. However, Thomas also indicated that his spiritual director guided him to listen to his consciousness and seek the truth about his life.

Single Gay Men

Most spiritual directors stated that they have contact with gay men. Their intervention focused on assisting gay men to arrive at self-acceptance and to view their sexuality as God's gift. However, following recognition, men tend to raise questions about how to live their identity in the light of the Christian faith. The path towards acceptance might be challenging as former expectations are purified. Men would need to affront these failures of how one imagined life to be but slowly discover a new freedom. A more significant challenge to integrate sexuality was noted. Directors added that often sexuality becomes the ultimate and most emphasized feature in the

19. "Separated or divorced, anke single gay men. Tidħol fi kriżi l-maskulinità. 'Għalfejn? Għalfejn jien raġel?' Again, losing ground, losing control, losing . . . that's the issue. Is-soltu n-nisa ngħidu jiżżewġu għax iridu t-tfal u r-raġel jiżżewweġ għax irid il-mara però it's not that clear cut. Jiġifieri raġel jiżżewweġ għax irid familja. Bħal meta mara tiżżewweġ, tridhom. Il-mara differenti, il-perspettiva differenti. Mara trid familja u, primarily, she is moved għax għandha bżonn ir-raġel biex ikollha t-tfal. Imbagħad ir-raġel jista' joqgħod. Ir-raġel jiżżewweġ għax irid familja u, ironically, what he searches in her is to enhance his masculinity, approves and also show off his masculinity. She becomes his extension. Il-mara tiżżewweġ biex ikollha t-tfal, imma mbagħad ir-raġel isir third or fourth class."

relationship with God. Part of the spiritual direction intervention would involve elevating this aspect in line with other human features.

> Jeremiah: With the few homosexual men whom I have encountered in spiritual direction, this is an issue, sometimes an issue which they need to explore more, sometimes a question of being liberated in. For example, coming to terms not so much with a person's homosexuality as coming to a recognition to this part of me as an image and likeness of God, and therefore also ordered towards my salvation, the consummation of my relationship with God. But then comes the very practical questions about what kind of relationship, what is conducive to growth in this relationship, it would be easy to simplify or oversimplify and focus on, "does that mean sexual relations are prohibited or not?" The challenge in spiritual direction would be not to focus on this as the first or the ultimate or the central matter, but to focus on relationship and then the expressions of that relationship which are conducive to growth or not conducive to growth. And growth not only in the relationship with the partner or the person, growth in the relationship with God and growth in the relationship with the wider world, which we belong, including the Church, which we belong. And there we are not only threading on sacred ground but on ground that is unexplored and has been unexplored for a long time.

Luke, Matthew, Philip and Andrew are the four participants who identified themselves as gay. The four narratives gave much attention to their coming out process, which is congruent with what spiritual directors have mentioned about this subgroup. However, the question of how to live sexuality is subject to the directees' confidence in being gay. Not all directees are fully assured in their identity, and for the most part, sexuality is still the central article that gears everything else in their life.

Gay Men in a Relationship

Gay men in a relationship made up the minor group out of the five that spiritual directors have as clients. Only two directors could share some features about their reality. One director noted that the significant challenge gay couples face is that they ritually challenge each other since they are both men or women, mainly who will control the relationship. It is different from the struggles that heterosexual couples face. Since both are men, they would recognize the patterns of fighting for control since they have the same features too.

> Moses: And then you have gay couples, both men and women. The major challenge is that they relate to each other through struggle. That is, they relate to each other, but their image is of two friends. They have to ritually fight. They settle down, but that's still there: the struggle and the question of who controls remains there. You could tell me, isn't it the same between a man and a woman? Yes, it's there, but in a different way.[20]

Another spiritual director also has contact with one gay couple who attends spiritual direction. He is aware that this is new ground for him to tread. Sometimes they attend as a couple, but often they attend the sessions separately. According to him, he does not recognize any major differences between gay and straight couples. The themes they discuss would be about values and prayer, but the couple also has a psychologist to speak about temperament and conflict issues. These topics would not be discussed during spiritual direction.

> Zechariah: I haven't found that many differences. There is a great sense of respect for one another. They don't try to get information on each other from me during the sessions because there is a great sense of openness between them. They are well trained in the spiritual life, and they go deep in the sense of the spiritual. What this couple have in their favor is that they are accompanied by another person to grow on a human level. They don't get their human relational aspects, their wellbeing, anger and conflict management in spiritual direction. They tackle these in another forum. They strike me a lot because it is only a few who take care of their life in this way. Just as when using a gym, in some way, they exercise in a spiritual and even a human gym. And both of them do it.[21]

---

20. "Imbagħad għandek gay couples, irġiel u nisa. The major challenge is li they relate from struggle. Jiġifieri they relate to each other imma l-image li tiġi hi ta' żewġt iħbieb, imma they need to ritually fight. Jiġifieri toqgħod imma hemm qiegħda. Struggle and who is going to control who tibqa' hemm. Tgħidli, bejn raġel u mara mhux hemm qiegħda? Iva hemm qiegħda, imma b'mod differenti."

21. "Ma tantx sibt differenzi. Hemm rispett kbir lejn xulxin. Ma jipprovawx jieħdu informazzjoni fuq xulxin mingħandi mis-sessions għax hemm openness kbira bejniethom. They are well trained in spiritual life and they go deep in the spiritual. Li għandhom favurihom din il- koppja li huma jimxu ma' persuna oħra to grow on a human level. The human relational aspects, their wellbeing, anger, conflict management ma jġibuħomx fi spiritual direction. Dawn jittekiljawhom ġo forum ieħor. Jolqtuni hafna għax ftit jieħdu ħsieb ħajjithom b'dan il-mod. Bħalma jmorru l-gym, jagħmlu

Luke and Andrew are the two gay men who form part of this subgroup. In both cases, they do not replicate the observation outlined by the spiritual directors, but one can argue that there is still a lack of true self-acceptance in Andrew's case. Luke, on the other hand, raises the theme of acceptance and prejudice within society. In his interview, he spent considerable energy in detailing others' reactions about the civil partnership, with some friends outrightly rebuffing him. Spiritual directors did not mention this scenario.

STYLES OF SPIRITUAL DIRECTION

Following delineation of the characteristics that men bring to spiritual direction, directors were invited to discuss their own particular style. What they mentioned were resources, self-care, and the challenging areas they have come across in this ministry.

As a rule, participants were hesitant with the term spiritual director. They prefer referring to their ministry as spiritual accompaniment or spiritual companionship. However, this contrasts with how spiritual directees refer to them. This study believes that this dilemma is a language issue. Colloquially referring to someone as *id-direttur spiritwali tiegħi* (my spiritual director) is easier said than *il-kumpann spiritwali tiegħi* (my spiritual companion) or *l-akkumpanjatur spiritwali tiegħi* (my spiritual accompanier). Moreover, spiritual directors tend to use verbs to describe their ministry, like *nikkumpanja* (I accompany), *nigwida* (I guide) or *nimxi magħhom* (I walk with them) rather than descriptive nouns like *jien l-akkumpanjatru spiritwali* (I am the spiritual accompanier) or *jien il-kumpann spiritwali* (I am the spiritual companion). Spiritual directors do not always categorize their style, but three distinct styles can be identified with contrasting features when placed along with each other. These styles are not mutually exclusive and often require common skills.

Spiritual Counsellors

From the data, six spiritual directors appear to view their ministry similarly to the service of a counsellor. Spiritual direction would be a well-defined plan with a specific timeframe. Spiritual direction is not expected to be a lifelong endeavor, and usually, directors have a quota of clients. Meetings are held regularly, usually once a month, with clearly stated objectives. At the end of a session, which often lasts not more than an hour, spiritual directors

---

gym spiritwali b'xi mod u gym anke uman. Jagħmluha t-tnejn."

would give a sort of task to the directee. The task would be specific to the client's needs, but a commitment to a fixed time to pray is a typical example.

Moreover, spiritual directors who understand their ministry in this way would advise clients to keep a journal and record their thoughts and feelings while praying. Later the journals would serve as tools to review progress. The resources that spiritual directors use are also well defined, such as adhering to a specific school of spirituality. Frequently, Saint Ignatius's spiritual exercises are the primary tools for directees who are beginners in their exploration of discernment or prayer. Lastly, boundaries between the director and directee are well defined. If spiritual directors are involved in other communities or have other professional roles in society, they would not allow their directees to confuse these roles. Often, they would not accept clients from these contexts. The only contact directees would have with the director is in the room where spiritual direction takes place.

Spiritual Fathers

Out of the ten spiritual directors, two relate to the style of spiritual fathers. They would have been involved in spiritual direction for a long time and built several communities. Mostly they would be friars and priests. Paternity becomes the fundamental center of their spiritual direction. They would have other talents but being a spiritual father would be the charism underlining their identity. In such a scenario, spiritual direction moves outside of the therapeutic room. Other environments where the director is involved become an extension of their ministry, and in some instances, directees would be channeled to participate in these communities. The frequency of meetings is less structured, and the relation between director and directee would last for a long time. The emphasis in this particular way of seeing the role of the spiritual father is that of being a facilitator between God and the soul in the process leading to union, also understood mystically in terms of the conception and birth of God in the soul. In this view, the director and directee are deeply involved in various activities and in each other's lives. Spiritual directors who understand their ministry in this way often guide men in various vocations, be it priesthood, marriage, or living a single life. As fathers, they are not only mentoring but are available to their spiritual children. They would often hold a dual motivation about spirituality: growth through intimacy and service through community building. Even the resources at their disposal reflect this motive. As an example, the importance of fasting as a spiritual exercise was noted. According to one spiritual director, through fasting, men learn to wait for grace and slowly surrender the need to control. It is an act of discipline which opens the self for the other and at the same time teaches prudence and humility. Discernment then is not confined in a set of exercises but is immersed in the dynamics of relationships, and like a father, directors are available to listen, to motivate and to support the soul.

Spiritual Friends

Four spiritual directors, from the way they described spiritual direction, appear to understand the ministry as resembling friendship. Instead of creating a safe space where the directee grows in knowing himself through formal support or expand into another human dimension within a community under the protection of someone bigger than him, spiritual directors who tend to adhere to this style have as their primary concern the creating of a space of almost friendship. They remark that the privilege aspect that emanates from spiritual directors as a guiding role or a father is suspended or camouflaged. They do their utmost to bring direction to look like two men who meet and talk with no expectations other than that which is assumed to exist in any friendship, that is, trust, care and availability. In doing so, expectations that men might have about directors are suspended to facilitate approachability, trust and intimacy. Directors describe their style as two who decide to go for a walk or table fellowship over a meal. The sessions become moments of rest and of dialogue. Ultimately these directors focus on preserving the freedom of their directees. They are aware of how sensitive men can be about control and meeting expectations. Being available to directees as they make sense of their lives is a central feature. However, they do so not through advice or suggestion but by listening and allowing the soul to find truth independently. They note that men often tend to regain control and receive enlightenment as they talk about their life. Suggesting answers would jeopardize the whole process. Spiritual friends do not get bothered if they do not hear from their directees for a long time since they assume that there are cases when men do not need contact as in any friendship. Their detachment gives back responsibility to the men whom they help. They do not pretend that directees have to seek their service session after session. If men decide to stop, they can do so without feeling the need to justify their actions.

Only a handful of the participants fit exclusively in the above styles. Often, directors draw from two styles and note that their methods of engaging with directees improved according to their experiences, primarily through continuous professional development and how they mitigated against challenges that they would have brought in supervision. This study will now proceed to outline standard features which are present in all three styles.

Goals

The common objective which all spiritual directors hold is to assist directees in growing in faith and wellbeing. Primarily, they guide men to deepen their relationship with God, bring further clarity of mind, and gradually work towards liberation from the exterior and interior obstacles that hamper movement in their relationship with God. However, it was noted that those who align with the style of spiritual fatherhood or spiritual friendship speak seriously about mysticism. They emphasize how the divine relationship with the soul is a spousal one and that the greatest struggle of men in spirituality is to surrender to God and receive his grace. This inevitable would entail helping men to familiarize themselves with the concept of God's mystery, suffering and patience.

Skills and Resources

All spiritual directors were aware of the various tools at their disposal. The differences lay in the timing of use. Spiritual directors evaluated three features prior to suggesting resources to their directees: the directees' cognitive abilities, their profession, and the type of spirituality they are already familiar with. The range of resources and skills mentioned are listed below.

1. Listening and empathy were the two fundamental skills that every director indicated as conducive to creating a trusting and non-judgmental environment. Spiritual directors shared that through their practice, they reviewed their levels of attentiveness on how well they listened and how they worded phrases when challenging directees not to upset them.

2. Another core group of resources mentioned by all spiritual directors was the knowledge they derived from psychology, specifically the tools used in retrospection, dream interpretation, and personality theory.

3. Directors' main analytic tool when evaluating the life of the directee was through the faculty of intuition. This skill was evident in all participants, but they cautioned that using it is subject to the training a director received and the depth in spiritual and life experiences. The challenging aspect in this regard would be the timing and how to communicate what

was intuitively deducted. Linked with this is their own experiences as men. Many of the issues that men exposed to spiritual direction like sexuality, affectivity, and relationships are also issues that spiritual directors had to make sense of in their own life. Through their own experience, they are aware of what the path of spirituality would entail.

4. The Bible, especially wisdom literature and the New Testament, was the leading resource spiritual directors used to encourage retrospection and discursive meditation. Often it was used as the instrument to encounter God and for discernment.

5. Ignatian spirituality, chiefly *the Spiritual Exercises of St. Ignatius of Loyola*, are also popular among spiritual directors. Not all use this manual, but those who do guide directees towards further self-awareness and vocational discernment.

6. Other spiritualities often referred to as the contemplatives are also popular among spiritual directors. These include Carmelite spirituality, Orthodox spirituality and the desert fathers. Seven out of the ten directors refer to these resources not as something they would recommend a directee to read unless specifically asked for but as a reference to review their practice.

7. When it comes to spiritual direction with a group of people, some spiritual directors probed the relationship between group dynamics, community living, and the insights they gained from Salesian, Benedictine and Franciscan spirituality.

8. Spiritual directors mentioned various books, theological exhortations, and music that enhance reflection, self-awareness, and retrospection.

9. Although not directly mentioned as a resource, spiritual directors who tend to their lay communities or are involved in different groups inevitably find that such communities become a resource for their directees. Under their director's eyes, directees would find a safe and creative space to relate and examine their spirituality.

Self-care

All spiritual directors contend that the need to disconnect from spiritual direction was important. Linked with this was to have supervision. Both mechanisms lead to better clarity of mind, one through rest by engaging in non-spiritual activities and through dialoguing with someone experienced in spirituality. This study found that well-established directors tend to seek supervision less than beginners since they feel they would cope on their own.

Learning not to burden themselves with other people's problems was the most complex challenge that many directors revealed they had to face. They overprotected their directees or found themselves ruminating about them. Often beginners in the profession tend to focus on the helping aspect of spiritual direction. However, later through supervision, this perspective shifts to one of accompaniment. Although the helping element remains, directors recognized that they do not have all the answers and that they need to surrender the person to God. As one spiritual director shared, detachment allows one to retain inner peace and a spirit of clarity.

Another mentioned benefit of supervision was that it offered a space for strong emotions to be expressed. A few directors mentioned that directees, as they share their burdens, also unload onto the director all the ugliness they encounter. Some directees would feel the need to enter into a process of catharsis for relief.

This study found a significant difference in the available support systems that spiritual directors have at their disposal. Friars, in particular, who live within a community have more opportunities to discuss complex cases they encounter. Some religious communities resort to group sessions where members meet to share through fellowship. However, not all friars have the same experience within their communities. One spiritual director noted that he does not trust his confreres due to a history of gossip, conflict and backstabbing. Rather than seeking support locally, he goes abroad. Travelling abroad for supervision is a common practice. The majority go abroad not due to conflict but because they find it rather hard to find a local spiritual director. As one participant explained, many of those who offer spiritual direction are his friends, and thus he would find it uncomfortable to seek supervision from them.

Challenges

Two main scenarios that affronted spiritual directors were when men resisted God's spirit for a long time and when transference within the client relationship occurred. However, one might argue that the challenges of boundaries are subjective to the style of spiritual directors mentioned earlier.

Spiritual counsellors tend to feel less confident with men who do not stick to a plan, appear to be wasting time or who expose delicate issues at an early stage. Moreover, if a person brings up issues that question their values or might lead to countertransference, they quickly refer to another director or refuse to be their spiritual directors.

Spiritual fathers struggle with clients who resist them personally or who try to manipulate the relationship. Directees, like sons, start playing the game and press buttons to control their spiritual fathers. Spiritual directors would see through these dynamics and suggest that it would be time for the directee to seek someone else.

Spiritual friends often struggle with people who approach them not from a friendship standpoint but from those who resort to tricks to gain attention or to get direct advice. In these situations, directors feel the need to protect themselves. One spiritual director shared how some people try to earn his admiration by lavishing him with compliments. Although he finds such behavior more common with women, this particular director feels uncomfortable with such people who approach him in this way.

FLUCTUATIONS IN SPIRITUAL DIRECTION

Although one can already deduce many advances and struggles, as stated in the previous sections, spiritual directors were invited to outline men's spiritual movement. This study will now focus on presenting them in terms of growth and resistance. As a general observation, spiritual directors agree that often progress takes considerable time. Like a rock being marked by water drops, the impact of spiritual direction is often hidden, bringing out a silent transformation. Although the following observations are separately illustrated for analytic purposes, one can note that each aspect directly links with the others. As one area improves, the others follow.

Areas of Growth

Improved Self-Awareness

Spiritual directors shared how spiritual progress relates to self-awareness. The issues that men expose in spiritual direction always had resonances in their interior life. In this respect, spiritual direction is very similar to counselling. As the issue was being managed, the person improved in becoming sensitive to himself. The entire progress, if done well and regularly, would stabilize the self in knowledge and confidence. Spiritual directors noticed that improvement happens in two areas: receptivity and affectivity. By suspending the need to be self-sufficient, they time out their aptitudes and, consequently, listen for feedback from their interiority. The listening part might bring out certain feelings that would scare or shock men, but progress in affectivity commences when men allow themselves to stay and reflect on these feelings. These dynamics were considered areas of growth since men would then pray with their whole self. As self-awareness purified the roots of the self, men would approach God more attuned with their discoveries. Men would approach the divine relationship with less cerebral import and begin to view it as a matter of the heart.

> Daniel: How would you describe the impact that spiritual direction does on the life of the spiritual directee? The impact would be a matter of insights. They discover, I say a word, and then they can gather the whole experience and give it a name or a phrase. They are then enlightened and grow. They usually react positively. It's always the Lord who brings peace and relief.
>
> Jeremiah: I would say growth in three dimensions. The first I would say is in the consistency of prayer, in other words, in the strength of the link with God, and this also applies to human relationships. Most relationships need to be cultivated, and to be cultivated, there has to be contact. If two married people never sit together for a meal, the chances are that their relationship will run into serious trouble at some point. If their only conversation is a shouted exchange and a warning of whoever is going to make the children's lunches or that the children are going late to school, eventually, things will run into real trouble. And it is the same with God. If at particular moments of the day I cannot sit down in the presence of God, or at least be aware of that presence, let alone speak to it or listen, then the relationship is problematic. So one area of growth would be in the consistency and depth of my prayer. A second area that I find, and this is always very deeply moving, is when this relationship is no longer only purely cerebral but it becomes a matter of the heart as well. Emotions come in, and there are some wonderful emotions. When people are moved to tears you know something quite deep is happening. Somewhat to my surprise, men are more easily moved to tears, nowadays many than I thought.

These spiritual directors' remarks fit with the observations on the origins of attachments (OB1), the consumption of attachments (OB2) and the formation of identity (OB4) in phase two of chapter three. In their exposition, spiritual directees exposed how reflection about their lives would be about taking a closer look at their values and desires, which were often acquired in childhood. Directees would begin to connect how they reacted when they failed or succeeded in consuming those attachments that brought them to the ideal. Furthermore, these expectations often reveal how a person is still an extension of his parents or, in the case of men who reject their parents' expectations, take a form of living as a rebellious act. Through the exercise of self-awareness, one begins to dissect, separate, and choose his identity anew. However, it must be remembered that men attend spiritual direction due to their desire to deepen their relationship with God but covertly, they would also be stating that their current identity fails to reach satisfaction. They would feel they are not good enough, and by attending spiritual direction, they would be already expanding the boundaries of their identity and further risk reviewing and amend it.

Heightened Enthusiasm for Spiritual Matters

In conjunction with self-awareness, spiritual directors noted that men exercise further freedom from introspection once the cycle is complete. They become creative and often take it upon themselves to continue discovering more about themselves. Being imbued with enthusiasm, they might start attending psychological sessions or begin to experiment with meditation. Prayer would revolve around these feelings with many interior satisfactions. It would be a phase where the soul feels alive and confident in God's relationship and itself. Particular previous behaviors stopped not simply because the directee realizes that it was harmful but because his new delight from his new identity becomes the source of satisfaction. The commitment to God and the spiritual path intensifies, and many new activities commence.

> Abraham: The growth I see is that in men, the younger ones must achieve. Achievement is for men, for the male. In girls, it is different. Men need to know they are achieving. Then they feel good, feel OK and feel on the right track. So, while they are in that phase, teenagers, young adults, possibly in their early 30s, the main focus is achievement. So, even in the spiritual life, if they struggle, thrive, try or rise, if they are shown they are achieving, then they are OK. Achievement also includes the targets, challenges, in their own character, way of understanding that needs addressing and say "I will work on it." They are totally *Pelagians*, thinking they are going to produce results. But I let them remain in their little illusion because they need to stay there, till when they come to the moment when they scream, "I can't do it." The next phase is then "go to Jesus." The next phase is faith. The first phase is believing in Jesus, and the second is faith. It's waiting for him, seeking what He wants, rather than what I want, or what I want him to do for me, which is the first

phase. The second is what does He want, and in actual fact, this is paralleled by the weeks of the month-long spiritual exercises.

The observation in phase two of chapter three about how identity continuously reconfigures itself (OB6) fits with these dynamics since the first act of self-awareness leads to temporary enjoyment and further invitation for introspection. The timing is subject to the client's temperament, but spiritual directees point to the celebration and enthusiasm that a proper act of mortification brings about. OB6 further points out that the depth of self-knowledge is unique to the person and not just a one-time exercise. With each episode, the soul is called to surrender something new.

Ability to Surrender

It was noted repeatedly by the spiritual directors interviewed that men find it harder than women to surrender control of their life. From the data, one notes that surrendering is the most challenging obstacle that men have to face. In trying to understand the levels of surrendering, it was noted that this inclination is linked with men's tendency to act rather than wait. Often the exercises of self-awareness create a subtle and hidden expectation. The exercises in themselves become operative to acquire favor from God. Men fall into this trap. They think that by working on themselves and performing many things for God, he will, in turn, favor them with prosperity, security and harmony. However, this might not always be the case. At one point, the levels of surrendering intensify. Once a man acts in a way to improve his life through self-awareness and strengthen his identity, spiritual directors point to the next phase: encountering failure. The type of failure encountered depends on the individual, but often it occurs swiftly and, in some cases, out of the blues. On seeing matters turning out not as one expected, men would feel God as silent in front of their disappointment. Spiritual directors note how this scenario is a susceptible one. Men might then experience resentment, anger and melancholy. It is within this scenario that spiritual directors note another development in the lives of men. Slowly and with much patience, men arrive at accepting that in the end, they cannot control all areas of life and that the relationship with God is not based on merit. Some directors noted that suggesting men to pray more or to exhort harder asceticism is damaging in this phase. Instead, men would need to be led to stop working for the kingdom and stay put with eyes open for what is coming. The blockage would not be something external to the self but the self itself. One spiritual director described this phase as descending into the abyss where the soul is devoid of all expectations. In front of God, there are no expectations, but from the abyss, one encounters the mercy and love of God. Spiritual directors underlined that the role of the director in this phase is vital since often men do not find solace from any other sources, and the spiritual director becomes the only person who offers compassion and companionship.

> Joshua: They would be going along their way, and the moment comes in their spiritual life when they feel they have to let go and abandon themselves to the mystery, to darkness, to the mystery of abandonment. And I can understand this, I know it from my own experience. "And at this point, one has to let go. No, one does not do what someone tells you to. At this point, one does not do anything." I have someone in mind: exactly when I told him this, I could see a deepening of his spiritual life. Something was blocking him, and from what he was telling me, I realized this at once—and then he could take off because that is the point other spiritual directors had got to: "you do this and that." No, not at all, "just let go."[22]

These observations relate to the appearance of failure (OB5) and the process of refinement of perception (OB8) in phase two of chapter three. The appearance of failure is the catalyst of spiritual growth, and the requirement to move beyond it is for the soul to surrender part of oneself. Often the soul approaches spiritual direction because it subtly is alerted by inner signs that matters are not functioning well. However, there is so much more to surrender. All men gather in one place, no matter their experience. They arrive to renounce all held ideas about themselves, and at the edge of meaning, they stand naked and transparent in front of God. What happens from this exercise of surrendering and reception is that the spiritual relationship matures into one where discernment clarifies, and the soul begins to relate directly with God without intermediaries but through accompaniment.

---

22. "Dawn li jkunu mixjin jiġu f'mument li fil-ħajja spiritwali jeħtieġ jitilqu r-riedni u jintelqu għal misteru, għall-misteru tad-dlam, għall-misteru tal-abbandun. U jien nifhmu, nafu mill-esperjenza tiegħi. 'Hawnhekk trid tintelaq. Le, ħalli milli tagħmel hekk, milli jgħidlek dak. Hawnhekk ma tagħmel xejn.' Għandi persuna f'moħħi li propju meta għedtlu hekk, minn dak il-ħin, tara l-approfondament spiritwali. Kien hemm blockage li jien mill-ewwel fhimtu minn dak li kien qed jgħidli u mbagħad seta' jtir għaliex diretturi spiritwali oħra waqfu s'hawn. 'U inti agħmel hekk u agħmel hekk.' Xejn minn dan kollu, 'intelaq.'"

Interior Liberation

Spiritual directors highlighted interior liberation as an aspect of growth. From the data, one can notice a variety of fluctuations about what they mean by it. One is directly linked with self-awareness. Men would be aware of their attachments and slowly, through discipline, renounce them. Certain addictions are given up, and lifestyles are amended in line with Christian values. Men would take it upon themselves to practice virtues.

> Adam: I feel it is life-changing. When someone takes the spiritual, as well as the psychological process seriously, there is an opening, something new. There is freedom because a person feels s/he has an issue. Every person has issues. A breakthrough shows in a person, even physically. Especially in men, as they are not very emotional. If it's not anger, but bursting into tears and apologizing profoundly, you'd have touched a raw nerve. It's like when a doctor touches you, and you say, "ouch!"[23]

The second aspect of interior liberation is secretive, and often, men would not be aware of the blockage they possess. Spiritual directors would notice them but at the same time feel powerless how to pull men from certain corners. Instead, they would remain patiently accompanying men until, through God's intervention, they arrive on their own. According to spiritual directors, this is another kind of interior liberation on a level of the spirit, and once men experience it, their desire for love is refined and, in turn, face life more prudently and meekly.

An Open Consideration to the Will of God

Similarly, the perspective men adopt towards God is also amended. If initially, they might be too sure of themselves, following purification, they grow in prudence. Pride takes for granted the other person, but the moments of suffering would make the relationship between the soul and God more explicit. Spiritual directors noted that men begin to focus less on peripheral objects and begin to make sense of God's will from the perspective of unconditional love. The risk of men to spiritualize every movement diminishes, and their

---

23. "Jien inhossha bhala lifechanging. Meta persuna vera tieħu bis-serjetà l-process spiritwali u anke psikoloġiku. Ikun hemm apertura, xi ħaġa ġdida. There is freedom għax persuna tħoss li għandha issue. Kull persuna għandha issue. Qisu meta tagħmel breakthrough il-persuna taraha anke fiżikament. Speċjalment l-irġiel għax ma tantx huma emotional. Jekk mhux anger, imma jinfaqa' jibki u ħafna sorry, imma tkun messejt raw nerve. Tabib qisu qed imissek u tgħidlu 'ajma.'"

perspective of God becomes generic. Instead of perceiving God as an external entity, men begin to relate with God as one who is accompanying the soul. The relationship becomes spousal even if not named directly as such. The only expectation that remains is the confidence that the soul receives in knowing that God always loves the person no matter what occurs in life.

> Jeremiah: And then the third would be liberated at least in part or experiencing some kind of monitory liberation from fears, from false images of self or false images of God, both, and false images of what it means to love God and to serve God, false images of what it is that gives one's life worth. These, too, are important markers. When a person no longer speaks about the life-mission in terms of things that I ought to be doing or choosing, [but] more about the unfolding of my life in relationship with others, what my presence in the world and my activity in the world and my prayer for the world is doing for the kingdom. These are important, I think. These are very, very important; they are the fruits of spiritual direction.

Furthermore, when considering the notion of the uncontained God (OB7) in phase two of chapter three, one can notice that after the process of mortification, the soul begins to learn and not to confuse that which is received from God and other things arising from their inner fluxes. God retains his uncontained nature, and men amend their perspective of what God truly wills through direct contact with his mystery which cuts in both ways: it dulls all expectations and yet provides love.

Ability to Stand Alone

Another sign of growth mentioned by some spiritual directors is when men acquire a disposition to relate with God on their own without any intermediaries. This capacity is not the same as self-sufficiency. On the contrary, men would have understood that they cannot aspire to be complete on their own, but they can live the fluctuations of spirituality more independently. Through these changes, one would live moments when faith is absent, or lack of love is felt. Men also learn how to express themselves on spirituality. There would be better clarity of mind and strength to live the tension in their present moment. By just praying, men would not be in a position to arrive at this state. Even spiritual direction changes. It becomes a relationship where the soul shares those moments of celebrations with someone else rather than seeking help constantly.

Jeremiah: The whole thrust of the spiritual life of the relationship with God is to acquire wisdom, isn't it? Again not in an intellect [way] but the wisdom of the heart, the heart that sees, the heart that knows, the hearts that feels and understands, the heart which is ready to pour out forgiveness, the heart that knows when it is prudent to hold back. So I prefer the word wisdom.

Samuel: Another growth is the ability to solely discern interior movements and how to react to them. Which means, you don't always have to come to me with whatever you need. You're used to being alone in front of God, you're learning, you're toying with discernment. Coming to me to talk about it together after is OK, but that is also internal freedom, as you're becoming more capable of getting in touch [with yourself], you ask, you search, even on a human level. Direction moves away from asking me to help you understand, to you have understood and have given me light. And that is extremely beautiful as the person grows.[24]

Resistances

All spiritual directors highlighted that the path of spirituality leads to a more profound realization of the relationship between the soul and God, but the journey entails many suffering moments. The soul is stretched and humbled in many ways. As much as progress occurs in men, so resistances emerge. The resistances mentioned by spiritual directors complement those mentioned by spiritual directees in (OB5) in phase two of chapter three. However, this study notes that the narratives by spiritual directees provide a fuller picture of their resistances.

Stubbornness

Some spiritual directors noted that man could be stubborn, and they express their disapproval by engaging in self-destructive activities as a sign of protest. They have observed men who would get drunk on weekends, take

---

24. "Growth oħra hi the ability to discern alone the interior movements and how to react with them. Jiġifieri mhux li għandek bżonn dejjem li tiġi għandi. Illi waħdek quddiem Alla drajt, qed titgħallem, qed tilgħab mad-dixxerniment. Ħalli wara tiġi titkellem dwarha flimkien, imma dik ukoll hi freedom interjuri għax qed takkwista l-kapaċità li taf tkun iktar in touch, issaqsi, tfittex inti, u anke fuq livell uman. Id-direzzjoni ssir mhux tgħidli u għinni nagħraf, imma għaraft u tatni dawl. U dik sabiħa ħafna għax il-persuna tikber."

drugs or engage in promiscuity. These actions would be an exclamation of the self who wants to hold control and freedom. Directors noted that the soul inevitably passes through these phases as it would be protesting against loss. Self-reliance and pride remain till the very end since the human mind is geared towards survival. However, one spiritual director remarked that men can also be creative. He shared how he encountered some who would want to have a tattoo to affirm their identity and preserve the woundedness that defines them. Another example is men spending time naked on their own. There would be nothing sexual about this exercise, but they would desire to be transparent and in the original state in front of God.

> Moses: Generally, a sign of resistance to God and a sign of not letting go is stubbornness. I am consciously in control, or alcohol. I go for it. I get dead drunk in one night. More than letting go, I can do what I want. I am free. One thousand per cent masturbation and pornography are always involved. It's not a sexual symptom. Not even promiscuity. It's a question of affirmation, freedom to be myself, to be in control. Alcohol, pornography, and masturbation, following which, something which is extremely interesting. The first time I met this. I underwent a search on a psychological level. Sometimes the need is to be free, including to be naked. Not to show off, or cruising, nothing sexual, just to be. Someone once told me this during a spiritual guidance [talk], but I did not ask why. It was very difficult for him to say it. He asked why and the reason came up. "I need and I feel the need to be in the original state." I don't see this as regression. It's coping, listening to oneself. I mentioned it [when I mentioned] alcohol. The cases I mentioned regarding alcohol are not even so serious, very manly. And pornography and masturbation [are] coping statements. And tattooing oneself! Some had tattoos done and argued with their wife. Some got tattooed behind their wife's back. Somewhere well hidden. If she realizes? In secret. At least the argument won't be a huge one as [the tattoo] doesn't show. It's a statement and an affirmation. In my opinion, masturbation and pornography in men are a way of telling God, "I am still in control." This corner, at least, is mine.[25]

---

25. "Generalment a sign of resistance to God and a sign of not letting go hi stubbornness. I am in control, jew alkohol, u tkun conscious. I go for it. Naghmel lejl insir hara. Imma iktar milli letting go, naghmel li rrid. I am free. One thousand per cent dejjem masturbation and pornography. It's not a sexual symptom. Lanqas promiscuity. It's a question of affirmation, freedom to be myself, to be in control. Alkohol, pornography and masturbation, imbaghad interessantissima din. L-ewwel darba li ltqajt maghha. Din ghamilt tfittxija fuq livell psikoloġiku. Ġieli l-bżonn ikun wiehed to be free, including li

Immobilization

Since the transformation of perception takes time and is subject to the soul's readiness, immobilization due to melancholy or self-pity is typical. Men would go round in circles trying to find a loophole since they would not have yet reconciled with what is required. Directors note that some people find it difficult to free themselves from their past. Some would come to spiritual direction with the same issues repeatedly but would seem not to want to grow out of them. In such cases, a few of the directors interviewed would terminate spiritual direction if they see no improvement after many sessions.

> Daniel: Immobilization, in the sense session after session and yet nothing is going on. I cannot pinpoint other [factors] at the moment. Challenges: to get out from the clutches of the past. The past always has a certain claim on the person. It's amazing how the past clutches at a person. However, the Lord frees from the past. And so, it can be a challenge. The past in the sense of childhood hurts, whatever form it can take.

Unwillingness to Suffer

Some men resist confronting themselves and their issues. Some directors noted how they encountered men who would reject their suggestions, such as seeking professional help. It would be evident that some would benefit from taking psychotherapy, and yet they strongly resist it. They become their own obstacle and expect that the spiritual director would sort out their problem.

> Abraham: Obstacles: not willing to pay the price is the main obstacle. Not being committed, being initially committed and then fizzling out. So many want to remain in control, even in a spiritual way, and I do not stomach that.

---

jkun għarwien. Not to show off, or cruising, nothing sexual, just to be. Kien hemm xi ħadd qalli f'direzzjoni spiritwali, imma ma saqsejtx għaliex. Biex qalagħha qala' ruħu. Saqsa għaliex u r-raġuni ħarġet. 'I need and I feel the need to be in the original state.' Ma narahiex regression. It's coping, listening to oneself. Semmejtha mal-alkoħol. Il-każijiet li semmejt tal-alkoħol lanqas huma daqshekk gravi, very manly. U pornography and masturbation coping, statement. U tattooing oneself! Kien hemm min għamel tattoo u ġġieled mal-mara. Hemm min għamel tattoo u l-mara ma tafx. Fejn ma jarax dawl. Tinduna? Bil-moħbi. Almenu l-ġlieda ma tkunx daqshekk kbira għax ma tidhirx. It's a statement and affirmation. Jien għalija fl-irġiel masturbation and pornography is a way of telling God, 'I am still in control.' Din ir-rokna għall-inqas hi tiegħi."

Adam: Sometimes, I have the profound intuition that a person would know what they want, deep down, even though they wouldn't know how to express it. I believe very much in this process. Deep down, they know what they want. If someone comes to tell me, for example, they have depression, this would be a case where I cannot offer my help. But they would say, "there's nothing wrong with me, I just get depressed out of nowhere," then you start to realize, it's impossible. And so it would be a question of some kind of obstacle, the person would be refusing to change.[26]

Sure, if I decide I don't want to get to this place because I don't want to change it, that becomes a big obstacle. And so we start examining a whole series of things. But I am not a magician, and if you don't help me, I cannot work miracles. It would be a case of a person who doesn't want to change. And certain people don't have depth. I have realized this in the case of certain people, and I have often have had some heated exchanges: in such cases, it would just be a waste of time.[27]

SOCIAL CONTEXT

When it comes to the social context, spiritual directors mentioned some scenarios within ecclesial circles and broader society that influence men's spirituality. Spiritual directors argued that men do not always mention specific social issues during spiritual direction, but they can identify the hidden links as directors. This theme was the least discussed, both by spiritual directors and directees since both sets of participants put more emphasis on their personal or professional experience. However, when considering the points that emerged, one can note that the social context can also result in a range of different expectations.

---

26. "Xi kultant jien ikolli l-intuition profonda li l-persuna taf xi trid. Deep down anke jekk ma tafx tartikula, nemmen ħafna fil-proċess. Deep down they know what they want. Jekk persuna tiġi u tgħidlek għandi depression serja, pereżempju, dan tip ta' każ li ma ngħinx persuni, imma jgħidu, 'jien m'għandi xejn, taqbadni depression mix-xejn,' u tibda tinduna, it's impossible. Allura jkun ostaklu għax ċertu persuni ma jkunux iridu jinbidlu."

27. "Dażgur, jekk jien niddeċiedi li din l-area ma rridx nidħol fiha because I do not want to change it, issir ostaklu kbir. Allura nibdew induru ma' ħafna affarijiet. Imma jien mhux magician. Jekk inti mhux ħa tgħinni, ma nistax nagħmel mirakli. Ikun persuna li dan ma jridx. Anke ċertu nies m'għandhomx depth. Ma' ċertu nies indunajt, u ġieli kelli xi battibekki, li ma' dan qed naħlu l-ħin."

Feminism

Some spiritual directors feel that feminism creates more pressure on men as to how they should behave. One example of social pressure is men's expression of disapproval and anger. Expressing these emotions has become an issue in society. Directors note that this should not be the case since that energy would then be transferred into harmful activity. They note how aggressiveness in society did not decrease with feminist intervention; instead, it increased, and it is not simply linked with how stressful life has become. When men intervene, for example, to discipline their children, such moments are interpreted as a threat. Even at the law courts, directors note that men feel vulnerable for the simple reason they are men.

> Moses: For instance, the fact that a man gets angry is becoming more of an issue. And I don't think this is right. Because it then spills over into other energies. Ultimately aggressivity is on the increase and not simply because of stress. I have had cases of men who do not even raise their voices at home. Because their son or daughter would threaten them, "I'll phone the social worker because you are abusing me." And so it is men who are suffering from this, not women. For instance, more than once or twice, I have even heard the comment that a man feels more vulnerable in court for the simple fact he is a man. That is to say, social pressure and social movements do exist as well as stereotypes.[28]

Another aspect associated with feminism is the subject of abortion. According to one spiritual director, the topic features in spiritual direction and men tend to bring questions about how to live in the social milieu and at the same time remain authentic and not allow being carried by such ideologies.

> Aaron: Feminism comes in with the issue of abortion. So, in a way, spiritual direction doesn't happen in a vacuum. It is happening in reality, and that reality is brought within the session. Some bring it more than others because the religious sisters focus more on what is happening in the community. They do not mention that many of these issues, but the men do. The issues as

---

28. "Eżempju li raġel jirrabja it's becoming more of an issue. Li jien ma nhossx li għandha tkun. Għax imbagħad qed tiġi sploduta f'enerġiji oħra. Ultimately aggressivity qed tikber u mhux minħabba stress biss. Kelli rġiel lanqas biss jgħollu leħinhom id-dar. Għax it-tifel jew it-tifla tgħidlu "nċempel is-social worker għax qed tabbużani." Allura l-irġiel qed ibatu minnha mhux in-nisa. Pereżempju anke, mhux darba jew tnejn, smajt il-kumment li raġel he feels more vulnerable in courts for the very fact he is a man. Jiġifieri social pressure and social movements jeżistu, u hemm stereotypes."

regards abortion, especially with the married man, he is strongly against it. I agree with him.

Moreover, some spiritual directors noted that the expectations and social constructs typically associated with men still persist. Malta remains quite hegemonic, with men still are expected to be the breadwinners. Contrary to what is happening abroad, spiritual directors note that Maltese men are still concerned about what they are bringing to the family rather than their career advancement.

> Samuel: In the case of men, the social context is a relevant factor—not that it isn't too in the case of women, but still there is a purely human factor: the reality of work. It might be something peculiar to Malta, but a man has a much greater awareness that he is the breadwinner. It is as if, even though a woman works, still she does it to make up for what the man cannot obtain, or she does it for her career. Of all the men under direction, there is only one case where the woman is officially the breadwinner, and the man takes care of the children. This is because she has a much better pay, besides having a professional job, and they have come to realize that money isn't everything. Moneywise, it's a better arrangement. Cognitively it was easy for them to come to this. However, the work milieu is important for a man's spirituality in Malta. In our culture, a man is still very much caught up in a sense of doing. And not only in order to develop his potential. Perhaps this is the Maltese context, but the idea of developing one's career here is not as pronounced as it is abroad. Here the overriding concern is to work to support one's family.[29]

Spiritual directors mentioned other topics about feminism that do not feature in spiritual direction but, according to them, might have implications in the way people perceive Christian spirituality. These are:

---

29. "Mal-irġiel il-kuntest soċjali jaffettwa, mhux għax man-nisa le, imma xorta hemm ħaġa li hi purament umana: id-dinja tax-xogħol. Issa forsi Malta imma r-raġel għandu wisq aktar is-sens li hu the breadwinner. Qisu l-mara taħdem, imma taħdem biex tikkumpensa dak li r-raġel ma jistax iġib jew għall-karriera. Mill-irġiel kollha li mmexxi raġel wieħed biss li l-mara hi officially the breadwinner u li qiegħed jieħu ħsieb it-tfal, u r-raġuni għax hi għandha paga ħafna aħjar u professjonista wkoll, u wasslu biex jara li l-flus mhux kollox. Moneywise taħdem aħjar. Cognitively it was easy for them to come to this. Imma l-kuntest tax-xogħol għall-ispiritwalità tal-irġiel f'Malta hi importanti. Ir-raġel għadu ħafna, fil-kultura tagħna, is-sens of doing. Mhux just biex jiżviluppa potenzjal ġo fih. Malta forsi din, imma l-idea li tiżviluppa karriera hi inqas fl-irġiel hawn milli barra. Hawn trid taħdem għall-familja."

1. The dangers of conforming to radical ideologies which leads to some people not attending mass since a man is saying it;[30]
2. The increased feminization of the church, which results in men distancing themselves from Christianity; and,
3. The display of the church as a defender of male privileges, which then leads to an assault by feminists.[31]

Sexuality

Although some spiritual directors acknowledge that through spiritual direction men are guided to self-acceptance and fuller integration, the moral aspect is still very rigid. Some point out that they take great care not to oppress the individual and, at the same time, not bring scandal to the church.

> Jeremiah: We live in a world, don't we, and also as a Church, where sexuality has really come into the sphere, where it plays a critical role in identifying people and a critical role as well in their relationship with the Church. Therefore, with God as well,

---

30. Deborah: "I know people who do not go to mass because a priest says it, a man, that is stupid. I go because I need the Lord. We fall into other traps, from one rigidity to another. I believe that in church, there would be women priest but there is only one priest in scripture and that is Christ. In the New Testament, there are no priests, only Christ. It seems to me that I have to have an open mind and an open heart, but I do not swallow every trend because it is one rigidity to another. In a couple of years, there will be something else. They do influence us, of course. Corruption has influenced us too. It is everywhere. Values have changed."

31. Jeremiah: "But I am very concerned, now as a Christian, rather than as a member of the Church, rather than as a spiritual director, though I suppose there may be some implications for people and their willingness to seek spiritual director. I am really concerned by two things: one is the increased feminization of the church, and the other is what I consider to be a feminist assault on the church, which presents the church as a bastion of male privilege and chauvinism. It never appeared during spiritual direction, and that's a separate conversation. Maybe we can have a separate conversation about this at another time because it is not directly related to spiritual direction, but maybe it can have implications about that. For example, from the point of view of the ministry of spiritual direction, the people coming forward now are not merely lay; they are essentially women. To be trained in the ministry of spiritual direction are overwhelmingly women. And this is part of the feminization of the church. If you look at the congregation, they are predominately women, mostly older women. But then, a very interesting observation, when I used to attend mass regularly at [hidden name] the good majority, a solid majority of the people who attend would have been young men. So, there is something in which the churches outside are pushing men away. I don't know why. And as I said, this is somewhat aside from spiritual direction, and maybe it can be a conversation we can take up another time. But yes, it is a concern that I have."

and it can be either a bond or a barrier to healthy relationships. Because it is new, one of the things that I feel a great obligation towards is that not only I do not oppress the individual nor bring scandal to the Church. Both they're not un-reconcilable, but finding the point at which can be reconciled isn't easy.

However, most directors point out how one cannot mature in spirituality if sexuality is not addressed. Often this is done through mistakes. When dealing with sexuality, one cannot see it from a perspective of coping with it or continence, but to use sexuality to draw one to a greater giving. If this does not happen, men get stuck in a moralistic perspective.

> Samuel: Direction involves more a question of being an essential component, helping a person to integrate their life story in the light of God. It involves the experience of being amoral, of first suspending the sense of morals in order first to achieve integration in the light of God, and once this is achieved, then one gets to that point. This is one theological problem we face. Spirituality is still considered part of morality, and it is not seen as freestanding. In my opinion, it has to break free even on the academic level. I'm not a lecturer, but I still think it's a conceptual mistake. I feel we have to have a lot of patience. It can be an obstacle, and it can be a huge discouragement for men. I see this more in those who want to move forward in the spiritual life and integrate it. Because one has to help a person to grow, even if they happen to be married. In treating the spiritual life with young people, I tell them that if they do not get involved with sex and money, they cannot live the spiritual life. Life has to be integrated even on the sexual level.[32]

> Zachariah: Even in the case of sexuality, it's more about chastity, and chastity not in the sense of continence but chastity in terms of just-love, according to Margaret Farley. We have emphasized other aspects too much: a strict identity, whether one

---

32. "Id-direzzjoni hi aktar xi ħaġa, parti essenzjali, li tgħin il-persuna tintegra l-lifestory fid-dawl t'Alla. Esperjenza li tkun amoralista li tissospendi l-morali biex l-ewwel tintegra fid-dawl t'Alla mbagħad tasal. Din hi problema teoloġika li għandna. L-ispiritwalità għadha parti mid-dipartiment tal-moralità, u mhux għal rasha. Fl-opinjoni tiegħi għandha tinħeles anke fuq livell akkademiku. Issa jien mhux lecturer imma hu żball kunċettwali. Jien inħoss li jrid ikun hemm ħafna paċenzja. It can be an obstacle and is a huge discouragement for men. Naraha iktar għal min irid jimxi u jintegra fil-ħajja spiritwali. Ghax inti trid tgħin lill-persuna tikber, u anke jekk miżżewweġ. Il-ħajja spiritwali maż-żgħażagh jien ngħidilhom jekk ma tmissx is-sess u l-flus ma tistax tgħix il-ħajja spiritwali. Il-ħajja integrata b'mod shih anke fuq livell sesswali."

is a Catholic or not, whether a person can receive Holy Communion or not, whether one is divorced or not, whether one is gay or not.[33]

This also applies to gay men. Many resort to spiritual direction who are authentic in their search, but sometimes their declaration of being gay is a political and cultural statement. In spiritual direction, these statements are often counterproductive. What is important is the path leading to love. However, the fact that gay men feel the need to make such declarations reflects the dichotomies which still exist in Malta and in the church.

However, from the data, not all spiritual directors might agree with this stance. Although they acknowledge that sexuality plays a role in spiritual progress, some directors feel that society has become obsessed with sexuality and gender theory, and they would guide one to live sexuality in light of chastity and Christian values.

> Deborah: Perhaps you may not agree with me, but I do believe that, at the moment, the world is obsessed with gender. Gender has always existed from creation, even a plant or animals. There is gender, but we are so obsessed with it that we have almost done it the beginning and end of everything. [. . .] I see issues of sexuality. Again, I go back to the basic principles: chastity is for all married or unmarried. We are sexual beings, but with some people, the sexual instinct becomes an internal issue. With others, it is in the background. As I said, we respond to that and sort that out and integrate it into our journey to God. God created sexuality but within a framework, within Christian life and human values.

A Fast-Paced Life

Some spiritual directors mentioned that life has become fast-paced. People are busy with multiple jobs and running from one activity to another. Nevertheless, directees do not wish to take their relationships and faith for granted. Due to time limitations, prioritizing spiritual direction over other matters is often challenging. They notice how the line of thought in directees is not clear. People come to the session stressed and rush to leave them.

---

33. "Anke sexuality, it's more about chastity, u chastity mhux in terms of continence imma chastity in terms of just-love ta' Margaret Farley. Kemm poġġejna enfasi fuq affarijiet oħra, bħall-identità stretta, jekk mhux Kattoliku jew le, jekk persuna tistax titqarben jew le, jekk hux divorzjat jew le, jew gay jew le."

Zechariah: The social context is so mixed and so complex. In Malta, we are even experiencing the country as a culture. We are going through great changes. We are losing a certain serenity and a sense of peace, as well as the idea of a stable life. This is something based on my own observations but also on what I hear around me. And so I get people coming who say "we'd like to come from time to time because we want to know at what stage we find ourselves in. We do not want to take life for granted, or faith for granted."[34]

Adam: For many persons who want to live out their spiritual life, time is a problem. Today many people have a first job, a second job, a third job, they have to prepare meals, face traffic, and life is completely full. Not one of all the people I see is a pensioner. And this means everyone is continuing to work. Often, time becomes an obstacle as in the case of persons who want to maintain a rhythm of prayer and reflection. There are some who have three or four children, and they face shouting and noise.[35]

Rigid Christian Movements

Another spiritual director spoke about how specific Christian movements remain rigid in their theology and present an aggressive attitude. Particularly when they argue against divorce or abortion, they generate more suffering than empathy. According to him, people who consider divorce or abortion do not do so for frivolous reasons. In his opinion, rather than exhorting what the church teaches, it would be better that if one had to speak, one does so to unite with the pain of others. One cannot pretend prompt solutions to these ethical issues, especially since they would be filled with people's suffering and redemptive experiences.

---

34. "Is-social context huwa tant imħallat, tant kumpless. F'Malta qiegħda tinħass, anke l-pajjiż bħala kultura. Għaddejjin minn bidla kbira. Ċertu serenità u paċi u ħajja stabbli qiegħda tintilef. Din hi osservazzjoni tiegħi, u anke x'nisma' minn dawn. Allura, 'nixtiequ niġu biex minn żmien għal żmien irridu nkunu nafu fejn aħna. We do not want to take life for granted, faith for granted.' Their family for granted, their relationship for granted."

35. "Ħafna persuni li jixtiequ jgħixu l-ħajja spiritwali jsibu problema bil-ħin. Illum ħafna persuni għandhom job one, job two, job three, isajru, traffic, il-ħajja hi mimlija. Il-persuni kollha li għandi ħadd minnhom ma hu pensjonant. Li tfisser li kulħadd għaddej bix-xogħol. Il-ħin isir ostaklu ġieli. Persuni anke biex iżżomm ritmu tat-talb u r-riflessjoni. Min għandu tlett itfal jew erbat itfal, għajjat, storbju."

Samuel: Sometimes I am worried because they are idealists but not Christians. Not so much in the context of dialogue but because they do not understand that it is not always the case that who gets an abortion, for instance, does so on ideological grounds but simply because that is their way out, and it's the same in the case of divorce. It's not a question of agreeing or disagreeing, but one cannot separate salvation from human suffering. Admittedly, one has to pronounce oneself in public, but certain pronouncements are better left unsaid because people get hurt by them: if one is going to say something and that's going to cause hurt, say it in such a way that you suffer with them, otherwise don't say anything at all. If I had to pronounce myself against divorce, I would be hurting people whom I am accompanying, and this sort of suffering shouldn't be imposed. The Church should be a spiritual director in these areas rather than bandying doctrine about and causing suffering. I get angry when I see this sort of thing, but at the same time, I say to myself that a person needs to grow and expand their horizon. And this is where the role of the spiritual director comes in, in order to help a person expand their horizon. I think that many of today's movements often go simply for black or white. They do not know how to live the grey areas, those that involve tension. This is also the case with certain young people who always want clear-cut answers.[36]

Alienation

One spiritual director shared his view that the church is in a sad state due to theological confusion. The theologies presented to people are opinions rather than solid teachings. According to him, this is a result following the Second Vatican Council. People are finding a church with different

36. "Xi kultant jinkwetawni għax huma ideoloġisti imma mhux Insara. Mhux inkwantu ta' djalogu, imma li ma jifhmux li min għamel abort mhux dejjem hu abort ideoloġiku imma s-salvazzjoni tiegħu. L-istess id-divorzju. Mhux li taqbel u ma taqbilx, imma ma tistax tifred is-salvazzjoni u t-tbatija tal-bniedem. Okay, titkellem fil-pubbliku, imma ċertu kliem aħjar ma jingħadx għax tweġġa' n-nies. Jekk ħa tgħid kelma, jekk ser tweġġa' għidha, halli tweġġa' magħhom, il-bqija tgħidhiex. Jien jekk ngħid kontra d-divorzju nkun qed inweġġa' nies li qed insegwi, u din it-tbatija mhix sew. Il-Knisja should be a spiritual director in these area milli toqgħod titfa' d-duttrina u tweġġa' n-nies. Meta ma narax dina nirrabja u fl-istess ħin ngħid li l-persuna għandha bżonn tikber u tespandi l-orizzonti tagħha. Hawn ir-rwol tad-direttur li jgħinek twessa'. Jiena ninnota li anke ħafna movimenti tal-lum ħafna drabi jkunu black and white. Ma jafux jgħixu l-grey areas, it-tensjoni. Anke ċertu żgħażagħ iridu dejjem clear cut answers."

messages and without a clear direction. Furthermore, he encounters many who are disappointed with their society. People have no means to stand on their own two feet, and the time of ideologies is over. He frequently encounters great unhappiness in people that translates into regret and alienation. Politicians' behavior, especially corruption, makes matters worse. Directees see themselves powerless in the face of such dynamics and lose their sense of belonging.

> Abraham: The most evident is the confusion of theologies in the Church. The different political affiliations to ideologies in the Church. I am afraid that the Church is in a terrible state. You have opinions, not solid teachings but opinions. And, I had to endure this, and I could see this in the making since I studied, which was the direct effect of the explosion of Vatican II. It was mainly up to the opinions of so-called theologians, so that's what we were learning: the opinions of Rahner, or the opinion of that one, the Protestants, Bart, and the rest of them. Opinions are fine, you form your opinion, and now we see the aftermath of so many years of very bad theology in the Church. Apart from very bad theology, no clear direction. I guess in anything, not even in the sacraments, not even in the basics of our faith anymore—all in disarray.
>
> ... disappointment with the world, with politics, and international politics. There is a deep sadness in people that they carry. It is not just disappointment it's despondent. I think they gave up on ideologies. The time of ideologies has gone. In the past, people created their worldview within an ideology; the us. Here in Malta, it is very tribal, and so it was very thriving: Nationalists, Socialists, football teams. The us and them. On a larger scale, this used to be ideology and specific persons who embody or personify the ideology. Even in the Church, you had ideologies. You had the bishop or the Pope. Those are gone. People have no means or formation to stand on their feet alone. Most [people] need to belong, and ideologies used to gather these people, including Catholic ideology, and now those are gone, and they have nothing. There are superficial ways to belong, but many are also beyond that. They have seen through the political social engineering. Many are even managing to see that they have been useful idiots for the powermongers. And they come and simply say, "Where are you [God]? What is happening? Where am I heading?"

With this last observation, phase three concludes. This chapter, together with chapter three, aimed to sketch a form of spirituality that arises from the lived experience of men but in dialogue with John of the Cross' spiritual doctrine and spiritual directors' professional experience. Nevertheless, the whole interpretive endeavor should not lead one to consider the aspects recorded as the definite constitutes of men's spirituality. Although the *map of the dark night* facilitates analysis and exposes salient patterns, any form of spirituality under examination must be understood in light of human development and its social praxis. Chapter 5 extends this discussion about men's spirituality by taking contemporary debates about masculinity onboard.

Chapter 5

Theoretical Considerations of Spirituality and Masculinity

Until now, this research discussed ten narratives of men who take their spiritual relationship with the divine seriously. In chapter three, John of the Cross' spiritual framework is used to explore the participants' stories and develop an understanding of their form of spirituality. In chapter four, spiritual directors working with a broader community of men provide clarifications relating to the diversity of forms and levels of transformation. In no way does this methodology offer a complete picture of men and their spiritual realities, but it yields many insights.

This chapter aims to relate the data that emerged from the lived experience to a selective theoretical corpus. Recognizing that the academic study of spirituality considers the layered transformative processes from the divine-human relation, this chapter will discuss three aspects: the human reality, how the divine reality reveals itself, and the mediated processes that bring out transformation. In order to remain faithful to the nature of this research methodology, human reality will be the gateway that leads us to identify something about the divine. Part one of this chapter considers human reality by examining theories about the study of self and masculinity. Since many theories study human reality from different academic fields, only a selection will be reviewed. Postmodern theories will be primarily emphasized since they are, at present, the major influencers, but one of their downsides is the danger of developing a fragmental and reductive self. Thus, part one begins by first presenting some theories of the self and then proceeds to consider different approaches to understanding masculinity. The decision to begin this chapter by presenting theories of self arises from postmodern concerns of reductionism in studying the human person. Theories of masculinity are not immune from this danger. Accordingly, to minimize it, the element of mystery in human development and further work towards the necessity of holding a unitive perspective of the self is introduced as a foundational vision.

The second aim of this chapter builds on the former by relating theory with how lived spirituality presents itself. Part two of this chapter discusses some features of the divine reality and the mediated process that seeks to access the divine. True to this project, but also for reasons of space, these aspects will be discussed primarily in relation to John of the Cross' spiritual framework. Lastly, this chapter considers the role of spiritual directors in helping male directees under their care. Thus, the last part of this chapter indicates possible mystagogical insights for further research.

PART ONE: SITUATING THIS STUDY IN THE CONTEXT OF CURRENT RESEARCH ON HUMAN REALITY

The Study of Self

The participants' narratives show that human reality is highly intricate and multifaceted. The same complexity is echoed in the academic study of the self. No single theory has been able to capture the totality of the self. Moreover, in different epochs, distinct accentuations about the nature of the self are witnessed, which have shaped pedagogical practices and political ideologies.[1]

Closer to our times, psychoanalysis, primarily through the work of Sigmund Freud, challenged the dominant discourse of free will and consciousness that defined the self and exposed how unconscious psychosexual drives affect personality and behavior.[2] The sociological viewpoint also evolved and showed how cultural and economic systems establish and administer identity.[3] Until late modernity, the self was viewed as a cohesive being, but after the Second World War, the centrality of the self and every

---

1. Due to space limitations, this chapter will not outline the various historical surveys of theories of self. For a general introduction, see Martini and Barresi, "History as Prologue: Western Theories of the Self." For an in-depth presentation, see Taylor, *Sources of the Self*; Martini and Barresi, *The Rise and Fall of Soul and Self*.

2. Martini and Barresi, "History as Prologue: Western Theories of the Self," 50.

3. Cooley, "Looking Glass Self"; Mead, *Mind, Self, and Society*; Durkheim, *Suicide*.

feature of its integrity were dismantled.⁴ Barresi and Martini point out how, in this period, "many theorists began to think of the self more as a product of culture than as its creator."⁵

While earlier approaches understood the power of identity formation as the responsibility of the self as a determined and active agent imbued by reason and principle, deconstructionists argued that social and cultural systems construct identities, also dismantling the assumption that absolute truth exists. Writing about how linguistic theories have given undue importance to speech rather than writing, Derrida criticized the West's overemphasis on *logocentric principles*, which assumed that the self had the mandate to bring order from chaos.⁶ This led him to assert that Western philosophy neglected to consider the conditions for what is affirmed and believed. How presence was formed had been taken for granted, and language kept repeating and controlling events that limit originality and possibilities. Deconstruction also inspired deconstructivism in the social sciences. Since Derrida argued that language is a system unto itself, even the self is shadowed by broader cultural and historical narratives that shape and control development. Whatever the self expresses must be thought of as already being said by a system that mitigates against dualistic values (good vs evil or beautiful vs ugly).⁷ Emphasis shifted from power to the self to power of a previous system that determines how language is applied and how life is understood. If language is understood similarly to an act of re-reading from an already narrated story, then ideals and conduct are also a product to satisfy a grand narrative. Since identity is constructed by sifting through memory, expression, socialization and interpretation, postmodernists argue that the whole process is fictitious, the self hides in its selectivity of past events and anything uttered is unoriginal.⁸

To further understand how deconstructive notions disturb the self, the concept of the *saturated self* by Kenneth Gergen will be presented.⁹ Gergen demonstrates in detail how society and culture changed due to postmodern thinking and technological advancements.¹⁰ He argues that a shadow

---

4. Martini and Barresi, "History as Prologue: Western Theories of the Self," 50.

5. Martini and Barresi, "History as Prologue: Western Theories of the Self," 51.

6. Bradley, *Derrida's "of Grammatology,"* 7 and 8; Gergen, *Saturated Self*, 107.

7. Derrida, *Limited Inc*, 93.

8. The concept of selectivity and writing as a fictitious process has been further developed in Frye, *Anatomy of Criticism: Four Essay*; de Man, *Allegories of Reading*; de Man, *Resistance to Theory*.

9. Gergen, *Saturated Self*.

10. Gergen, *Saturated Self*, 18–47.

of suspicion altered social relations and cultural expression.[11] Since deconstructivism beckoned that the status quo be confronted, the assumed order in social relations changed drastically. Gergen explains how:

> The postmodern condition more generally is marked by a plurality of voices vying for the right to reality—to be accepted as legitimate expressions of the true and the good. As the voices expand in power and presence, all that seemed proper, right-minded, and well understood is subverted. In the postmodern world, we become increasingly aware that the objects about which we speak are not so much "in the world" as they are products of perspective. Thus, processes such as emotion and reason cease to be real and significant essences of persons; rather, in the light of pluralism, we perceive them to be imposters, the outcome of our ways of conceptualising them. Under postmodern conditions, persons exist in a state of continuous construction and reconstruction; it is a world where anything goes that can be negotiated. Each reality of self gives way to reflexive questioning, irony, and ultimately the playful probing of yet another reality. The centre fails to hold.[12]

Subsequently, the upheavals had profound implications for how the self is considered and the construction of identities.[13] A plurality of options and at the same time a deep-seated reservation towards them characterizes the postmodern consciousness. As voices bombard the self, none offer true fulfilment. Although past ideals promulgated by Romanticism and the Enlightenment period still linger and govern many social institutions and cultural narratives, the barrage of voices is ever increasing. Globalization and access to new technologies amplified the multiplicity of identities available for the self. A market marked by "multiplicity of incoherent and unrelated languages of the self" is offered and shifting from one identity to another feels like a necessity.[14] Society saturates itself, and consequently, the self is overwhelmed. The voices and options are not simply peripheral but *populate the self*, yet none have the privilege and authority to convince.[15] Gergen argues that an ever-increasing intensity weighs down on the self and a *pastiche personality* develops.

---

11. Gergen, *Saturated Self*, 31, 94, 105 and 24.
12. Gergen, *Saturated Self*, 7.
13. See Grodin and Lindlof, *Constructing the Self in a Mediated World*, 1–11.
14. Gergen, *Saturated Self*, 6.
15. Gergen, *Saturated Self*, 49 and 69.

> The pastiche personality is a social chameleon, constantly borrowing bits and pieces of identity from whatever sources are available and constructing them as useful or desirable in a given situation.[16]

Identities are not just a matter of fluidity and productivity but turn into personas: images strategically constructed to manipulate others for validation.[17] The self also questions the authenticity and sincerity that govern relationships. Relationships develop as a means for instrumental action and function more to gain something out of them. As these features keep unfolding, identities lend themselves to an ethos of narcissism and insensitivity, and thus relationships develop superficially and in isolation.[18] Gergen further argues that the self faced by the gravity of dismantlement adopts an ironic personality. The predominant form of language of the self becomes a language of disconnect from the seriousness and illusions of reality.[19] However, constantly relying on irony does not solve the crisis of existential meaning; instead, the sorrow accentuates and turns the self into a cynic. According to Gergen, these dynamics intensify the need to *know thyself*, but the impasse of trust intensifies. For this study, the observations by Gergen are essential as they act as a sign that describes the present context that forms Maltese men. The participants of this study sought spirituality and spiritual direction to know themselves. However, they are *a priori* living in a postmodern society that grants them a plurality of choices that the self can appropriate, whilst beliefs previously upheld without question are doubted at the same time. Increasingly, the responsibility to find meaning falls directly upon the self.

Since postmodernists' theories compelled a reconsideration of beliefs held in all levels of society, the assumed gender order was inevitably challenged. With the rise of feminism, masculinity began to be questioned and reconsidered as well. A plurality of voices about masculinity began to emerge. Since this study focuses on men, these developments are of immense significance, and in the next section, masculinity will be examined.

---

16. Gergen, *Saturated Self*, 150.

17. Alan Downs explores the various strategies that gay men adopt to acquire validation in Downs, *Velvet Rage*.

18. Grodin and Lindlof, *Constructing the Self in a Mediated World*, 135–37.

19. Gergen, *Saturated Self*, 15 and 16.

Human Reality and Masculinity

Before feminism awakened a gender-specific examination, the constitutions of masculinity were taken for granted. R. W. Connell, in her pioneering work *Masculinities,* endeavored to explore how masculinity was constructed.[20] Her inquiry led her to trace the history of Western understanding of masculinity. She observed how "definitions of masculinity are deeply enmeshed in the history of institutions and economic structures."[21] Masculinity is not an immovable idea that one possesses prior to and separate from interaction, but according to Connell, masculinity is fashioned through social relations. Rather than speaking of one masculinity, Connell observes a diversity of masculinities. In particular, she criticized male sex role theory, which delineated the conduct and relationships between men and females based on demarcations and expectations exclusive to the sexes. She regarded this theory rooted in complementarity as a late-nineteenth-century reaction against the emancipation of women.[22]

However, for Connell, establishing the diversity of masculinity is not enough. She also leads her inquiry toward recognizing *hegemonic masculinity*.[23] Observing how different masculinities compete in the gender order, she found that an explicit masculinity in line with the values of a patriarchal society is systematically recognized as the ideal by secular and religious institutions. Promoted as the ideal image, it subordinates femininity and regulates other forms of masculinities. Hegemonic masculinity becomes mainstream since it achieves what a patriarchal society values at a given time. Connell shows, however, that even hegemonic masculinity is subject to change. It should not be considered a single form of masculinity that has stood out over time. In different periods, hegemonic masculinity might be constituted by other features to satisfy specific economic and social demands. Connell further identifies three ways other "lesser" masculinities relate to the hegemonic one: subordination, complicity, or marginalization. The hegemonic masculinity not only carries admiration for its virility but is granted the power to subdue.[24] Connell cautions that how a man moves from one form of masculinity to another is not an act of frivolous decision-making but is subject to the demands of hegemonic masculinity.

20. Connell, *Masculinities.*
21. Connell, *Masculinities,* 29.
22. Connell, *Masculinities,* 21–27.
23. Connell, *Masculinities,* 37.
24. "Perceived fear, anger and humiliation influence how people reason and react to threats. Fear can become institutionalized." Crawford, "Human Nature and World Politics: Rethinking 'Man.'"

Underneath masculinities, deep compulsive forces support a gendered sense of meaning.[25]

As the feminist voice gained traction in North America, a reactive men's movement emerged in the late 1970s to heal a perceived male identity crisis.[26] The mythopoetic men's movement emerged. Relying on Carl Gustaf Jung's theory of universal archetypes,[27] the mythological research of Joseph Campbell,[28] and Mircea Eliade's work on initiation,[29] such authors, formulated self-help books and supportive communities to answer the challenges men faced in society. Robert Bly's *Iron John: A Book About Men* is probably the most influential piece of writing.[30] Blaming feminist movements, industrialization, and the absent father in many boys' lives, Bly argues that male energy has weakened. To restore masculinity, a man had to disconnect from the city, be initiated with pre-industrial archetypes of manhood, and reconnect with *deep masculinity*. Other authors followed suit.[31] A global network entitled *ManKind Project*, influenced by the mythopoetic men's movement was established in 1984 and is present in more than twenty-three nations.[32] Other Christian movements like the *Promise Keepers*[33] emerged, which relied upon Muscular Christianity as a philosophical approach.[34] Similarly to mythopoetics, criticism against these movements is strong since they promote the recovery of traditional male roles for privileged white, heterosexual males based on dualistic sexual scripts and simplistic Biblical hermeneutics.[35]

25. Connell, *Masculinities*, 76.

26. See Farrell, *Liberated Man*. See also National Organization for Men Against Sexism (NOMAS).

27. Papadopoulos, *Handbook of Jungian Psychology*.

28. Campbell, *Hero with a Thousand Faces*.

29. Doty and Beane, *Myths, Rites, Symbols*.

30. Bly, *Iron John*.

31. Moore and Gillette, *King, Warrior, Magician, Lover*; Keen, *Fire in the Belly*. Donovan, *Way of Men*; Donovan, *Becoming a Barbarian*.

32. Website of *ManKind* Project: https://mankindproject.org/.

33. Promise Keepers is an American Evangelical Christian offshoot founded in 1990. See (Organization) Promise Keepers, *Promise Keepers Men's Study Bible*; Bartkowski, *Promise Keepers*.

34. Muscular Christianity is a philosophical approach that has its origins during the Victorian era. It promoted virility, self-sacrifice, discipline, and active involvement in appropriating Christian ideals. A resurgence of this movement appears today due to fears that the church has become too effeminate: Burke-Sivers, *Behold the Man*; Richards, *Be a Man!*

35. Eldén, "Gender Politics in Conservative Men's Movements"; Kimmel, "Reading Men." For a comprehensive account of these movements, see Gelfer, *Numen, Old Men*.

Although the mythopoetics movement gained much popularity in media and internationally, Michael A. Messner, in *Politics of Masculinities: Men in Movements,* explored other ways that American men reacted to the changes that held definitions of masculinity were undergoing.[36] His particular interest was to explore how men organized themselves politically to defend their cause or make sense of the changes. He identified eight *terrains* of political expression: men's rights advocates, radical feminist men, social feminist men, men of different ethnicity, gay male liberationists, *Promise Keepers,* and the mythopoetic men's movement.[37] Messner acknowledges that men are finding it challenging to discover how to be a man in American society. He identifies three causes: a rise of unemployment in American cities, a government that seems uninterested in nurturing social hope, and the critical voice of feminists that question roles traditionally held by men, such as being the breadwinner for their families.[38]

Similarly, Michael Kimmel argues that men in the United States have experienced a crisis of masculinity.[39] Modernization, cultural and social changes, and the formation of women's movements brought about a profound and combined impasse for men to secure their particular privileges and power in society. Kimmel identifies three responses: masculinist organizations that responded to modernization's challenges, antifeminists who worked against the emancipatory action of women, and profeminist movements that took on board and supported the growth of women's suffrage.[40] Although R. W. Connell agrees with Kimmel's observations that ideologies of masculinity are passing through change due to modernization and feminism, she does not consent to the notion of a crisis of masculinity. According to her, masculinity is a social configuration of practices, and a system of gender configurations cannot have a crisis.[41] Connell is correct in her observations, but her same comments are leveled ten years later to men's studies for becoming stagnant for offering "a plethora of fixed and fluid 'type' of masculinities" with little consideration of how men negotiate

---

36. Messner, *Politics of Masculinities.*

37. These eight terrains are not mutual exclusive. Also, when Messner's research was published, he used the term "men of colour." Due to criticism towards this term, this study opted to change it to reflect men who share different attributes (cultural heritage, ancestry, religion and physical appearance) that distinguish them as a group.

38. Messner, *Politics of Masculinities,* 5–7.

39. Kimmel, "Men's Responses to Feminism at the Turn of the Century"; Kimmel, *Manhood in America.*

40. Kimmel and Mosmiller, *Against the Tide.*

41. Connell, *Masculinities,* 84.

their masculinity.[42] After hegemonic masculinity research, the inclination to name masculinity as a social construct that shapes the behavior of men continued. Thereafter, one encounters *inclusive masculinity, mosaic masculinity, hybrid masculinities, metrosexual, hyper-masculinity, soft masculinity, caring masculinity,* and *heroic masculinity*.[43] The list goes on. Andrea Waling notes that men's studies at present "understand and theorize masculinity as something to which men are victims of, or possess in a set of masculinity categories or tropes."[44] However, there is little insight into how men reflect, negotiate and engage with their masculinity. She advocates a return to post-structural feminist theory so that men's studies investigate how men engage with their masculinity, especially concerning inequalities, power, the role of agency, and the concept of emotional reflexivity.[45]

If one considers how the different and competing social configurations define masculine practices, one cannot ignore that the social impact ultimately falls within the remit of the self. Messner argues that while one needs to acknowledge a crisis of identity in men, scapegoating women is not a solution. Although in the 1980s and 1990s, there was a commitment to recovering male friendships and helping men become more responsible as fathers and husbands, the fear of women taking the traditional roles of men as leaders endured. Messner proposes that to work towards social justice, there must be a respectful dialogue since men are inevitably changing but might not necessarily do so as feminists hoped. There is a plurality of reactions, with many men ignoring or not even considering the feminist arguments.[46]

While in politics and the social sciences, some level of antagonism between feminism and men's movements continues today, the momentum of academic research on masculinity has expanded into other academic disciplines and beyond North America.[47] However, the present terrain remains

42. Waling, "Rethinking Masculinity Studies." For a broader discussion on crisis and masculinity, see Edwards, *Cultures of Masculinity*, 6.

43. It is not the purpose of this chapter to examine every hyphenated form of masculinity. For a detailed presentation and analysis of these theories and the criticism leveled against them, see Waling, "Rethinking Masculinity Studies." Moreover, the issue of the fragmental study is not a rare phenomenon in men's studies only. As we will see in the next section, this problem runs into other domains. Moreover, it might be argued that although men's movements inspired by the mythopoetics defend traditional masculinity and neglect the feminists' views, they were more able in offering men practices and spaces to engage with their masculinity through self-help books and initiations.

44. Waling, "Rethinking Masculinity Studies," 90.

45. Waling, "Rethinking Masculinity Studies," 98.

46. Messner, *Politics of Masculinities*, 16.

47. It is not the aim of this chapter to go through all the academic material about

confrontational. Defenders of traditional masculinity remain while others consider traditional masculinity as the main problem in men's lives that needs to be eradicated. In theology, the study of men and masculinity has also made its entrance, primarily in two main areas: biblical hermeneutics and pastoral/spiritual care.

Eric C. Steward notes that while the study of men as gendered beings has a short history, biblical hermeneutical studies that employ masculinity theories to consider hegemonic masculinity and the various levels of complicity, subordination and marginalization among various masculinities are even more recent. Although in the past biblical figures have been a topic of exploration, only recently is a critical interrogation of masculinity as gender being applied.[48] In *Men, Spirituality and Gender-Specific Biblical Hermeneutics*, Armin Kummer enters into a lengthy review of masculinity and Christian spirituality influenced by the mythopoetics.[49] He notes how authors across different Christian denominations have been inspired by and responded to Bly's work.[50] However, criticism of these ideas is plentiful. Although the emphasis on the warrior archetype differs between authors, fierceness, bravery, and strength remain the stereotypical tropes that describe men and their attitudes. In some cases, biblical hermeneutics are not adequately exercised or separated from personal conclusions. Some authors even went far as promoting male aggressiveness. Although relating to the anima is considered necessary so that men enhance their capacity to stay with their feelings, remnants of the sex-role theory remain strong in these authors. Often, they promote that men should be more involved in combative roles than in other activities like the arts.[51]

---

masculinity. However, as a way of example, one can notice a growing interest in tracing the historical forms of masculinity. See Arnold and Brady, *What Is Masculinity?*; Forth, *Masculinity in the Modern West*; James, *Women, Men and Eunuchs*. The sociological perspective continued to solidify and expand into other social systems too, see Adams and Savran, *Masculinity Studies Reader*; Kimmel, *Handbook of Studies on Men and Masculinities*. In literature see Hobbs, "Masculinity Studies and Literature."

48. Stewart, "Masculinity in the New Testament and Early Christianity."

49. Kummer, *Men, Spirituality, and Gender-Specific Biblical Hermeneutics*, 5.

50. Example: Rohr, *Adam's Return*; Rohr and Martos, *From Wild Man to Wise Man*; Grün, *Lottare E Amare Come Gli Uomini Possono Ritrovare Se Stessi*; Arnold, *Wildmen, Warriors and Kings*; Pryce, *Finding a Voice*; MacDonald, *When Men Think Private Thoughts*. Many of these authors discontinued treating spirituality and masculinity in their future publications and shifted in discussing practical theology or spirituality. Quite recently, a dissertation also takes onboard St Ignatius as an example of deep and mature masculinity see Burdziak, "Spirituality of Catholic Men During Midlife."

51. Kummer, *Men, Spirituality, and Gender-Specific Biblical Hermeneutics*, 31 and 32.

However, in the area of pastoral care, new research is emerging. Since pastoral care and counseling have well-being and mental health at their core, there is a mutual interest in theory, assessment tools and intervention strategies. Anthony Isacco and Jay C. Wade, in their book *Religion, Spirituality and Masculinity*, explore the relationship of how men use their religious affiliations, spirituality lifestyle, and masculinity, presenting a vast amount of research evidence that determines positive and negative factors for mental health and wellbeing.[52] Isacco and Wade approach masculinity as an ideology that men hold as a personal definition and cultural construct. By taking onboard masculinity ideology, they agree with the gender-role strain perspective regarding hegemonic masculinity and its relationship with other "lesser" masculinities.[53] Masculinity ideology is understood as a worldview a person has regarding beliefs and attitudes that agree to particular cultural and social defined standards for male behavior.[54] Isacco and Wade outline three types of masculinity ideologies:

Traditional Masculinity Ideology

This ideology is closely linked with hegemonic masculinity. It is the type of masculinity mainstream society tends to encourage: to be competitive, self-reliant, aggressive, and sexually primed. Mental health and physical problems correlated with how much men conform to these norms. Conformity or endorsement with traditional masculinity is closely connected to how men respond to substance abuse, domestic abuse, anger issues, rigid sexual identity, and are more prone to romantic relationship difficulties and low self-esteem.[55] Although conforming to traditional masculinity ideology has positive benefits like social and financial rewards, it appears that the psychological and health problems outweigh the benefits. Although by not conforming to such ideology men would face rejection by others, complying with traditional norms has also been connected to reluctance to seek psychological help, higher risk of psychological distress, depression, low self-esteem, poor health behaviors, romantic relationship dissatisfaction, and the retention of sexist and homophobic attitudes.[56]

52. Isacco and Wade, *Religion, Spirituality, and Masculinity*.
53. Isacco and Wade, *Religion, Spirituality, and Masculinity*, 38.
54. Pleck et al., "Masculinity Ideology and Its Correlates"; Isacco and Wade, *Religion, Spirituality, and Masculinity*, 38.
55. Mahalik et al., "Using the Conformity to Masculine Norms Inventory to Work with Men in a Clinical Setting."
56. Isacco and Wade, "Review of Selected Theoretical Perspectives and Research in

Positive Masculinity

In the face of the negative consequences that traditional masculinity ideology can foster in men and boys, a paradigm to develop and identify positive ways for men to express masculinity has been established. The Positive Psychology Positive Masculinity paradigm (PPPM) developed by Mark S. Kiselica, Sheila Benton-Wright and Mark Englar-Carlson seeks to identify positive masculine features for the self and others to engender.[57] Through their research, they developed eleven domains of positive masculinity: male self-reliance; the worker-provider tradition of men; men's respect for women; male courage; daring and risk-taking; the group orientation of men and boys; male forms of service; men's use of humor; and male heroism. One notices that certain traits relating to traditional masculinity could be considered positively, like self-reliance and risk-taking. Thus, traditional masculine ideology is not mutually exclusive to the positive masculinity paradigm. There can be positive and negative characteristics. Moreover, the eleven positive domains are not exclusive to men. Women can also own and participate in these features.

Precarious Manhood

In precarious manhood, masculinity is viewed as something that requires validation from others. Boys are faced with a set of rigid expectations that they must meet. Failure to comply leads to pushback, bullying, abuse, and the threat of violence and expulsion from other boys, men, girls, and women. Here one encounters masculinity which needs to be displayed and performed, but it is also fearful and defensive masculinity since men use different strategies to compensate for validation and protect the vulnerable self against all the demands and expectations.[58] Vandello and Bosson present three central ideas of precarious manhood:[59]

    i. Masculinity is a precarious and elusive social status, which must be worked for and earned;

---

the Psychology of Men and Masculinities."

57. Englar-Carlson and Kiselica, "Affirming the Strengths in Men"; Kiselica and Englar-Carlson, "Identifying, Affirming, and Building Upon Male Strengths"; Kiselica et al., "Accentuating Positive Masculinity."

58. Isacco and Wade, *Religion, Spirituality, and Masculinity*, 41.

59. Vandello et al., "Precarious Manhood."

ii. The earned and privileges of the social status of masculinity are unstable and transitory; and

iii. Since others endorse masculinity, men have to work hard at presenting and regulating themselves, consciously or unconsciously, to achieve status and validity.

Although these theories provide a richer perspective of how men make sense and construct their masculinity, Anthony Isacco and Jay C. Wade, drawing from their professional experience, found "that many men will not be able to describe their masculinity ideology; so to ask them directly to describe their masculinity beliefs may result in very little knowledge that would be of use to the therapist."[60] Thus they advise that the onus rests upon the therapist to observe how masculinity ideologies manipulate men's lives.

The last example mentioned in this section serves to emphasize further the number of competing ideas about masculinity today: the debate that took place after the publication of the *APA Guidelines for Psychological Practice with Boys and Men*.[61] From the outset, the guidelines define gender as socially constructed; moreover, they pronounced that traditional masculinity is the cause and culprit of men's low mental health and violence, and this forms the basis of their approach. Debates about these guidelines dominated the media. While some backed the guidelines, others considered them misguided for framing traditional masculinity as pathological. In addition, many found the guidelines offensive for not valuing the dedication of men in wars and for considering masculinity only as a social construct with many political undertones.[62]

Although more recent authors have moved away from the Jungian perspective, attitudes towards the feminist notion of the social construction of masculinity still tend to be antagonistic. However, feminist insights are being taken on board. Nonetheless, even in theological circles, the danger of reductionism and fragmentation persists. These pitfalls will now be discussed.

---

60. Isacco and Wade, *Religion, Spirituality, and Masculinity*, 45.

61. American Psychological Association, *A.P.A. Guidelines for Psychological Practice with Boys and Men*.

62. Gurian, *Masculinity Is Not Our Enemy*; Whitley, *Why the A.P.A. Guidelines for Men's Mental Health Are Misguided*; Peterson, *Some Thoughts on the A.P.A. Guidelines for Psychological Practice with Boys and Me*.

The Dangers of Reductionism

In the face of the multiplicity of voices competing to make sense of masculinity, personal meaning appears remote. Connell mentions that when men shift from one form of masculinity to another, it is not a frivolous act,[63] and Gergen points out that the various voices vying within the self for validation lead the self to hold multiple and fragmented identities, so that ultimately the center fails to hold due to the many levels of fragmentation populating the self.[64] Connell mentions sex change as a form of exit for men from the patriarchal order,[65] while Gergen points to the importance of recovering relationships and creating new narratives by accessing the *sublime*.[66] However, various questions arise. How are we to make sense of this center that contains self-meaning? Are we to see this center that fails in front of all the multiple voices only as a sociological phenomenon? Are men only seeking to satisfy a social script?

Apart from the dilemmas the subjective self faces to make sense of itself, the postmodern era also gave rise to much unintegrated academic research. Martini and Barresi argue that deconstructive theories such as feminism and post-colonialism and traditional schools of thought like psychology that took onboard deconstructive insights inevitably sustained a further fragmentary approach to the notions of self:

> Currently, in the science of psychology, when the notion of self shows up, it tends to be in one of its many hyphenated roles, such as self-image, self-conception, self-discovery, self-confidence, self-esteem, self-knowledge, self-acceptance, self-reference, self-modelling, self-consciousness, self-interest, self-control, self-denial, self-deception, self-narrative, and self-actualisation. To some extent, the notion of identity has suffered a similar fate, as notions of racial identity, ethnic identity, sexual identity, gender identity, social identity, political identity, and so on have come even in scientific contexts to take prominence over the notion of personal identity.[67]

---

63. Connell, *Masculinities*, 76.

64. Gergen, *Saturated Self*, 7. "If there is one great intellectual challenge for our day, it is the pervasive sense that we are in danger of losing our sense of the human." Williams, *Being Human*, 23.

65. Connell, *Masculinities*, 85.

66. Grodin and Lindlof, *Constructing the Self in a Mediated World*, 127.

67. Martini and Barresi, "History as Prologue," 51.

Many academic disciplines started to engage with the notion of self, and although they gave rise to a variety of information, they produced *hyphenated* selves: isolated concepts of the self with no unity.[68] Against the multiplicity of academic voices vying to declare something about the self, Martini and Barresi comment that only the "carefully initiated [few] can wade into the waters of theoretical accounts of the self without soon drowning in a sea of symbols, technical distinctions, and empirical results, the end result of which is that the notion of the unified self has faded from view."[69]

Moreover, to remain faithful to the spirit of deconstructionism, one must also consider that both past and emerging discourses about self and identity are satisfying a narrative of sorts. It can be an emancipatory narrative as in the case of feminists, but it can also be conservative and apologetic as in the case of advocates of traditional masculine roles. The result is that one runs the risk of understanding the self selectively and reductively. How can one speak of the self and its apparent center of gravity without falling into such dangers?

Attempts to unify the multi-layered fragments about the self are beginning to appear, such as the *network self*.[70] The *network self* recognizes and takes on board a view of the self as embedded but related and intersected within itself (genetics, psychology and emotions) and out of itself with others (social roles, gender, religion and race).[71] However, for Kathleen Wallace, the self is not simply immersed in rationality. She also views the self as in-development or as a process. She attempts to merge the self as relational with the autonomous and responsible qualities.[72] Wallace formed the *cumulative network model* of the self (CNM). According to CNM, "the self is a complex of plural constituent relations, that is, a network of traits, with synchronic unity and a process, that is, a temporal spread with diachronic unity."[73] Interestingly, she points out that even individuals can feel fractured when others overemphasize one trait of a given identity as a defining feature for the whole self.[74]

While studies about the self have to consider the various interdependent levels of inquiry across disciplines, a spiritual perspective articulating something of the reality of the self must also recognize the element of

---

68. See Leary and Tangney, *Handbook of Self and Identity*.
69. Martini and Barresi, "History as Prologue," 52.
70. Wallace, *Network Self*.
71. Wallace, *Network Self*, 2 and 23.
72. Wallace, *Network Self*, 7.
73. Wallace, *Network Self*, 8, 24, 27–34.
74. Wallace, *You Are a Network*.

mystery. Considering mystery or mystical theology in front of a postmodern reality where there is no direct reference to any totalizing meaning, and self meaning has equally become saturated finds its worth.[75] The importance of mystery also emerges from the contribution of participants in this study. Most spiritual directors recognized how making sense of God's mystery is primarily that characteristic that defines their caring role, while directees, even if not uttered directly, desire to blend how God mysteriously participates in the mysterious unfolding of their life.

Human Reality and Mystery

Taking mystery as an essential ingredient in human development should not discourage further research into the various disciplines. It should be considered as a reminder that the self will never be captured by one single theory. Mystery becomes an entry that lessens reductionism and considers all viewpoints, even if they appear divergent. To examine how mystery is so intertwined with human development, firstly, the self, no matter if male or female, will be examined from a biblical perspective through the observations made by Kees Waaijman. Thereafter mystery will be further discussed from a human development perspective through the work of Franco Imoda. Kees Waaijman shows how the biblical self is similarly dynamic, vast, mobile and escapes being condensed to a single impression.[76] The self, theologically often referred to as the soul, escapes any reductionism:

> [The self is] a reserved space which can open itself up but simultaneously has the ability to close itself; a source of life but with the capacity to jam up within itself; surrender in love but also capable of devouring one's life; it can live together in peace with the core of one's personality but also depress the inner self; it can turn inward and be besides itself.[77]

Delving deeper into these fluctuations of the soul (nephesh, psyche), Waaijman outlined seven characteristics. Three of these describe the soul's substance, while the remaining four concern themselves with the soul's activity.

---

75. Mark McIntosh draws many scenarios where mystical theology can provide insight, for example, in dialogue with theories of human consciousness, theories of oppression and marginalization, theories of postmodernism and theories of creation see McIntosh, "Mystical Theology at the Heart of Theology." See also Bingemer, "Mystical Theology in Contemporary Perspective."

76. Waaijman, *Spirituality*, 435.

77. Waaijman, *Spirituality*, 436.

The first aspect views the soul as embodying an inner space that fosters reflection and feelings (Gen 18:12; 1 Kgs 3:28). It delineates itself from the immediate social context through separation and communication with the social others (Gen 46:15, 18, 22, 25–27). Its inner space develops into a center that maneuvers the soul into different operations. It promotes the construction of one's identity (Gen 14:21; 36:6) and elicits responsible conduct towards oneself and others (Lev 4:2; 5:17). However, although the soul's interior space is separate and fenced from others, its barrier is weak. The Psalms provide various scenarios of how the soul is robbed of its security.[78] Waaijman, commenting on the narrative about Job, exposes how the inner space of the soul is two-sided: the soul has an exterior, social configuration which Satan was granted the power to assault, and it has an interior part that is intangible and hidden from Satan.[79] How the soul handles its security is of utmost importance. If the soul exclusively identifies itself with the exterior enclosure, it turns into a *dead soul* (Lev 21:11; Num 6.6).

> Against this background it is completely understandable that Jesus sharply opposed all identification with one's external soul, particularly with its social position: "Whoever comes to me and does not shun father and mother, wife and children, brothers and sisters, and even his own soul, cannot be my disciple." (Luke 14:26).[80]

The second aspect of the soul is the connection between being needy and being sensitive.[81] The soul is felt as empty and retains an unquenchable thirst and hunger to possess and own (Isa 29:8; Prov 10:3; Isa 32:6). At the same time, the soul is filled with emotion to move towards the marvelous for its delight. A sense of fluidity is noticed. Sometimes the soul experiences peace (Prov 18:20) and, at times, fear (Lam 1:20). The soul is the place where tenderness and intimacy are engendered. The third feature of the soul is associated with its life core, the essence that grants the earthly form to become a living soul through God's breath (Gen 2:7; Isa 42:5; 57:16). "The two together, the soul form and the breath of life, constitute the human being."[82] The fusion of body and spirit make a living soul (Gen 2:7) able to think, relate, develop and grow: *to be*.

The fourth feature is the identity of the soul through the presentation of the *I*. Through the manifestation of the *I*, the soul seeks to acquire worth

---

78. Pss 40:13; 116:3; 149:8; 105:18; 80:13; 52:7; 140:12; 109:13, 15; 101:8.
79. Waaijman, *Spirituality*, 437.
80. Waaijman, *Spirituality*, 438.
81. Waaijman, *Spirituality*, 438–39.
82. Waaijman, *Spirituality*, 439.

and admiration (Ps 116:15).[83] An interaction between the soul and the *I* ensues. The soul can nurture and strengthen identity (Prov 23:7; Song 6:12), or it can engulf it in discouragement (Job 10:1). The fifth feature that Waaijman notices relate to the different movements of the soul.

> The soul goes out, goes forth, goes up, goes down, goes out into space, goes into the depths. That is its nature. On account of this mobility *nephesh* is analogous to *ruach*. *Ruach* brings to the fore the mobility of *nephesh*, its inner drive: "My soul yearns for you in the night, my draft within me earnestly seeks you" (Isa. 26:9).[84]

The soul can ascend either in pride (Ps 24:4) or in prayer (Ps 25:1). It can descend either in sorrow or guilt (Ps 16:10) or denunciation (Ps 35:13). The sideways movements are either a state of expansion (Ps 118:5; Isa 60:5) or an ambivalent distraction (Isa 5:14). In addition, the soul can step out of itself to search (Song 5:6) or destroy the other (Ps 35:25; 28:13). The sixth feature is the ability for the soul to accompany and rest with the other (Matt 11:28-29). The preceding features of thirst and need propel the soul to go forth and seek contact and intimacy. Love admits the other to becoming part of the soul. Waaijman here refers to the love Jonathan held for David:

> The soul of Jonathan became tightly bound to David's. Jonathan came to love him as its own soul (...). Jonathan and David made a pact because Jonathan loved him as his own soul. He took off the cloak he was wearing and gave it to David, and his coat of mail too, even his sword, his bow and his belt (1 Sam. 18:1-4).[85]

The giving of clothes symbolizes how the soul expands and extends through and because of love. The resting attribute of the soul is then one of attachment or of *becoming*. The final feature of the soul is the capacity to lay down its life for others. It is the mark of love exemplified by Jesus (John 15:12-13; Matt 20:28; John 10:11, 15; 10:17-18) and the mark of those who follow Him. In abiding to love, the soul lives under the certainty of being outpoured, annihilated, and sacrificed.[86] Nevertheless, Christian salvation rests in such a paradox. The soul in losing itself saves itself (Matt 10:39; 16:25; Mark 8:35; Luke 9:24; John 12:25).

The Christian understanding of the soul based on its biblical manifestations is a matrix of various enigmatic references. The self flows from the privilege of *being* an *imago Dei* (Gen 1:26-28), and its *becoming* aims

---

83. Waaijman, *Spirituality*, 441.
84. Waaijman, *Spirituality*, 442.
85. Waaijman, *Spirituality*, 444.
86. Waaijman, *Spirituality*, 445.

towards the *imitatio Dei*, taking as the means thereto participation of its freedom in creation and ultimately imitating and following Christ. Thus, the science of self is in likeness with and finds fulfilment within the nature and mystery of God. What becomes apparent from these observations is that the biblical human self is also fragmentary in its operations, but it is slowly being led to embrace wholeness compatible with God's wholeness.[87] Instead of taking each aspect separately with the risk of fragmenting the self or extracting some qualities of likeliness that the self shares with the nature of God, some authors give consideration to the mystery aspect in human reality.

This section will now turn to Franco Imoda's observations by examining how mystery emerges instinctively from a person's lived experience and then by discussing in-depth the paradigm Imoda constructed to reduce reductivism. One could argue that the paradigm Imoda develops views the self from a unitive perspective that meets the present needs in studying the self. Imoda takes mystery as a fundamental ingredient in studying the self and the various levels of its development.[88] He presents six *a priori* scenarios in which mystery is manifested in lived experience and from which the self cannot disengage. Here it appears that there could be no self without mystery since mystery points towards development: an unfinished self that seeks to become.

a. **Life as a journey in time:** Journeying is the metaphor of life, encompassing living as an adventure and a collection of fragmented experiences to create a coherent, meaningful existence. Mystery is expressed within the promise of temporality that aims to recover a hopeful vision of life from falling into oblivion. This is synonyms to Hamlet's famous quote "to be or not to be."[89] The self does not know from where it came, and similarly, the future is a mystery.

b. **Laughter and Play:** The ability to laugh necessitates immersion in reality. At the same time, a withdrawal from the efforts, illusions, and personas one creates. Humor is a statement of doubt towards the images one makes of the self to be validated in the world. Play, on the other hand, allows the discovery of something new. It allows the self to be surprised by joy through going beyond expectations.[90]

---

87. Wilson, "Christian Theological Understanding of the Self," 35.
88. Imoda, *Human Development*.
89. Imoda, *Human Development*, 13 and 14.
90. Imoda, *Human Development*, 15–17.

c. **Seeking:** The self holds a desirous, curious, and open passion towards life. Mystery appears through the seeking and the going forth in exploration. The habitat of the self ever desires to move, yet within the exploration itself, the self seeks to find a home to call its own. Seeking and belongingness come together under cover of mystery.[91]

d. **Pain:** Pain splits the soul in two by distinguishing between the actual circumstances and the ideal. The self experiences fragility and an attack on its person, yet it remains aware that things might change. Pain then becomes the paradoxical bridge that creates within the soul a desire to bring together the ideal within the actual reality it lives.[92]

Pain is the locus of mystery precisely because, while it is the necessary way by which reality with its "painful" limits imposes itself, it at the same time impels the person beyond his actual reality towards a "meaning" for its painfulness, to be found "elsewhere."[93]

e. **Solitude:** Similar to seeking, the soul is also split into two activities. On one side, it seeks deep intimacy through the gift of giving self and on the other hand, it fears its survival and backtracks away from the gazes of others. Intimacy comes with a risk. It seeks to love, and simultaneously, there is the threat of allowing another person inside the deepest intimate center of the self.[94] Love and risk go hand in hand.

f. **Dissatisfaction:** The last feature is synonymous with the "restless heart."[95] The soul is torn between two kinds of activities: a willingness towards delight, pleasure, the exclusion and expulsion of suffering, and a deep desire towards happiness or joy as the apex of human perfection.[96] However, Imoda does not view these two realities dualistically.

The central point of the anthropology is not to be found in focusing exclusively on the aspect of limitedness or on that

---

91. Imoda, *Human Development*, 17–20.
92. Imoda, *Human Development*, 20–22.
93. Imoda, *Human Development*, 21.
94. Imoda, *Human Development*, 22 and 23.
95. Augustine, *Life and Writings of Saint Augustine*, I, 1 in Imoda, *Human Development*, 23.
96. Imoda, *Human Development*, 23–26.

of infinitude, but rather on the tension between the two. This point could well be termed the theme of "mediation" or of the intermediary.[97]

What Imoda suggests is that the self is in itself a series of *in-betweenness* unable to rest in one place, be it satisfaction, pain, solitude, or intimacy. The constant need for the self to appropriate various possessions and temper dissatisfaction does not bring stability and fulfilment. No status, possession or achievement satisfies human desire.

These six features are part of the givenness of life. Typically, the self lives unthreatened in the context of reality. The Cartesians inform us that the self takes onboard the exploration and understanding of mystery involved in life. However, Imoda further adds that there will be instances in life when the self cannot suspend the presence of mystery. He calls them *moments of truth* that come about suddenly and unexpectedly out of disappointments, tragedies, and failures. The self descends into helplessness until meaning is brought back. A *totalising effect* takes hold of the self. All its support, held values, ideas, and perspective no longer offer support and constancy. The entire life with all its constituents is brought into question. According to Imoda, the self is defenseless against these dynamics and has to live in an intermediatory state until truth reveals itself once again. In recapturing a refiner truth of life, the self also renounces something already held in its life. Imoda calls this the element of *annihilation*. Thus, in many ways, the self will never be the same again.[98]

In light of this mystery, Imoda proposes three parameters that should form part of any discourse about human reality. His framework seeks to coordinate integration between the anthropological reality of human development with the scientific eye that many academic disciplines continuously provide. By doing so, he hopes that the personal mysterious element of human development is respected and allowed to be developed in its uniqueness and not simply reduced to a blind spot or something abstract.

First Parameter: Otherness, Individual and Environment

The development of the individual occurs in continuous relation with others.[99] The self as a subject stands in front of an infinite number of objects. Potentiality is infinite, but the fact that the self only becomes through

---

97. Imoda, *Human Development*, 24.
98. Imoda, *Human Development*, 27–31.
99. Imoda, *Human Development*, 72–78.

interaction is a limit imposed by reality. Thus, alterity expresses both infinity and limitation. Self as a subject by its own part cannot become. It always requires otherness.[100] One notes that even the beginning of becoming human is already shaped by otherness. The subject is conceived through the unity of two individuals, its genetic makeup is given, yet the self is inimitable. The self comes into existence within a physical body, compelled with a mind and an energetic spirit that brings forth movement, presentation, and expression. The self is a sapient and intuitive being. A natural intelligence emerges where the self utilizes all the variety of bodily objects at its disposal for survival. These objects and capacities are closer than any cloth that later covers them. In its nakedness, the self relates to its body and slowly develops various mental capacities, movements, and perceptions. The self could have been formed in an infinite possible way, yet it was given a body, mind and spirit that uniquely limits it.

In exploring these dynamics, one encounters consciousness of the self, which remains a puzzling topic even today. Locke understood consciousness as "the perception of what passes in a man's own mind."[101] However, the understanding of consciousness extends to an awareness of oneself and one's thoughts, feelings and the subtle intuition or sense of wakefulness of selfhood. Richard Maurice Bucke distinguished between three types of consciousness that a human person can possess: *simple consciousness*, which is an awareness of the body; *self-consciousness*, awareness of being alive; and, *cosmic consciousness*, which is an awareness of life and the order of the universe.[102] It is also the world of the neural basis of self where theories from neuroscience are applied to understand the biological changes and brain activity when the self exercises introspection and self-awareness.[103] Evolutionary psychology also fits in this first parameter since their theoretical approach focuses on how certain psychological traits have evolved and adapted through the interplay of natural selection in human evolution.[104] Evolutionary psychology frameworks have developed personality models like the Big Five Model[105] and the HEXACO Model,[106] which situate and organize these personality traits to explain how selection has shaped persons

---

100. See Williams, *Being Human*.
101. Yaffe, "Locke on Consciousness, Personal Identity and the Idea of Duration."
102. Bucke, *Cosmic Consciousness*.
103. Lou et al., "Towards a Cognitive Neuroscience of Self-Awareness."
104. Schiralli et al., "Evolutionary Personality Psychology."
105. Costa and McCrae, "Four Ways Five Factors Are Basic."
106. Lee and Ashton, "Psychometric Properties of the Hexaco Personality Inventory."

and further identify why certain traits are preferred over others, especially in certain specific environmental contexts.

At the other pole, we encounter various foreign environments and objects to the body that push for interaction. Even here, one notes the interplay of infinite and limited possibilities. From all the possible contexts that the self could have been situated, it is limited to a particular immediate family, context, and country with its religious and cultural features. With globalization and access to new technologies, the self encounters an unlimited variety of cultures and philosophies of life, but the immediate context primarily shapes the self. The immediate social systems act as pedagogical instruments that form identity with their symbols and philosophical and linguistic capabilities. Here one enters the realm of sociology and social psychology. George Herbert Mead, for example, distinguishes between the *me* as a socialized aspect of the person while the *I* retains the active agency of the person. Thus, while the self is a social product, it retains creative and purposive freedom. Another example is identity fusion, which distinguishes between the personal self and the social self and examines how the self unites within particular groups through a sense of shared oneness.

Imoda referring to De Finance's theory, provides examples of how the self confronts the other.[107] The self can deny, annexe, utilize, withdraw, or commune with the other. These reactions expose a delicate balance between the subject (self) and the object (other). The tension between the two is mitigated by either suppressing subject or object or adapting to the difference. An interpretive exercise precedes action on behalf of the self. The tension that the other brings out exposes how the path of becoming is one of struggle and anxiety.

Second Parameter: Temporality; Past and Future

Temporality signifies that human development occurs over time.[108] The unfolding of the present is a result of past actions with an outlook to appropriate a future. Past and future can be considered as interior others that the self has to acknowledge. There is no individuality without a past. What has formed the self consequently seeks a future to answer the incompleteness of the past self. The past then embodies the personal history of the self, while the future points to the world of opportunities, possibilities, and the desire of a future self. Past and future are connected. Again, an equilibrium

---

107. Imoda, *Human Development*, 73.
108. Imoda, *Human Development*, 78–89.

emerges between two poles. There can be no past without a future and vice versa. Both embody the self.

Imoda notes that the self cannot be open for the future unless the past is befriended and accepted as a limit and possession.[109] A variety of questions emerge: is the self a prisoner of the past? Does absolute freedom on the part of the self appropriate the future? Imoda notes that a balanced self, first and foremost, has to accept the givenness of the past that the self has received. The past foreshadows the free will of the self and engenders responsibility.[110] Within the awareness of responsibility, the self enters the realm of the future. There would be no responsibility unless the self has yet to reach a better state of itself. However, focusing on the future without proper attention to the past puts the self in danger of owning unrealistic goals.

The recognition of the unconscious mind opened various theories on how hidden processes like forgotten memories and implicit knowledge influence the self and its behavior. The way how the past shapes the self is the realm of psychology and psychoanalysis.[111] Here the various driving forces of the self are encountered: the will to pleasure developed by Sigmund Freud, the will to power from Adlerian psychology and Viktor Frankl's will to meaning. Jungian theory of archetypes and how a self possesses a collective unconscious also finds its place here. On the side of the future self, one finds the theories of Carl Rogers with his distinction between the real self and the ideal self.[112] While the real self is the actual present self that was formed through past experiences, the ideal self is the hopeful and idealized self that one wishes to attain, which is usually influenced by role models and the pressures of society and culture. Donald Winnicott distinguishes between the true self (an authentic and spontaneous feeling of aliveness) with the false self (the masks, personas or facades that a person defensively adapts to hide the self),[113] and Abraham Maslow's hierarchy of needs motivate the self to reach its full potential through attaining self-actualization— to become the most that one can be.[114] The last example mentioned here is Erik Erikson's stages of psychosocial development, which identifies eight stages that an individual must pass through to attain a continuous healthy and sense of well-being.[115]

---

109. Imoda, *Human Development*, 80.
110. Imoda, *Human Development*, 82 and 83.
111. Gardner and Miller, *Exploring Depth Psychology and the Female Self*.
112. Rogers, *On Becoming a Person*.
113. Winnicott, *Maturational Processes and the Facilitating Environment*.
114. Maslow, "Theory of Human Motivation."
115. Erikson, *Childhood and Society*.

Third Parameter: Structure, Processes and Stages

The first two parameters show that there is no absolute subject or object that defines the self, similarly past and future refer to each other. The self is caught in interpreting and using different instruments to make sense of the four fields of tensions. This third parameter takes on board the *in-betweenness* of these four poles.[116] It is a mysterious endeavor in itself. The interaction of the former parameters, which is a struggle, regards life as a continuous interpretive and an intersubjective endeavor. Rather than a quest of the self to capture something that absolutes itself, the self enters a trial-and-error *modus operandi*. The *in-betweenness* calls forth dialogue, testing and critical reflection with a multiplicity of mediations. By mediations, Imoda understands all the objects, methods, stages, and processes that the self uses to bridge the gap between knowing and unknowing, having and not having, stability or chaos, but a contradiction emerges:

> Since mystery expresses itself, but also approaches and makes itself known, always and only through mediations, and since no one of these mediations can exhaust the mystery, we find ourselves face to face with an almost innumerable series of mediations.[117]

Such intermediate instruments try to distil the mystery surrounding reality and grant a map to the self to navigate life through knowledge, advice, and practical help. In that sense, mediators are pedagogical. However, the quest itself remains elusive, and the self knows and feels incomplete. As much as mediation does not fully capture the reality of the self, the self cannot proceed without them. Each school of thought that fall into the different poles mentioned in the previous paradigms describes and explains something about the self but inevitably propose guides, principles, and advice. The list of mediations is infinite.

It comes as no surprise that the self feels lost amongst a plurality of voices on how to become. The postmodern perspective suspends and questions each of these mediations and the narrative behind them. As much as postmodernism transfers responsibility onto the self to make sense of life, a problem of trust also emerges. The self faces new questions: which mediation is safest, reliable, and genuine? Who knows me best?

If one had to categorise and list all the possible mediations in human reality, it would be an impossible task. Instead, this study will focus on the

---

116. Imoda, *Human Development*, 89–100.
117. Imoda, *Human Development*, 90.

narrative approach since it acts as an instrument applied in therapeutic relationships, which the self uses to make sense of life.

The Narrative Approach

The narrative view takes into account how the self's understanding of life emerges similar to a story. Mary Schechtman distinguishes between two elements: a sense of self that must be narrative and that the lives of selves are narrative in structure.[118] Thus, the narrative approach acts as a hermeneutical stage where the self can objectify, present, and make sense of its individuality and temporality to a listener. The self is thus responsible and actively aware of its life rather than merely having a past.[119]

Discourse about life, spirituality, masculinity, and the self is brought forth in the form of a story, and the metaphor of journeying is often used.[120] The experiences of the self are selectively organized in a plot made of different experiences.[121] Life stories are revisited with the hope of finding meaning within them.[122] Many researchers expose the processes that occur as a person engages in narration and the benefits such an approach yields to well-being.[123] Some benefits can be noticed in the narratives in chapter two, such as sexual acceptance, clarification of one's vocation, integration with the affective dimension, and greater community involvement through shared belongingness. The groundwork processes of the narrative approach are derived from hermeneutical studies and applied to psychological development theory.[124]

A person constructs a representation of their self—an identity—by separating through reflection from the sameness of reality; simultaneously,

---

118. Schechtman, "Narrative Self," 394.

119. Schechtman, "Narrative Self," 394.

120. Writing about spirituality as a journey is seen in autobiographies like Augustine, *Life and Writings of Saint Augustine*; Thérèse de Lisieux, *Story of a Soul*; Stein, *Life in a Jewish Family*. Also allegorically in Bunyan, *Pilgrim's Progress*; Hurnard, *Hinds' Feet on High Places*.

121. See how the role of the metaphor shapes discourse and identity formation in Lakoff and Johnson, *Metaphors We Live By*.

122. Ruffing, "Ancestry, Place[S], and Identity in Spiritual Direction Narratives"; Tilley, *Story Theology*.

123. McAdams, "Psychology of Life Stories."; McAdams and McLean, "Narrative Identity"; McLean et al. "Selves Creating Stories Creating Selves"; Bauer et al., "Narrative Identity and Eudaimonic Well-Being."

124. Ricœur, *Time and Narrative*; Ricœur, *Oneself as Another*; Ricœur, *Figuring the Sacred*; Thiselton, *Hermeneutics*; Warnke, *Gadamer*.

that person is shaped unconsciously by the immediate context. One configures an unfinished autobiography by reviewing past experiences and speaking about oneself in the form of a story.[125] McAdams views the life story model as a form of "quality or flavouring of people's self-understanding, a way in which the self can be arranged or configured."[126] The story of the self is intended to distil confusion, acquire meaning and be unique.[127] The self not only engages in interpreting inward feelings and memories but also other stories outside of the self.[128] Within the exploration of other stories,[129] the self constructs a personal ideology and a *habitus*.[130] The self is both author and reader who ultimately sustains a volitional character to attain self-actualization—the *telos* of individual stories.[131] The narrative approach assumes that the person has the agency and capacity to reflect and

125. "Selves are fundamentally agents on this view, and agency requires narrative. To be agents we must be intelligible to ourselves and to others; our actions must be meaningful and significant in a way that cannot be captured in purely naturalistic terms, but requires that we interpret our behaviours in the context of a narrative." Schechtman, "Narrative Self," 395.

126. McAdams, "Psychology of Life Stories," 102.

127. Lilgendahl and McAdams, "Constructing Stories of Self-Growth."

128. ". . .selves are embodied creatures, embedded in a social context in which they interact with others. The idea that selves are agents brings with it the idea that selfhood is something that emerges in a community, further distinguishing the narrative conception of self from the Cartesian picture of an isolated and independent thinking subject." Schechtman, "Narrative Self," 404.

129. By other stories, one can include all secular forms like films, games, literature and people's experiences, and religious texts, especially the Bible and the lives of saints. Each story invites the self to relate and appropriate meaning. Also, identity is formed subject to how the self perceives and adapts to how others respond to the self. See Mead, *Mind, Self, and Society*.

130. In sociology, *habitus* is a combination of habits, perceptions, and a disposition towards life. Primarily the *habitus* is learnt through imitation. Pierre Bourdieu differentiates between the hexis (automatic physical inclinations like bodily disposition) and habits (mental and emotive schemes that evoke how the self perceives feels, and acts). See Bourdieu, *Outline of a Theory of Practice*. The concept of habitus was also a key topic in medieval philosophy, see: Larrivee and Gini, "Is the Philosophical Construct of 'Habitus Operativus Bonus' Compatible"; Faucher and Roques, *Ontology, Psychology and Axiology of Habits (Habitus) in Medieval Philosophy*.

131. Tilley, *Story Theology*. Primarily Christian desire and identity is educated by imitating Jesus through immersion in the Gospels see Kempis, *Imitation of Christ*. See also Origen, *De Principiis* 4.2.4; Newitt et al., "Narrative Identity." Andrea Canales also presents how the poetry of John of the Cross begins from lyrical poetry and moves to prose, for it recounts a story of a soul who cannot rest until it finds the Beloved. It invites the reader to follow suit see Canales, "La Noción Del Movimiento En El Cántico Espiritual B De San Juan De La Cruz." The link with spiritual identity and the Romantic ideal of art and poetry has been explored in Schmelzer, "(Neo)Platonic Thought in Saint John of the Cross and Stéphane Mallarmé."

compose a meaningful sense of self which provide "some degree of unity and purpose."[132] In line with this approach, models outlining spiritual phases emerged to facilitate progress and provide a blueprint for spiritual development.[133] Autobiographies become a space in which the reflexive self, the *I*, can construct, discover and discern solutions when problems are faced. Although the self constructs a linear story, it is also through difficulties that the story alters. Identity becomes a representation of the self that stabilized after disruption and can further be expressed among other stories or identities.[134] These dynamics expose how the mechanism of identity formation is ultimately a linguistic endeavor rather than merely a biological or psychological disposition.[135] Identity would be established upon *thematic coherences* (themes, values, principals) that support, direct and simultaneously mold purposeful individuation—a unitive *who I am* symbol distinguishable among other possible identities in the world.[136] Spiritual experiences become significant turning points that configure, reconfigure and stabilize a spiritual identity. The adventures of the self are recorded as movement from stability to change and stability once again. If stability succeeds, hurdles turn into trophies that forge a stronger identity. However, if unsuccessful, the self is engulfed by further confusion.[137] The narrative approach provides access to how the individual enters the arena of making sense and living mystery. Mystery is encountered through the tension of continuing desiring a fuller realization of self. It is within the listening of the narrative of the self that we encounter the various instruments which were applied first to understand oneself and second to capture something about God.

Having crossed through a lengthy theoretical terrain about human development, it is worth turning back to the participants in this research and reconsidering their experience. In the participants' narratives in chapters two and three, a list of mediations are encountered: the application of the Ignatian spiritual exercises, discursive meditation and the use of

132. McAdams, "Psychology of Life Stories"; Singer et al., "Self-Defining Memories, Scripts, and the Life Story."

133. Some examples: Climacus, *Ladder of Divine Ascent*; Fowler, *Stages of Faith*; Hagberg and Guelich, *Critical Journey*.

134. Zahrai, "Narrative Identity."

135. Schechtman, "Narrative Self," 402.

136. See the concept of *experiential gestalts* in Lakoff and Johnson, *Metaphors We Live By*, 77–86. See also Habermas and Bluck, "Getting a Life"; Markus and Nurius, "Possible Selves."

137. Parallelism can be observed with Todorov's cycle of narratives and scripts: (1) equilibrium, (2) disruption of the equilibrium, (3) acknowledgement of the disruption, (4) an attempt to solve and (5) regaining a new equilibrium: Todorov, "2 Principles of Narrative."

imagination, liturgy, devotional practices like saying the rosary, fasting and dedicating fixed time to prayer, reading scripture and community involvement through shared belongingness, evangelization, voluntary work and sharing of experiences. All these mediating instruments have one ultimate purpose: granting to the self insights, delight, and access to the divine reality and consequently harmonizing the self among the four fields of tension of individuality, otherness, past and future.

Imoda explains how the self enters the tension by applying different mediations that try to stabilize reality and manage mystery. Mediations are not simply external instruments applied by the self but are in themselves concrete life experiences, and each mediation, lifestyle, practice and experience carries three distinctive opportune moments (*kairos*).[138]

1. **Moment of Presence**: Imoda describes this first moment of presence as a recovery of equilibrium in front of the chaos of infinite possibilities. The self is not lost but stable through achieving a certain sense of peace, meaning, continuity and success. Life feels under control, and any issue encountered that threatened identity destabilization is tempered and resolved. It is a moment that affirms the reality of the self since it achieved, solved, and succeeded in capturing meaning. The struggle led to delight. This path takes onboard the agency of the self to make sense of its reality and look for the everlasting and meaningful. The path of desire and affirmative growth seeks to cultivate what the self already owns and make it better by seeking the best.[139]

    The narratives in this study provide us with an array of examples of how the self recovers a sense of stability, balance, and security. One can note, for example, the various consolations of joy and delight received from prayer, new awareness, and integration of some aspects of the self, a rediscovery of trust and hope in oneself and God and an existential clarity of who one is.

2. **Moment of Absence**: Absence teaches the self that every reality touched upon is not enough and does not satisfy entirely. The self is marked by need and desire. The stability that past mediations had provided does not last, and the recovered meaning is quickly lost. The self encounters deprivation, tension, and emptiness yet again, which propels the self to seek re-equilibrium.[140]

---

138. Imoda, *Human Development*, 126.
139. Imoda, *Human Development*, 126–28.
140. Imoda, *Human Development*, 129.

Desire, poised amid the disequilibrium between the patterns of having and not having, of knowing and not knowing, but especially of being and not being, acts as the mainspring of becoming and developing towards what the person truly is.[141]

We encounter here moments of waiting and abandonment, the encountered voice of life that utters 'No!' to the self, the various degrees of failures, disappointments, rejections by others and the sudden loss of comfort and possessions. Imoda lists a variety of examples and also includes the *dark night of the soul*. He notes that this *kairos* of absence often bring destruction, but they become opportunities for further growth and transcendence.

3. **Moment of Transformation**: Transformation is synonymous with an alliance of the preceding two moments of presence and absence. In their unity, the self develops gradually through equilibrium between discovering, questioning, and transcending. If the self only encounters disappointment, it becomes too cynical and defensive, while if satisfaction and delight are always experienced, the self becomes numb and uninterested in the search. Life and death meet. The unity of presence and absence also highlights that no intermediate mediation can fully capture the self or the reality that the self is called to fulfil. The opportune time when experiences, styles, and processes stop granting meaning propels the soul to search for a refined way of relating. The self that expands faces loss, but the self recovers a refined existential reason for doing so through that loss. The whole process does not rest on an illusion, but it points towards a more profound realization of self which is given rather than grasped. Thus, human development in light of Christian mystery becomes redemptive.[142]

Much more could be said about the self and the various mediated instruments of development offered to it. However, this study will now move forward in exploring how John of the Cross views the self and the role that the *dark night* plays in transcending all mediated instruments at the disposal for the self to find fulfilment.

---

141. Imoda, *Human Development*, 128.
142. Imoda, *Human Development*, 129–33.

PART TWO: COMPARATIVE COMMENTARY WITH JOHN OF THE CROSS' SPIRITUAL FRAMEWORK

In this second part, the three opportune moments of presence, absence, and transformation discussed by Imoda will be related to John of the Cross' spiritual framework. Each opportune moment will be expanded by referring to the dynamics exposed in previous chapters and also referring to some mediated instruments researched internationally and in Malta.[143]

It has been noted in chapter one of this study that each aspect of the *dark night* focuses on a particular faculty of the soul. The *active night of sense* takes into consideration the soul's capability to pursue and affix to external objects, the *active night of spirit* deals with interior possessions that the soul, through its intellect and memory, can experience, while the *passive nights of sense and spirit* propel a transformation in the likeness of God. John of the Cross dissects the soul according to the analytic tools of his time, but in line with Sam Holes' observations, John of the Cross understands the soul as a physical and spiritual unitive entity.[144] The term soul is thus not separate and distinct from its body. Accordingly, in this section, the two terms of self and soul are applied interchangeably, denoting the same understanding. Although John of the Cross dissects the *dark night* in four aspects matching the aptitudes of the self, the *dark night* is a single flow leading the self within the dynamics of affirmation, negation, and transformation. The purpose of this section is to discuss these fluctuations. One notices how every material or immaterial instrument first affirms, then it expires and pushes the self towards a refiner device. These observations reflect upon John of the Cross as a theologian. Although he is often relegated as an apophatic theologian, the role of desire in his poems and commentaries indicates that his doctrine encompasses both apophatic and cataphatic aspects.[145] However, in discussing transformation and union, John of the Cross moves beyond these two theological branches. His spiritual doctrine might suggest implications for understanding the connected aspects of masculinity, human, and spiritual development.

---

143. For the most part, Maltese academic discourse on men and gender relies on international theories of masculinity. Academic research on Maltese masculinities is scarce. Only a few studies have been conducted like Caruana, "Is Masculinity in Crisis?"; Briguglia and Caruana, "Why Do Men Join the Men's Rights Movement in Malta?"; Cauchi, "Masculinities in Male Administrative Staff at the University of Malta."

144. Hole, *John of the Cross: Desire, Transformation, and Selfhood*, 2. See also Payne, *John of the Cross and the Cognitive Value of Mysticism*, 16–18.

145. Mahoney, "Understanding the Christian Apophaticism of St. John of the Cross."

The Way of Affirmation: my house being now all stilled

In this path, the primary mediated instrument that the soul uses is its desire, specifically desire which is affirmed by positive results, satisfaction, expression, and meaning. John of the Cross views desire as the primary cause of movement [fired with love's urgent longings], the mean that directs progress [the one that burned in my heart] and the final endpoint [the Lover with his beloved; I caressing him; I parted his hair].[146] By affirmation, the soul recovers a sense of confidence in these three parts: the source of desire which is interior to the soul, the means that shape behavior and the results of satisfying desire. Sam Hole describes John of the Cross as a theologian of desire.[147] He notes four contributions laid out by John of the Cross that elevate the Saint as a unique theologian of desire:[148]

1. John of the Cross views desire in its entirety. He does not focus on a particular part of human desire like passions or sexuality. In his poetry and commentaries, one notices a soul which continuously yearns and seeks, but no fragment of its desire is repressed. Thus, John of the Cross does not exclude one area of human desire in favor of another. Instead, he treats desire as an integrated phenomenon.[149]

2. John of the Cross views desire as manipulable energy that can produce life or lead to destructive outcomes. The spiritual ascent that he proposes is then a pedagogical effort that slowly redirects human desire to befriend those repressed parts of desire and lead desire to its proper course of action. Since he understands desire as the primary force that shapes a Christian life, he assists the soul in making sense of its desire and guides the soul to be at peace within its own *house*.[150]

146. The poetic quotations in this section are from the *Noche Oscura*.
147. Hole, *John of the Cross*.
148. Hole, *John of the Cross*, 2–9.
149. Sam Hole notes that Anders Nygren predominately influenced the dominant modern theological view of desire. He presented two opposing desires of love: agape and eros. Eros was deemed as an unacceptable desire for a Christian. However, in John of the Cross, one notices that erotic love is not repressed. Rather, it is embraced and elevated as the figurative language that best describes the relationship between the soul and God. Hole, *John of the Cross*, 9, 13–16, 106, 93–94. See also Nygren, *Agape and Eros*. Due to space limitations, the modern rekindling towards the study of desire is not presented. However, Sam Hole provides a brief historical analysis in Hole, *John of the Cross*, 9, 25–61. Also see Sheldrake, *Befriending Our Desires*; Williams, "Deflections of Desire." James Alison also attends to the nature of desire by applying René Girard's mimetic theory in Alison, *Raising Abel*; Alison, *Joy of Being Wrong*.

150. Various figures in the Christian tradition that take into consideration discernment of desire. For example, John Climacus, Ignatius of Loyola, Evagrius Pontus and

3. Once the soul is tranquil with its desire, John of the Cross proposes further movement. Two types of desires emerge in his writings: human desire, which is subject to lack and divine desire, which originates and functions through abundance.[151] These two desires are in constant tension but are not opposed to each other. John of the Cross proposes a method where human desire can disengage from projecting satisfaction and lack unto God. Hole notes that for John of the Cross, transformation is not about satisfaction. The ultimate aim of desire is to partake in divine desire. Like human desire, divine desire is exposed through its origins, means, and ends, but instead of being governed by lack, it is operative through abundance.[152] There is no selfish endpoint in divine desire. For John of the Cross, the *dark night* terminates all acts of projections onto God, but the soul is further introduced to a transformation of desire that participates in the same desire of the Trinity.

4. Since the divine is revealed through the soul's progressive ascent through managing and making sense of desire, Hole notes that John of the Cross clarifies that the study of spirituality should not be reduced to a subdivision of theology. Rather, spirituality, understood from the dynamics of desire, becomes the central feature of theological discourse. The facet of experience cannot be reduced as a secondary characteristic as God's salvific mission is ultimately revealed through it.[153]

From the data derived from this research, desire played a significant role in shaping behavior and seeking happiness. Time after time, dynamics of repression of a particular aspect of desire, often the sexual, was noted. Spiritual progression entailed a personal reconsideration of those desires that were ignored until the soul befriended and embodied them as a positive quality of being human. The metaphor of the *house* symbolizes the self with all its *rooms* that are required to be *stilled*. If an aspect is intentionally or unintentionally repressed, it would inevitably wreak havoc in a person's life. In line with John of the Cross, affirmative spirituality is first and foremost about healthy human development. The divine cannot begin to be sought unless the human aspect is involved and taken care of.

From the experiences shared by spiritual directors and directees, there would be a spiritual blockage until a harmony of desires is achieved. Those

---

the Desert Fathers in Hole, *John of the Cross*, 16–18, 194–98.

151. From the poems *Canticle* and *Flame of Love,* divine desire is not simply a recognition of God in creation, but the transformation that the soul undergoes elevates its desire to the same desire that governs the Trinity. Hole, *John of the Cross*, 4.

152. Hole, *John of the Cross*, 19, 198–200.

153. Hole, *John of the Cross*, 201–04.

participants who started off repressing their sexual dimension had to accept it before progressing further in purification. The same is true for those who enjoyed the pleasures of life addictively without considering their moral compass or those who faced emotional abuse. No part of desire can be repressed or cut off. As the spiritual directors pointed out, much of spiritual growth concerned itself with human flourishing like deeper self-awareness of feelings and desires that the self owns, the different past and present influences that shape desire, increased enthusiasm to own a healthier life perspective, facing fears, discovering interior expression and freedom, and broader critical discernment. All interior, exterior, past and imagined pieces of the self begin to clarify and emerge as voices that the self can give into or detach. Thus, the self embraces a fuller appreciation of all the fragments it possesses and has influenced its development.[154]

Research by Isacco and Wade also points to these affirmative dynamics.[155] They present a range of evidence that points to a positive relationship between mental health, prayer, and religious/spiritual involvement. The eleven healthy characteristics proposed in the paradigm of Positive Psychology Positive Masculinity (PPPM) include three connected with religious participation: male relational and caring styles termed as *action empathy*, belongingness within a fraternal organization that has a shared mission with others, and enhancing leadership and team orientation.[156] Isacco and Wade note that although men might not attend traditional Sunday services, they often express their spirituality through social-oriented activities within particular communities they feel comfortable in.[157] Isacco and Wade also note that when prayer is understood as a coping tool, men benefit from a process that leads to calmness. They see prayer positively linked with an ability to request guidance, surrender control, foster self-acceptance, better problem-solving and connectedness, and provide a space for the expression of feelings.[158] Breslin and Lewis also explored the link between prayer and health. They found that prayer has a positive impact on neurological and cardiovascular processes in the body, leading men to recognize the need to

---

154. In the *Canticle*, Stanza 1, no 1, John outlines ten things that a person becomes aware of: obligation towards God for saving the soul, much of the soul's life has passed, that life is short, the path leading to salvation is constricted, the just are rarely saved, things of the world are vain and deceitful, everything fails and finishes, time is uncertain, heaven's accounting is strict, perdition is very easy.

155. Isacco and Wade, *Religion, Spirituality, and Masculinity*, 77.

156. Kiselica et al., "Accentuating Positive Masculinity."

157. Isacco and Wade, *Religion, Spirituality, and Masculinity*, 82.

158. Isacco and Wade, *Religion, Spirituality, and Masculinity*, 85.

engage in healthier behavior like abstaining from substance abuse.[159] The list of affirmative results is extensive, ranging from physiological to psychological and social support. One last example is social isolation, which can lead to depression and suicide. A strong link can be found between church attendance or other involvement in religious/spiritual activities, which act as a buffer against loneliness and positive mental health outcomes.[160]

The Sunday mass attendance census in Malta has been the predominant measurement that directed discourse about religious involvement. However, for the last five decades, Sunday mass attendance has been falling.[161] The statistics presented in the 2017 census show that only 36.1% of the Catholic population in Malta attended mass on census day. Compared to the census of 2005, a decrease of 14.5% in attendance was recorded. The ratio between men and women was balanced, with slightly more than half of mass attendees being women (53.1%).[162] Projections show that attendance will continue to drop. Previous censuses had already exposed the tendencies towards decline and propelled some investigation into how the faithful are engaging with spirituality. In 2014 a census was carried out about the level of participation by the youth in various religious movements in Malta. The census provided rich numerical data about membership numbers and outlined a series of reasons why members attend these groups.[163] The majority of the respondents who participated in these groups also participated in arts, sports, other spiritual activities, and fellowship. They listed several positive benefits: involvement in these groups becomes part of their identity, they feel a sense of commitment towards their groups or movements, experience a sense of belonging towards the group.[164] These positive results correlate with research on well-being. New research linking spirituality and well-being has begun to appear in Malta, although local research is still scarce. During the run-up for Malta to host the European Capital of Culture in 2018, Marie Briguglio and Ariana Sultana examined the relationship between cultural participation and life satisfaction. Many cultural activities in Malta are directly linked with religion, like the *festa*,[165] carnival and

---

159. Lewis et al., "Prayer and Mental Health."

160. Isacco and Wade, *Religion, Spirituality, and Masculinity*, 84.

161. (Discern) Institute for Research on the Signs of the Times, *Malta Sunday Mass Attendance: Census 2017*.

162. (Discern) Institute for Research on the Signs of the Times, *Malta Sunday Mass Attendance: Census 2017*, 18.

163. (Discern) Institute for Research of the Signs of the Times, *Grassroots*.

164. See also Inguanez and Gatt, *Enigmatic Faith*.

165. The Maltese *festa* is a religious event in Malta. Every village has a patron saint, sometimes two and a religious celebration is held every year. The festivities extend also

Good Friday.[166] Their research found evidence that although the Maltese participate less in culture than other European nations, there are higher levels of life satisfaction among Maltese who participate in cultural life.[167] Life satisfaction was found to be positively associated with having a social life, mental and physical health, environmental quality, government trust and being Catholic.[168] Moreover, Marie Briguglio found that while church attendance adds no further engagement towards responsible environmental commitment, participation in socio-cultural religious activities and self-assessed spirituality have a positive correlation with various environmental initiatives.[169]

These examples point to the way in which desire, when positively validated by others, infuses other dimensions of life, bringing forth further satisfaction, responsibility, and meaning. It is desire that keeps the center of identity intact, but it is always relational. Thus, an affirmative desire exposes a context that validates and provides space for that desire to be affirmed. As seen in the preceding chapters, most spiritual directors dedicate much of their time to encouraging their directees by owning a loving and non-judgmental attitude. Some directors even offer directees to join communities that might provide belongingness, friendship, and opportunities to engage in social activities. Even the directees' narratives expose how the very first step of spiritual growth is human flourishing. However, the equilibrium that an affirmative desire produces is not enough, and it is quickly challenged.

The Way of Negation: where have you hidden?

The mediated instrument in this way is again desire, but instead of being affirmed, it is denied. The *dark night* begins to approach when the assurance that an affirmed desire produces in the self starts to be challenged by unforeseen life circumstances. The same mediated instruments that have worked in the past expire in producing satisfaction, equilibrium and

---

into the secular with fireworks, processions, and bands.

166. About young people's membership in the festa and cultural identity, heritage and creativity see Avellino and Avellino, "Youths' Expression of Cultural Identity through the Visitor Encounter." On higher levels of well-being among participants see also Briguglio and Sultana, "Effect of the Maltese Festa on Well-Being."

167. Briguglio and Sultana, "Man Cannot Live on Bread Alone."

168. Briguglio and Sultana, "Man Cannot Live on Bread Alone," 27. See also (NSO) National Statistics Office, *Culture Statistics*.

169. Briguglio et al., "Environmental Engagement, Religion and Spirituality in the Context of Secularization."

meaning. Desire as the cause originating from within the self intensifies [left me moaning; tell him I am sick, I suffer, and I die; extinguish these miseries], desire, as mean, is lost [I went out calling you, but you were gone; you fled like the stag; tell me, has he passed by you?], and desire as an end escapes capture [you fled like the stag; where have you hidden? This heart, don't you heal it?].[170]

To further elucidate the *dark night*, the theology of impasse by Constance FitzGerald will be briefly presented.[171] FitzGerald views the *dark night* both as a personal and societal experience of impasse. By impasse, she means how a soul experiences total blockage in life and feels "that there is no way out, no way around, no rational escape from, what imprisons one, no possibilities in the situation."[172] Reason and the capacity to solve problems do not yield any result. Furthermore, there is a sense of hopelessness in finding a solution. "Every logical solution remains unsatisfying, at the very least" and limitation seizes the desire of the soul.[173] Movement is brought to a halt. The past does not provide solace, the present instruments at the disposal of the soul, like the capacity to imagine a way out, are rendered useless, and the future "has the word limits written upon it."[174] This experience affects self-image and self-confidence, but the soul is left alone as others do not yield any relief through their advice and empathy. These others are the intermediate voices that fail too, and the soul inhabits uncertainty, hopelessness, and rejection.[175] However, FitzGerald does not limit the experience of impasse only as a subjective event of a soul. She further explores how the experience of God and spirituality emerge from a concrete historical context. It is within such social context that the soul is faced with resources that can support or worsen its condition:[176]

> If we deal with personal impasse only in the way our society teaches us—by illusion, minimization, repression, denial, apathy—we will deal with societal impasse in the same way. The "no way out" trials of our personal lives are but a part of the far more frightening situations of national and international impasse that

---

170. The poetic verses in this section are from the *Cantico Espiritual*. For a short survey of the dark night see two sermons given by Rowan Williams entitled "The Dark Night" and "A Ray of Darkness" in Williams, *Ray of Darkness*, 80 and 99.

171. Cassidy and Copeland, *Desire, Darkness, and Hope*.

172. Cassidy and Copeland, *Desire, Darkness, and Hope*, 78.

173. Cassidy and Copeland, *Desire, Darkness, and Hope*, 79.

174. Cassidy and Copeland, *Desire, Darkness, and Hope*, 79.

175. Cassidy and Copeland, *Desire, Darkness, and Hope*, 88.

176. Cassidy and Copeland, *Desire, Darkness, and Hope*, 91.

have been formed by the social, economic and political forces in our time.[177]

FitzGerald notes that the signs of the times are permeated with a stubbornness of impasse that remains present even with all the hard work levelled against it. "Not only God and the loved one fail us, our institutions fail us [too]."[178] The *dark night* as a societal impasse exposes the shadow that dominates human desire through its expressions of violence, control and cold reasoning.[179] For FitzGerald, the persistent presence of impasse is an assertion that old methods of social relations must give way to superior ones. One area to which she dedicates much attention is the experience of feminine impasse as a critique of institutions and "ultimately of Christianity, with its roots in sexist, patriarchal culture."[180] She notes that in the face of such impasse, feminists, even if they do not realize it, are embracing the call of the *dark night* and transcending the broken symbols that govern and control the experience of God.[181] Other authors who enter into dialogue with FitzGerald take her theology of impasse and expand it into other areas such as climate change, white supremacy and the devastating effects of the Covid-19 pandemic.[182] Perhaps the experience of impasse can also be related to the understanding of present-day masculinity.

Going back to the narratives in chapters three and four exposes numerous instances of breakdown when desire was negated. The setbacks were obstacles that threatened identity cohesion. The fear of chaos in the life of the person loomed intensively. Disruption in movement and dislocation of identity appears in participants' lives either as a persistent sensation of interior hollowness that interrupts equilibrium or as a forceful and often abrupt event of failure. At one point in their life events, the self reaches a

---

177. Cassidy and Copeland, *Desire, Darkness, and Hope*, 92.
178. Cassidy and Copeland, *Desire, Darkness, and Hope*, 93.
179. Cassidy and Copeland, *Desire, Darkness, and Hope*, 93.
180. Cassidy and Copeland, *Desire, Darkness, and Hope*, 94.
181. Cassidy and Copeland, *Desire, Darkness, and Hope*, 99.
182. To name a few, see the articles by Laurie Cassidy, Susie Paulik Babka, and Margaret R. Pfeil articles in Cassidy and Copeland, *Desire, Darkness, and Hope*, 103, 73 and 211. Steven Payne offers seven points to consider when applying the symbol of the *dark night* to global challenges: (1) it is transitory towards transformation in love (2) it is not a return to the old ways (3) it cannot be applied to every painful life experience (4) it may vary according to time, place and needs (5) it cannot be aligned to any tragic event as God's deliberate action (6) it must be made sense of with every generation, independent of societal progress, and (7) it will always exist as a boundary of knowledge about God: Payne, "Dark Night of the Soul, Yesterday and Today." Perhaps here Edith Stein's reflections on the relation between cosmic night and mystic night are important to consider in Stein, *Science of the Cross*, 64.

level of negation in which all that constitutes its identity is doubted and suspected as insufficient means to attain order. That desire which was so affirmed is now radically denied. Nothing brings solace, and the center that holds meaning is at the brick of collapse. These dynamics led directees to reconsider their held desires and located them as expectations that others held for them. Thus, desire begins to be purified. The expectations also reveal the norm that defined masculinity. Disruption of not meeting these ideals signify a loss of self meaning, but moreover, the self is displaced in the whole social sphere. The self would be fearful and vulnerable in front of others and prone to exclusion, wrongdoing, and alienation. Even the method of attaining spiritual enlightenment required refinement. Rather than holding a mechanical method based on merit and discipline, a relational approach began to appear.

These dynamics can be related to John of the Cross' understanding of appetites. He considers them as the first external attachment and obstacle in spirituality. Within the definition of appetites, one can include all the self's fragments—visible and invisible—used to construct an identity. The fragments, which are things of the world, were not an issue for John of the Cross. He sees harm when the self defines itself through fragments.[183] Fragments being neutral objects become charged with personal and social delight when the soul consciously or unconsciously agrees to prefer them. These parts of identity also satisfy a social and cultural order.[184] Hence the delights that the soul receives from the appetites would be socially sanctioned as fitting. In line with John of the Cross' insights, it is quite natural for the soul to mistake joy and satisfaction from appetites and the approval it receives from the social context with God. When failure was encountered, participants resisted change and confrontation. The resistance can be attributed to fear but also ignorance to the depth of critical reflection. These views appear in the *active night of the spirit*. Proper use of the intellect, memory and will commences not when the path is easy and life is taken for granted, but when some identity features do not grant satisfaction and belongingness. Although the soul would resist change, the interior faculties would operate to recapture stability. In particular, discursive meditation, as a spiritual exercise, would be employed as an intermediary means to review identity and

---

183. *Ascent*, Book 1, chs. 1, 3 and 4; Burrows, *Ascent to Love*, 26–36. "Only when love has grown to a certain point of depth and commitment can its limitations be experienced. Our senses are carried to deeper perception, as it were, by exhaustion." in Cassidy and Copeland, *Desire, Darkness, and Hope*, 83.

184. Jack Mulder Jr. utters similar tones in his adaption of John of the Cross's spiritual framework on the theme of racism in the mystical life in Mulder, "Whiteness and Religious Experience."

hopefully discover new insights that can justify the soul's desire. Through the use of imagination, re-readings, meditation, and scripture study, the soul would be thirsty to find new fragments to own an identity closer to the call for perfection and quench the negation. One can also notice how when participants engage in the various exercises of mortification, their masculinity, even if they did not explicitly name it, would be reviewed. They would resist and grief aspects of their masculinity and rediscover others. The components of new masculinities would be subject to their selectivity, context, and aptitudes, but their need to fit into a social role kept resurfacing and often, it was pronounced under cover of discerning God's will.

John of the Cross endorses these initiatives, and one could also include modern practices such as retreats, counselling, and psychoanalysis since these introduce the soul to the path of mortification, bring new insights and engender responsibility. The soul is now active in bringing transformation to its own life. However, John of the Cross repeats that they are not a guarantee and safe instrument to what God wills. In other words, John of the Cross is advocating the soul to stop projecting events of affirmation or despair onto God. A new kind of love that is more transparent as a style of communication with God requires transcending not only the fragments to be replaced by other fragments but a transcendence of the whole method of relationship.[185] Contemplation is introduced here since it transcends every mediated instrument available to the soul. One can notice how easily the mortification process can be manipulated. Not only can the self selectively choose what to engage with, but the process itself can become mechanical, and a means to produce delight. Moreover, in the wrong hands, the process of mortification can lead to spiritual abuse.[186]

As an example of how institutions can contribute or hinder spiritual progress, research by Angele Deguara on sexual morality and religious beliefs among LGBT and cohabitating Catholics, will be presented. Unsurprisingly her research reveals how social and religious institutions that negatively view same-sex desires contribute to poor mental health in LGBT persons. Against such a harsh climate, LGBT individuals face a shattering experience of their inner state since they would be engulfed in various negative feelings like guilt, fear, and disempowerment.[187] Such experiences of rejection and pronounced judgement propel LGBT persons to re-examine their relationship with God. The experience of impasse can be seen against the need to grow spiritually, and yet religious institutions hinder

185. Cassidy and Copeland, *Desire, Darkness, and Hope*, 85.
186. Diederich, *Broken Trust*.
187. Deguara, "Between Faith and Love?," 85.

self-development and identity formation through its condemnation. Deguara found that such experiences lead to further low self-esteem, depression and suicidal thoughts.

On the other hand, Deguara noted that divorcees or cohabiting Catholics experienced more shame than guilt due to their experiences of judgement and exclusion.[188] The labelling of them as sinners and the prohibition to take holy communion bring much shame.[189] As Deguara observes, the experience of personal and social impasse propels a variety of strategies for the self to reevaluate itself through self-reflection, consulting a psychotherapist, a psychologist or spiritual director:[190]

> The reconstruction of a fragmented self and the development of a positive self-identity can be an onerous, relentless process but it is also a means of self-realization and spiritual growth. Most LGBT Catholics in my study eventually tend to embrace both the LGBT and Catholic aspects of their identity rather than reluctantly having to give up one of them.[191]

Paradoxically, as FitzGerald notes, the experience of impasse is an opportunity for the soul to discover a newer perspective beyond what the social offer.[192] Isacco and Wade note that the type of God-image a person hold is the primary source that provides meaning, purpose, hope and comfort. They also note that the relationship with God is also the place where a person can *wrestle with*, express disapproval and blame God.[193] The experience of impasse exemplified in the research by Angele Deguara accentuates the *wrestling with* God, since the LGBT person's only source of hope against an institution that judges would rest solely on that person's relationship with God.[194]

These observations by Deguara are also apparent in the participants' narratives in chapters two and three. Participants in this research sought help from spiritual directors since they could not perceive anything in their immediate reality that granted solace. In separating from their context, they sought a director to recover and reconfigure their identity. Since few men genuinely embody the ideal requirements of hegemonic masculinity, men

---

188. Deguara, "Between Faith and Love?,"130.
189. Deguara, "Between Faith and Love?," 94 and 95.
190. Deguara, "Between Faith and Love?," 210.
191. Deguara, "Between Faith and Love?," 241.
192. Cassidy and Copeland, *Desire, Darkness, and Hope*, 80.
193. Isacco and Wade, *Religion, Spirituality, and Masculinity*, 58.
194. About the various God-images that LGBT embrace, see Deguara, "Between Faith and Love?," 171.

inevitably live a frustrated identity continuously measured by patriarchal ideals. When men arrive at this level of purification, they can encounter blame, misinformation, or lack of concern from those around them. Within such a scenario, those whom the participants turned to for help can either bring further harm by relegating back to the ideals that govern gender order or encourage a fuller re-examination of masculinity. In line with these thoughts, one could argue that the significant harm that the mythopoetics did was that they turned spirituality into a weapon. Rather than approaching the effects of postmodernism as an opportunity for more profound critical self-evaluation, they altered the traditional form of detachment into a reactive and stubborn endeavor that promoted self-reliance. The hero journey that the mythopoetics constantly use, also signified as one who goes to the wilderness or the desert, is not a process that reinforces held ideas but instead humiliates them and engenders poverty of spirit.

Within these dynamics, the postmodern critique of gender cannot be ignored. Part of the reclamation of incompleteness leads one to notice how identity is formed by the expectations of the immediate others and how it carries social tones. Inevitably entering into a process of mortification distils personal desires from expectations and displaces in many aspects men in the whole social gendered order. Moreover, the process of mortification can also be a selective endeavor by the soul. Since the soul will not willfully harm its survivability, only an experience of the impasse will force the soul to examine other areas that remain untouched.

The Way of Love

In the preceding sections, human development was presented as a personal project within a context that provides and simultaneously controls the kind of stories one can configure. Spiritually speaking, the soul progresses in constructing or fine-tuning an identity through the process of managing its desire through moments of struggle, mortification, transcendence, and affirmation. The multiplicity of voices that bombard the soul are the different voices in the soul (past influences and futuristic ideals) and external expectations that continuously control and judge the soul's desire. All these voices constantly affirm or deny. Here part of the transformation entails the soul to own a self-confident discerning attitude when and how to give in to such voices. However, this transformation, although it is commendable, it is incomplete.

All participants of this research experienced aspects of mortification, but they remained part of society. Part of their reconfiguration of identity relates to the existence of a pastiche personality. They searched, imitated, and negotiated their identity in different settings, but such maneuvers did not last long. The continuous experience of dissatisfaction exposes a gradual disempowerment of the self to hold a center.[195] In the severity of such a crisis, the self sees life bankrupt from any form of meaning.[196] Only nothingness would be envisaged as a future outcome in front of all the voices bombarding the self.[197] The remaining hope would rest in God, but even their faith would be questioned.[198] In supplicating God, the soul perceives not a distinct voice of assistance but His silence. God's silence carries a heavier weight than all the other voices.[199]

In such a scenario, the insights of John of the Cross concerning the *passive night of sense* are worthwhile. None of the qualities, skills, and information that the soul encounters are a reliable means to access, contain or recognize God. God's silence only signifies that a more profound purification occurs within the soul where all the interior voices are dulled.[200] In such a desperate state, the soul would be supplicating for something or an other to find meaning. Slowly the soul is being found by God, not through signs and objects that the world tried to form it, but through nakedness and poverty of spirit.[201] John of the Cross speaks of a different type of transformation, which occurs in the substance of the soul where desire is transformed from

---

195. John of the Cross relies on a philosophical maxim that two contraries cannot coexist in the same person. Here one notices a multiplicity of contraries in the same person; *Ascent*, Book 1, ch. 4; *Night*, Book 2, ch. 6; Book 2, ch. 5.

196. Similar to trauma: "Trauma not only fractures time, but also challenges our representation of it. Trauma thus provokes the rethinking of endings, endings beyond which we cannot imagine but nonetheless survive." In Arel and Rambo, *Post-Traumatic Public Theology*, 8. Also, here one can note how the soul would be suffering in the form of affliction, which is a different type of suffering further discussed in Weil, *Waiting for God*, 117–36; Farley, "Serving the Spirit of Goodness."

197. Also see Brooks, "Disenchanted Self."

198. On psychological nihilism see Grodin and Lindlof, *Constructing the Self in a Mediated World*, 135.

199. "The Father spoke one Word, which was his Son, and this Word he speaks always in eternal silence, and in silence must it be heard by the soul." *Sayings*, 100.

200. "Silence is something to do with acknowledging a lack of power." Williams, *Being Human*, 80. See also the chapter entitled, "Saying the Unsayable: Where Silence Happens" in Williams, *Edge of Words: God and the Habits of Language*.

201. A synonymous term is the emptying of the self: "a progressive emptying of the self—a loss in the credibility of subjectivity, agency, the 'I' at the centre of being." in Grodin and Lindlof, *Constructing the Self in a Mediated World*, 128. Or as Thomas Merton states the soul is now being found by God "beyond experience, in 'unknowing,' and we should never grasp the experience for its own sake." Merton, *Course in Christian Mysticism*, 55.

lack to one which operates through unlimited abundance.[202] In other words, the silence of God is an interior pronunciation that halts the soul from projecting affirmative or negated desire unto Him. God's silence appears to be a wake-up call for the soul to stop giving tribute to Him for the goodness that the soul receives from the world and to stop pronouncing blame to Him when desire is denied. John of the Cross points out that God's desire functions beyond such human limited processes; His love is unconditional no matter if the soul feels affirmed or negated in the world.[203]

Martin Buber is introduced here since he accentuates similar thoughts. Buber starts by distinguishing two primary ways in which the self lives and enters a relational existence: *I-Thou* and *I-It*. He and she can replace *It*.[204] Human existence and relationships emerge from an *I* addressing the *Thou* or the *It*. The existence of the *I* is always dependent and in relation to either a *Thou* or an *It*.[205] The realm of *I-It* is one where the *I* engages in a world of activities: *I* perceive, *I* think, *I* feel, *I* imagine, *I* remember, and *I* do. Every object produced by these verbs are *its*. It also includes what others teach the *I* like how the *I* should speak, think, and desire.[206] The foundation of the *I-Thou* mode of existence operates differently. When the *Thou* reveals itself, there are no in-between objects. The verb happens while subject and object are voided. Unlike the *it*, which needs to refer to other objects, the *Thou* has nothing that bounds it.[207] However, as the meeting between the *I* and the *Thou* occurs, the *I* tries to bind the *Thou* through the various fragments it extracts from the encounter.[208] The *I* calls these fragments experiences of the *Thou*. Buber explains that although the *I* will extract knowledge, memories and feelings, such experience is limited. Existence is independent of the many experiences the *I* can extract. No matter what the *I* experiences, it is subject to a series of secondary things which are independent of the givenness of the actual encounter. The experience itself becomes a possession that the *I* only has based on a series of things. The world, life or the *Thou*

---

202. The substance of the soul refers to the innermost depths or center of the subject see Payne, *John of the Cross and the Cognitive Value of Mysticism*, 42.

203. "Bear in mind that your flesh is weak and that no worldly thing can comfort or strengthen your spirit, for what is born of the world is world and what is born of the flesh is flesh. The good spirit is born only of the Spirit of God, who communicates himself neither through the world nor through the flesh." *Sayings*, no 43.

204. Buber, *I and Thou*, 3.

205. Buber, *I and Thou*, 4.

206. Buber, *I and Thou*, 37–39.

207. Buber, *I and Thou*, 4, 39–43.

208. Buber, *I and Thou*, 5.

permits to be experienced but it operates independently of such bounds.[209] Thus for Buber, experience is in itself an activity that finds its place in the realm of *I-it*.

Buber takes the example of the *I* observing a tree.[210] The *I* first meets the tree (an *I-Thou* moment), and then the *I* will analyze and extract knowledge about the tree. However, whatever the *I* obtains, does not affect the tree. What remains is the givenness and appearance of the tree. It is natural for the *I* to give attention to the fragments, but unless every fragment is relegated back to the unitive tree, the *I* diminishes the proper regard for the tree. Such an example is also directed to the relation with the divine *Thou*:

> Just as the melody is not made up of notes nor the verse of words nor the statue of lines, but they must be tugged and dragged till their unity has been scattered into these many pieces, so with the man to whom I say *Thou*. I can take out from him the colour of his hair, or of his speech, or of his goodness. I must continually do this. But each time I do it he ceases to be *Thou*.[211]

Real life just happens; "the *Thou* meets me through grace—it is not found by seeking."[212] It is not a result of fragmented *its* that the self prepares, discerns, extracts, and imagines. All the verbs, together with their objects, expire. The moment the *I* begins to focus on what it has gained or what is expected from the *Thou*, the *Thou* recedes in the background. In other words, the *Thou* is more than any fragment the *I* can conjure. For Buber, "the eternal source of art" is for the *I* to meet the form of the *Thou* in silence and be open to the endless possibilities that are being offered. However, in doing so, the *I* needs to sacrifice and relinquish all the *its*, including its speech and its need to objectify. The total absorption in the present encounter between the *I* and the *Thou* just happens. In that meeting point, all unconceived and unprepared actions and effects occur in a continuous present.[213]

> What, then do we experience of *Thou*?
>
> Just nothing. For we do not experience it.
>
> What, then, do we know of *Thou*?

---

209. Buber, *I and Thou*, 5.
210. Buber, *I and Thou*, 7 and 8.
211. Buber, *I and Thou*, 9.
212. Buber, *I and Thou*, 11.
213. Buber, *I and Thou*, 13.

Just everything. For we know nothing isolated about it any more.[214]

For this discussion of masculinity and human/spiritual development, the *I-it* includes all the mediated instruments that the soul has appropriated according to its experience that act as the in-between filters that the soul uses to distil mystery and capture life, relations, itself, and God. These include everything the world can offer: archetypes, culture, world views, social constructs and expectations; all voices which ultimately limit the direct contact and givenness of any pure *I-Thou* relationship. The transformation that Buber and John of the Cross refer seeks to transcend this mode of filtering and abandon the held narrative one wants as it interferes and keeps the *Thou* far. However, Buber agrees with John of the Cross that until the soul realizes that every means is an obstacle, and every means will collapse or expire, the actual encounter does not come about. The soul lives through the pedagogical path of affirmation and negation to arrive at the total annihilation of all its possessions.[215] The aim is not to repress but to recover that original, mystical, and mysterious encounter with the *Thou* that precedes the *I-it*.

Traditionally the phases of the *dark night* were covered within the threefold path of purgation, illumination, and union. The three effects cannot be viewed in a linear or mechanical way; rather they operate simultaneously. As a deeper purgation reaches the soul, a new light is received, fulfilling a closer union. Moreover, if one takes the two-fold process of affirmation and negation, these three conditions appear differently depending on who controls them. In the *active night of sense and spirit*, the soul works through the purgation by means of mortification—selectively reviewing and constructing an identity that is perceived as faithful to the call for holiness. Illumination is still affected but limited to the soul's willingness to participate in psychospiritual exercises. The gifts received would be about the human condition. In the hands of the soul, the achievement would be like tending a field—the substantial union that always exist between God and creatures. These processes are consistent with the *I-It* realm, even if the desire is to reach God. Even here, the concept of God is understood in terms of *its* perspective, one *it* among others. However, when God finds the soul in its poverty, purgation and illumination torment the soul. Since purgation and illumination bypass the boundaries of identity, knowledge blinds the intellect, and the will suffers. The soul would not know where exactly it stands in the light of the union of likeness to God. However, the soul does

---

214. Buber, *I and Thou*, 11.
215. Buber, *I and Thou*, 12.

not need to know. The minute the soul tries to understand God, the pure encounter turns into an *it*. Faced by such inevitable human operation, both Buber and John of the Cross agree that the soul, at least in this life, oscillates between the *I-it* and *I-Thou* modes of relations.[216] Since identity forms part of the *I-It*, it is an activity about the temporal past that the soul tries to preserve.[217] The pure continuous relation as an *I-Thou* is impossible in this life. After settling in the *dark night*, which is the realization of these two realms of relating, the soul would view its identity of this world as a trivial matter since the whole fruits produced by the path of affirmation and negation become less important to define the *I* concerning God.

Understood in the light of this discussion of John of the Cross' doctrine, growth is a progressive threefold development, with its beginning and endpoint in God, and Christ is the prototype which the soul should imitate. The first exercise of the soul is self-acceptance of all that constitutes it: all that has formed its identity and desire. The soul's desire is befriended in view of its past influences and the various means of how it was and can be expressed and fulfilled in this life. The second exercise of growth is also self-acceptance, but this time the celebration and affirmation of life are contrasted with limits, loss of meaning and disequilibrium. Even the soul's aptitudes, such as imagination and discernment, will cease to grant fulfilment and satisfaction at some point. Here the soul encounters a God who is perceived as silent and more immense. The act of self-acceptance encompasses mystery, fragility, and loss of control, but these moments of impasse become opportunities for further growth. The third aspect of growth is the way of love. Here growth requites that the soul not only befriend these two aspects of human development and acceptance but remains open to the divine relationship with God. This openness oscillates between two modes of desiring: the soul knows it holds a desire governed by human lack but is willing to approach the divine and plead that its desire is transformed into divine desire operating from divine abundance. In this scenario, the surest instrument at the disposal of the soul to communicate with God is not its imagination or any aptitude but contemplation, a loving and faithful general observation of God. Hence, the third aspect of growth is again an act of self-acceptance through which the soul participates in a continuous act of contrition and conversion.

Faced by tribulation, John of the Cross advises a soul to stop trying to find a remedy by turning towards creatures or by entering into any form of

---

216. *Night,* Book 2, ch. 18, no 4.
217. Buber, *I and Thou*, 13.

spiritual activity that has expired in granting value.[218] Instead, he advises the soul to wait silently and slowly turn a general loving observation (contemplation) towards God.[219] In this scenario, affirmation and negation become one since the soul's fluctuations were not associated with God but resulted from the consequences of subscribing to many hollow identities.[220] The *dark night* becomes an invitation to the soul to allow itself to be found and be intuitive within a reality that preceded the world and to start a transformation appropriate to its uniqueness.[221] Through these dynamics, one realizes how the journey was, in fact, God's desire in the first place. Faith is not simply something that the soul has or a conjured or declared voice (an *it*). Instead, the soul encounters faith in its givenness as a secret ladder but also an impasse that disguises; this is a mysterious reality that shrouds God but simultaneously purifies and invites towards a loving relationship with no intermediate instruments except a total free givenness.[222] The soul thus sub-

218. *Night*, Book 1, ch. 10, no 1; The first encounter of the passive dark night can be associated with trauma. Studies of trauma suggest that recovering the story of trauma could not fully be captured in language, see Arel and Rambo, *Post-Traumatic Public Theology*, 6.

219. Rom 6:4–6; 12:2; *Night*, Book 1, ch. 10, no 4; Fitzgerald, "Impasse and Dark Night," 94. Here a spiritual death signifying the paschal mystery appears while the waiting for God prefigures the silent Saturday before the resurrection, see Martini, *Our Lady of Holy Saturday*. This negation is also about any initiative to recover "deep masculinity." The whole method becomes redundant for a more profound spirit within the self has no gender, and escapes appropriation by the faculties of the self.

220. After *the passive night of sense*, human desire would remain lacking in relation to the perfection of God, but this lack would be "compatible with the divine abundance." in Howells, "From Human Desire to Divine Desire in John of the Cross."

221. *Night*, Book 1, ch. 1: "Even the manifestations of the passive night of sense and spirit typically associated with ectasy cannot be considered as extraordinary in themselves rather such transiet acts would be a reaction of the body undergoing further purification." Garrigou-Lagrange and Doyle, *Christian Perfection and Contemplation According to St. Thomas Aquinas and John of the Cross*, 35. Gergen's solution points to the concept of the *sublime* as "a power or force that was beyond and prior to human capacity for rational articulation." Grodin and Lindlof, *Constructing the Self in a Mediated World*, 137.

222. *Ascent*, Book 2, ch. 1, no 1; *Night*, Book 2, ch. 15, no 1; ch. 17, no 1. "The crossroad in question here is that between *meditation* and *contemplation*. Previously, perhaps using an Ignatian method, one has exercised the spiritual powers in the hours of meditation—the senses, imagination, understanding, the will. But now they won't work. All efforts are in vain. The spiritual practices that up to now have been a source of inner joy become a torment, intolerably dull and fruitless. But there is no tendency to occupy oneself with worldly things. The soul desires more than all else to remain still, without bestirring itself, allowing all its faculties to rest. But this seems to them to be sloth and a waste of time. That is more or less the state of the soul when God wishes to lead it into the *Dark Night*. In usual Christian parlance, such a condition will be called 'a cross.'" Stein, *Science of the Cross*, 6:61.

mits to the strangeness of a divine-abundant and divine-mysterious desire through contemplation and becomes disguised from the world and from itself in faith.[223]

Before ending this section, a question will be posed: *What constitutes the new identity resulting from contemplation?*[224] In other words, what type of man emerges from this form of relating as *I-Thou*? From the narratives of this study, only one participant, Peter, provided a glimpse of what contemplation might look like and thus, results are sketchy. In trying to answer the question, one has to imagine how one would relate with God without projecting affirmative and negated desire unto God or, as Rowan Williams aptly states:

> . . . we need to abandon the attempt to assemble a list of actions that put God in our debt we have to recognise once and for all that God's unconditional activity cannot be moulded by our finite actions and that God's mind cannot be changed by human effort. To belong among God's people is to have let go of the idea that we can have a claim on God's favour and accept that we must be radically receptive to God's initiative.[225]

All *its* that categorize life and limit God begin to lose their import, and one begins to cross into the realm of mystics where poetry is more valid and authentic than any objectifiable word. Mystics attempt to shape into words that loving dialogue that arises between the soul and God.

Moreover, a new identity or new masculinity might not be an appropriate term following the experience of the *passive night of sense*.[226] It ap-

---

223. Contemplation here is understood as *infused contemplation*, "that which tire mystics speak of, is a loving knowledge of God, which is not the fruit of human activity aided by grace, but of a special inspiration of the Holy Ghost; so that it is not producible at will, as is an act of faith." in Garrigou-Lagrange and Doyle, *Christian Perfection and Contemplation According to St. Thomas Aquinas and John of the Cross*, 45 and 46.

224. How John of the Cross views contemplation entirely contrasts with how Christian authors on masculine spirituality view it. Here contemplation becomes the only remaining active instrument that the self adopts to "access" God to allow being known by Him. It is not to be understood as a passive feminine aspect that the self taps into to feed the active masculine side. If the masculine/feminine binary still exists, then the soul is still operating within the dynamics of *the active and passive night of sense*. Moreover, the substance of the soul is not the same as "deep masculinity." The wildmen, warriors, magicians, and kings archetypes must be darkened by faith too see: 1 Kgs 19:11–13, Tobit 2:7–10 and Job 3.

225. Williams, "Mystical Theology and Christian Self-Understanding," 14.

226. Col 3:3; Gal 2:20; This "new identity" escapes enclosure, but it is open to otherness. The soul would not only further desire the Beloved but begin to desire the desire of the Beloved: Williams, "Deflections of Desire"; Howells, "From Human Desire to Divine Desire in John of the Cross." Also important to note that when the contemplative

pears that while identities, masculinities, genders and all other constitutes are an entry point to spiritual perfection, in the end, they become empty containers in relation to a larger divine reality. The soul realizes how all the objects of this world are foolish with God.[227] However, if one conceives of masculinity and spirituality through its manifestations and mystery, then the investigation places masculinity within a temporal spectrum with its origin in the body, but it is further developed, administered, regulated, and objectified through interaction. Masculinity becomes a mediated instrument in itself, and like any other object the self was granted access to, it is affirmed, negated, transcended, and ultimately redeemed at the opportune moment. This process might suggest that when contemplation permeates desire, the soul relegates all fragments making up identity and masculinity against the pure *I-Thou* background, which supersedes the same processes of affirmation and negation. If contemplation reverses relations upside down, then as Buber notes: "just as prayer is not in time but time in prayer, sacrifice not in space but space in sacrifice,"[228] so it is with men and their subjective masculinity: men do not meet God through a particular form or time, but it is God-form, as unconditional and abundant desire that meets the man; everything else about reality is abolished.[229] Hereafter, the soul with God would escape reductivism about each others' nature and that of the relationship governing the two. The self also disposes authorship of its own story and allows itself to be surprised and taken up by the mysterious *I-Thou* relationship. These events recover for the soul that divine union exemplified in the biblical allegorical narrative before Adam and Eve consumed the fruit of the tree of knowledge.[230]

The participant Peter acknowledged three aspects: unlimited and unconditional love, receiving beyond what could have been imagined, and God patiently accompanying the soul. The three features accentuate John of the Cross' thoughts. The world in all its objects and relations cannot provide and support existential meaning to the soul as it does not contain an infinite and unconditional desire for love. The soul with all talents and insights realizes how powerless it is to imagine how God's love can be.[231] However, com-

---

life begins the asceticism in the active night does not cease rather, "the exercise of the different virtues becomes truly superior when the soul receives the mystical grace of almost continual union with God." in Garrigou-Lagrange and Doyle, *Christian Perfection and Contemplation According to St. Thomas Aquinas and John of the Cross*, 25 and 42.

227. 1 Cor 3:19.
228. Buber, *I and Thou*, 9.
229. Buber, *I and Thou*, 9.
230. Gen 3.
231. Fitzgerald, "Desolation as Dark Night."

ing to encounter something about God's love, the soul begins to consider its identity from the Beloved mark that nothing of the world is capable to love the soul as God.[232] This discovery leads to the third feature that God is patiently accompanying the soul. Projection by the soul onto God as an external figure diminishes and identity begins to be seen from an *I am* to a *We are* perspective independent of the world.[233] God then does not remain an external and distant entity to the soul. Slowly, through contemplation, the soul begins to embrace the loving dialogue with the Beloved that indwells within the soul.[234] The preservation of the *I-Thou* becomes the center that holds and sustains the self.

Having examined how the self is understood and how the three paths of affirmation, negation and transformation interact with John of the Cross, this chapter will move into the last phase of this research. In part three, a discussion will follow about possible ways to enrich spiritual direction with men.

PART THREE: SPIRITUAL DIRECTION WITH MEN

The previous sections show how human development is an intricated matter. The process can be summarized by noticing that the self tries to answer two interior questions. The first question is, *who am I?* In many ways, different external voices temper the anxiety that this question causes to the self by pointing to material and immaterial identity constructs. Thus, part of the spiritual growth necessitates that the self responsibly steps forward to examine what has been assumed as part of its life. Furthermore, the inescapable trials of life and the experience of failure, while they intensify the desire for the self to find an answer to its existence, they also unveil another critical question: *who knows me best?*[235] This question is about whom the

---

232. Col 3:10, 12, 14; cf. Eph 4:1–6; Gal 2:9. See also Blommestijn et al., *Footprints of Love*. In their book these authors highlight a variety of features that the *dark night* realizes in the soul: hoping without memory, to be unconditional open to God's future and disinterested love.

233. Bernard of Clairvaux expresses similar thoughts in Clairvaux, *Five Books on Consideration*.

234. "You were more inward to me than my most inward part and higher than my highest." Augustine, *Life and Writings of Saint Augustine* 3.6.11.

235. These two questions, *who am I* and *who knows me best,* are similar to Barry and Connolly's questions that they apply to define spiritual direction: *who is God for me* and *who am I for God* in Barry and Connolly, *Practice of Spiritual Direction*, 5. Henri Nouwen also begins treating the importance of spiritual direction from this perspective in Nouwen et al., *Spiritual Direction*. Rowan Williams notes that "the question put to the believer is about the ultimate direction of his or her life: *for the sake of what* do we

self shall trust as the most secure and reliable source of truth. In essence, spiritual growth entails opening, partaking, and responding to the different instruments that initially grant meaning but later expire in value. For the Christian person, God would be the ultimate answer to the second question, and John of the Cross' doctrine is centered on the necessity for the self to detach from any subjective concepts and experiences that limit God's loving spirit. In other words, a process of unlearning is necessary so that the self loses itself entirely in order to be regained anew. Thus, spiritual effort encompasses two activities: to know through seeking, gaining, and reviewing experiences of God and to be known where the self makes itself available and willing to be found by God through contemplation. To be found by God is synonymous with John of the Cross' understanding of union with God.

These two dynamics of spirituality are recognized in the mission of spiritual direction.[236] Directors offer both knowledge and a method of how God can be accessed as the most reliable source of truth. It is agreed that spiritual direction aims to guide others to become aware of God's presence in human experience and to elicit responsibility and determination in how a person responds to God's transformation.[237] This goal brings forth a continuous reflection of one's thoughts, feelings, and actions if taken seriously. Hence, the continuous relationship between the directee and director can be described as a form of prayer requiring a profound attitude of listening both to the self's operations and God's actions.[238] Through spiritual direction, the directee is introduced to a style or a variety of ways of prayer. Prayer in all its forms is a mediated instrument in which the self participates by listening to itself. It fosters an approach to life with new intentionality so that life has "the potential to become an avenue towards the Sacred."[239] From this emerge the two functions of spiritual direction: discernment of experience and facilitation to the encounter with God. These two roles will be briefly discussed in this last part in conversation with the discussion above concerning masculinity and the dynamics of identity formation.

Discernment of Experience

Spiritual direction can be considered as another space for the self to explore itself. Although it occurs under the premise of discerning God's will and

---

live?" Williams, *Wound of Knowledge*, 167.

236. For a brief history of spiritual direction, see Leech, *Soul Friend*, 30.
237. Buckley, *Sacred Is the Call*, 19 and 22.
238. Buckley, *Sacred Is the Call*, 28 and 33.
239. Buckley, *Sacred Is the Call*, 45.

action in the person's life, much of its work is less about knowing God and more about understanding how the self is constructed, how the self responds to desire, how the self seeks refiner sources of existential meaning and how the self try-outs new forms of selfhood.[240] In addition, spiritual direction allows the possibility of trying things out by cooperating with someone experienced in spiritual dynamics and slowly acquiring the habit to remain mindful of God's presence.[241] Sue Pickering defines spiritual direction as:

> Taking place when one person (the director) prayerfully supports and encourages another person (the directee) to attend and respond to God. As a fellow pilgrim, the spiritual director accompanies the directee on this journey of faith. The real "director" is God the Holy Spirit, who initiates and inspires the directee's deepening relationship with the Trinity, with his or her own self, with other people, and with the realities of life in the global village of the twenty-first century.[242]

From the observations gathered from the previous sections, several operations can be outlined that directors participate in when directing men. Here they will be briefly discussed.[243]

Objectifying the Self

Like other talk therapies, spiritual direction assists directees to draw their identities into view as much as possible. It is a process of objectification through language and critical reflection.[244] A men-specific objectification emerges by attentively listening to how men describe themselves, what is sensitive to them, how they position themselves in the social contract, what is revealed and potential blind spots that are hidden from the directee.[245] The parameters outlined by Franco Imoda in phase one of this chapter find their place here.

---

240. Seeking self-meaning is the initiator of the examination of religious experience in Barry and Connolly, *Practice of Spiritual Direction*, 17.

241. Barry and Connolly, *Practice of Spiritual Direction*, 17.

242. Pickering, *Spiritual Direction*, 3.

243. Each aspect is discussed separately but should not be considered exclusively.

244. The role of spiritual directors has been named as *interpreters of experience* in Dyckman and Carroll, *Inviting the Mystic, Supporting the Prophet*, 24.

245. See the *Johari Window* as a self-help heuristic technique that assists persons in understanding themselves and their relationship to others better in Luft and Ingham, *Johari Window*.

Part of the journey of spirituality is befriending and exploring each of the aspects of human development with greater scrutiny. Often the entry point to self-awareness is desire. Janet Ruffing explains that any relationship with God encourages the directee to explore and share desire. In her experience, she shares that exploration of desire can be a frightening experience for directees. Therefore, the spiritual director contributes by providing a space to support and encourage exploration.[246] Agreeing with Ruffing, part of the objectification of the self is firstly to name what one desires and then examining how true that desire is genuine and realistic. From what has been observed from the previous chapters, desire is the gateway for spiritual exploration, but along the way, desire is sifted from expectations and illusions that have populated the self through socialization.[247]

Objectifying the self resonates with an improved self-awareness as one of the areas of growth that spiritual directors mentioned in chapter four. Moreover, working with men requires particular import in the realm of feelings, especially in patiently allowing the directee to express emotions, responding nonjudgmentally and offering solace with complicated feelings like grief, vulnerability and shame.[248] Thus, all of the objectifying the self does is aimed for greater self-awareness as an act of repentance for God's grace.[249]

However, this remaining mindful of God's presence has its dangers. In chapter four, spiritual directors pointed out that men seek spiritual direction less than women.[250] This observation is also backed by current discourse from pastoral care research.[251] Part of the disinterest is attributed to conventional ideas that men should strive to control one's life and be independent. However, when considering the multiplicity of voices vying for validity, one cannot ignore that the spiritual voice is immersed in competition.

However, in chapter four, spiritual directors noted that the primary reason why men approach spiritual direction is when their current lifestyle

---

246. Ruffing, *Spiritual Direction*, 15.

247. Dunne, *Spiritual Mentoring*, 19–22; Grosse, *Eight Masks of Men*.

248. Donald Bisson shares similar thoughts: "When men grow in befriending their emotions, the positive results seep into renewed images of God, better relationships and discovery of inner reality." Bisson, "Melting the Iceberg," 30–37.

249. Dunne, *Spiritual Mentoring*, 32.

250. I am hesitant to use the phrase "feminization of the Church" as such discussion gives into the politics of hegemonic masculinity and muscular Christianity. The arguments are often based only on church attendance and do not consider other religious or spiritual activities.

251. Knieling, *Männer Und Kirche*; Kuratle and Morgenthaler, *Männerseelsorge Impulse Für Eine Gendersensible Beratungspraxis*.

would not be functioning as planned. If there is stability with a man's knowledge, then there is a tendency to ignore other examples even if they seem better. Failure becomes the catalyst for men to seek new avenues. This growing mindfulness towards God's presence can become a significant obstacle since a man can apply it mechanically, feeding into the desire to be perfect rather than real. What transpires is a self that merely substitutes one construct to another, and although substitution brings a lifestyle change, the self remains the center of attention. Within such dynamics, the element of struggle appears to be the determinate factor of undoing gender and spiritual development. Disappointments pull men into embodying a form of marginality—an internalized shameful feeling that impends, estranges, and dislocates men from owning a centered and stabile perspective about them in the world. The subjective phrase that captures these feelings is *not good enough*. Thus, when men approach spiritual directors, it should not be viewed lightly, as it signifies that they are attempting to break away or cope with the demands of masculinity. Men would be giving a chance to the spiritual voice, but at any point in time, a soul can change its mind and take other voices onboard, even radical once. Since one of the purposes of spiritual direction is to assist a soul in discerning God's voice amidst the multiplicity of voices, the direction of men unavoidably becomes deeply involved in doing, undoing and redoing masculinity.[252] If one takes on board these observations, then directors have to embrace a men-specific spiritual direction style.[253] Three principles would guide direction: owning a sensitive gaze to how men behave, noticing how gendered subjective concepts get mixed up with God and perceiving how held masculinities are being put into question. At the directee's own pace, directors have to reflect on the interplay between spirituality and gender in unlearning and rediscovering new terrain for identity formation. In the end, spiritual directors guide the soul that the expectation of *being good* to earn God's grace needs to be abandoned.[254]

---

252. See West and Zimmerman, "Accounting for Doing Gender"; Butler, "Performing Feminisms."

253. See Cervantes, "Manhood and Spirit," 179.

254. Kuratle and Morgenthaler pronounce similar thoughts: "Having to be a man, and yet not really being able to, since a man's concrete life always shamefully falls behind the demands of masculinity . . . So against lots of resistance, an externalising style of problem-solving needs to be overcome by therapeutic talk and a new language has to be practices for their problems, emotions and desires, a language that goes beyond the socially constructed forms of masculinity." Kuratle and Morgenthaler, *Männerseelsorge Impulse Für Eine Gendersensible Beratungspraxis* 30; Translation from Kummer, *Men, Spirituality, and Gender-Specific Biblical Hermeneutics*, 49.

Quantifying and Producing the Self

Spiritual directors contribute directly to how the self involves itself in spiritual matters by providing options to spiritual directees that foster a prayerful attitude. Interestingly, church attendance was not the primary feature that directors looked at when speaking about male directees. Instead, they mentioned other spiritual exercises like finding time alone to pray, going for walks in the countryside, meditating with the Bible, reading a book, adhering to spiritual direction sessions and discursive meditation. Participating in liturgy might have been taken for granted, but it exposes that men might be quantifying themselves in spiritual matters in a broader way.[255] Some spiritual directors expressed the necessity that directees learn to establish a routine or find time to pray and be with God.

Similarly to the previous operation, spiritual directors are deeply involved in encouraging their directees to flourish and express their spirituality in various ways.[256] To do and to labor has already been noticed as the preferred spiritual manifestation for men, and with each spiritual direction session, men are inevitably propelled toward editing, promoting and presenting the self to others and God. The self engages with various initiatives from evangelization, detaching from attachments, exploring an aspect of themselves and the apostolate as expressions of the soul's commitment to love.

Another feature about men that seems to fit here is the attitude of wanting to *do for the kingdom*. Spiritual directors noted that when men see value in growing committed to God's presence, they seek to express their loyalty through activities and practical experiences. In many cases, this attitude of doing for God reflects a mindset of bargaining: if the self shows its commitment to God, surely God will favor in equal terms the self. So again, the self remains the center of attention. These observations connect with Donald Bisson's concerns that men bring in spiritual direction.[257] He lists five challenges that spiritual directors will face when working with men:

1. The dichotomy between doing and being, which Bisson connects with social conditioning. According to him, the encouragement of performance and competitiveness limits the movement of the spirit.

---

255. See the six steps that men can do to grow in awareness and movement to spiritual depth in Bathum, "Discovering Creative Depth Within." Also see Jackson, "State of the Churches in Europe."

256. Often, the term used is to teach directees how to listen and respond to God. Pickering offers a list of different methods in Pickering, *Spiritual Direction*, 43–116. See also: McHugh, *Listening Life*.

257. Bisson, "Melting the Iceberg," 125.

2. Valuing thoughts over feelings. It is challenging for men to stay with feelings of vulnerability, grief, dependency, and shame. These bring a great challenge for spiritual directors, especially when considering that relating with God will inevitably stir many emotions.

3. Men's awareness of their bodies. According to Bisson, men deny their bodily needs, which can lead to addictions. He links these dynamics with the stereotypes that control how men should behave.

4. Homophobia. In particular, Bisson observes how the fear of being labelled gay influences how men view the call for intimacy with Jesus, their expression of deep feelings, and their understanding of friendship with other men and women.

5. Spiritual closet. The previous challenges yield a spiritual closet, which Bisson explains to mean that men hide their spiritual desires and instead sublimate over performance, religious talk, and achievement rather than focusing on the relationship with God. When these operations fail, men would inevitably reach a state of powerlessness.

It is within such observation that gender sensitivity in spiritual direction is of utmost importance. These dynamics result from a culture that ingrains stereotypical gendered assumptions about relationships, which in this study, one could notice being transmitted through the different expectations that parents, the religious institutions and the social context hold. Thus, by discerning experience, the spiritual director is to be conscious of gendered ways a man seeks God's movement, and that resistance will surely surface when such mechanical ways and expectations of relating fail.[258]

The danger with objectification, quantification and production of the self is that both spiritual directors and directees can view them as the end of spiritual growth rather than the preliminary features. As noted, it is straightforward for the self to think that the spiritual relationship with God will fluctuate according to how much they produce, participate, or remain committed to spiritual activities. Therefore, although directees need to be encouraged to celebrate and exercise what has been gained or discovered with each spiritual milestone, spiritual directors must be attentive to other hidden dynamics: what is genuinely propelling all the spiritual activities; what is being closeted and tugged away from awareness; who is really addressed in all these activities? In the end, the spiritual journey points to one critical quantifying or productive aspect for which the self should strive: greater transparency, intimacy and authenticity with God.[259] Anything

---

258. Bisson, "Melting the Iceberg," 122.

259. "God desires the smallest degree of purity of conscience in you more than all

else, done in the name of God, appears to be at risk of being vane.[260] Thus, spiritual directors should remain conscious and ready when the opportune moments arrive, and all these instruments of awareness, expressions and performances expire. They expire not into nothingness but for a superior operation to emerge.

Regulating the Self

If spiritual directors sustain a continuous relationship with their directees, directors develop into a source that endorses or questions conduct even if directors do not desire this. This is beyond the spiritual director's control: inevitably, every therapeutic relationship brings forth an influential and a power dynamic. How much directees attach importance to their directors' validation is related to the directees' needs of dependency, their self-confidence, and their interior freedom. Whether directees look at their spiritual director as a counsellor, friend, or father figure, the spiritual director will grow to be a reliable measurement that judges and confirms conduct. However, one could argue that some models are more likely to foster a dependent relationship, leading to manipulation from both directees and directors.[261] Although the three styles of spiritual direction that emerged from chapter four (spiritual counsellor, spiritual father, and spiritual friend) reflect each director's personality and charisma, they are continuously adapted according to the experience gained from what directees expect from directors.

Gary W. Moore and David G. Benner identify two axes that influence spiritual directors' styles: *authority* and *orientation*. Often spiritual directors who find little value in authority feel uncomfortable with the term director and prefer being known as spiritual friend or companion. However, when spiritual direction is associated with the priesthood, authority is unavoidably brought into the picture. Orientation demarcates the various activities related to spiritual directors, such as teaching, mentoring, healing, guiding, or sponsoring.[262] Moreover, these two axes are shaped and influenced by the particular theological tradition or denomination that the spiritual director ascribes to.[263] However, when we consider spiritual direction as gendered,

---

the works you can perform." *Sayings*, no 12. See also *Sayings*, 59, 60, 72, and 73.

260. To speak about beginners' motivations for consolation and satisfaction, John of the Cross uses the seven capitals sins as a basis for his argument in *Dark*, Book 1, chs. 1–13.

261. Hoyeau, *La Trahison Des Pères*.

262. Moon and Benner, "Spiritual Direction and Christian Soul Care," 20 and 21.

263. For particular styles of spiritual direction that emerge from different Christian

projection might be another hidden axis that influences directors' style. Spiritual directors carry a gendered character, and directees will unconsciously or consciously notice it. In the end, directees choose their spiritual director, not the other way round, and they must do so from a pool of potential candidates. One could argue that directees choose a director with a gendered identity that they are attracted to and reflects their needs.[264] When directees spoke about the close friendship with their director or recognized that their director answered many of their fatherly needs, they would unintentionally reveal that they were attracted and wished to own similar masculinity to their director.

The dangers of participating in this operation of the self are twofold: ignorance and role confusion. Spiritual direction automatically presents alternative masculinities to the directees. Thus, a gender-based self-reflection on the style a director uses is critical. It would expose patterns of perceptions and behaviors that might reinforce certain masculinity beliefs and provide proper preparation when encountering contradictory examples in directees. If such reflection does not occur, what a spiritual director has not yet considered in terms of personal preferences of masculinity, stereotypical mindsets and the complicit enjoyment of certain privileges would be ignored when directees bring them up in spiritual direction. A supposedly gender-neutral approach makes spiritual direction ignorant of gender dynamics.[265]

Furthermore, spiritual directors have the responsibility to notice how directees become attached to them. In this study, some scenarios exposed how directors were conscious that some directees viewed them as father figures or intimate friends with many expectations and unresolved feelings. For male directors, a genuine examination of their own masculinity can provide the necessary precaution and preparation to know what type of directees they tend to attract and prepare the necessary response when their role is confused either with God's image or with other figures in the directees' life story. This observation applies to female spiritual directors as well. Although only one female spiritual director participated in this study, and so results are inconclusive, it does not exclude the possibility that when a man chooses a female spiritual director, it resonates back to other figures in the directee's life story. Moreover, female spiritual directors might

---

denominations and traditions, see Moon and Benner, *Spiritual Direction and the Care of Souls*.

264. As much as directees choose their spiritual directors, directors behave the same way when choosing their supervisors.

265. Pickering suggests different areas that directors need to listen to and respond to reduce the danger of projection in Pickering, *Spiritual Direction*, 122–42.

contribute further beyond the three spiritual director's styles outlined in this study. One encounters, for example, the style of spiritual mothers in Julian of Norwich, also known as Mother Julian and spiritual midwifery.[266]

Emancipating the Self

Interior liberation was one of the areas of growth that was repeatedly mentioned by spiritual directors who participated in this study. Furthermore, when considering the doctrine of John of the Cross and the study of human development, it is clear that spiritual growth goes hand in hand with greater awareness of self and purification of desire. Awareness inevitably brings forth a better recognition of how the self is populated, especially about stereotypes, expectations, and aspirations of others, but at the same time, it is a humble recognition since the mystery that clouds God also clouds the self. Not only is the self heavy with so many demands and stereotypes imposed by others, but they camouflage the deepest desires of the self and distort God's image. Emancipation begins immediately from the moment a directee seeks direction since seeking spiritual direction requires the directee to take the risk of being transparent, honest, and committed to the real. The previous operations of the self (objectifying, producing, and quantifying) find their true purpose within emancipation of the self from all forms of limitations that impede union with God. Spiritual direction aims to liberate and purify the soul as much as possible from objects, visible and invisible, external, and interior, socially, and emotionally sanctioned and projected onto God that control and limit the relationship itself.[267] It is no wonder that spiritual directors encounter so much resistance from directees as the process of emancipation cuts deep into the core of the self.

Resistance is the greatest obstacle in spiritual growth. It is a natural unconscious response that the self falls into to defend itself from uncertainty and uncontrollable change. However, Ruffing goes a step further. Through her experience as a spiritual director, she has come to believe that resistance is unconscious but often willfully employed by the self to evade the implications that a spiritual relationship with God brings about.[268] This study confirms this paradoxical observation since the directees who acted

---

266. Guenther, *Holy Listening*, 81.

267. "The work of the director is to lead the soul to this full surrender and freedom of spirit, according to its own capacities, in the way of evangelical perfection, 'which is detachment and emptiness of sense and spirit.'" Merton, *Course in Christian Mysticism*, 196.

268. Ruffing, *Spiritual Direction*, 33.

as participants in this study have acknowledged the various ways how they deliberately evaded confronting the real matter they thought had to be dealt with. Thus, by implication, one can understand that life will indeed be changed when seeking God. As much as God affirms the self, losing is an inevitable experienced too. These observations have also been noted by spiritual directors who participated in this research when they spoke about men's attitudes when God is felt close. Men tend either to evade or to be stubborn, which leads to an inability to surrender control.[269] Even prayer can be a form of resistance. Prayer here encompasses all forms of spiritual exercises. However, the self can unconsciously or consciously abandon a prayer routine, choose another spiritual director, choose a method that grants emotional delight, own a mental state that distorts openness to God, or even change communities. All such evasions highlight how the self wants to remain centered on its own.

Loss of control is inevitably one of the implications of spiritual growth. However, the dynamics of fear and flight from God should not be seen as contradictory to the primary desire of the self to be intimate with God. Resistance should be respected and considered as a training ground. Even if the self is stubbornly resisting and struggling, it is instantaneously being fashioned by mystery. At one point, the struggle melts, but such an opportune moment is beyond the spiritual directors' control. Resistance points us to the merit of the *passive night of sense and spirit*. Since the spiritual relationship concerns itself between the self and God, God will bring forth further transformation. God always knows best the contours and operations of the soul, and it is within such dynamics that it is not the self who seeks God, but it is Him who works for the self to be found. John of the Cross reassures the soul that through such purification, God struggles with the soul and achieves more than if he had to create the soul from nothing since nothing does not resist back.[270] However, spiritual directors will inevitably encounter the ripple effects of resistance, sometimes even directly, since a directee can merge the role of the director with that of God. Indeed, resistance is the greatest challenge since, as directors shared, at one point in the spiritual journey of their directees, what often they encounter is a continuous pattern of evasion, stubbornness and struggle to surrender to God. It is

---

269. Tad Dunne suggests that training in spiritual direction should help mentors be with directees when they encounter failure and understand what kind of experience to anticipate with God. However, spiritual growth is precisely the loss of the self which also means the inability to anticipate anything about God in Dunne, *Spiritual Mentoring*, 5.

270. *Ascent*, Book 1, ch. 6, no 4.

then no wonder that spiritual directors name patience as one of the critical virtues in giving spiritual direction.

Moreover, a further need for the *passive night of sense and spirit* is exposed when considering the limitations of spiritual directors. Resistance can also be reinforced by spiritual directors either by giving out signals of disapproval, withdrawal, discomfort, helplessness or even by simple nonverbals that the directee can misunderstand. As much as the self cannot control the relationship with God, it is with spiritual directors and the dynamics of spiritual growth in their directees.[271] Another form of resistance in spiritual growth lies within the director independent of directees. Although the focus of this study was primarily to look at how directees express their masculinity and how directors respond, inevitably, some dangers were observed about directors. Like directees, directors resist due to character formation, socialization, and experiences of life. Since these dangers appeared directly in the narratives of directees and some directors even revealed them, they will be listed below, but further research is required in these areas.[272]

1. **The danger of pride**: spiritual directors might fall into the trap that their track record of supporting others, training and personal spiritual experiences warrants incredible confidence in how spiritual growth is brought forth. Pride then leads to other forms of behavior like judging others involved in church ministry as amateurish, abandoning directees who do not fulfil their demands, cynicism about life and the church, gossip, and separation from those who hold a different perspective from theirs.[273]

2. **The danger of impatience**: resistance is an inescapable reality in spiritual growth, and for the most part, it is the central area where God's grace will be exposed in the life of the directee. Often resistance is so persistent, repetitive and sometimes defying that the directors grow annoyed, exhausted and disenchanted.

3. **The danger of unresolved sexual issues**: like the directees, directors are not exonerated from sexual dynamics. Often, this results from unexplored areas in oneself, which leads to role confusion, unwarranted emotional expectations, and disappointments. In some cases, the ministry of spiritual direction is viewed as a vocation that substitutes and justifies their unfulfilled desire to enter into a romantic relationship, not being a father and loneliness. Underneath confusion of roles

---

271. Ruffing, *Spiritual Direction*, 46.
272. These resistances are not mutually exclusive.
273. See Capps, "Don Quixote as Moral Narcissist."

emanates a confusion of desire which the director needs to befriend and separate from the ministry of spiritual direction.[274]

4. **The danger of superficiality**: two areas of superficiality can be deduced. The first area is the lack of continuous professional development. Some might be unwilling to be educated by new knowledge about human relations, interpersonal skills, and spiritual growth dynamics. There might be tendencies to sideline knowledge that emerges from other academic disciplines that question and confront the moral principles of the church. The second area is to disregard and forget that the essential mission of spiritual direction is not a type of counselling. If spiritual direction is reduced to guiding directees to abide by the moral principles of the church, giving emotional support or talk therapy, then spiritual development turns into role conformity and life management. However, spiritual direction entails more than just learning how to handle everything one needs to live a productive, happy, and fulfilling life. As seen from the ten narratives of directees in chapter two, sin, disordered desires, and suffering become an entry to salvation since through these happenings, the directees' desires are clarified. Superficiality breeds ignorance and a form of spirituality of boxes where directees are led to fit in ready-made identities.

Directors might be aware or unaware of how they respond to these forms of resistance in themselves. However, spiritual abuse takes form when directors give way to such risks. The same tenets that guide spiritual growth, like forgiveness, trust, and mercy, are easily manipulated or abandoned to protect one's reputation, control others or guard against identity defamation. Hence, all these resistances points to the fact that when emancipation occurs, it is primarily brought about by God, and in the process, both the directee and director experience it. So much so that sometimes the mistakes of a director become the catalyst for further spiritual awakening in directees.

The mysterious ways how the emancipation of the soul is brought about reveals God's presence. Disinterest love finds its merits within such context since it acts as a buffer when spiritual directors need to let go of their control in their guidance.[275] While it is of utmost importance that spiritual directors remain present in providing support and care, often described as something unique and rare by directees since very few people would understand their interior struggles, the director does not allow himself or herself to be inordinately attached to their directees. The directors have to keep in

---

274. Silver, *Trustworthy Connections*.
275. Blommestijn et al., *Footprints of Love*, 156.

check which desires are being fulfilled through their involvement since inordinate attachment can lead to distorted responsibility and spiritual abuse. Disinterested love allows the director to begin to see the other with the eyes of God and allow mystery to accomplish itself.[276]

Thus emancipation of the self includes two crucial operations: purification and transcendence. However, the timing when the soul experiences them is so subtly mysterious. As much as satisfaction, delight and affirmation are desirable, grief, negation and loss are inescapable realities of life. A twofold drive marks life: life gives, forms, and at the same time, it takes back and destroys. The self, grown by the labors of mortification, is further emancipated through surrendering itself. Similarly, to any worldly object, feeling, form, masculinity and possession, grief would not last forever; the oils of the lamps will give way, and it would be foolish for the self to seek the old and lost identity in any form.[277] As the self embraces the cross of loss, it grows in freedom and transparency. Hence part of the emancipation of the self is to learn to temporarily appreciate what is given, and at the same time, the self is ready to surrender them at the opportune moment. The self pre-empts the operations of this world and remains free by comprehending how all voices are already finished.[278]

As for transcendence, when the self learns that although nothing in this world can last forever, the soul begins to operate with a new hopeful perspective. It remains deeply involved within the world, but it transcends everything of it. It neither falls into pessimism nor delusion. Transcendence builds on loss, and yet loss has not the final word. While grief signals the struggle when the self lets go, transcendence is the actual moment when the self is being found anew. Transcendence satisfies a lesser hope where the self is satisfied temporarily by new discoveries that others bring but remains reclined on divine providence.

One aspect of human development that this study exemplifies is how sexuality is closely related to the spiritual. As shown in chapter three, many of the directees spoke about their spiritual and sexual development effectively interchangeably. Emancipation was witnessed when spiritual directors reinforced a continuous presence that positively allowed directees to speak and accept one's sexuality, sustain complicated feelings of infertility, fears of rejection, expose homophobia or when disappointments and conflict emerged in relationships. Since sexuality is the most private aspect of

---

276. Blommestijn, "Learning to See the Other with the Eyes of God in St. John of the Cross."

277. Matt 25:1–13.

278. *Counsels*, no 7.

the self, it becomes a gateway and a reflection of spirituality: the expectations governing identity also control how sexuality is objectified, quantified, and produced. If societal expectations judge an identity as *not good enough*, then sexual expectations bombard men that they are *not man enough*. Thus, spiritual emancipation always involves the sexual since sexuality is the most personal, intimate, and secretive aspect of the self. Struggling reappears again since resistance to spiritual emancipation reflects the undoing of man's efforts to manage and camouflage his sexuality so that he achieves the expectation to be *man enough*. It must be pointed out how the coming out experience of gay men is a real example that exposes a split between spirituality and sexuality that needs healing. Furthermore, the coming out acts as a symbol that should speak to all men no matter their sexual orientation. From this study, one can notice various coming out experiences in men: coming out of oppressive expectations, of inordinate roles, coming out to love, to their deepest desire and ultimately to God. Thus, no wonder many gay authors consider the coming out experience as a sacrament.[279]

Preparing for the Mysterious Encounter

The first aspect of spiritual direction is a lengthy preparation that points to what John of the Cross calls contemplation. The operations of the self that spiritual directors participate in can be seen as a process of mortification leading to wholeness.[280] The discovery of self is equivalent to the operations of the *active night of sense and spirit*, figuratively seen as the Bride (soul) searching for the Beloved (the one who truly knows the soul). However, the self remains centered on itself. Here God becomes the "spiritual director" that elevates the soul and brings further decentralization.[281] Directors need to be aware of three signs that John of the Cross notes when the transition to contemplation begins. These are:

1. A continuous experience of dryness and dissatisfaction in prayer and life. The same operations of the self previously supported by spiritual directors now feel empty and devoid of any satisfaction and delight.

---

279. Goss, "Integration of Sexuality and Spirituality"; Fortunato, *Embracing the Exile*; Glaser, *Coming out as Sacrament*; McNeill, *Freedom, Glorious Freedom*.

280. "The goal of a Christian life becomes not enlightenment but wholeness—an acceptance of this complicated and muddled bundle of experiences as a possible theatre for God's creative work." Williams, *Wound of Knowledge*, 2.

281. "One can deliver oneself up to crucifixion, but one cannot crucify oneself. Therefore that which the active night has begun must be completed by the passive night, that is, through God himself." Stein, *Science of the Cross*, 6:74.

Although the desire for God remains strong, the self experiences dissatisfaction with any instrument that previously grasped something about the divine.

2. An understanding that turning back to the old self is not a viable solution. The self faces hopelessness and disinclination to use its abilities to grasp the divine, knowing they will grant nothing of value. The self is fearful that while God is desired, an internal obstacle impinges on any employment of its powers.

3. A desire of the soul to be in solitude, in silence and with a loving gaze for God. The only words that describe what the self desires are marked by simple phrases like wanting to be with God. For John of the Cross, when the soul utters its simple desire to rest in God achieves contemplation, the highest form of prayer.[282]

Neither spiritual directors nor the self is the initiators of these three operations. However, indirectly, spiritual directors can either assist the soul by validating the course of events or hinder further by provoking more arduous spiritual activities or judging directees. No theological exhortation or moral statement can quench this divine operation. Unless one does not enter a process of affirmative, honest, and empathic conversation, all prepositional assertions will fail to bear fruit since it is God who brings the soul to hold this new identity. Hence a defining part of the mission of spiritual direction is to be sensitive to when such opportune moments appear to be fulfilled.

In this study, the role of spiritual direction has been described as resembling that of a counsellor, a friend, or a father. In contrast, Shaun McCarty describes spiritual directors as *mystagogues*.[283] By this term, he means that spiritual directors are seen as guardians and stewards of mystery with the primary function to facilitate others to be attentive, relate and abandon themselves to mystery. As McCarty explains, becoming a mystagogue has more to do with experience than training; consequently, directees learn how to relate to mystery through *contagion* rather than infusion.[284] By contagion, one can understand what has already been iterated that a spiritual directee, in choosing and sticking with a spiritual director, unconsciously admits a desire to become like his spiritual director, specifically how the director lives their spirituality as a person of faith. Through the relationship, the director teaches the directee how to relate to mystery by evoking questions, fostering

---

282. *Sayings*, no 82, 88, and 119; *Ascent,* Book 2, chs. 13 and 14; *Night,* Book 1, ch. 9.
283. McCarty, "Spiritual Directors," 3.
284. McCarty, "Spiritual Directors," 3.

a contemplative attitude, and encouraging directees to seek answers at their own pace. However, the most powerful means of *contagion* is that spiritual directors are an example for their directees.

Moreover, if we take John of the Cross' doctrine, the role of a mystagogue is to be attentive to the language of directees, which without the directees' knowledge would be desiring that the opportune moments for spiritual growth take form. As has been already noted, the language of desire is wrapped in a paradox of wanting and evading, metaphors that form passions and profound silence that is louder than words. This language reflects the inability of the self to capture mystery and paradoxically the inability of the self to name what it actually desires. The *I know not* invocation that John of the Cross mentions as a result of contemplation cuts in two ways: it is pronounced in front of the inability to contain God's love and the inability of the self to know itself in front of such love.[285] The divine love is too expansive that although it populates the self, it is still shrouded in mystery, so much so that the self shares in its mystery as well.

Furthermore, a profound awareness required by the mystagogue relates to purification and transcendence. A spiritually grown self acquainted with the cycle of purification, transcendence, and taking onboard faith as the only means to be found by God will grow in desiring what John of the Cross calls the annihilation of the self. In other words, purification and transcendence also become the instruments that begin to expire. The self would desire a spiritual death in all things esteemed, especially those lingering fragments that still stain and control individuation. Ultimately the soul would want to break free from the cycle of affirmation and negation and hopes to lie in the beatific vision. The soul remains engaged within the world but does so more serenely and, at the same time, carrying a deep longing for union to be settled once and for all. Spiritual directors should then remain concerned with the eschatological self that is slowly emerging. It is a new self which, in line with Saint Paul, is being clothed by the mystery of Christ:

> As many of you as were baptized into Christ have clothed yourselves with Christ. There is no longer Jew or Greek, there is no longer slave or free, there is no longer male and female; for all of you are one in Christ Jesus. And if you belong to Christ, then

---

285. "I entered into unknowing/and there I remained unknowing/transcending all knowledge." A poem by John of the Cross entitled, "Stanzas concerning an Ecstasy Experienced in High Contemplation."

you are Abraham's offspring, heirs according to the promise. (Gal. 3:23-29)[286]

Similarly, John of the Cross teaches that the soul must pass through all the night phases and realize that nothing of this world, including gender and the activities and practices that previously brought spiritual delight, can grasp God and the soul. Thus, while the soul remains in the world, it knows that ultimately everything is in vain.[287]

Much more might be said about the role of spiritual directors in guiding men, and there is still much to explore. This chapter has sought to make a beginning by relating the data that emerged from the lived experience of the directees and directors who took part in this study to a theoretical corpus and, on the basis of this analysis, to expand on the layered transformative process between the divine-human relationship. Part one of this chapter considered human reality and human development by situating the discussion on a postmodern platform, which led to the necessity not to limit any discussion about the self reductively. A necessary precaution against reductionism is to include mystery as a central characteristic of human development. Part two continued to expound on mystery by outlining how the self is affirmed, negated, and transcended by laying out examples specifically from men's studies and masculinity. Part three built on the preceding sections by expounding further on the operations of spiritual direction and emphasized how the very true nature of spiritual direction is directly linked with being stewards of mystery. Having now considered the dynamics of spiritual growth envisaged by John of the Cross and the multiple resonances it brings about in the lives of men, this study will move to its concluding part by suggesting what needs to be reclaimed in men's spirituality.

---

286. See "The Soul's Tricolored Garment" in Stein, *Science of the Cross*, 6:158.
287. John 15:19; John 17:14-16; Rom 12:2.

Conclusion

As this study draws to a close, it is important to recollect the purpose of this research and to reflect on the significance of its results. This study set out to explore three research questions: can a form of spirituality about men be identified and described, how can this spirituality be examined, and what needs to be reclaimed?

This project is the first comprehensive investigation of masculinity from the perspective of John of the Cross, and the first two questions have been considered in much detail in this study. By attending to the narratives of directees and directors and correlating them with John of the Cross' spiritual framework, we encounter a form of spirituality shaped by many aspects: visible, invisible, exterior, and interior. The form is made up of endless fragments that sketch a contour, but desire invigorates the core of the form and propels movement. This research has also shown that speaking of men's spirituality undoubtedly comprises a gendered style of living. All the aptitudes of the self, exerted through intellect, memory and will, are directed to attain validation from others. Thus, men learn and embody a gendered manner of acting, thinking, feeling, remembering, and valuing.

These findings make several contributions to the current literature on spiritual direction. They show how men's gendered manner of being human is also projected onto their relationship with God, and thus men also own a gendered style of approaching, praying, and thinking about God. What underpins this mode of being is a desire based on a sense of lack which propels the self to satisfy the emptiness by struggling and laboring to achieve meaning. Desire as lack is equivalent to survivability in the world. Others teach the self how to earn worth, but they also declare something about God. Men relate to God according to their perceived experience of God through the eyes of others. If God is aligned to fulfilled expectation, then validation is assumed as endorsed by God. Likewise, if God is associated with unfulfilled expectations, then God is resented. This inner rhythm of desire as lack consequently exposes gendered ways men face fears, negotiate their identity, resist change, seek support, and confront disappointment. Failure is indeed a catalyst of change, but the merit of John of the Cross emerges when considering how he distinguishes between two types of failure: failure that can be mitigated, solved, or managed, but desire as lack endures, and the kind of failure best described as an impasse, which impedes mitigation, voids options and materializes the self's fear. Here desire as lack leads to hopelessness and despair, but failure as impasse is an entry to God's transformation. The *dark night*, understood as an impasse, is a spiritual pedagogy that illustrates the operations of desire as lack from its affirmative and negative consequences. Ultimately, it leads to the transformation towards a desire of abundance and the nakedness of spirit. Experiencing failure of the first kind stimulates self-agency and flexibility of identities, and like at the market, the self can choose which new theory or unexplored spiritual practice to try out and gain insight. As observed in chapter four, spiritual direction is often sought by men in these experiences of failure. However, in the experience of impasse, men and all their instruments, including spiritual direction, are disempowered, but the self is led towards transformation. According to John of the Cross, the solution rests in allowing this perceived disempowerment to take its course while holding a contemplative or a general loving observation approach to God.

These also results contribute to the study of masculinity by exposing that while masculinity is an entry point in the spiritual relationship through its expression and participation in affirmative and negative events, in front of the impasse of faith, the self is led away from gendered ways of relating with God. However, this does not mean that masculinity is taken away. Rather masculinity is endowed with the seven virtues and remains engaged in the immediate context. Moreover, the self gradually frees itself from living in the world according to the laws of survivability and detaches from relying upon any gendered modes to encounter God. It is here that a limitation of this study arises but at the same time lays the groundwork for future research in masculinity and mystical theology. None of the male directees interviewed present an example of this new masculinity. Indeed, the term new masculinity might not be appropriate following the merits of the *passive night*, but it is being used here to remain faithful to the subject matter. In this scenario, any term we can think of must be yoked with Paul's assertion of being clothed in Christ (Gal 2:20). Even if directees offer examples of spiritual growth, they act as vague semblances that the union with God will accomplish. Maybe capturing it in plain language is impossible since what is received through the *passive night* is ultimately a mystical experience.

Notwithstanding this limitation, there is a need for further exploration of this new masculinity. One area is through dialogue with the mystics, by attuning to mystics' responses to the gendered socio-religious context of their time and, more importantly, how their gendered mode of being was transformed through their relationship with God. Their merits can also enlighten further results in the theories of self and masculinities. As noted in chapter five, theories of self have become fragmented while theories of masculinities either emphasize the negative qualities and consequences of subscribing to "types" of masculine ideologies or defensively reinforce the affirmative qualities without proper engagement with the harms. In all circumstances, proper regard to the self as a unitive entity drifts further away, and men remain torn in arguments of victimization or perpetrators. This study establishes a qualitative perspective that respects the unitive self even if it is a mystery in itself. Perhaps the significant contribution of this study to masculinity research is that it relegates discourse about gender with self and human development theories. In doing so, the self is respected as a unitive being, always moving towards living its mystery. The perspective that we bring about spirituality changes as well. Instead of regarding it simply as a means towards positive well-being or as a form of escapism from social responsibility, spirituality is understood as a *science of the self*—a method of thinking and practicing the self through affirmative, negative, and transformative modes of being in real and intense life impressions. Spiritual direction finds its mission within these continuous developmental dynamics, guiding towards more transparent openness towards the divine mystery. This study's contribution to research on spiritual direction is that it exposes how gender dynamics are not external to spiritual direction. On the contrary, spiritual direction is saturated in such subtleties, so gender dynamics cannot be side-lined. The insights gained from this study show that although a Christian denomination's particular tradition shapes the specific functions of spiritual directors, gender dynamics are ultimately the conduits that mold the relationship and the various operations of spiritual direction. Moreover, if transformation, as understood by John of the Cross, is an exit from gender dynamics, then this is the case also for spiritual directors. The primary role of spiritual directors that distinguishes their mission from that of other therapeutic professionals and, at the same time, negates any gendered modes of being is that of *mystagogue*. As stewards of mystery, their secondary gendered roles of guiding, supporting, teaching, and sponsoring are ultimately voided so that God emerges as the only Bridegroom that encounters the soul.

Perhaps by attending to the three modes of how masculinity is affirmed, negated, and transformed, we can answer the third research question about reclamation. In doing so, we also reclaim something new about how masculinity can be understood and how spiritual support to men can be better provided. The first reclamation is about affirmation and responsibility, which resonates with the call to ascend. The self is motivated to live and enjoy life by capturing a presence of meaning and peace. At first, this reclamation is limited to the expectations of parents and social systems, but through the experience of struggle, the self grows in reviewing, purifying, and discovering its true desire. The reclamation of affirmative masculinity inspires the self to be the best it can be and grasp success. It resonates with the celebration of life and self-actualization. Perhaps the transfiguration of Christ captures this scenario.[1] The link is Christ *ascending* to Mount Tabor as He *anticipates* the glory that awaits Him. Similarly, the self ascends and labors to grasp that glory that is already anticipated. Even spiritual direction finds its place in the transfiguration story within the image of Elijah and Moses, with whom Christ consults and discerns. Through the spiritual operations of objectifying, quantifying, and producing, spiritual directors support and guide their directees to succeed in the ascent of life and aspire to bring positive results in well-being. However, this reclamation is incomplete.

Following the events of the transfiguration, Christ quickly reminds the three disciples that he will suffer. The second reclamation is the way of the cross, which is the inevitable experience of absence, negation, and loss to which the self must surrender itself. This reclamation is an acceptance by the self that it cannot control everything in life, that the world is limited, and that the nature of the self cannot be reduced to a pattern of having and not having. However, acceptance of life as a descent does not come about out of thin air. Gendered ways of resisting and the struggles of the self with the encounter of impasse are the same avenues that lead to transcendence. Hence, this reclamation should propel spiritual directors to respond with compassion to their directees' resistances, remembering that God will meet the soul through the ensued chaos of escapism, stubbornness, and protest. Only God can bring into effect perfect emancipation of the self, and it requires perseverance until the soul realizes that the experience of impasse is not an attack on its person but is liberation from living desire as lack. The most excellent Biblical example for this reclamation is Christ's abandonment and annihilation on the cross. Spiritual direction is also here prefigured in the image of Mary and the beloved disciple, who accompany Christ from a distance, observing, perplexed and unable to do anything in

---

1. "The Transfiguration, like all of the biblical events in the life of Christ, was not an event that occurred because Christ needed it. Jesus had no self-serving reason to change the way he looked or the colour of his clothes. The event happened for the benefit of those who witnessed it." Andreopoulos, *This Is My Beloved Son*, 35.

the ensued chaos. Nevertheless, it is from the chaotic circumstances that the third reclamation begins to emerge.

If we had to stop with the second reclamation, the feeling that ensues is one of resignation and passivity in front of undesirable but inevitable consequences of life. However, the findings of this research suggest otherwise. The first reclamation leads to the second, and similarly, the third reclamation results from the preceding two. It is a reclamation that can only be fulfilled after the self experiences and transcends the fluctuations of affirmation and negation. In other words, it is a reclamation of masculinity that begins to share in the new creation of Christ's resurrection. God clothes the self with a superior identity in likeness to His desire as abundance. Apart from the living flame of love that unceasingly consumes and emanates love, John of the Cross also leaves us with another poem that perhaps foreshadows how desire as abundance might look.[2] In the metaphor of the eternal spring, the self recognizes God's love in its flows, rises and unconditional outpourings of love. However, the setting is always at *night*. This reclamation develops at *night* and succeeds from the pure encounter with God as *I-Thou* by resting onto faith and allowing God's mystery to take hold of the self. The self remains in the world, and until union with God truly comes into effect, and the soul departs this world, it keeps participating in different gendered modes of relating but without being held by them. No idea or experience is allowed to become an ideology that limits the self, relationships with others and God.

One of the metaphors of John of the Cross to display the interior disposition that follows in this third reclamation appears through the *solitary sparrow*.[3] A fragile creature who seeks the highest place rising above all objects of the world that can capture it, and there alone in silence and solitude stripped from experiences and owning no definite color of self-centeredness, holds its beak in the wind and sings in response to the love and inspiration of the Beloved. This metaphor should not lead us to think of John of the Cross' spiritual framework as escapism from the world. On the contrary, it affirms that the only way men can be perfected, reconciling all the fragments of their being, is through dark faith and a transformation of desire. The solitary sparrow signifies where the soul finds its sustenance, but following transformation, it returns to the world with a new self-giving and self-humbling attitude.

---

2. See John of the Cross's poem, "Song of the soul that rejoices in knowing God through faith."

3. *Sayings*, 121; Ascent, Book 2, ch. 14, no 11; Canticle, Stanza 14 and 15, no 24.

Bibliography

Adams, Rachel, and David Savran. *The Masculinity Studies Reader.* Oxford: Blackwell, 2002.
Adriansen, Hanne Kistine. "Timeline Interviews: A Tool for Conducting Life History Research." *Qualitative Studies* 3 (2012) 40–55.
Alison, James. *The Joy of Being Wrong: Original Sin through Easter Eyes.* New York: Crossroad, 1998.
———. *Raising Abel: The Recovery of the Eschatological Imagination.* London: SPCK, 2010.
American Psychological Association. *A.P.A. Guidelines for Psychological Practice with Boys and Men.* American Psychological Association, 2018.
Andreopoulos, Andreas. *This Is My Beloved Son: The Transfiguration of Christ.* Brewster, MA: Paraclete, 2012.
Arel, Stephanie N., and Shelly Rambo, eds. *Post-Traumatic Public Theology.* Cham: Palgrave MacMillian, 2018.
Arnold, John, and Sean Brady. *What Is Masculinity?: Historical Dynamics from Antiquity to the Contemporary World.* Basingstoke, UK: Palgrave Macmillan, 2013.
Arnold, Patrick M. *Wildmen, Warriors and Kings: Masculine Spirituality and the Bible.* New York: Crossroad, 1995.
Atkinson, Robert. "The Life Story Interview as a Mutually Equitable Relationship." In *The Sage Handbook of Interview Research: The Complexity of the Craft*, edited by Jaber F. Gubrium et al., 115. 2nd ed. London: Sage, 2012.
Augustine. *The Life and Writings of Saint Augustine.* Boston: Wyatt North, 2012.
Avellino, Marie, and Chantal Avellino. "Youths' Expression of Cultural Identity through the Visitor Encounter." In *Young People and the 'Festa' in Malta*, edited by Andrew Azzopardi, 109–28. Malta: Best Print, 2015.
Barry, William A. *Spiritual Direction and the Encounter with God: A Theological Inquiry.* Mahwah, NJ: Paulist, 2004.
Barry, William A., and William J. Connolly. *The Practice of Spiritual Direction.* San Francisco: HarperOne, 2009.
Bartkowski, John P. *The Promise Keepers: Servants, Soldiers, and Godly Men.* London: Rutgers University Press, 2004.
Basit, Tehmina. "Manual or Electronic? The Role of Coding in Qualitative Data Analysis." *Educational Research* 45 (2010) 143–54.
Bathum, Mike. "Discovering Creative Depth Within." In *The Spirituality of Men: Sixteen Christians Write about Their Faith*, edited by Philip L. Culbertson, 93. Minneapolis: Fortress, 2002.

Bauer, Jack J., et al. "Narrative Identity and Eudaimonic Well-Being." *Journal of Happiness Studies* 9 (2006) 81–104.
Beel, Nathan, et al. "Counseling Men: Treatment Recommendations from Australian Men's Therapists." *Journal of Men's Studies* 28 (2019) 101–21.
Bernard, Charles André. *Il Dio Dei Mistici: Le Vie Dell'interiorità*. L'abside: Saggi Di Theologia 12. Milan: Paoline, 1996.
———. *Teologia Mistica*. L'abside: Saggi Di Teologia 41. Milan: Paoline, 2005.
———. *Teologia Spirituale*. L'abside: Saggi Di Teologia 30. Milan: San Paolo, 2002.
Bingemer, Maria Clara Lucchetti. "Mystical Theology in Contemporary Perspective." In *The Oxford Handbook of Mystical Theology*, edited by Edward Howells and Mark A McIntosh, 86–105. Oxford Handbooks. Oxford: Oxford University Press, 2020.
Bisson, Donald. "Melting the Iceberg: Spiritual Direction for Men." In *Spiritual Direction in Context*, edited by Nick Wagner, 30–37. New York: Morehousing, 2006.
Blommestijn, Hein. "The Dark Night in John of the Cross: The Transformational Process." *Studies in Spirituality* 10 (2000) 227–41.
———. "Learning to See the Other with the Eyes of God in St. John of the Cross." In *Esperienza E Spiritualità: Miscellanea in Onore Del R.P. Charles André Bernard S.J.*, edited by Herbert Alphonso, 195. Rome: Pontificia Università Gregoriana, 2005.
Blommestijn, Hein, et al. *The Footprints of Love: John of the Cross as Guide in the Wilderness*. Leuven: Peeters, 2000.
Bly, Robert W. *Iron John: A Book about Men*. New York: Addison-Wesley, 1990.
Bourdieu, Pierre. *Outline of a Theory of Practice*. Translated by Richard Nice. Cambridge Studies in Social and Cultural Anthropology. Cambridge: Cambridge University Press, 1977.
Boyle, M. O'Rourke. "A Beautiful Ending: Juan De La Cruz's 'Cantico Espiritual.'" *The Journal of Theological Studies* 54 (2003) 530–69.
Bradley, Arthur. *Derrida's "Of Grammatology."* An Edinburgh Philosophical Guide. Edinburgh: Edinburgh University Press, 2008.
Braun, Virginia, and Victoria Clarke. "Using Thematic Analysis in Psychology." *Qualitative Research in Psychology* 3 (2006) 77–101.
Briguglia, Michael, and Christabelle Caruana. "Why Do Men Join the Men's Rights Movement in Malta?" *Interface: A Journal for and about Social Movements* 10 (2018) 279–96.
Briguglio, Marie, et al. "Environmental Engagement, Religion and Spirituality in the Context of Secularization." *Environmental Research Letters* 15 (2020).
Briguglio, Marie, and Ariana Sultana. "The Effect of the Maltese Festa on Well-Being: An Economic Analysis, with a Focus on Youth Participation." In *Young People and the 'Festa' in Malta*, edited by Andrew Azzopardi, 51–73. Malta: Best Print, 2015.
———. "Man Cannot Live on Bread Alone: Cultural Participation and Life Satisfaction in Malta." In *Capitalising on Culture? Malta and the European Capital of Culture*, edited by V. A. Cremona, 15–36. Msida: Malta University Publishing, 2017.
Brooks, E. M. "The Disenchanted Self: Anthropological Notes on Existential Distress and Ontological Insecurity among Ex-Mormons in Utah." *Cult Med Psychiatry* 44 (2020) 193–213.
Brubaker, Rogers. "Digital Hyperconnectivity and the Self." *Theory and Society* 49 (2020) 771–801.
Buber, Martin. *I and Thou*. Translated by Ronald Gregor Smith. Edinburgh: T. & T. Clark, 1937.

Bucke, Richard Maurice. *Cosmic Consciousness: A Study in the Evolution of the Human Mind*. 2nd ed. Connecticut: Martino, 2010.

Buckley, Suzanne M. *Sacred Is the Call: Formation and Transformation in Spiritual Direction Programs*. New York: Crossroad, 2005.

Bumpus, Mary Rose, and Rebecca Bradburn Langer, eds. *Supervision of Spiritual Directors: Engaging in Holy Mystery*. Harrisburg, PA: Morehouse, 2005.

Bunyan, John. *Pilgrim's Progress: In Today's English*. Chicago: Moody, 1984.

Burdziak, Michael J. "The Spirituality of Catholic Men During Midlife: An Ignatian Perspective." DTh diss., La Salle University, 2020.

Burke-Sivers, Harold. *Behold the Man: A Catholic Vision of Male Spirituality*. San Francisco: Ignatius, 2015.

Burrows, Ruth. *Ascent to Love: The Spiritual Teachings of St. John of the Cross*. London: Dimension, 2006.

Bushlack, Thomas J. "Shadows of Divine Virtue: St. John of the Cross, Implicit Memory, and the Transformation Theory of Infused Cardinal Virtues." *Theological Studies* 81 (2020) 88–110.

Butler, Judith. "Performing Feminisms: Feminist Critical Theory and Theatre." In *Performing Feminisms: Feminist Critical Theory and Theatre*, edited by Sue-Ellen Case, 270. Baltimore: Johns Hopkins University Press, 1997.

Campbell, Joseph. *The Hero with a Thousand Faces*. Bollingen Series. Oxford: Princeton University Press, 2004.

Canales, Andrea. "La Noción Del Movimiento En El Cántico Espiritual B De San Juan De La Cruz." *Mysterion* 12 (2019) 99. www.mysterion.it.

Capps, Donald. "Don Quixote as Moral Narcissist: Implications for Mid-Career Male Ministers." In *The Spirituality of Men: Sixteen Christians Write about Their Faith*, edited by Philip L. Culbertson, 66. Minneapolis: Fortress, 2002.

Caruana, Christabelle. "Is Masculinity in Crisis? A Sociological Analysis of Men Who Joined the Men's Rights Movement in Malta." BA honors thesis, University of Malta, 2015.

Cassidy, Laurie M., and Shawn M. Copeland. *Desire, Darkness, and Hope: Theology in a Time of Impasse: Engaging the Thought of Constance Fitzgerald, O.C.D*. Collegeville, MN: Liturgical, 2021.

Cauchi, Keith. "Masculinities in Male Administrative Staff at the University of Malta." Master of Gender Studies, University of Malta, 2019.

Cervantes, Joseph M. "Manhood and Spirit: Awareness, Reflection, and Life Transitions." In *A Counselor's Guide to Working with Men*, edited by Matt Englar-Carlson et al., 179. Alexandra, VA: American Counseling Association, 2014.

Chowning, Daniel. "Free to Love: Negation in the Doctrine of John of the Cross." In *St. John of the Cross: A Guide in Understanding the Mystical Doctor*, edited by Stephen Payne. Washington, DC: ICS, 1992.

Clairvaux, Bernard of. *Five Books on Consideration: Advice to a Pope*. Cistercian, 2004.

Climacus, John Saint. *The Ladder of Divine Ascent*. Boston: Holy Transfiguration Monastery, 2012.

Coe, H. John. "Musings on the Dark Night of the Soul: Insights from St. John of the Cross on a Developmental Spirituality." *Journal of Psychology and Theology* 28 (2000) 293–307.

Col, Rossanno Zas Friz De. "Spirituality and the Search for a Triple Unity." *Studies in Spirituality* 24 (2014) 1–23.

The Collected Works of Saint John of the Cross. Translated by Kieran Kavanaugh and Otilio Rodriguez. Washington, DC: ICS, 1991.

Connell, Raewyn. *Masculinities*. Cambridge: Polity, 2005.

Conrad, Browyn Kara. "Neo-Institutionalism, Social Movements, and the Cultural Reproduction of a Mentalité: Promise Keepers Reconstruct the Madonna/Whore Complex." *Sociological Quarterly* 47 (2016) 305–31.

Conway, Colleen M. *Behold the Man: Jesus and Greco-Roman Masculinity*. Oxford: Oxford University Press, 2008.

Cooley, Charles Horton. "The Looking Glass Self." In *Human Nature and Social Order*, 179–85. New York: Charles Scribner's Sons, 1902.

Costa, Paul T., and Robert R. McCrae. "Four Ways Five Factors Are Basic." *Personality and Individual Differences* 13 (1992) 653–65.

Crawford, Neta C. "Human Nature and World Politics: Rethinking 'Man.'" *International Relations* 23 (2009) 271–88.

Cristóbal, Serrán-Pagán y Fuentes. "The Active Life and the Contemplative Life in St. John of the Cross: The Mixed Life in the Teresian Carmelite Tradition." *Religions* 11 (2020) 509. https://doi.org/10.3390/rel11100509.

———. "Divine Mercy in Thomas Merton and St. John of the Cross: Encountering the Dark Nights in the Human Soul." *Merton Annual* 30 (2017) 117–30.

Culligan, Kevin Gerald. "Toward a Contemporary Model of Spiritual Direction: A Comparative Study of Saint John of the Cross and Carl R. Rogers." *Ephemerides Carmeliticae* 31 (1980).

Davies, Oliver, and Denys Turner. *Silence and the Word: Negative Theology and Incarnation*. Cambridge: Cambridge University Press, 2008.

Deguara, Angele. "Between Faith and Love? Sexual Morality and Religious Belief among Lgbt and Cohabiting Catholics in Malta and Sicily." PhD diss., University of Malta, 2018.

Delap, Lucy, and Sue Morgan, eds. *Men, Masculinities and Religious Change in Twentieth-Century Britain*. Edited by John H. Arnold et al. Genders and Sexualities in History. London: Palgrave Macmillan, 2013.

Derrida, Jacques. *Limited Inc*. Edited by Gerald Graff. Evanston: Northwestern University Press, 1988.

Diederich, Remy F. *Broken Trust: A Practical Guide to Identify and Recover from Toxic Faith, Toxic Church, and Spiritual Abuse*. Quezon: LifeChange, 2017.

Dodd, Michael. "John of the Cross: The Person, His Times, His Writings." In *St. John of the Cross: A Guide in Understanding the Mystical Doctor*, edited by Stephen Payne, 5. Washington, DC: ICS, 1992.

Dogmatic Constitution on the Church: Lumen Gentium. Boston: Pauline, 1965.

Dombrowski, Daniel A. *St. John of the Cross: An Appreciation*. Albany: State University of New York Press, 1992.

Donovan, Jack. *Becoming a Barbarian*. Milwaukie, OR: Dissonant Hum, 2016.

———. *Way of Men*. Milwaukie, OR: Dissonant Hum, 2012.

Doty, William G., and Wendell C. Beane, eds. *Myths, Rites, Symbols: A Mircea Eliade Reader*. New York: Harper & Row, 1976.

Downey, Michael. *Understanding Christian Spirituality*. Mahwah, NJ: Paulist, 1997.

Downs, Alan. *The Velvet Rage: Overcoming the Pain of Growing up Gay in a Straight Man's World*. Da Capo Lifelong, 2012.

Doyle, Dominic. "Changing Hopes: The Theological Virtue of Hope in Thomas Aquinas, John of the Cross, and Karl Rahner." *Irish Theological Quarterly* 77 (2012) 18–36.
Dreyer, Elizabeth A., and Mark S. Burrows, eds. *Minding the Spirit: The Study of Christian Spirituality*. Baltimore: Johns Hopkins University Press, 2005.
Dunne, Tad. *Spiritual Mentoring: Guiding People through Spiritual Exercises to Life Decisions*. San Francisco: HarperSanFrancisco, 1991.
Durkheim, Emile. *Suicide: A Study in Sociology*. London: Routledge, 2002.
Dyckman, Katherine Marie, and L. Patrick Carroll. *Inviting the Mystic, Supporting the Prophet: An Introduction to Spiritual Direction*. New York: Paulist, 1981.
Edwards, Tim. *Cultures of Masculinity*. London: Routledge, 2006.
Eldén, Sara. "Gender Politics in Conservative Men's Movements: Beyond Complexity, Ambiguity and Pragmatism." *NORA—Nordic Journal of Feminist and Gender Research* 10 (2002) 38–48.
England, F. "An Architectonics of Desire: The Person on the Path to Nada in John of the Cross." *Acta Theologica* 33 (2013) 79–95.
Englar-Carlson, Matt, and Mark S. Kiselica. "Affirming the Strengths in Men: A Positive Masculinity Approach to Assisting Male Clients." *Journal of Counseling and Development* 91 (2013) 399–409.
Erikson, Erik H. *Childhood and Society*. New York: Random, 2014.
Farley, Wendy. "Serving the Spirit of Goodness: Spiritual and Theological Responses to Affliction in the Writings of St. John of the Cross and Louise Erdrich." In *Post-Traumatic Public Theology*, edited by Rambo S. Arel S., 115–34. Cham: Palgrave Macmillan, 2016.
Farrell, Warren. *The Liberated Man: Beyond Masculinity: Freeing Men and Their Relationships with Women*. New York: Bantam, 1975.
Faucher, Nicolas, and Magali Roques. *The Ontology, Psychology and Axiology of Habits (Habitus) in Medieval Philosophy*. Cham: Springer, 2018.
Fitzgerald, Constance. "Desolation as Dark Night." *The Way*, Supplement 82 (1995) 96–108.
———. "Impasse and Dark Night." In *Living with Apocalypse: Spiritual Resources for Social Compassion*, edited by Tilden Edwards, 94. San Francisco: Harper & Row, 1984.
Forth, Christopher E. *Masculinity in the Modern West: Gender, Civilization and the Body*. New York: Palgrave Macmillan, 2009.
Fortunato, John E. *Embracing the Exile: Healing Journeys of Gay Christians*. San Francisco: HarperSanFrancisco, 1994.
Fowler, James W. *Stages of Faith: The Psychology of Human Development and the Quest for Meaning*. Rev. ed. New York: HarperCollins, 1995.
Fox, Barbara F. "The Dark Night of the Soul: Conscious Suffering, Meaning and Transformation." Master of Arts in Counseling Psychology, Pacifica Graduate Institute, 2014.
Freeman, James M., and David L. Krantz. "The Unfulfilled Promise of Life Histories." *Biography* 3 (1980) 1–13.
Frohlich, Mary. ""O Sweet Cautery": John of the Cross and the Healing of the Natural World." *Horizons* 43 (2016) 308–31.
Frye, Northrop. *Anatomy of Criticism: Four Essays*. Oxford: Princeton University Press, 1957.

Gan Chong Beng, Peter. "Union and Difference: A Dialectical Structuring of St. John of the Cross' Mysticism." *Sophia* 48 (2008) 43–57.

Gardner, Leslie, and Catriona Miller, eds. *Exploring Depth Psychology and the Female Self: Feminist Themes from Somewhere*. London: Routledge, 2021.

Garrigou-Lagrange, R., and M. Timothea Doyle. *Christian Perfection and Contemplation According to St. Thomas Aquinas and John of the Cross*. St. Louis: Herder, 1937.

Gelfer, Joseph. *Numen, Old Men: Contemporary Masculine Spiritualities and the Problem of Patriarchy*. Edited by Lisa Isherwood and Marcella Althaus-Reid. Gender, Theology and Spirituality. London: Routledge, 2016.

Gergen, Kenneth J. *The Saturated Self: Dilemmas of Identity in Contemporary Life*. New York: Basic Books, 1991.

Glaser, Chris. *Coming out as Sacrament*. Louisville: Westminster John Knox, 1998.

Good, G. E., et al.. "Men and Therapy: Critical Concepts, Theoretical Frameworks, and Research Recommendations." *Journal of Clinical Psychology* 61 (2005) 699–711.

Goss, Robert E. "The Integration of Sexuality and Spirituality: Gay Sexual Prophets within the Ufmcc." In *The Spirituality of Men: Sixteen Christians Write about Their Faith*, edited by Philip L. Culbertson, 200. Minneapolis: Fortress, 2002.

Green, Deirdre. "John of the Cross and Mystical Unknowing." *Religious Studies* 22 (1986) 29–40.

Grodin, Debra, and Thomas R. Lindlof, eds. *Constructing the Self in a Mediated World*. Edited by Kenneth J. Gergen and John Shotter. Inquiries in Social Construction. London: Sage, 1996.

Grosse, Frederick G. *The Eight Masks of Men: A Practical Guide in Spiritual Growth for Men of the Christian Faith*. London: Haworth Pastoral, 2019.

Grün, Anselm. *Lottare E Amare Come Gli Uomini Possono Ritrovare Se Stessi*. Rome: San Paolo Edizioni, 2007.

Guenther, Margaret. *Holy Listening: The Art of Spiritual Direction*. New York: Cowley, 1992.

Gula, Richard M. *The Call to Holiness: Embracing a Fully Christian Life*. New York: Paulist, 2003.

Gurian, Michael. *Masculinity Is not Our Enemy*. https://gurianinstitute.com/masculinity-is-not-our-enemy-2/.

Habermas, T., and S. Bluck. "Getting a Life: The Emergence of the Life Story in Adolescence." *Psychol Bull* 126 (2000) 748–69.

Hagberg, Janet O., and Robert A. Guelich. *The Critical Journey: Stages in the Life of Faith*. Salem, WI: Sheffield, 2005.

Halberstam, Jack. *Female Masculinity*. Durham: Duke University Press, 2018.

Herráiz, Maximiliano, ed. *Obras Completas: A Cargo De Maximiliano Herrálz*. Salamanca: Sígueme 2007.

Hinkle, Christopher. "A Delicate Knowledge: Epistemology, Homosexuality, and St. John of the Cross." *Modern Theology* 17 (2002) 427–40.

Hoare, Liz. *Using the Bible in Spiritual Direction*. New York: Morehouse, 2015.

Hobbs, Alex. "Masculinity Studies and Literature." *Literature Compass* 10 (2013) 383–95.

Hole, Sam. *John of the Cross: Desire, Transformation, and Selfhood*. Oxford: Oxford University Press, 2020.

Howells, Edward. "From Human Desire to Divine Desire in John of the Cross." *Religious Studies* 55 (2018) 405–17.

Howells, Edward, and Mark A. McIntosh, eds. *The Oxford Handbook of Mystical Theology*. Oxford Handbooks. Oxford: Oxford University Press, 2020.
Hoyeau, Céline. *La Trahison Des Pères*. Paris: Bayard Culture, 2021.
Hurnard, Hannah. *Hinds' Feet on High Places*. Shippensburg: Destiny Image, 2005.
Imoda, Franco. *Human Development: Psychology and Mystery*. Leuven: Peeters, 1998.
Inguanez, Joe, and Rebecca Gatt. *Enigmatic Faith*. Floriana: Institute for Research on the Sign of the Times (Discern), 2015.
Institute for Research of the Signs of the Times (Discern). *Grassroots: The Youth Ministry Scape in Malta*. Malta: Progress, 2014.
Institute for Research on the Signs of the Times (Discern). *Malta Sunday Mass Attendance: Census 2017*. Malta: Progress, 2018.
Isacco, Anthony, and Jay C. Wade. *Religion, Spirituality, and Masculinity: New Insights for Counselors*. New Jersey: Routledge, 2019.
———. "A Review of Selected Theoretical Perspectives and Research in the Psychology of Men and Masculinities." In *The Psychology of Men and Masculinities*, edited by R. F. Levant and Y. J. Wong, 139-68. Washington, DC: American Psychological Association, 2017.
Jackson, Darrell Richard. "The State of the Churches in Europe." *Review and Expositor* 115 (2018) 157-74.
James, Liz. *Women, Men and Eunuchs: Gender in Byzantium*. London: Routledge, 1997.
Johnson, Adam. "The Crucified Bridegroom: Christ's Atoning Death in St. John of the Cross and Spiritual Formation Today." *Pro Ecclesia* 21 (2012) 392-408.
Joiner, Thomas E. *Lonely at the Top: The High Cost of Men's Success*. New York: Palgrave Macmillan, 2011.
Jones, Simon R. "Re-Expanding the Phenomenology of Hallucinations: Lessons from Sixteenth-Century Spain." *Mental Health, Religion and Culture* 13 (2010) 187-208.
Jordan, Ana. *The New Politics of Fatherhood: Men's Movements and Masculinities*. Genders and Sexualities in the Social Sciences. Edited by Victoria Robinson and Diane Richardson. New York: Palgrave Macmillan, 2019.
Keen, Sam. *Fire in the Belly: On Being a Man*. London: Bantam, 1991.
Kempis, Thomas à. *The Imitation of Christ*. New York: Dorset, 1952.
Kimmel, Michael S. *Handbook of Studies on Men and Masculinities*. California: Sage, 2009.
———. *Manhood in America: A Cultural History*. Oxford: Oxford University Press, 2018.
———. "Men's Responses to Feminism at the Turn of the Century." *Gender and Society* 1 (1987) 261-83.
———. "Reading Men: Men, Masculinity, and Publishing." *Contemporary Sociology* 21 (1992) 162-71.
Kimmel, Michael S., and Thomas E. Mosmiller. *Against the Tide: Pro-Feminist Men in the United States, 1776-1990: A Documentary History*. Boston: Beacon, 1992.
King, Nigel. "Using Templates in the Thematic Analysis of Text." In *Essential Guide to Qualitative Methods in Organizational Research*, edited by Catherine Cassell and Gillian Symon, 257. London: Sage, 2004.
Kiselica, Mark S., et al. "Accentuating Positive Masculinity: A New Foundation for the Psychology of Boys, Men, and Masculinity." In *A.P.A. Handbook of Men and Masculinities*, 123-43. Washington, DC: American Psychological Association, 2016.

Kiselica, Mark S., and Matt Englar-Carlson. "Identifying, Affirming, and Building Upon Male Strengths: The Positive Psychology/Positive Masculinity Model of Psychotherapy with Boys and Men." *Psychotherapy: Theory, Research, Practice, Training* 47 (2010) 276–87.

Knieling, Reiner. *Männer Und Kirche: Konflikte, Missverständnisse, Annäherungen.* Göttingen: Vandenhoeck & Ruprecht, 2011.

Kummer, Armin M. *Men, Spirituality, and Gender-Specific Biblical Hermeneutics.* Leuven: Peeters, 2019.

Kuratle, David, and Christop Morgenthaler. *Männerseelsorge Impulse für eine Gendersensible Beratungspraxis.* Stuttgart: Kohlhammer, 2015.

Lakoff, George, and Mark Johnson. *Metaphors We Live By.* Chicago: University of Chicago Press, 2017.

Larrivee, Denis, and Adriana Gini. "Is the Philosophical Construct of 'Habitus Operativus Bonus' Compatible with the Modern Neuroscience Concept of Human Flourishing through Neuroplasticity? A Consideration of Prudence as a Multidimensional Regulator of Virtue." *Frontiers in Human Neuroscience* 8 (2014) n.d.

Leary, Mark R., and June Price Tangney, eds. *Handbook of Self and Identity.* London: Guilford, 2014.

Lee, Kibeom, and Michael C. Ashton. "Psychometric Properties of the Hexaco Personality Inventory." *Multivariate Behav Res.* 39 (2004) 329–58.

Leech, Kenneth. *Soul Friend: Spiritual Direction in the Modern World.* Harrisburg, PA: Morehouse, 2001.

Lewis, Christopher Alan, et al. "Prayer and Mental Health: An Introduction to This Special Issue of Mental Health, Religion and Culture." *Mental Health, Religion and Culture* 11 (2008) 1–7.

Lilgendahl, Jennifer Pais, and Dan P. McAdams. "Constructing Stories of Self-Growth: How Individual Differences in Patterns of Autobiographical Reasoning Relate to Well-Being in Midlife." *Journal of Personality* 79 (2011) 391–428.

Lisieux, Thérèse de. *Story of a Soul: The Autobiography of St. Thérèse of Lisieux.* Translated by John Clarke. Washington, DC: ICS, 1996.

López Baralt, Luce. "The Poetics of Silence in the Spiritual Canticle of St John of the Cross." *Concilium* 5 (2017) 35–47.

Lou, H. C., J. P. Changeux, and A. Rosenstand. "Towards a Cognitive Neuroscience of Self-Awareness." *Neurosci Biobehav Rev* 83 (Dec 2017) 765–73.

Luft J., and Ingham H. *The Johari Window: A Graphic Model of Interpersonal Awareness. Proceedings of the Western Training Laboratory in Group Development.* Los Angeles: University of California, 1955.

MacDonald, Gordon. *When Men Think Private Thoughts.* Nashville: T. Nelson, 1997.

Mahalik, J. R., et al. "Using the Conformity to Masculine Norms Inventory to Work with Men in a Clinical Setting." *Journal of Clinical Psychology* 61 (2005) 661–74.

Mahoney, A. Timothy. "Understanding the Christian Apophaticism of St. John of the Cross." *Logos: A Journal of Catholic Thought and Culture* 7 (2004) 80–91.

Man, Paul de. *Allegories of Reading: Figural Language in Rousseau, Nietzsche, Rilke, and Proust.* London: Yale University Press, 1982.

———. *The Resistance to Theory.* Theory and History of Literature 33. Minneapolis: University of Minnesota Press, 2002.

Maria, Oliveira Cleide. "The Dark Night Metaphor in Saint John of the Cross; Spiritual Itinerary." *Horizonte* 10 (2012) 779–803.
Markus, Hazel, and Paula Nurius. "Possible Selves." *American Psychologist* 41 (1986) 954–69.
Martini, Carlo Maria. *Our Lady of Holy Saturday: Awaiting the Resurrection with Mary and the Disciples*. St. Louis: Liguori, 2004.
Martini, Raymond, and John Barresi. "History as Prologue: Western Theories of the Self." In *The Oxford Handbook of the Self*, edited by Shaun Gallagher, 50. Oxford Handbooks. Oxford: Oxford University Press, 2014.
———. *The Rise and Fall of Soul and Self: An Intellectual History of Soul and Self*. New York: Columbia University Press, 2006.
Maslow, Abraham. "A Theory of Human Motivation." *Psychological Review* 50 (1943) 370–96.
Matthew, Ian. *The Impact of God: Soundings from St John of the Cross*. London: Hodder & Stoughton, 1995.
McAdams, Dan P. "The Psychology of Life Stories." *Review of General Psychology* 5 (2001) 100–22.
McAdams, Dan P., and Kate C. McLean. "Narrative Identity." *Current Directions in Psychological Science* 22 (2013) 233–38.
McCarty, Shaun. "Spiritual Directors: Teachers and Guardians of Mystery." In *Spiritual Direction in Context*, edited by Nick Wagner, 1–9. Morehouse: New York, 2006.
McCluskey, Kirsty Jane. "An Interview with Rowan Williams." *Theology* 117 (2014) 163–68.
McGinn, Bernard. "The Biblical Mysticism of John of the Cross." *Medieval Mystical Theology* 27 (2018) 103–17.
———. "The Letter and the Spirit: Spirituality as an Academic Discipline." *Journal of the Society for the Study of Christian Spirituality* 1 (1993).
———. "Mystical Consciousness: A Modest Proposal." *Spiritus: A Journal of Christian Spirituality* 8 (2008) 44–63.
McHugh, Adam S. *The Listening Life: Embracing Attentiveness in a World of Distraction*. Downers Grove, IL: InterVarsity, 2015.
McInnis, Judy B. "Eucharistic and Conjugal Symbolism in the Spiritual Canticle of Saint John of the Cross." *Renascence* 36 (1984) 118–38.
McIntosh, Mark A. "Mystical Theology at the Heart of Theology." In *The Oxford Handbook of Mystical Theology*, edited by Edward Howells and Mark A. McIntosh, 25. Oxford Handbooks. Oxford: Oxford University Press, 2020.
McLean, K. C., et al. "Selves Creating Stories Creating Selves: A Process Model of Self-Development." *Pers Soc Psychol Rev* 11 (2007) 262–78.
McNeill, John J. *Freedom, Glorious Freedom: The Spiritual Journey to the Fullness of Life for Gays, Lesbians, and Everybody Else*. Maple Shade, NJ: Lethe, 2009.
Mead, George H. *Mind, Self, and Society: From the Standpoint of a Social Behaviorist*. Edited by Charles W. Morris. Chicago: University of Chicago Press, 1934.
Merton, Thomas. *A Course in Christian Mysticism: Thirteen Sessions with Famous Trappist Monk*. Edited by Jon M. Sweeney. Collegeville, MN: Liturgical.
Messner, Michael A. *Politics of Masculinities: Men in Movements*. Lanham, MD: Alta Mira, 2000.

Messner, Michael A., Max A. Greenberg, and Tal Peretz. *Some Men: Feminist Allies in the Movement to End Violence against Women*. Oxford: Oxford University Press, 2015.

Minnema, Lourens. "Spatial Imagery as Key to Two Mystical Experiences of Transformation: A Comparison between Teresa of Avila and John of the Cross." *Mental Health, Religion and Culture* 15 (2012) 587–609.

Moon, Gary W., and David G. Benner. "Spiritual Direction and Christian Soul Care." In *Spiritual Direction and the Care of Souls: A Guide to Christian Approaches and Practices*, edited by Gary W. Moon and David G. Benner, 11. Illinois: InterVarsity, 2004.

———, eds. *Spiritual Direction and the Care of Souls: A Guide to Christian Approaches and Practices*. Illinois: InterVarsity, 2004.

Moore, Robert L., and Douglas Gillette. *King, Warrior, Magician, Lover: Rediscovering the Archetypes of the Mature Masculine*. New York: HarperOne, 1990.

Muesse, Mark. "Don't Just Do Something, Sit There: Spiritual Practice and Men's Wholeness." In *The Spirituality of Men: Sixteen Christians Write About Their Faith*, edited by Philip L. Culbertson, 3. Minneapolis: Fortress, 2002.

Mulder, Jack. "Whiteness and Religious Experience." *International Journal for Philosophy of Religion* 89 (2020) 67–89.

Muto, Susan. *John of the Cross for Today: The Ascent*. Notre Dame: Ave Maria, 1991.

———. *John of the Cross for Today: The Dark Night*. Notre Dame: Ave Maria, 1994.

National Statistics Office (NSO). *Culture Statistics*. Valletta: National Statistics Office, 2003.

New Testament Masculinities. Edited by Stephen D. Moore and Janice Capel Anderson. Atlanta: Society of Biblical Literature, 2003.

Newitt, Lee, et al. "Narrative Identity: From the Inside Out." *Counselling Psychology Quarterly* 32 (2019) 488–501.

Nouwen, Henri J. M., et al. *Spiritual Direction: Wisdom for the Long Walk of Faith*. London: HarperOne, 2006.

Nygren, Anders. *Agape and Eros*. Translated by Philip S. Watson. Philadelphia: Westminster, 1953.

Pable, Martin W. *The Quest for the Male Soul: In Search of Something More*. Notre Dame, Ind.: Ave Maria, 1996.

Page, Nick. *The Dark Night of the Shed: Men, the Mid-Life Crisis, Spirituality and Sheds*. London: Hodder & Stoughton, 2015.

Papadopoulos, Renos K., ed. *The Handbook of Jungian Psychology: Theory, Practice and Applications*. London: Routledge, 2006.

Pax, Clyde. "Companion Thinkers. Martin Heidegger and Saint John of the Cross." *Philosophy Today (Celina)* 29 (1985) 230–44.

Payne, Steven. "The Dark Night of the Soul, Yesterday and Today: Revisiting John of the Cross's Classic Text and Symbol." *Studies in Spirituality* 31 (2021) 85–101.

———. *John of the Cross and the Cognitive Value of Mysticism*. The New Synthese Historical Library Texts and Studies in the History of Philosophy. Edited by Norman Kretzmann. Dordrecht: Kluwer Academic, 1990.

Peck, M. Scott. *The Road Less Travelled: A New Psychology of Love, Traditional Values and Spiritual Growth*. London: Penguin Random, 2012.

Peterson, Dave. "Some Thoughts on the A.P.A. Guidelines for Psychological Practice with Boys and Men." https://www.nas.org/blogs/article/some_thoughts_on_the_a.p.a._guidelines_for_psychological_practice_with_boys.
Pickering, Sue. *Spiritual Direction: A Practical Introduction*. London: Canterbury Norwich, 2014.
Pleck, J. H., et al. "Masculinity Ideology and Its Correlates." In *Gender and Social Psychology*, edited by Oskamp S. and Costanzo M. California: Sage, 1993.
Plummer, Ken. *Documents of Life 2: An Invitation to a Critical Humanism*. 2nd ed. London: Sage, 2001.
Promise Keepers, (Organization). *The Promise Keepers Men's Study Bible: New International Version*. Grand Rapids: Zondervan, 1997.
Pryce, Mark. *Finding a Voice: Men, Women and the Community of the Church*. London: SCM, 1996.
Radcliffe, Timothy. *What Is the Point of Being Christian?* London: Burns & Oates, 2005.
Richards, Larry. *Be a Man! Becoming the Man God Created You to Be*. San Francisco: Ignatius, 2009.
Ricoeur, Paul. *Figuring the Sacred: Religion, Narrative, and Imagination*. Edited by Mark I. Wallace and translated by David Pellauer. Minneapolis: Fortress, 1995.
———. *Oneself as Another*. Translated by Kathleen Blamey. Chicago: University of Chicago Press, 1992.
———. *Time and Narrative*. Chicago: University of Chicago Press, 1990.
Rogers, Carl. *On Becoming a Person: A Therapist's View of Psychotherapy*. London: Robinson, 1977.
Rohr, Richard. *Adam's Return: The Five Promises of Male Initiation*. New York: Crossroad, 2004.
Rohr, Richard, and Joseph Martos. *From Wild Man to Wise Man: Reflections on Male Spirituality*. Ohio: St. Anthony Messenger, 2005.
Roy, Louis. "Expérience Du Silence De Dieu Chez Jean De La Croix." *Prêtre et Pasteur* 115 (2012) 79–86.
Ruffing, Janet. *Spiritual Direction: Beyond the Beginnings*. New York: Paulist, 2000.
Ruffing, Janet Kathryn. "Ancestry, Place[S], and Identity in Spiritual Direction Narratives." *Narrative Works* 8 (2019).
Sánchez-Costa, Enriques. "El Pájaro Solitario Sanjuanista: Una Aproximación." *RILCE: Revista de Filología Hispánica* 24 (2008) 407–19.
Sanderlin, David. "Charity According to St. John of the Cross: A Disinterested Love for Interesting Special Relationships, Including Marriage." *Journal of Religious Ethics* 21 (1993) 87–115.
———. "Faith and Ethical Reasoning in the Mystical Theology of St. John of the Cross: A Reasonable Christian Mysticism." *Religious Studies* 25 (1989).
Schechtman, Mary. "The Narrative Self." In *The Oxford Handbook of the Self*, edited by Shaun Gallagher, 394–416. Oxford Handbooks. Oxford: Oxford University Press, 2014.
Schermer, Travis W., and Cornelius N. Holmes. "Will to Masculinity: An Existential Examination of Men's Issues." *Journal of Humanistic Counseling* 57 (2018) 191–207.
Schiralli, Katerina, et al. "Evolutionary Personality Psychology." In *Encyclopedia of Evolutionary Psychological Science*, edited by Todd K. Shackelford and Viviana A. Weekes-Shackelford, 1–13. Cham: Springer, 2019.

Schmelzer, Felix K. E. "(Neo)Platonic Thought in Saint John of the Cross and Stéphane Mallarmé." *Hipogrifo. Revista de literatura y cultura del Siglo de Oro* 6 (2018) 505–23.
Schneiders, Sandra M. "Religion and Spirituality: Strangers, Rivals, or Partners?." *The Santa Clara Lectures* 6 (2000) 1–26.
———. "Spirituality in the Academy." *Theological Studies* 50 (1989) 676–97.
Seale, Clive, and Carol Rivas. "Using Software to Analyze Qualitative Interviews." In *The Sage Handbook of Interview Research: The Complexity of the Craft*, edited by Jaber F. Gubrium et al., 427. London: Sage, 2012.
Segal, Lynne, ed. *Slow Motion: Changing Masculinities, Changing Men*. New York: Palgrave Macmillan, 2007.
Sheldrake, Philip. *Befriending Our Desires*. Collegeville, MN: Liturgical, 2016.
———. "The Study of Spirituality." *The Way* 2 (1999) 162–72.
Silver, Anne Winchell. *Trustworthy Connections: Interpersonal Issues in Spiritual Direction*. Cambridge, MA: Cowley, 2004.
Singer, J. A., et al. "Self-Defining Memories, Scripts, and the Life Story: Narrative Identity in Personality and Psychotherapy." *Journal of Personality* 81 (2013) 569–82.
Skotnicki, Andrew. "By the Secret Ladder: Christian Mysticism and Liberation of the Imprisoned." *Theology Today* 66 (2009) 33–44.
Springs, Steele. "The Multistate Paradigm and the Spiritual Path of John of the Cross." *The Journal of Transpersonal Psychology* 26 (1994) 55–80.
Stein, Edith. *Life in a Jewish Family: Edith Stein—an Autobiography*. Translated by Josephine Koeppel. Collected Works of Edith Stein. Washington, DC: ICS, 1999.
———. *The Science of the Cross*. Volume 6. Edited by L. Gelber and Romaeus Leuven and translated by Josephine Koeppel. Washington, DC: ICS, 2002.
Stewart, Eric C. "Masculinity in the New Testament and Early Christianity." *Biblical Theology Bulletin* 46 (2016) 91–102.
"The Study of Christian Spirituality E La Teologia Spirituale." *Evolving Methodologies (Metodolgie di Evoluzione)* 12 (2009).
Suárez, Lucero González. "El Amado Del Cántico Espiritual, De San Juan De La Cruz. Una Fenomenología Hermenéutica Del Ágape Como Esencia Del Esposo Cristo." *Cuestiones teológicas* 41 (2014) 377–401.
Taylor, Charles. *Sources of the Self: The Making of the Modern Identity*. Cambridge: Harvard University Press, 1989.
Thiselton, Anthony C. *Hermeneutics: An Introduction*. Grand Rapids: Eerdmans, 2009.
Tilley, Terrence W. *Story Theology*. Collegeville, MN: Liturgical, 1990.
Todorov, Tzvetan. "The 2 Principles of Narrative." *Diacritics* 1 (1971) 37–44.
———. *Theories of the Symbol*. New York: Cornell University Press, 1987.
Turner, Denys. "The Art of Unknowing: Negative Theology in Late Medieval Mysticism." *Modern Theology* 14 (2002) 473–88.
Twitchell, James B., and Ken Ross. *Where Men Hide*. New York: Columbia University Press, 2006.
Vandello, Joseph A., et al. "Precarious Manhood." *Journal of Personality and Social Psychology* 95 (2008) 1325–39.
Waaijman, Kees. "Spirituality as Transformation Demands a Dynamic-Structural Approach." *Studies in Spirituality* 1 (1991) 25–35.
———. *Spirituality: Forms, Foundations, Methods*. Leuven: Peeters, 2003.

———. "Towards a Phenomenological Definition of Spirituality." *Studies in Spirituality* 3 (1993) 5–57.

Waling, Andrea. "Rethinking Masculinity Studies: Feminism, Masculinity, and Poststructural Accounts of Agency and Emotional Reflexivity." *Journal of Men's Studies* 27 (2018) 89–107.

Wallace, Kathleen. *The Network Self: Relation, Process, and Personal Identity*. New York: Routledge, 2019.

———. "You Are a Network." Edited by Sam Dresser. https://aeon.co/essays/the-self-is-not-singular-but-a-fluid-network-of-identities.

Wang, David C. "Two Perspectives on Spiritual Dryness: Spiritual Desertion and the Dark Night of the Soul." *Journal of Spiritual Formation and Soul Care* 4 (2018) 27–42.

Warnke, Georgia. *Gadamer: Hermeneutics, Tradition and Reason*. Cambridge: Polity Press, 1987.

Weil, Simone. *Waiting for God*. New York: Capricorn, 1959.

Werblowsky, R. J. Zwi. "On the Mystical Rejection of Mystical Illuminations: A Note on St. John of the Cross." *Religious Studies* 1 (1966) 177–84.

West, Candace, and Don H. Zimmerman. "Accounting for Doing Gender." *Gender and Society* 23 (2009) 112–22.

Whitley, Rob. "Why the A.P.A. Guidelines for Men's Mental Health Are Misguided." https://www.psychologytoday.com/us/blog/talking-about-men/201902/why-the-apa-guidelines-mens-mental-health-are-misguided.

Wiethaus, Ulrike. "Christian Piety and the Legacy of Medieval Masculinity." In *Redeeming Men: Religion and Masculinities*, edited by Stephen B. Boyd et al., 48. Louisville: Westminster John Knox, 1996.

Williams, A. N. "The Doctrine of God in San Juan De La Cruz." *Modern Theology* 30 (2014) 500–24.

Williams, Rowan. *Being Human: Bodies, Minds, Persons*. London: Society for Promoting Christian Knowledge, 2018.

———. "The Deflections of Desire: Negative Theology in Trinitarian Disclosure." In *Silence and the Word. Negative Theology and Incarnation*, edited by Oliver Davies, 115. Cambridge: Cambridge University Press, 2002.

———. *Edge of Words: God and the Habits of Language*. London: Bloomsbury, 2014.

———. "Mystical Theology and Christian Self-Understanding." In *The Oxford Handbook of Mystical Theology*, edited by Edward Howells and Mark A. McIntosh, 9–22. Oxford Handbooks. Oxford: Oxford University Press, 2020.

———. *A Ray of Darkness: Sermons and Reflections*. Lanham: Cowley, 1995.

———. *Where God Happens: Discovering Christ in One Another*. Colorado: New Seed, 2007.

———. *The Wound of Knowledge: Christian Spirituality from the New Testament to St John of the Cross*. London: Darton, Longman & Todd, 2014.

Wilson, Kenneth. "A Christian Theological Understanding of the Self." In *The Theological Roots of Christian Gratitude*, 31–49. Basingstoke, UK: Palgrave MacMillan, 2015.

Winnicott, Donald W. *The Maturational Processes and the Facilitating Environment: Studies in the Theory of Emotional Development*. London: Routledge, 1990.

Wynn, Mark. "Mystery, Humility and Religious Practice in the Thought of St John of the Cross." *European Journal for Philosophy of Religion* 4 (2012) 89–108.

Yaffe, Gideon. "Locke on Consciousness, Personal Identity and the Idea of Duration." *Nous* 45 (2011) 387–408 [electronic: 1–22].

Yeon, Pia Attard. "Divine Love as the Ultimate Source for Human Union: Theology of the Body and St John of the Cross." Master of Arts in Spirituality, University of Malta, 2011.

Zahrai, Larysa. "Narrative Identity: Formation Mechanism." *Journal of Vasyl Stefanyk Precarpathian National University* 7 (2020) 85–91.

Index

NOTE: Page numbers with "n" indicate notes; "t" indicates a table.

Aaron (director), 191–92
abortion, 191–92
Abraham (director), 165–66, 182, 189, 198
action empathy, 233
active night of sense
    attachment to external objects, 230
    the intellect, 24
    obstacles and warnings, 109, 110t
    overview, 15–21
    psychological focus during, 151
    remedies and outcomes, 111t, 119–28
active night of spirit
    holding on to attachments, 145
    the intellect, 31
    and loss of meaning, 110
    the memory, 32–34
    mortification, 245
    obstacles and warnings, 110t, 128–37
    overview, 21–41
    psychological focus during, 151
    recognizing interior elements, 230
    remedies and outcomes, 111t, 138–41
    the will, 34–41
actual detriments (*passive night of spirit*), 46–47
Adam (director), 190, 196
affirmation, way of, 231–35
alienation, 197–99

Andrew (directee), 103–6, 119, 127–28, 137, 147–48, 172–73
anger, 42–43, 45, 61, 66, 68, 70–71, 81, 105, 125, 133, 191
annulment, 79–80, 85, 116, 124, 140
Anthony of Padova, Saint, 101
APA Guidelines for Psychological Practice with Boys and Men, 212
appetites. *See also* mortification
    controlling, 20–21, 26
    countering, 41
    denudation of, 111t, 119
    harms from, 15–18, 17nn12–13, 18n15, 36, 109, 238
    natural vs. voluntary, 15–18
    recognizing and addressing, 19–20n25, 109–10t, 190–21
    voluntary, 15–16
The Ascent of Mount Carmel (John of the Cross), 14–15, 21–24, 41, 109
attachments
    consuming or rebelling against, 145–46
    harms from, 73, 147–50
    origins and characteristics, 112, 114, 145, 151–52, 238, 262–63
    remedy, 119–20, 181–82
authenticity, 20, 41, 81, 100, 111t, 156, 204, 256

Barresi, John, 202, 213–14
Benner, David G., 257–58
Benton-Wright, Sheila, 211

in-betweenness, the self and, 224
biblical hermeneutics, 209
Bisson, Donald, 255–56
Bly, Robert, 206, 209
Bourdieu, Pierre, 226n130
Briguglio, Marie, 234–35
Brother Sun, Sister Moon (film), 91
Buber, Martin, 243–46, 249
Bucke, Richard Maurice, 221

Campbell, Joseph, 206
celibacy/chastity, 96, 104, 119, 136, 139, 169, 194–95. *See also* sexuality
charity, 22, 26, 30, 42, 52
Connell, R. W., 205, 207
consciousness, types of, 221
consolation, 23–24, 38, 44, 131, 145, 150, 153, 257n260
contemplation
 adaption to, 44, 264
 entering, signs of, 264–65
 infused, 45
 the mysterious encounter, 46, 239, 246–47, 247n223
 the *passive night of sense*, 111t, 141
 processes associated with, 26–28
 as a resource, 178
control, male need for, 153, 160, 163–65, 175–76, 188, 260. *See also* surrender
cumulative network model of self (CNM), 214

Daniel (director), 167, 181, 189
the *dark night*. *See also active night of sense; active night of spirit; passive night of sense; passive night of spirit*
 applying to global challenges, 237n182
 characteristics, 41–45
 "dark night of the soul," xi
 importance, 14
 purgation, illumination, and union, 245
 role in transcending the self, 229, 238
 secretive knowledge of, 50
 as a unified entity/experience, 230
The Dark Night (John of the Cross), 14–15, 109
death
 and abandonment, 47–48
 of loved ones, 119, 127
 spiritual, transformation and, 23, 229, 266
Deborah (director), 193n30, 195
deep masculinity, 206
Deguara, Angele, 239–40
Derrida, Jacques, 202
desolation/despair, 23, 90, 140–42, 150–51, 157, 236, 265, 269
directees. *See* spiritual directees and specific individuals
discursive meditation. *See* meditation
dispensation issue, 72
dissatisfaction
 anxiety and, 156
 directees' experience of, 50, 139
 and doubt, 58, 63–65
 as leading to transformation, 5–6
 with material existence, 35
 the restless heart, 219
Drachma LGBTIQ+ community, 97, 97n82
drug dependency, 59–63, 66–69, 77–78, 112–13, 120–22, 124, 129, 130–31, 188. *See also* attachments *and individual directees*
Dunne, Tad, 260n269

Eliade, Mircea, 206
Elijah (priest), 87–88
emptiness, inner, 17, 22, 109, 110t, 148–51, 228, 268
Englar-Carlson, Mark, 211
Erikson, Erik, 223

failure
 as catalyst for change, 44, 128, 150, 254, 269
 and resistance to change, 238, 250
 sadness/shame as response to, 145, 183, 148
 and self-acceptance/self-love, 125, 169

as warning, 110
faith
  ability to stand alone before God, 186
  accessing God's divine essence, 21–22, 58, 247
  as both blinding and illuminating, 40–41, 40n117
  linking with faith and hope, 22
  as obstacle, 110t
Farley, Margaret, 194
fatherhood
  challenges associated with, Peter's example, 58
  directees' responses to, 143, 146–47
  God's, 167–68
  spiritual, 31, 175–76, 177
feminism, 191–93, 204–7, 213
FitzGerald, Constance, 236–40
formal locutions, 30
Francis of Assisi, Saint, 91, 116
Frankl, Victor, 223
freedom. *See* liberation/freedom
Freud, Sigmund, 201, 223
friends, spiritual, 176–77

gay men in a relationship
  active night of spirit, 136–37
  challenges, 172–74
  directee's experience, 96–102, 103–7
  external attachments, 118–19
  gay subculture, 104
  remedy and outcomes, 126–28
gender
  binaries, limits of, 248n224
  impacts on experiencing Christianity, 2
  postmodern critique, 241
  sensitivity to, and spiritual direction, 256–57
Gergen, Kenneth, 202–4, 213
God. *See also* spirituality/spiritual journey; the soul
  dual qualities, 40n117
  fatherhood, 165
  silence of, 242–43
  as unapproachable, 110
  will of, 161
God, union with. *See also* surrender; *individual directees and directors*
  connecting to through Christ, 34, 73–74, 165, 246
  experiencing, 29–30, 46–47, 61–62, 111t, 232
  fluctuating process for, 151–52
  as God's desire, 247–48, 260
  impacts of contemplation, 249–50
  and interior stillness, 39, 44, 242
  I-Thou, I-It relationships (Buber), 243–46
  obstacles to, 15, 109, 128–37
  preparation for, 264–65
  role of faith, 40–41
  role of meditation and mortification, 239
  role of spiritual direction, 251
  and self-acceptance/self-love, 34, 152, 180–82
  spiritual betrothal, 44, 111t, 142
  and spiritual objects, 39–40
  and supernatural goods and exercises, 38–39
  the three reclamations, 270–72
  the uncontained God, 151
  unique qualities, 144
  wood fire metaphor for, 48–50
God's love
  accepting, 141, 143
  and beauty/goodness, 16n7
  desire for, 20, 46–47, 63, 159
  experiencing, 15–16, 48–50, 111t, 138, 141, 168
  focusing on, 33
  ubiquity of, 186
  as unconditional, 243
  as unique, 239
grief/bereavement. *See* sadness/grief

habitual detriments (*passive night of spirit*), 46
healing, true, 40, 42, 122, 131, 151, 264
heat/wood fire metaphor, 48–49, 48n152
hegemonic masculinity, 205–6, 208, 210
herd metaphor, 46n141

Hole, Sam, 222, 230–31
the Holy Spirit
    challenges relating to, 18–19, 165
    receiving, 32, 50–51, 78, 243n203, 252
hope
    linking with faith and charity, 22
    as path to love, 138
    role in the obscuring of memory, 32
the house metaphor, 232
human development
    healthy, and union with God, 232
    limits of perception, 16
    mystery as part of, 215–25
    otherness, individual and environment, 248n226
    and spirituality, 39, 253

identify, reconfiguration, 149–50
identity. *See also* the self
    and Christian practice, 2
    contemplation and, 248, 248–49n226
    dynamics of formation, 147–48, 202
    the hyphenated self, 214
    life story model, 225–27, 226n129
    multiple possibilities, 203
    reconfiguration of, 241–42
    the saturated self, 203
    of study participants, criteria, 227
Ignatian of Loyola, Ignatian spirituality, 135–36
    teachings of, use by spiritual directors, 178
imago Dei/imitatio Dei, 34, 217–18
Imoda, Franco, 220–29, 252
impasse, theology of, 236–41
the intellect (*active night of the spirit*)
    characteristics, 24–25
    as obstacle, 110t, 128
    purification of, 21–22
    supernatural knowledge from, 25–28
    and visions, 28–29
intuition skills, 177–78
Iron John: A Book About Men (Bly), 206
Isacco, Anthony, 210–12, 233, 240

I-Thou, I-It relationships (Buber), 243–47, 249–50, 272

James (directee), 63–69, 112–13, 121–22, 130–31, 146–48, 170
Jeremiah (director), 162, 169, 181, 186–87, 193–94, 193n31
John of the Cross. *See also active night of sense; active night of spirit; dark night; passive night of sense; passive night of spirit; spirituality/spiritual journey*
    on attachments, 145
    on contemplation, 246–47, 247nn223–224, 264–65
    on desire, 231
    guidelines for mitigating failure, 269
    influence of, xi
    on resistances/obstacles, 128, 149
    revelation of personal spiritual journey, 14
    on self-annihilation, 21–24
    solitary sparrow metaphor, 272
    on spiritual betrothal, 142
    spiritual doctrine, relevance to men's spirituality, 4
    spiritual poetry, 14
    understanding masculinity through conversation with, 2
    understanding appetites, 238
    understanding the soul, 230
    unique perspective, 144
John the XXIII, 101, 136
Jonathan, love for David, 217
Joshua (director), 157, 163–64, 168–69
joy/delight, 34–37, 35n99
Jude (directee), 80–85, 115–16, 133, 140, 146–48, 171
Jung, Carl Joseph, 206

Kimmel, Michael, 207, 207n37
Kiselica, Mark S., 211
Kummer, Armin, 209

Lewis, Christopher, 233
liberation/freedom. *See also* appetites
    from divine union, 19

as focus of spiritual friends, 176
and grief, 151
as outcome, 111t
and the self, 187–88, 222–23, 257, 263
views on, 63
listening skills/empathy, 177
lived experience, 5n18, 9n24
The Living Flame of Love (John of the Cross), 14–15, 48n152, 53, 53n175, 232n151
Locke, John, 221
locutions, 30–31
logocentric principles, Western focus on, 202
love. *See also* God's love; sexuality
and becoming like the beloved, 16n8
and sexuality, 194–95
the soul's capacity for, 217
steps of, 50–52
unconditional, Peter's struggles with, 143
Luke (directee), 96–99, 101–2, 118–19, 126–27, 136–37, 147–48, 172–73

Malta. *See also* individual directees and directors
Common Entrance Examination (CE), 60n17
cultural participation, 234–35
educational institutions teaching spiritual direction, 7
Mużew (Museum), 55–56, 55n5, 96, 98, 101, 169
Society of Christian Doctrine, 55nn5–6, 96
speaking English in, 59, 59–60n16
traditional gender roles in, 192
ManKind Project, 206
Marley, Bob, 113
married straight fathers
active night of sense, 109–11, 120–21
active night of spirit, 129–30, 138–39
directees' experiences, 55–63

relationship issues, 166–68
Martini, Raymond, 202, 213–14
Masculinities (Connell), 205
masculinity
diverse perspectives on, 204–8, 208–9n47
incorporating into spiritual journey, 255–56, 270–72
and male-specific objectification, 252–54
new constructs for, 239
pastoral perspectives, 210–12
precarious manhood, 211–12
reductionist voices, 213
as self-sufficiency, 160
spiritual components, 3
and spiritual emancipation, 249, 264
theological approaches, 209
and theory of the self, 204
traditional assumptions, 205
Maslow, Abraham, 223
material goods, possessions, 35
Matthew (directee), 90–94, 116–17, 125, 134, 141, 147–48, 172
Matthew, Gospel of, parable of the sower, 120–21
McCarty, Shaun, 265
McIntosh, Mark, 215n75
Mead, George Herbert, 222
meditation
in-betweenness of the self, 224
contemplation vs., 247n22
and delight, 41–44
John's views on, 25–27
as spiritual exercise, 20, 58, 130–31, 133, 150–53, 182, 227
for transcending resistance, 27, 238–39
and understanding appetites, 20
memory, 21–22, 32–33
Men, Spirituality and Gender-Specific Biblical Hermeneutics (KUMMER), 209
men's studies, xii, 1
Merton, Thomas, 3, 242n201, 259n267
Messner, Michael A., 207–8
moments of absence/presence/transformation, 228–29

Moore, Gary W., 257–58
moral goods, 37–38
mortification
  and asking for help, 149
  as a continuous process, 149–50
  as remedy, 111t, 119
  resistance to, 148–49
  and spiritual growth, 125–26, 186
  as tool for transformation, 239, 241–42
Moses (director), 157, 160, 164, 166–67, 170, 173, 188, 191
Muesse, Mark, 2
Muscular Christianity, 206, 206n34
Mużew (Museum). See Malta
mystical theology/mystery
  as arising from lived experience, 218–25
  characteristics and value of, 2–3
  enabling encounter with, 264–67
  and human development, 215
  the self and, 220–24
mythopoetics (men's spiritual movements), 1, 206–7

narrative approach to self-understanding, 225–29
Nathaniel (directee), 69–73, 113–14, 122–23, 131, 139–40, 147–48, 170
natural goods, 36
natural memory, 31
negation, way of, 235–41
network self, 214
night metaphor, 15–45
Nouwen, Henri, 88–89, 135
Nygren, Anders, 231n149

obsessive-compulsive disorder, 67
original sin, 47
otherness, role in human development, 220–21, 248n226

pain, as a mystery, 219
parenting
  fathers vs. mothers, 146–47
  and responses to parental expectations, 145–46
  struggles with, 58, 143
passive night of sense
  obstacles and warnings, 110t, 111t, 142
  overview, 41–42, 42n118
  purification of the soul, 141
  relationship between God and humans, 141
  remedy and outcome, 142
  spiritual marriage, 52–53
  as transformation of the soul, 45, 230, 242, 249, 260
  unintentional selfishness, 41–45
passive night of spirit
  characteristics, 46
  imperfections associated with, 46, 144
  obstacles and warnings, 110t, 111t
  soul's torment during, 47–48
  as transformation of the soul, 230, 260
pastiche personality, 203–4
Paul (directee), 59–63, 111–12, 120–21, 129–30, 139, 147, 167
Payne, Steven, 237n182
Peers, E. Allison, xi
Peter (directee), 55–59, 111, 120, 129, 138–39, 141–43, 153–54, 167, 248–50
Philip (directee), 85–90, 117–18, 125–26, 135, 147–48, 172
Pickering, Sue, 252, 258n265
play, laughter, as a mystery, 218
Plummer, Ken, 10
positive masculinity, 211
Positive Psychology Positive Masculinity paradigm (PPPM), 211, 233
praxis (lived experience), 5
prayer
  Buber's views, 249
  as a form of resistance, 260
  growth in, characteristics, 182
  importance, 67, 78, 92, 96–97, 121–22, 130–31, 134–37, 140
  prayer groups, 76
Preca, Saint George, 102
pride, 261

Promise Keepers, 206–7, 206n33
purgation, 43, 46, 245
purification, 18, 20, 263

qualitative research, 11–12
quietness/stillness, spiritual, 26, 32, 39, 44, 111t, 138. *See also* contemplation

Radcliffe, Timothy, 2
Reconciliation, Sacrament of, 82
Religion, Spirituality and Masculinity (Isacco and Wade), 210–12
remora metaphor, 19n24
renunciation
    acts of, 141
    as remedy, 20, 111t
    and resistance to surrendering, 150
    timing of, 25–26
resistance
    to emancipation of the self, 259–60
    forms of in spiritual directors, 261–62
    immobilization as, 189
    stubbornness as, 187–88
revelations (*active night of spirit*), 29–30
Rogers, Carl, 223
Ruffing, Janet, 259–60, 2534

sadness/grief, 43, 64, 69, 131, 151
Samuel (director), 160, 162–63, 167–68, 187, 192, 194, 197
Schechtman, Mary, 225, 226n125, 226n128
the self. *See also* human development; identity
    alterity/otherness, 220–22
    in-betweenness, 224
    emancipation of, 259
    identity creation by, 225–27
    moments of absence/presence, 228–29
    nakedness of, 111t
    narrative approach, 225–29
    objectifying, 252–53
    parameters of human reality, 220–24
    postmodern theories of, 202–4
    preparing for the mysterious encounter, 263–65
    quantifying and producing, 255–57
    questions about, 250–51
    self-regulation, 257
    studies of, 201–4
    transcending, 263–64
    transparency towards God, 152
self-awareness. *See also* identity
    asking for help, 149
    directees' struggles with, 67, 73, 76–77, 79–80, 85–86, 88–90, 120, 124–25, 131, 133, 138–40
    enhanced, 111t
    the fragmented self, 213–14
    goals, 259
    historical studies of, 201–4
    and introspection, 149
    men's challenges with, 128, 255–56
    relationship to spiritual growth, 180–82
    response to inner emptiness, 150–51
    role of spiritual direction, 251
    the saturated self, 202–3
    self-acceptance, 135–36, 139, 141, 193–95
    self-annihilation, 21–24, 112t
    types of consciousness, 221–22
    and understanding appetites, 19–20n25, 20
self-emptying, 242n201
self-pity, 163, 189
sensory goods, 37
separated straight men
    directees' experiences, 74–85
    external attachments, 114–16
    masculinity crises among, 170–71
    obstacles and warning, 131–33
    remedy and outcomes, 123–26, 139–40
sexuality. *See also* celibacy/chastity; gender
    accepting, 116–17, 126–27
    coming out process, 88–90, 94–97, 103–4
    and identity, 72

sexuality (continued)
- inclusion of in spirituality, 85, 193–95, 239–40, 264
- moral conduct, 163
- promiscuity, 59–61
- of spiritual directors, 261–62
- struggles with, 65, 128, 137, 139–41, 171–72

silence, God's, 142, 242–44, 242nn200–201, 247, 265–66, 272

single gay men
- directees' experiences, 85–95
- external attachments, 116–17
- obstacles and warnings, 134–36
- remedy and outcomes, 125–26, 141
- struggles with self-acceptance, 171–72

single straight men
- directees' experiences, 63–74
- diverse needs of, 168–70
- obstacles and warnings, 130–31
- remedy and outcomes, 139

solitary sparrow metaphor, 272

solitude, 67, 82, 136, 219, 265

the soul
- attachments of, as limiting union, 150
- birth of God in, 175
- constant inbetweenness of, 220
- *dark night* of, as growth opportunity, 229, 267
- denuding of appetites and gratifications, 19–20
- God's desire for union with, 247–48
- as the life core, 216
- as manifestation of the *I*, 216–17
- misery of, 47–48
- need for intimacy, 216–17
- need for introspection, 149–50
- as a physical and spiritual unitive entity, 230
- plasticity of, Biblical examples, 215–16
- and willing sacrifice, 217

The Spiritual Canticle (John of the Cross), 14–15, 19–20n25, 40n117, 46, 109, 232n151, 232n154

spiritual counsellors, 174–75

spiritual directees
- characteristics, 144–54, 160–64, 168–71, 180–85
- contexts associated with, 159
- demographics of directees, 158
- focus on moral conduct, 162–63
- projection onto directors, 258–59
- reasons for seeking spiritual direction, 155–58, 251–64
- resistance by, 179
- sample choice/composition, 9
- struggles of, 163–65
- understanding of God's will, 161–62, 185–86
- women vs. men, 160–61, 163

spiritual directors
- authority, 257–59
- challenges, 179–80, 255–56
- functions, overview, 250–51
- gender sensitivity, 172–74, 254, 256–58
- limitations of, 259, 261–62
- as mystagogue, 265
- quantifying and producing the self, 255–57
- resistance to, 187–90
- responsibilities and goals, 20, 44, 149, 177, 178, 190–99, 240, 252
- sample choice/composition, 6–8, 6n21, 10
- self-care, 178–79
- skills and resources, 177–78
- style differences, 174–77, 257–58
- supervisors, 179

Spiritual Exercises of St. Ignatius of Loyola, 178

spiritual feelings (*active night of spirit*), 31

spirituality/spiritual journey. *See also* individual spiritual directees and directors; sadness/grief
- areas of growth, 4, 22–24, 39, 180–82, 185
- beginner characteristics, 31, 42–43, 181
- challenges, 32, 171–72, 195–96, 260
- expecting God to do the work, 133

failure as catalyst for, 184
fundamental role of faith, 24
impediments, 151–52, 191–93, 195–97, 239–40
links with theology, 3
locations, 30–31
mediations, 227
and new masculinities, 268–72
persevering, 19–20, 19n23
phases of the dark night, 46–53, 264–65, 267
the proficient, characteristics, 42, 44
revelations, 29–30
resistance, 187–90, 259
and sexuality, 193
and social identity, 166
spiritual marriage, 52–53
and spiritual objects, 39–40
spiritual poverty, 110t
spiritual reclamation, 4
spiritual unctions, 25
and strength of will, 34–35
studying, methodology for, 5
and supernatural knowledge, 25–28
surrender, 183–84
threefold development process, 246–47
true healing, 40
and understanding human development, 39, 253
visions, 28–29
Waaijman's categories, 5, 9n24
warnings associated with prosperity and enthusiasm, 110
the way of affirmation, 231–35
the way of love, 246–48
the way of negation, 235–46
spiritual marriage, 52–53, 111t
spiritual memory, 32, 34
spiritual objects, 39–40
Steward, Eric C., 209
stillness. *See* quietness/stillness
straight single men
   obstacles and warnings, 112–14
   remedy and outcomes: *active night of sense*, 121–23
study design
   analysis approach, 11

data gathering/interviews, 10–11
ethical considerations/limitations, 12–13
hypotheses, 3–4
life story model of self, 225–27, 226n130
methodology, 4–6, 10–11, 11n33
study participants, 6–8, 6n21, 9, 227–28
suffering
   avoiding, 187, 189–90
   for Christ, 24
   hope for reward, 38, 89, 137, 161
   by men vs. women, 163, 191
   and trauma, 169, 196–97, 196n196
   value of, 24, 35, 45, 48, 52, 177, 185
superficiality, 262
supernatural goods and exercises, 38–39
supernatural knowledge, 25–28
surrender, 52, 150, 163–64, 177, 179, 183–84, 259n267, 260–61, 263, 271

temporality, 218, 222–23
theology of virtues, as outcome during the *active night of spirit*, 111t
Thomas (directee), 74–76, 114–15, 123–24, 131–32, 139, 171
torment. *See* suffering
traditional masculinity ideology, 210
transcendence, 111t, 263–64
transformation
   and the equilibrium between presence and absence, 229–30
   factor allowing recognition of, 5–6
   as outcome during the *passive night of sense*, 111t
trauma, 242n196, 247n218

unconscious mind, 223
unintentional resistances, 110t
unintentional selfishness (*passive night of sense*), 41–42

Vatican Council II, 4
venial sins, 16n6
visions (*active night of spirit*), 24–31

Waaijman, Kees, 5, 9n24, 215–16
Wade, Jay C., 210–12, 233, 240
Waling, Andrea, 208
Wallace, Kathleen, 214
Why Be a Christian? (Radcliffe), 2
the will (*active night of the spirit*), 21–22, 34–41, 34–35n98
Williams, Rowan, 3, 248, 250–51n235
Winnicott, Donald, 223

women
  female spirituality, 2
  marital struggles, 75, 77–78
  mothers, 146–47
  and relationships, 166–67
  as spiritual directees, 160–61, 163

Zachariah (director), 194–95
Zechariah (director), 173, 196

www.ingramcontent.com/pod-product-compliance
Lightning Source LLC
Chambersburg PA
CBHW071233230426
43668CB00011B/1412